Everyday Law
for Consumers

The Everyday Law Series

Edited by Richard Delgado and Jean Stefancic
University of Pittsburgh Law School

Everyday Law for Individuals with Disabilities
Ruth Colker and Adam Milani (2005)

Everyday Law for Children
David Herring (2006)

Everyday Law for Consumers
Michael L. Rustad

Everyday Law for Gays and Lesbians
Anthony Infanti

Forthcoming

Everyday Law for the Elderly
Lawrence Frolik

Everyday Law for Latino/as
Steve Bender, Joaquin Avila, and Raquel Aldana-Pindell

Everyday Law for African Americans
Harold McDougall III

Everyday Law for Consumers

Michael L. Rustad

Paradigm Publishers
Boulder • London

Copyright © 2007 Paradigm Publishers

Published in the United States by Paradigm Publishers, 3360 Mitchell Lane Suite E, Boulder, CO 80301 USA.

Paradigm Publishers is the trade name of Birkenkamp & Company, LLC, Dean Birkenkamp, President and Publisher.

Library of Congress Cataloging-in-Publication Data
Rustad, Michael.
Everyday law for consumers / Michael L. Rustad.
    p.   cm. — (The everyday law series)
  Includes bibliographical references and index.
  ISBN 978-1-59451-452-4 (acid-free paper)
  1. Consumer protection—Law and legislation—United States—Popular works.   I. Title.

KF1610.R87 2007
343.7307'1—dc22

                                                                2007016919

Printed and bound in the United States of America on acid-free paper that meets the standards of the American National Standard for Permanence of Paper for Printed Library Materials.

Designed and Typeset by Mulberry Tree Enterprises.

11   10   09   08   07   1   2   3   4   5

Contents

Preface and Acknowledgments

Consumer law is a broad subject covering the sale of goods and comes into play to protect you in a broad range of financial transactions, including consumer loans, credit repair, credit, consumer leases, usury, interest rates, Internet transactions, distance contracts, home shopping, television advertisements, door-to-door sales, and telephone solicitations. All Americans are consumers whenever they purchase goods or services for personal, household, or family use. Consumers are entitled to the rights and remedies of state and federal consumer protection rules and regulations.

The primary emphasis of this book is on "what to do" about a broad range of consumer problems when hiring a lawyer is not an option. If you know about your rights before they are infringed upon, you will be in a better position to avoid problems or obtain redress if need be. Forewarned is forearmed when it comes to protecting your rights. With the knowledge and resources from this *Everyday Law* book, you can become an effective advocate for yourself and protect your rights in the consumer marketplace.

Series editors Richard Delgado and Jean Stefancic assisted me in developing the proposal for this book. Diane D'Angelo provided extraordinary support locating consumer protection statutes, rules, and regulations. I also appreciate the help of Danielle LaVita in formatting the chapters. William Berman, a law professor at Suffolk and head of Suffolk University Law School's Housing and Consumer Protection Clinic, provided useful insights on legal services for low-income consumers. I appreciated the suggestions of Jean Girard, CPA, on consumer lending issues. Thanks to Ellen Shapiro, administrative attorney for the Massachusetts Court System, for her useful suggestions on consumer law. Bill Farrell, Esq., a clerk/magistrate in the Department of the Trial Court, Boston Municipal Court, Dorchester Division, provided me with valuable materials on small claims, as did Sean P. Coleman, assistant clerk magistrate at the Natick District Court. I learned a great deal from the many clerk magistrates and assistant clerks who were my students when I served as a faculty member in the District Court Symposium on Small Claims and Consumer Law sponsored by the Flaschner Judicial Institute.

My colleague Joseph McEttrick provided me with valuable materials on state lemon laws and unfair and deceptive trade practices, including Chapter 93A actions. I greatly benefited from materials provided by my contracts teacher and colleague, Richard Perlmutter. Extra special thanks go to these talented Suffolk University Law students: Daryl Abbas, Danielle Bouvier, Matthew Bowie, Nicole Chiesa, David Cormier, Shannon Downey, Kara Fratto, John Gillis, John Hebb, Leah Levy, Suzanne Manning, Meghan Marfioni, John Martin, Nicole Nelson, and Ana Sa, who took the time to review and edit this manuscript. David Cormier and John Martin also wrote useful helpful hints for redressing consumer problems. Danielle Bouvier, Shannon Downey, and Nicole Chiesa provided research assistance and made editorial suggestions on individual chapters. Jen D. Frank of the Syracuse College of Law also provided useful editorial suggestions and research assistance during the summer of 2006. Luisa Chau, Esq., a member of the New York Bar, spent many hours editing and shaping sections of this book. She provided me with useful practical pointers as well as an insightful perspective on New York's strong tradition of consumer protection. I am very grateful for the steadfast commitment of my students and former students.

My family has been supportive and encouraging, as usual. James Knowles Rustad, M.D., is a musician and a consumer as well as producer of musical products for sophisticated consumers. Tune him in at http://www.JamesRustad.com. Erica Knowles Rustad, who is a second-year law student at Fordham University Law School, offered useful suggestions for the book, often based on her experiences working in the retail world. My wife, Chryss J. Knowles, is a consumer par excellence, and I would like to thank her for editing this book.

Michael L. Rustad

Acronyms and Abbreviations

AAA	American Arbitration Association
AG	Attorney General
APR	Annual Percentage Rate
BAPA	Bankruptcy Abuse Prevention and Consumer Protection Act of 2005
BBB	Better Business Bureau
B2C	business-to-consumer
CAFA	Class Action Fairness Act
CAN-SPAM	Controlling the Assault of Non-Solicited Pornography and Marketing Act
CCPA	Consumer Credit Protection Act
CDA	Communications Decency Act
CFR	Code of Federal Regulations (implements statutes)
Ch. 93A	Massachusetts' Unfair or Deceptive Trade Practices Act
CLA	Consumer Leasing Act
CMR	Code of Massachusetts Regulation
COPPA	Children's Online Privacy Protection Act
CPSC	Consumer Product Safety Commission
CRA	Community Reinvestment Act
CRA	Credit Reporting Agency
CUTPA	Connecticut Unfair Trade Practices Act
C2C	consumer-to-consumer
DOT	Department of Transportation
ECOA	Equal Credit Opportunity Act
EFTA	Electronic Funds Transfer Act
et seq.	*et sequential* (and the following sections of statutes)
FAA	Federal Arbitration Act

FACT	Fair and Accurate Credit Transactions Act
FBI	Federal Bureau of Investigation
FCBA	Fair Credit Billing Act
FCIC	Federal Citizen Information Center
FCRA	Fair Credit Reporting Act
FDA	Federal Drug Administration
FDA Act	Federal Food, Drug, and Cosmetic Act
FDCPA	Fair Debt Collection Practices Act
FDIC	Federal Deposit Insurance Corporation
FPLA	Fair Packaging and Labeling Act
FRB	Federal Reserve Board
FTC	Federal Trade Commission
FTCA	Federal Trade Commission Act
GAO	Governmental Accountability Office
G-L-B Act	Gramm-Leach-Bliley Act
GPS	global positioning system
HIDC	Holder-in-Due-Course Doctrine
HIPAA	Health Insurance Portability and Accountability Act of 1996
HMDA	Home Mortgage Disclosure Act
HMO	health maintenance organization
HOEPA	Home Ownership and Equity Protection Act
HUD	Housing and Urban Development
IC3	Internet Crime Complaint Center
ISPs	Internet service providers
LSC	Legal Services Corporation
MGLA	Massachusetts General Laws
NADA	National Automotive Dealers Association
NAMB	National Association of Mortgage Brokers
NCL	National Consumer League
NCUA	National Credit Union Administration
NDA	new drug application
NFIC	National Fraud Information Center
NHTSA	National Highway Traffic Safety Administration
OCC	Office of the Comptroller of the Currency
PIRG	Public Interest Research Group
RCW	Revised Code of the State of Washington
Reg. B	FTC Regulations Implementing the Equal Credit Opportunity Act
Reg. CC	Availability of Funds and Collection of Checks
Reg. E	FTC Regulations Implementing the Electronic Funds Transfer Act
Reg. M	FTC Regulations Implementing the Consumer Leasing Act

Reg. Z	FTC Truth-in-Lending Act Regulations
RESPA	Real Estate Settlement Procedures Act
Rest. 2d Contracts	Restatement (Second) of Contracts
Rest. 2d Torts	Restatement (Second) of Torts
RISA	Retail Installment Sales Act
SEC	Securities and Exchange Commission
TILA	Truth in Lending Act
UCC	Uniform Commercial Code
UCCC	Uniform Commercial Credit Code
UCITA	Uniform Computer Information Transaction Act
UDTPA	Unfair and Deceptive Trade Practices Act
UETA	Uniform Electronic Transactions Act
USC	United States Code
USDOJ	U.S. Department of Justice
USDOT	U.S. Department of Transportation
VIN	vehicle identification number
VSA	Vermont Statutes Annotated

1

Introduction

Chapter 1 introduces you to the big picture about consumer law. Modern consumer law has evolved out of centuries of experience and must continue to evolve into the twenty-first century. The values and needs of society have transformed businesses from entities that serve the interests of only their shareholders to those that serve the public interest as well. Modern consumers are indebted to the consumer activists of earlier eras who took direct action to establish consumer rights, including the creation of governmental units for consumer protection.

The rest of the chapters of this book provide you with practical legal strategies for taking direct action to protect your rights in consumer transactions. Each chapter explains your rights, focusing on what practical steps you can take to protect them. Although you cannot learn all consumer rights and remedies from this book, you will have the basis for taking action to resolve many consumer complaints. Even if you decide to retain a lawyer, you will gain a basic understanding of consumer law rights, which will help you to effectively use legal services and win your case.

The chapters in Part I explain how self-help remedies enable you to obtain individual justice in the consumer marketplace. Chapter 2 is a comprehensive guide on how to take direct action by filing private lawsuits and complaints to vindicate your rights under state or federal consumer law. Chapter 3 provides specific information on what you need to know before you go to small claims court. Chapter 4 gives you guidance on finding an attorney and using his or her services effectively. The emphasis of this book is on self-help, but in some cases, it is necessary to retain a lawyer, notably in products liability, consumer class actions, bankruptcy, and medical malpractice actions.

Chapter 5 is a guide to mandatory arbitration and alternative dispute resolution in consumer transactions. Businesses of all types, from nursing homes, employers, financial services companies, and countless other companies selling goods or rendering services to consumers often present consumers with arbitration agreements. When the parties agree to arbitration, a third party decides the hearing and settlement of their dispute by agreement. When consumers agree to arbitration, they are giving up their right to a jury trial and other important legal rights before a dispute has arisen. This chapter explores the advantages and disadvantages of alternative means of dispute resolution.

Part II focuses on your rights and liabilities when it comes to consumer contracts, tort actions, and defective products. Chapter 6 arms you with knowledge about how to protect your rights and avoid infringing the rights of others in commonly occurring consumer problems. Chapter 7 introduces you to your rights and remedies in consumer transactions resulting in personal injury. The remainder of the book applies all of these general principles to common problems that confront many Americans such as: "Automobile Sales, Services, and Financing" (Chapter 8), "Obtaining Credit" (Chapter 9), "Banking, Credit Cards, and Debit Cards" (Chapter 10), "Credit Reports and Discrimination in Lending" (Chapter 11), "Your Debtor's Rights and Remedies" (Chapter 12), "Protecting Home Sweet Home" (Chapter 13), and "Consumer Protection in Cyberspace and Identity Theft" (Chapter 14). The theme of each substantive chapter is that informal resolution of consumer problems is often the best option.

Consumer class action is one avenue not covered in this book for consumers. That vehicle, which has been advancing rapidly in recent years, enables hundreds, sometimes thousands, of consumers victimized by shoddy products to join in a single suit against the company that has caused them harm. A class action lawsuit is a highly technical, but extremely powerful, device that always requires an experienced attorney. Because it enables a large group to sue for their combined damages, the potential recovery—and the socially beneficial effect of the suit—may be large.

Overview of Consumer Law

A "consumer" is an individual who enters into a transaction primarily for personal, family, or household purposes. The term *consumer product* is normally used for items purchased for personal, family, or household purposes.[1]

Countless Federal Trade Commission (FTC) regulations as well as hundreds of state and federal statutes governing such diverse topics as discriminatory credit, credit card charges, product warranties, door-to-door sales, and telemarketing, employ this definition. If you are purchasing goods or services outside your trade, profession, or occupation, you are a consumer protected by many mandatory consumer protection laws at the state and federal levels.

"Consumer transactions" may be broadly defined as the advertisement, offer for sale, sale or distribution of any merchandise or service to an individual for purposes that are primarily personal, family, or household. Consumer protection statutes are enacted by Congress and state legislatures, whereas the common law is judge-made law. If you are purchasing goods and services as part of your business, trade, or profession, the Uniform Commercial Code (UCC) and the common law will likely govern these transactions.

Consumer protection comprises public regulations of food, drugs, and products, as well as private remedies including class action lawsuits for defective goods, products, and services. American consumer law includes private remedies and public regulation of consumer transactions. In order to file a consumer lawsuit, you must establish the merchant's or creditor's liability. You are entitled to statutory or common law remedies if a seller delivers nonconforming goods, a property owner fails to return a security deposit, or a creditor fails to give you statutorily mandated disclosures before lending you money. A growing number of federal and state statutes, as well as the common law, help you obtain redress for economic losses, damages, or injuries arising out of consumer transactions. Consumer law is a matter of personal and corporate responsibility for causing damages or injuries. Judge-made laws, such as the common law of contracts and torts, supplement state and federal statutes.

Consumer law also prevents, punishes, and deters false, misleading, or deceptive acts or practices. Fraudulent trade practices, such as tampering with odometers, fraudulent packaging of products, or marketing dangerously defective consumer products deserve civil penalties by federal and state regulators. Even weight loss advertisements in major media outlets frequently employ dubious weight loss claims that constitute misrepresentation or outright fraud. Lenders who rip off taxpayers cheat all American taxpayers.

Many Americans are unaware of how to register a complaint about fraudulent business practices with federal and state agencies. The primary emphasis of this book is to help you vindicate your consumer rights and remedies, even if you cannot afford a lawyer, which is typical of most American consumers. Contingency fee lawyers will not find the typical consumer law case to be cost-justified, which is why you need knowledge of consumer law to take direct action.

Consumer law in the twenty-first century gives you rights and remedies not found in an earlier era. Prior to the last half of the twentieth century, the ethic was *caveat emptor*—buyer beware. In a society without consumer protection, you would have had to put up with systematic fraud such as odometer tampering, the sale of flood-damaged cars, discriminatory mortgages, and unregulated businesses and services. The consumer law protections you enjoy today are the result of a larger social movement by consumer activists, muckraking journalists, and brave individuals to uncover predatory practices that target low-income and middle-income consumers. Today, consumer law protects all Americans, though many statutes still specifically highlight systematic social problems experienced by Americans with limited means. However, as long as you are purchasing goods or services in your personal, family, or household capacity, you have all local, state, and federal statutory protections as well as common law rights, which are discussed in the subsequent chapters of this book.

Consumer law includes two components: public consumer law and private consumer regulation. The distinction between public law and private law deals with the difference between regulation and litigation. The FTC and other federal and state agencies enforce public consumer law, whereas consumers litigate by filing private civil actions. At the state level, the attorney general (or designated agency) has the primary role of enforcing statutes prohibiting unfair and deceptive acts and practices in consumer transactions. Federal and state agencies regulate and file criminal and civil actions on behalf of the consuming public. In contrast, private consumers file individual lawsuits to vindicate their rights. Private product liability actions are necessary when manufacturers breach their fiduciary duty by failing to protect consumers by adequately testing products.

Public Consumer Law

Public consumer law is a subset of administrative law that governs the relationships between the business community and the government. Federal and state agencies enforce public law consumer regulations through civil penalties as well as criminal law fines that go to the state or federal treasury. The executive branch of our government enforces administrative law, whether at the state or federal levels. Government regulators or prosecutors assess civil or criminal penalties against companies that charge excessive credit charges, roll-back odometers, or "flip" home mortgages, and they redress other public consumer law abuses discussed in this book. The FTC, the Securities and Exchange Commission (SEC), and other federal and state agencies are playing an increasingly prominent regulatory role protecting consumers in cyberspace, which is the subject of Chapter 14. The Federal Bureau of Investigation (FBI), for example, arrested a former employee of Internet Wire for writing a bogus news release about shares of Emulex common stock. That false communication caused countless investors to suffer economic injuries.

The public law of consumer protection is one of the broadest fields of law that protects you in the event of consumer bankruptcy, shoddy service contracts, fraudulent automobile repairs, used car warranties, and countless other unfair and deceptive acts and practices. Consumer law also covers consumer rights and remedies in alternative dispute forums such as arbitration, mediation, and small claims courts. The public branch of consumer law rids the marketplace of unfair and deceptive trade practices and acts harming all Americans. Public state and federal agencies have well-established mechanisms for investigating consumer complaints. You can help serve the public interest by making consumer complaints, which call marketplace abuses to the attention of government officials.

Your single best source for federal statutes, regulations, and rules is the Internet. Every consumer protection agency maintains a website with comprehensive information about public consumer law. The FTC website displays information on hundreds of statutes that it enforces and administers, including the Truth in Lending Act (TILA; Title I of the Consumer Credit Protection Act), the Consumer Leasing Act (CLA), and the Fair Debt Collection Practices Act (FDCPA), to name just a few.[2]

Every jurisdiction has enacted scores of consumer laws protecting you in your capacity as a consumer. Every state has enacted general consumer protection statutes arming you with remedies to redress unfair and deceptive trade practices. In addition, specific state laws address particular programs such as garnishment—a creditor's attachment of a portion of your wages or property to repay a debt. The amount that a creditor may garnish is a matter of state law. In addition, creditors may seize your real or personal property to enforce a security agreement or lien on sales or services. In almost every consumer case, one must consider both federal and state statutes. The FTC, the Consumer Product Safety Commission (CPSC), the U.S. Postal Service (USPS), and the Food and Drug Administration (FDA) are the chief constables of consumer protection among hundreds of federal agencies protecting consumers. You can make direct consumer complaints to these federal agencies; complaint forms are available online. (See http://www.ftc.gov.)

State legislatures around the country enacted general purpose consumer protection statutes punishing and deterring unfair and deceptive trade practices acts in the 1960s and 1970s. Consumers, for example, may recover attorney's fees under a lemon law if they are the prevailing party in either a lawsuit or arbitration proceeding. All but a few states operate websites where you may download consumer protection statutes and their implementing regulations. California, New York, and Massachusetts are among the states that accept online complaints and provide you with an easy-to-use online complaint form that will save you postage and time.

Public consumer law also includes state enforcement by consumer protection divisions of state attorneys general or consumer affairs bureaus of state agencies. Your state's attorney general or designated agency is the place to lodge complaints about state consumer law rules and regulations. You can learn more about your state's consumer protection units by doing a simple Google search to locate your state's consumer protection website. Specific state statutes address everyday consumer transactions, including used car sales, the labeling of commodities, car repair, the packaging of goods, and the sale and lease of goods, among many other commercial transactions.

Local consumer protection agencies at the city or county level enforce state regulations in California, New York, Massachusetts, and other consumer-friendly jurisdictions.

Many state attorneys general devote significant resources to public education, including useful practical guides on how to protect your rights. Keep in mind that the purpose of public consumer law, at the federal and state level, is to detect and punish conduct inimical to a large number of consumers, not just the individual.

To obtain an individual remedy, you need to turn to private consumer law. Fortunately, the majority of state and federal consumer protection statutes encourage consumers to file individual lawsuits by permitting the award of attorney's fees and costs plus double or treble damages to a prevailing consumer.

Private Consumer Law

Private consumer law encompasses remedies initiated by aggrieved consumers to redress personal injuries, financial losses, or property damages caused by defective goods, products, or services. Public consumer law seeks to regulate the consumer market and protect you from predatory or unfair practices, whereas private lawsuits are the only practical means to get your money back. Since governmental agencies cannot redress individual consumer problems, direct action by private consumers and their attorneys supplements public regulations. If a seller or service provider has defrauded you, you will likely want your money back and you will need to file your action in court. Small claims courts, the subject of Chapter 3, are special courts whose purpose is to enable you to represent yourself in an informal proceeding. However, every small claims court has a cap or limit on the amount you can claim.

Private consumer law coexists with public law, which means that you will have the right to take direct action as well as rely upon public enforcement by federal consumer protection agencies. Many federal and state statutes encourage individual consumers to file lawsuits, which also benefit the larger public by exposing dangerous or fraudulent practices. Verdicts under TILA are limited to modest statutory damages; the possibility of winning attorney's fees and costs will even the playing field. The Equal Credit Opportunity Act (ECOA), for example, permits individual loan applicants to file private lawsuits in federal district court to recover money damages. Since a private litigant may recover attorney's fees and costs, it is possible to find legal representation, even though the actual damages may be slight.

If you do pursue self-help remedies, your arsenal will consist of state and federal consumer protection statutes as well as contract and tort remedies. Federal and state statutes provide mechanisms for you to file private actions to vindicate your rights. Many state statutes enable you to recover double or treble damages to punish and deter egregious consumer abuses. Public regulators and prosecutors may enforce consumer statutes, but their enforcement actions rarely result in a settlement for individual consumers.

You can file a private lawsuit to redress economic or personal injuries caused by unfair or deceptive trade practices, defective products, mismanaged medical care, negligently performed services, or discrimination by lending institutions. In complex cases such as mass products liability or toxic torts, you will need to retain an attorney to pursue your claim. If you cannot afford one, your only recourse is to take self-help measures to vindicate your rights.

Why Do We Need Consumer Law?

With the distinction between private and public consumer law in mind, what function does consumer law play in American society? The overarching goal of consumer protection is to punish and deter unfair or deceptive acts or practices that harm a substantial number of consumers. Consumer protection law sends a signal that society will not tolerate sellers, merchants, or creditors that do not treat American consumers fairly.

Example: Action against Fraudulent Trade School. The students of a school providing training in the field of sonography filed an unfair and deceptive trade practices action because they were misled by the school. The school told the students that they would receive job offers in the profession after completing their final examination. However, this was not possible because the school did not offer clinical training in a medical setting, a prerequisite for students taking the licensing examination, the American Registry for Diagnostic Medical Sonographers (ARDMS) test. The court trebled actual damages because of the defendant's egregious deception and awarded the plaintiffs $287,892 under the New Jersey Consumer Fraud Act. The parties settled a punitive damages claim, and the court awarded counsel fees and costs to the plaintiffs (*Brown et al. v. Haas et al.*, No. L-2352-04 [Middlesex Cty., N.J., Feb. 2005]).

Many federal and state statutes, such as the New Jersey Consumer Fraud Act, award double or treble damages to prevailing plaintiffs in egregious cases. Juries award punitive damages when sellers or merchants are recklessly indifferent to the public safety or rights of American consumers. The purpose of consumer law is to eliminate unfair and deceptive trade practices.

Example: H&R Block. The website Wallstreetfraud.com reported a 2006 lawsuit against H&R Block filed by New York's attorney general (New York AG) for the tax preparer's deceptive sales of a flawed "Express IRA" product that was loaded with hidden fees and exposed many clients to tax penalties. The lawsuit charged H&R Block with pressuring its customers into purchasing a financial services product in which up to 85 percent of the 150,000 consumers lost money due to the hidden fees and potential tax penalties. The purpose of the New York AG's lawsuit was to prevent other working families from investing in a flawed financial services product.

Example: Yogurt Shop. A famous *Seinfeld* episode centered on misleading "low carb" claims made by a New York City yogurt shop. The character Cosmo Kramer invested in a nonfat yogurt shop that proved to be a flop after Jerry and Elaine found that the yogurt tasted suspiciously good and that they were gaining weight from eating the product. Elaine, good consumer that she was, took direct action by having the yogurt tested. The results led to the closing of the yogurt business.

Anti–Consumer Law Activists

Self-styled neoconservatives argue that consumer law drains the business community. These conservatives argue that the market is self-correcting and that consumer protection agencies should either be scaled back or consigned to the dustbin of history. Nevertheless, before we rush to judgment and abolish consumer law, we need to understand its history and purposes. The remainder of this overview chapter provides a brief glimpse into the hazards and risks presented before consumer protection and tells the story of how the social movement to develop consumer-oriented business practices has improved American society.

Life without Consumer Law

What if there were no state and federal consumer laws or common law remedies to detect, punish, and deter unfair and deceptive trade practices? First, it is likely that the quality of products and services you purchase would be shoddier and more dangerous. In the caveat emptor era, unsafe and defective food, drugs, and medical products were tested first on consumers rather than in the research laboratory. If products were not labeled accurately, it is likely that food, drugs, therapeutic devices, and cosmetics would expose you to preventable dangers. If there was no law on pricing, it is likely that you would have no basis for comparison shopping. If there were no tort remedies for dangerously defective consumer products, your family, community, or church would be your only safety net. If there was no CPSC, tens of thousands of injuries or deaths would be caused by excessive preventable dangers not detected and removed from the consumer marketplace. No government regulators would compel manufacturers to remove dangerously defective products from the marketplace, even if there were known dangers or a developing profile of danger. Such was the case, to a great extent, before consumer law evolved to what it is today.

   If there were no laws against medical malpractice or regulating the treatment of injured patients or nursing home residents, there would be no remedy for substandard medicine or care. Without a tort system, there would be no way to recoup medical costs, lost earnings, or other damages. Without a tort system, railroad workers would lose their jobs when they lose limbs in coupling accidents. The charitable railroad would likely reassign the amputee to a desk job offering lower pay. Without tort remedies, the chances are good that the corporate wrongdoer would not pay the true costs of injuries because they would not be accountable for injuries caused. If no tort system or other private consumer protection remedy existed, bad actors would not be meaningfully deterred from engaging in predatory trade practices. In the absence of a tort system, the cost of injury is borne by the victim and the victim's family, church, and community. Corrective justice requires that wrongdoers pay the true cost of their activities.

The History of Consumer Law

Throughout most of history, caveat emptor was the prevailing ethic, and buyers had no recourse for many fraudulent sales or services. The modern history of consumer law did not evolve until the 1960s when Congress and state legislatures passed scores of statutes to vindicate the rights of ordinary Americans in the marketplace. Consumer law reallocated losses and damages to the seller. Consumer protection replaced the ancient rule of caveat emptor (let the buyer beware) with *caveat vendito* (let the seller beware).

To paraphrase Woody Allen, the sale of goods and services in the late nineteenth and early twentieth centuries was divided into the horrible and the miserable. Meat products posed great health risks to the consuming public because of the industry's unsanitary slaughterhouses. Additionally, the waste materials from the slaughterhouses contaminated the water supply and made life unpleasant for anyone in the neighborhood.[3] Chicago's stockyards mechanized the killing of livestock on a large scale. Companies such as Swift and Armour boasted of the "cleanliness of their productive facilities."[4] The manufacturers used everything but the oink, including animal bones in china plates and cups and glycerin in explosives.[5] However, horrendous conditions belied the public relations voice of the meat packers in an era where there was no federal inspection of slaughterhouses and "sanitation was nonexistent."[6]

The meatpacking industry was a clear example of the downside of consumer sovereignty that elevated profits over consumer safety. Farmers sold cattle fattened on "whisky malt" or the refuse mash of the breweries, which caused them to develop boils. The boils on these mash-fed cows splattered assembly line workers with foul-smelling ooze. Boils were part of the "embalmed beef" that had killed several times as many U.S. soldiers as all the bullets of the Spaniards in the Spanish American War (1898).[7] During this era, farmers actually welcomed the onset of tuberculosis in their cattle because they would fatten up more quickly. Fraudulent commodity sellers would purchase rancid butter, oxidize it, remove the odor, and return it with skim milk to resell it as butter bricks in the cities. No government inspectors kept these dangerous foods out of the marketplace.

In 1905, Upton Sinclair published his novel *The Jungle,* and reaction came in the form of a public outcry in which meat sales dropped by 50 percent in a short period.[8] Shortly after the novel's publication, Congress also reacted by enacting the Meat Inspection Act of 1906, which mandated meat inspections for the first time. Sinclair and the muckrakers also inspired legislation such as the Pure Food and Drug Act of 1906 and the Filled Milk Act in 1923 to curb the practice of adding fat, oil, and other adulterants to milk.

In 1934, the Office of Drug Control initiated an investigation of products containing dinitrophenol, a dangerous substance used in diet drugs, which were responsible for many deaths and injuries. However, since the federal statute did not mandate drug effectiveness, the federal authorities could not seize dangerous or worthless drugs and could only issue warnings to the public.[9] The turning point in federal governmental regulation over drugs and medicine came only in the wake of the mass disaster of Elixir Sulfanilamide. This deadly concoction caused the death of over 100 American children in 1937. The untested elixir contained diethylene glycol, a chemical analogue to antifreeze.[10] The demand for the elixir came in the wake of the marketing of sulfanilamide, a "miracle" drug used to treat streptococcal infections, which was used safely in tablet and powder form.

In June of 1937, a sales representative for S. E. Massengill reported that consumers were requesting that the miracle drug be produced in a liquid form so it would be easier to administer to children. The company's chief chemist and pharmacist discovered that sulfanilamide would dissolve quickly in diethylene glycol.[11] Massengill then placed the drug on the market without taking the elementary step of studying the safety of this compound.[12] The company treated consumers as guinea pigs: a deadly decision because the compound caused certain kidney failure.[13]

Every victim of Elixir Sulfanilamide poisoning suffered kidney failure and the cessation of urine flow, followed by severe abdominal pain, nausea, vomiting, stupor, and convulsions leading to death.[14] The children who took the drug suffered blindness, and the lucky ones fell into a comatose or semi-comatose state and died after a few days.[15] Taking this untested medical compound was a certain death sentence because there was no antidote or treatment available for diethylene glycol poisoning.[16]

In June of 1938, President Franklin Delano Roosevelt signed the Federal Food, Drug, and Cosmetic Act (FDA Act), which mandated the testing of drugs for safety before marketing. The 1938 statute required pharmaceutical companies to submit a new drug application (NDA) to the FDA. Congress also assigned the task of policing the labeling of drugs to the FTC. The FDA Act required makers to label drugs with instructions for safe usage.[17] Today, the FDA regulates drugs and medical devices, and the agency's two most important regulatory statutes are the FDA Act and the Fair Packaging and Labeling Act (FPLA).

Consumer Protection in the Twenty-First Century

Throughout the 1960s and 1970s, U.S. presidents delivered consumer messages to Congress each year. President John F. Kennedy proposed a Consumer Bill of Rights in his 1962 Consumer Message to Congress.[18] The Consumer Bill of Rights included "the right to safety; the right to be informed; the right to choose; and the right to be heard in government decision-making."[19] President Lyndon Johnson also urged Congress to support new consumer legislation in his 1966 Consumer Interests Message.[20] It is difficult to imagine a contemporary president singling out consumer protection as a topic worthy of a major policy speech.

Today, you are living in a decidedly anti–consumer law climate. Tort reformers call for reduced governmental regulation of business transactions and restricted remedies to redress corporate wrongdoing. Yet the corporate scandals of WorldCom, Tyco, Adelphia, and Enron provide a compelling justification for greater consumer protection in the twenty-first century. Enron's fraudulent accounting practices ultimately cost American investors billions of dollars.[21] As a result, increased trading prices for energy caused consumers around the country to experience higher home heating bills. For example, in Utah, consumers paid 38 percent more to heat their homes in 2005 than in 2004.[22] Internet stock manipulation and duplicitous accounting practices harm both investors and the general public.

Additionally, the cutting edge of consumer protection involves regulating unfair and deceptive swindles in cyberspace. A consumer purchasing a fake Louis Vuitton bag, advertised on eBay as authentic, needs to know what steps to take to mitigate her damages. This type of fraudulent activity on Internet sites is just the latest evidence that consumer protection is a necessary guardian in the new millennium.

Notes

1. This is the standard definition of "consumer product" used in countless federal and state statutes. The Fair Debt Collection Practices Act, for example, defines consumer debts as "arising out of . . . transaction[s]" that "are primarily for personal, family, or household purposes," 15 U.S.C. § 1692a(5).

2. Federal Trade Commission, http://www.ftc.gov/ (last visited June 17, 2007).

3. Kenneth F. Kiple, *Cambridge History of Food*, Vol. 2 (Cambridge: Cambridge University Press, 2000), p. 1315.

4. Ibid., p. 18.

5. Ibid.

6. Ibid.

7. Ibid.

8. Ibid.

9. Ibid.

10. Ibid.

11. U.S. Food and Drug Administration, *Taste of Raspberries, Taste of Death: The 1937 Elixir Sulfanilamide Incident*, available at http://www.fda.gov/oc/history/ elixir.html (accessed November 20, 2006).

12. "Documentary Examines Sulfanilamide Death of 1937." A full account of this mass torts disaster, quoting FDA historian John Swann in the documentary *Taste of Raspberries, Taste of Death*, is available at http://www.ashatorg/news/showarticle .cfm?id=3659 (accessed November 19, 2006).

13. FDA, *Taste of Raspberries, Taste of Death*, available at http://www.fda.gov/ oc/history/elixir.html (accessed July 20, 2006).

14. Ibid.

15. Ibid.

16. Ibid.

17. FDA, *A Brief History of the Center for Drug Evaluation and Research*, available at http://www.fda.gov/cder/about/history/histext.htm (accessed November 19, 2006).

18. Robert J. Hobbs and Stephen Gardner, *The Practice of Consumer Law: Seeking Economic Justice* (Boston: National Consumer Law Center, 2003), p. 7.

19. Ibid.

20. Ibid., p. 26.

21. Jonathan R. Laing, "Personal Wealth: Meet Mr. Pressure," *The Edge* (Singapore), December 19, 2005.

22. Dave Anderton, "Huntsman Sr. Fears Traders Manipulate Natural Gas," *Deseret Morning News* (Salt Lake City), December 10, 2005.

Part I

Private Consumer Remedies

2
Taking Direct Action by Filing a Complaint

As I was writing this chapter, I heard a knock on my door. It was a home improvement contractor asking me if I would like an estimate to have my driveway resurfaced. It was a classic example of a consumer transaction involving both goods and services. Nevertheless, consumers should think twice before entering into home improvement contracts of all kinds. Real diligence is especially in order when responding to unsolicited door-to-door offers. Door-to-door sales and services have a long history of consumer fraud. In this case, the contractor had solid references from neighbors and was not known for shoddy work. Mailings and telephone calls provide another popular avenue for consumer fraud. Recently, I received a fraudulent email solicitation that announced me as the winner of an international lottery: "Congratulations! You may receive a certified check for up to $400,000,000 U.S. CASH! One lump sum! Tax free! Your odds to WIN are 1–6. . . . Hundreds of U.S. citizens win every week using our secret system! You can win as much as you want!"

It was a wonderful opportunity for financial freedom—for the con artist, that is. If you have been informed that you were the winner of a Canadian, Australian, El Gordo, or El Mundo lottery, you have nothing to lose—but your entire bank account. The international lottery is just the latest example of a fraudulent consumer transaction. Scam artists have been conning consumers since antiquity.

A Canadian telemarketer targeting consumers with low or bad credit ratings has recently victimized American consumers. During the telephone calls, employees fraudulently offered consumers pre-approved, low-interest MasterCard or Visa credit cards, as long as the consumer agreed to permit the crooks to debit their bank accounts for a fee ranging from $175 to $199. Next, the company would ask the consumers for bank account numbers and

14

routing information in order to debit the accounts later. However, none of these consumers ever received a credit card because the fraudulent seller had no authority to issue MasterCard or Visa credit cards.[1]

In a famous *Seinfeld* episode, Jerry coached Elaine on the strict rules of a soup restaurant owner known as "The Soup Nazi." When Elaine failed to have her money ready, it infuriated the Soup Nazi and he tossed her from his store, screaming, "No soup for you!" Later, Elaine found the Soup Nazi's recipes and distributed them widely in an act of vengeance, ruining his business. Elaine's action was an example of self-help in response to a consumer problem. As Elaine demonstrated, consumers are not powerless in response to unfair, arbitrary, or capricious actions by sellers. Consumer law is a field in which you do not need a lawyer for every problem.

Each chapter of this book stresses direct actions that may be taken by consumers to protect their rights. Consumers do not need to passively wait for regulators to protect them. Instead, they can induce action by taking self-help measures such as filing complaints with agencies, writing letters of complaints to businesses, resolving disputes through informal settlement mechanisms, or filing lawsuits. In fact, many state and federal consumer protection statutes rely upon consumers to file actions that expose unfair or deceptive practices affecting other consumers.

Nearly every state has a general consumer protection statute, called Unfair and Deceptive Trade Practices Acts (UDTPA) or Little FTC Acts. Many of these statutes enable consumers to file direct actions by awarding double or treble damages, attorney's fees, and costs. In taking direct action, you are helping other consumers by identifying dangerous or unfair practices. As a "private attorney general" you may also recoup money damages for any losses or damages you suffered as an individual, while benefiting the larger public by exposing systematic consumer abuses. The private attorney general is a distinctively American legal institution. In Sweden, as in many other European countries, a consumer files a complaint with the ombudsman, who then attempts to resolve the dispute with the merchant. The American way is for consumers to be self-reliant in redressing harms done to them.

You purchase a lemon automobile, for example, in which the windshield wipers work in any and all conditions except rain. Public regulators have no authority to file a lawsuit on your behalf. You can vow never to purchase another car and accept the loss or you can take direct action to get a refund or replacement vehicle that works.

Consumer law is a response to widespread abuses such as predatory home improvement contracts, hidden finance charges, rent-to-own, used car sales financing, uninhabitable mobile homes, odometer rollbacks, overcharges for extended warranties, fraudulent mortgages, refinancing, racial and gender discrimination against customers, and unfair debt collection practices. Consumer law is not an easy body of law to describe because it consists of both public regulation and private remedies.

Before beginning the study of self-help remedies, you need a general roadmap to your statutory and common law rights. The remedies discussed in this section are broadly related to the entirety of consumer rights as discussed in subsequent chapters. Many law books for the layperson give too much attention to statutes and case law without enough practical advice on how to rectify abuses. Consumers may have an adequate cause of action, but this is only the first step. The most important step is to determine who can provide help.

This chapter presents practical steps you can take to redress consumer protection issues with the merchant and with a regulatory agency. If you have a problem with consumer goods or services, begin by complaining to the company. If informal attempts to resolve problems are ineffective, you can consider filing a lawsuit or file a complaint with a consumer protection agency or attorney general's office. In most cases, you do not have to go further than your immediate seller, lender, or merchant. The most effective method used to address a complaint to the seller, lender, or merchant is to write an informal letter with respect to your complaint.

Example: Model Complaint Letter to a Retail Store. The Hawaiian attorney general gives the following suggestions for writing an effective complaint letter:

- Address the letter to a manager who has real authority — someone who can solve the problem. That is usually the head of customer service department or a top officer such as the president of the company.
- If you are getting this information from the Internet, then you must be able to type! Type your letter.
- Start out with data. State (a) when you bought the product, (b) where you bought it, (c) the name and model of the product, and (d) the serial number, if you have it.
- State the problem clearly. Be brief. Do not rant and rave (even if you are feeling that way!). Be businesslike and objective. Companies receive many letters from "crackpots," and such letters are ineffective.
- State what you want. Do you want a refund? Do you want to exchange the product? If so, for what? Do you just want an apology?
- Send copies of relevant documents like receipts. Do not send original receipts. Keep them.
- Set a specific time for them to respond. A reasonable time is usually ten business days or more.
- Make sure you give your phone number (specify whether it is daytime or nighttime or give both) and your address, your email address, and other contact information.
- Keep a copy of everything you send. It is also a good idea to send a certified letter with return receipt requested for big-ticket items.

Retail sales tend to receive high scores on customer service because unhappy customers are not good for business. Businesses compete with each other to win you as a customer. The competition in the consumer marketplace ratchets up expectations about the quality of consumer products and services. From our daily bowl of cereal to the car we drive, we have an ever-expanding array of choices. Given this wide selection, national companies are normally quick to resolve problems. For example, a Massachusetts couple was experiencing trouble with their two-year-old Apple iBook laptop and returned it to the Apple store in the South Shore Plaza in Braintree, Massachusetts, for repairs. When the repairs were unsuccessful, the manager returned from the backroom with a new laptop and an apology for their inconvenience.[2] Work with customer service because in many cases, businesses still have a customer satisfaction model. Sometimes a firm will not only right wrongs but may even offer you incentives (free stuff!) to entice you to use their products or services again.

Complaints to the Merchant

Do not delay in contacting the merchant. Delay can result in problems with the statute of limitations, but there is also the maxim that you should not "sleep on your rights." The doctrine of laches may bar a claim if you unreasonably delay notifying the merchant.[3] Under UCC Article 2, prompt notification of defects in goods is an absolute necessity. I once had a client who purchased a customized office chair that cost several thousand dollars. My client was a professional with back problems who needed a tailor-made chair at work. The chair delivered by the company was made of first-rate materials. The quality was high and so was the store's service.

My client returned her customized chair for adjustments on several occasions. She gave them one last chance to make the proper adjustment, but the company was not successful. The chair did not fit her needs, but she got busy with family and work issues and waited several months before returning the chair to the store and asking for a full refund. The salesperson was initially reluctant to return the purchase price and instead offered store credit. The store gave my client a prompt refund after she contacted the manager with whom she dealt. My client was fortunate to receive the refund because by waiting several months, she was sleeping on her rights.

If you have a problem with goods or services, voice your complaint seasonably and reasonably. Delay is the handmaiden of having either an unsatisfactory or no remedy. By doing nothing, you are accepting goods or products with their defects. You cannot, for example, revoke acceptance of goods unless you give the seller prompt notice as to why the goods substantially impair your use. If you fail to give the seller seasonable notice, you are in effect waving goodbye to your buyer's rights. Retailers may have a more liberal return policy than required by the law. It is not enough in most states to print the return policy on the receipt. Many states require retailers to post their return policy in a prominent place in their retail establishment.

Place any complaint you have with services or goods in writing, preferably a typed document formatted in a professional manner. Save your correspondence in a special file if you are making a complaint by email. It is best to write a formal letter of complaint. Be sure to date the letter and caption it as a complaint. Provide a clear and concise account that explains your problem with the goods or services. Also, it is important to avoid hyperbole and gratuitous insults. Do not threaten legal action in the first letter. Follow up with a telephone complaint or a complaint in person and create a log of the person you spoke with and the substance of the conversation.

Create the log while your memory is fresh. Be sure to jot down the time, date, and place of communication as well as anything else you believe to be relevant. If you are unable to get satisfaction after writing a letter and doing a follow-up, you may consider writing a letter that suggests further actions may be necessary. Even at that stage, however, do not threaten legal action. The informal method of adjudication is often the best way to resolve disputes. First, try to resolve your complaint directly with the merchant, creditor, or seller. If you are still unable to resolve the problem, you may need to take further action, such as making a complaint to a federal or state regulatory agency or a private lawsuit.

Before you confer with a lawyer, assemble a file about the dispute that contains a brief chronology of the dispute, relevant records, receipts, and any other documents that may serve as evidence in the event of litigation. You should then direct future communications to your attorney once you have retained counsel.

What to Do: Letters of Complaint

Your first and often best line of defense is a direct complaint to the seller, lender, or merchant.[4] Many of your remedies are contingent upon giving the seller reasonable and seasonable notice of your claim, so a complaint letter may also serve that function. Your letter should minimally give accurate contact information (name, address, telephone, and email), the reason you are writing, and a demand for an appropriate remedy.

The notice must be reasonably specific and seasonable so the seller has an opportunity to "cure" the problem (see UCC §2-508). The term *reasonableness* is a commonsense standard, not a fixed rule. Courts define the proper amount of time to act differently in a consumer transaction than in a business-to-business transaction. The important point is to make a complaint to the direct seller that gives fair and reasonable notice.

Consumers must send a demand letter before filing a UDTPA lawsuit or have their action dismissed. In Massachusetts, for example, you must send a thirty-day demand letter that explains why the business violated the consumer's rights and what damages are involved.

If cable service is the problem, a minor outage due to a storm would not be grounds for a complaint, but you do have a cognizable complaint if there are an unreasonable number of interruptions with the service. However, please note that the UCC does not apply to consumer services' transactions. If you are writing a letter of demand because of a Truth in Lending Act, Equal Credit Opportunity Act, Magnuson-Moss Warranty Act, or other violation, refer to the relevant statute and briefly explain why the applicable statute applies to your facts.

Every sale of goods accords buyers an array of rights and remedies under Article 2 of the Uniform Commercial Code, which governs the sales of goods in every state but Louisiana. UCC Article 2 requires you to notify buyers and specifically delineate the problems with goods, whether you are rejecting goods or revoking acceptance of goods. In order for you to obtain a remedy, you must notify the seller of the specific problems with goods or services within a reasonable time after discovering problems with goods or be barred from *any* remedy (see UCC §2-607(3) [a]). Disappointed buyers will have no remedy at all unless they can prove by a preponderance of the evidence that they gave the seller or merchant a timely opportunity to cure the problem. The UCC gives the seller a second chance to make things right.

Your demand letter has legal significance because it establishes that you have given "notice," which is a requirement before pursuing a remedy under your state's UDTPA. Most, if not all, consumer laws require you give the merchant notice before pursuing claims. Make certain you give written notice because telephone or oral notices create a problem of proof. You may give a reasonable notice by email as well as by regular mail. A seller is also entitled to notice before a buyer files suit for breach of warranty or breach of the sales contract. See UCC §2-607(5) [a] (2003).

The complaint letter discussed above applies equally to services and the sale of goods covered by UCC Article 2. If you are rejecting or revoking acceptance on goods, you will need to delineate the specific problems with the goods. The standard of performance for UCC Article 2 is the "perfect tender rule." This means that if the goods fail to conform in any respect, the seller is in breach and is subject to the right of cure. The concept of "workmanlike" is based on a flexible industry standard that is equally applicable to plumbing, masonry, and scores of other services. A contractor who installed a defective chimney liner, which caused a fire to erupt in the fireplace, would be liable for negligent installation.

The standard of performance for consumer sales is "perfect tender" (UCC §2-601), but this pro-consumer standard does not apply to services contracts, which have a less rigorous performance standard: Was the work performed in a competent manner? If professional services were rendered, did a profession such as medicine, dentistry, or law recognize them within the standard of care? When professional services are rendered, those rendering them may make mistakes but are not liable unless they have violated a

standard of care or best practices in their field. A doctor may, for example, misdiagnose breast cancer, but there is no negligence if professional standards of care such as tests and procedures were followed. Be sure to adjust your complaint depending on whether you are addressing deficiencies in sales or services.

Remember to retain a copy of the complaint that you send. Save all emails and make a log of *all* telephone conversations you had with sellers, creditors, professionals, or their agents. Be sure to include the date and responsible party. Always ask the name and position of someone making representations about store policies or your transactions. Retain all originals documents, including receipts and other records. Attach copies of receipts, repair records, or other documents to your letter.

Many states have enacted Unfair and Deceptive Trade Practices Acts, which requires consumers to write a demand letter as a predicate to filing a lawsuit for unfair or deceptive trade practices. Maine's Unfair Trade Practices Act is typical in requiring that the consumer "must first inform the business and give the business an opportunity to make a settlement offer" (Maine Unfair Trade Practices Act, 5 M.R.S.A. 213 (1) [A]). Maine's attorney general has also drafted specific demand letters at http://mainegov-images.informe.org/ag/dynld/documents/clg3.pdf.

A UDTPA lawsuit may be filed only if the seller or company does not adequately respond to your complaint letter. A company's failure to respond to your reasonable demand letter may also be an aggravating circumstance bolstering your contention that you have been treated unfairly. Whether you file suit in small claims court or retain an attorney in a high-stakes case, you will need to give the seller or merchant reasonable notice prior to filing suit.

Determine Who Is at Fault

The first step in resolving your consumer complaint is to determine all parties potentially at fault. When you encounter a problem with a product or service, you should complain to the firm you think is responsible. In most cases, that company will be able to resolve the issue. If a seller delivers dangerously defective goods or products that do not work, you are likely to have more than one avenue of complaint. Make a direct complaint to your immediate seller with a copy to the manufacturer or other parties in the chain of distribution. In a product liability action, every party in the chain of distribution is potentially liable for the consequences of dangerously defective products. Consumers can take direct action to protect their rights in most economic loss cases. Note that consumers, like merchants, are also subject to the general standard of reasonableness. It is unreasonable, for example, to purchase a prom dress and then return it the night after the prom. You are not acting in good faith if you purchase Halloween decorations and return them November 1 after using them without a problem.

Suppose you have a problem with a short-wave radio. You can complain to the immediate seller. If that is ineffective, complain directly to the company that made the radio and that has the responsibility to uphold the key warranties. Warranties pass through the direct seller to you. I once had a problem with a short-wave Grundy radio, and my local Staples refused to give me a refund. In contrast, Grundy promptly sent me a new one, which today remains in excellent working condition. You may be asked to speak with a service representative about a problem; if you do, treat that person courteously, and most reputable companies will do the right thing.

However, suppose your first attempts at resolving a problem are fruitless. Take the case of Carla Consumer, who spent a miserably wet weekend in the White Mountains of New Hampshire because the tent the Tents-R-Us sales representative recommended was not suitable for outdoor camping.

Example: Letter about a Defective Product

Company Official
Complaint Division
Title, Company
Street Address
Town, State, Zip Code

Your Name
Your Address
Your Town, State, Zip Code

RE: Defective Tent

September 30, 2007

Dear Complaint Department:
　　On August 16, 2007, I purchased a Weathermaster tent from the Tents-R-Us branch store, located in the Hanover Mall in Hanover, Massachusetts. I have included a photocopy of the receipt and proof of purchase with this letter. I am seeking a refund because the tent was defective in not being suitable for outdoor camping because it was not waterproof.
　　I specifically asked Joe Smith, the clerk in your store in the Hanover Mall, for advice in purchasing a tent suitable for outdoor camping. My husband also explained to Mr. Smith that we had never camped before and needed his advice in purchasing a tent suitable for spring or summer camping that would keep my family dry, even in torrential rains. Our family went on a Labor Day camping trip to Conway, New Hampshire.
　　We followed your sales representatives' instructions for assembling the tent and used the tent on the nights of September 1–3. The Tents-R-Us tent failed to perform according to specifications in your literature and the representations made by Mr. Smith. It rained the night of September 3, and the tent

leaked in several places, making for a miserable night of camping. Enclosed please find a sales receipt for the tent for $137.50. I am seeking a prompt refund for the full amount and the cost of postage to send the defective tent to your store.

I look forward to your prompt reply and a full resolution to this matter.

Sincerely yours,

Carla Consumer
Address
Telephone
Email Address

If the seller is unwilling to repair, replace, or refund the goods, you have recourse under your state's Article 2 of the UCC. A few states, notably Massachusetts and Maryland, prohibit sellers from disclaiming or limiting implied warranties. The Magnuson-Moss Warranty Act (15 U.S.C. §§2301–2312) requires sellers such as Tents-R-Us to provide minimum warranties if a consumer product fails. If a seller does not use the label "full warranty" or "limited warranty," the consumer-buyer will have the right to pursue statutory damages. The Magnuson-Moss Warranty Act will apply to the tent and virtually any other consumer product that costs more than $10.

The most important feature of Magnuson-Moss in this case is that Tents-R-Us may not entirely disclaim or modify any implied warranty to a consumer. It is a consumer transaction, so the seller will be required to give Carla a remedy because the tent was defective, malfunctioned, or failed to conform to the written warranty. Tents-R-Us is liable in this example, and Carla Consumer will receive money damages.

Since she relied upon the expertise of the seller to supply her with a suitable tent for outdoor camping, Carla will likely have remedies under UCC Article 2 as well. A seller is liable for a fitness warranty if the buyer relies upon a seller's expertise, for example, in recommending a tent suitable for camping out on Mount Washington. The tent may have been suitable for backyard camping but not for serious mountain campers. If it turned out that the buyer knew that a particular tent was selected to be used for mountain camping, the seller would be liable if the tent was unsuitable for rugged terrain. A seller is liable for supplying goods that are fit not only for their ordinary purpose but also for any specific purpose.

Suppose Tents-R-Us gave Carla the recommendation to buy the Weathermaster Tent, which was suitable for mountain camping, and she reasonably relied upon his expertise. If the Weathermaster Tent leaked like a strainer, it would be deemed unsuitable for mountain camping. Given that it was Carla's specific purpose to use the tent for camping, Tents-R-Us will be liable for violating the implied warranty of fitness for a particular purpose. The fitness warranty applies because Carla relied upon the seller's expertise about a particular purpose for the tent. In this case, Carla reasonably relied upon the seller's skill and judgment.

Because Carla reasonably relied upon the knowledge of Tents-R-Us in supplying her with a waterproof tent and the product did not meet her representations, the immediate seller is liable for breaching the implied warranty of fitness for a particular purpose. Rainstorms are well within the expected use of tents. Additionally, if a seller deliberately misleads a buyer, he will also be liable under a state's Unfair and Deceptive Trade Practices Act.

Carla Consumer will also have causes of action for other UCC Article 2 warranties. In the "leaky tent" example, the seller will also be liable for breaching an express warranty if it was advertised as "waterproof." An "express warranty" is entirely a matter of contract, wherein the seller may define or limit his obligation respecting the subject of the sale and provide as to the manner of fulfilling the warranty or the measure of damages for its breach. Any affirmation of fact or promise made by the seller to the buyer that relates to the goods and becomes a part of the basis of the bargain creates an express warranty that the goods will conform to the affirmation or promise. Waterproof means that the fabric has been coated with polyurethane and the seams have been taped, making the tent impermeable to water. If the seller did not use a coating that made its outdoor tent waterproof, Tents-R-Us is liable for breach of an express warranty.

Assume that the tent manufacturer's literature stated that the tent sold to Carla had a "1,500 mm coating." The abbreviation *mm* refers to the amount of water the fabric will hold before it leaks. The performance standard for a 1,500 mm coating is very high. This performance standard requires that a tent withstand a 1,500 mm column of water for more than one minute before a single drop permeates the fabric. A tent with this rating should easily be strong enough for an ordinary rainstorm in the White Mountains. In fact, a 1,500 mm tent is strong enough to withstand rain from a 75-mph hurricane-force storm. If a tent advertised as having a 1,500 mm rating leaked, there would be clear liability for an express warranty.

The definition of an express warranty found in every state makes a seller accountable for "any affirmation of fact or promise made by the seller to the buyer which relates to the goods and becomes part of the basis of the bargain" (see UCC §2-313). Express warranties require no special language. Any seller's statement that relates to its goods—advertising, sales literature, television advertisements, and seller's statements—can constitute an express warranty. It is not necessary for the Tents-R-Us sales staff to use magic words such as "warrant" or "guarantee." Sellers need only make a statement about the features of the tent, and the express warranty is created. Express warranties are nondisclaimable once made. Seller statements about features of the materials used in the tent and the ability to withstand wind or rain go to the "basis of the bargain." Carla thought she was purchasing a tent that would have been suitable for use in extreme conditions at high altitude, such as Everest Base Camp. However, this case was not even appropriate for the relatively tame White Mountains terrain.

Tents-R-Us is also potentially liable for the implied warranty of merchantability because the tent was not fit for its ordinary purpose of being used on camping trips. Merchantability means that goods must pass without objection in the trade under the contract description. If the contract is for an outdoor camping tent, the fact that it leaks violates the seller's obligation to supply a "merchantable" tent. Even if the direct seller did not make any statements about the qualities of the tent, he will nevertheless be liable if the tent was not fit for its ordinary purpose. Carla Consumer will have a cause of action against the tent manufacturer for breach of the implied warranty of merchantability as well. Of course, a consumer can only recover once, even though two defendants are potentially liable for the breach of warranty. If the Tents-R-Us manufacturer marketed its product with national advertising, packaging, or labeling representing that the tent was waterproof, it will also be liable for the breach of an express warranty.

Gather Your Facts

Spend a few minutes jotting down the specific grounds for why you think you have rights or remedies under state or federal warranty law. If the product you purchased did not work, describe what went wrong. If a lender failed to give disclosures, give the circumstances. Explain why you are unhappy about the product or service. Also, jot down the date of purchase, any verbal exchanges you might remember having with the seller or service provider, and any other information pertinent to the product or service. Back up your statements with copies of key documents such as receipts, bills of sales, or loan documents.

Decide Where to Send the Letter of Complaint

You might have to do a little research to learn the identity of the person in charge of the organization. You need to address the letter to someone high up enough in the organization to take your letter seriously. For instance, you might want to call the store where you purchase your goods and ask for the manager's name and contact information. Fortune 500 companies, as well as large or medium-sized businesses, will typically have contact information posted on their websites. Navigate their website to find the appropriate contact person or department. In addition, most large organizations have customer service departments whose entire reason for existence is resolving issues for unsatisfied customers. If you are dealing with a small business, you should send your letter directly to the owner or manager. If you think you incurred personal injury because of the use of a defective product or service, consult a private attorney. Do not try to handle personal injury claims on your own.

Contingency fee attorneys will not typically be available except for high-stakes cases such as products liability, medical malpractice, or class actions. Class actions make it cost-justified to join the claims of other consumers where they have been overcharged. In a class action, the attorney is paid out of the class action settlement, or the defendant pays the fee if a statute provides for cost shifting. You will need the expertise of a lawyer to pursue complex cases in which you are seeking punitive damages against improper billing, excessive charges, or chiseling consumers. In these cases, the expertise of an attorney specializing in your kind of case is a necessity. However, if you are trying to get resolution on defective products or unsatisfactory services, this section applies to you.

Identify All Responsible Parties
Sue all responsible parties to protect your rights. The court will determine who is ultimately responsible for your claim. In products liability action, you will file lawsuits against your immediate seller, distributors, and any other party in the distribution chain, including the maker of component parts.

In a medical malpractice action, you will frequently file suit against the hospital as well as individual providers, such as doctors, nurses, or other staff who treated you. Similarly, you may file suit in a fair credit case against a mortgage broker as well as a mortgagee. Do not name parties who are not responsible for your injury. Determine who is responsible for your personal injury, property damages, or other financial losses. Identify all potentially responsible parties and send the demand letter to any party with potential liability to you. Many companies have complicated corporate organizations (and reorganizations), so identifying responsible parties may not always be a simple task.

Manufacturers' Warranties
In the case of goods, check your warranties booklet and try to determine whether goods you purchased are covered by the manufacturer's warranty. Try to call the warranty hotline. In many cases, you will receive an offer for repair, replacement, or refund. Focus on the disclaimers on the warranties to see if any of them apply to you. The Magnuson-Moss Warranty Act is a federal act that prevents the seller from disclaiming implied warranties of merchantability.

Make Clear and Convincing Explanations
You are unlikely to receive prompt remedial measures or other actions from a seller unless you state your case clearly and in a credible way. In order to obtain recovery, you need to establish that you did not misuse or abuse the goods. It may be a good idea to demonstrate your knowledge of the law, but do not go overboard. As a consumer, you have federal and state rights and remedies, and merchants have a corresponding duty to respect your rights.

Give the merchant a fair opportunity to redress your concerns before filing a complaint with a government agency. Complaints to the FTC and other federal or state agencies should be made only after you have exhausted informal methods of dispute resolution with your direct seller or the manufacturer. Should informal methods fail, you can then move onto a "demand letter." Your complaint letter must give a clear account of what remedy you are seeking and why you are entitled to a refund, replacement, or other compensation.

Provide Documentation

Whenever possible, provide photocopies, not originals, or relevant documents such as receipts, advertisements, or warranties. In order to receive a refund you will need to prove that you purchased the product and that the injury you suffered or losses sustained were not due to your contributory negligence or misuse of a product. In other words, you must demonstrate a causal connection between what the seller did and the injury suffered by the consumer. When writing the complaint about defective goods or services, recount facts and dates.

Remember to be thorough but concise when drafting your consumer complaint. In certain cases, you may need a notary public to attest to the authenticity of a signature on a document by signing the document and affixing his or her stamp. A notary public is authorized by the state to administer oaths, certify documents, and attest to the authenticity of signatures. A certified document contains the notary's seal that establishes the document as genuine, and it may be introduced as evidence at a trial or administrative hearing. An official record keeper, clerk of the court, or any other authorized person, including an attorney, may certify a document. A certified statement has been sworn to before a notary public as a true statement.

Use a Professional and Courteous Tone

Draft your letter with a professional and courteous tone and presentation. Never make empty threats, such as "I intend to take this case to the U.S. Supreme Court." Briefly state the problems with the product or service. Sergeant Joe Friday, the central character in the TV program and recent movie *Dragnet,* had a famous catch phrase, "Just the facts, ma'am." It is also good advice for complaint letters: "Just the facts, and the reasons why you deserve relief!" Your objective in making a demand is to seek compensation for monetary losses or property damages. Convey the message that you are only seeking a remedy that you are entitled to under state or federal law.

Whether you are drafting a complaint letter or making a personal complaint, avoid insulting the sales staff or company. Briefly state the problems with the product or service. Avoid exaggeration, hyperbole, or gratuitous insults. Insults will reduce your chances for a prompt recovery and will only lead to greater sales of antacids. Most businesses will view well-documented complaints as an opportunity to make you happy and restore goodwill.

Often, you will be dealing with a managerial employee, not an owner or actual manufacturer. Therefore, the person you are dealing with did not personally manufacture or service a defective product. Like umpires in baseball, they are only doing their job. Do not unload on managers or sales clerks. Accurately summarize any representations made by sales staff or advertising or instructions on packaging that you relied upon. Your letter should state your expectations and the problems you have with products or services.

Be Cautious When Citing Legal Statutes

Do not cite statutes or regulations unless you are certain they apply. In most consumer cases, your state's UDTPA is broadly applicable. Article 2 of the UCC applies to all consumer sales. If a car dealer reset the odometer on your car to reduce the mileage, you can safely cite your state's UDTPA as well as the federal act prohibiting such odometer tampering.

Exhaust All Available Dispute Mechanisms

As a consumer, you have federal and state rights and remedies. Give the merchant a fair opportunity to redress your concerns before filing a complaint with a government agency. Do not make formal complaints with agencies until you have exhausted informal methods of dispute resolution with your direct seller.

Massachusetts Consumer Protection Act, Chapter 93A, provides Massachusetts consumers with the right to take private civil action and recover damages when they are victims of unfair and deceptive trade practices. Section 9 of Chapter 93A (Massachusetts's UDTPA) permits you to recover losses of money or property from such practices, but you must send the business a thirty-day demand letter. The statute requires you to explain and document specific monetary or property losses. You have the burden of proving both the injury suffered and the damages sought. If the business or other defendant offers you a settlement within this thirty-day window and you reject it, your rejection of the offer may become evidence used in court. A defendant can present evidence of a spurned settlement offer, and if the settlement was reasonable, the legal consequence is that your recovery may be limited to actual damages.

Before you send your UDTPA demand letter, be sure that you have pursued all informal methods of settlement. A UDTPA demand letter gives the business one last opportunity to settle the claim. Check the UDTPA statute in your jurisdiction to determine any procedural steps you must take before filing suit.

When you send a demand letter, you are communicating a direct message to the seller or creditor that you are serious and that you are exercising your rights under your state's consumer protection statute. Consumer law evens the playing field, especially when it provides for the possibility of treble damages, attorney's fees, and costs. If a merchant flatly refuses to give you a statutorily guaranteed remedy, remind them that if you are required to file a UDTPA action, they may end up paying your attorney fees as well as double or treble damages. A UDTPA letter implies that it is better to settle your claim than pay your attorney fees as well as the seller's own fees in answering your statutorily based complaint.

Every state requires consumers to serve merchants with a demand letter before filing a UDTPA action. The following steps are drawn in large part from the Massachusetts attorney general's website and can easily be adapted to fit other states' regulations. Check your state's statute to determine what actions you need to take to trigger your rights (see Appendix A for a list of statutes). You can also find this information on your state attorney general's website. Appendix B provides you with help locating your state's attorney general online. Appendix C provides detailed contact information. In addition, consumer protection regulations are available in hard copy form in most community libraries.

Step One. Give accurate contact information, including your full name and address. Also, enclose your email address. You must be sure to make clear that a UDTPA claim is being asserted. Caption your letter citing the applicable UDTPA statute by checking Appendix A at the end of this book. A Massachusetts consumer, for example, should caption the letter as follows: "Re: Chapter 93 Demand Letter."

Step Two. Describe clearly and briefly what the seller, merchant, or creditor did that you consider unfair or deceptive. Be specific. Give dates, times, and supporting details backed by documentation. Recount the dates, price paid, and other relevant facts involved in the consumer transaction.

Step Three. Explain the injury, property damages, or financial losses you suffered because of the unlawful act. Document how you suffered economic injuries or other damages from an unlawful act such as:

- Failure to return a security deposit, resulting in the loss of money;
- Sale of a defective household appliance, resulting in the ownership of a useless and worthless product;
- Failure of the TV technician to fix a broken set, resulting in payment for services improperly performed;
- Purchase of goods through "bait and switch" tactics, resulting in owning unwanted goods that are more expensive than originally planned;
- Sale of a lemon automobile or a dangerous defective used car; or
- Odometer tampering or rollback cases.

Step Four. Be sure to send the demand letter to all prospective respondents. In addition, always send two copies of your demand to each respondent— one by certified or registered mail so that you have a copy of the receipt and a second copy by regular mail in the event that the merchant refuses to accept the certified copy. You will need to prove that you gave the merchant thirty days to respond before filing a lawsuit under your state's UDTPA statute.

Example: UDTPA Demand Letter. A demand letter is a requirement for any consumer complaint. However, a Chapter 93A demand letter takes a particular form according to Massachusetts law. At a minimum, you will need to specify what unfair or deceptive act or practice you were victimized by and describe your financial injuries. The purpose of the demand letter is to offer the other party a chance to settle your claim. You will need to consult your state UDTPA to determine what should be contained in a model letter used in your jurisdiction. In the following sample demand letter, consider a hypothetical situation in which a parent has purchased a used car for a daughter who is heading off to college. Pay attention to how the letter utilizes the tips above and really creates an explicit description of why the consumer is entitled to relief. This letter helps demonstrate how statements from a seller as well as your own statement of needs to the seller are of paramount importance when establishing your credible expectation of a warranty. Any reader will be able to insert the facts of their own specific case within the portions printed in italics.

(Name, Address)

Dear Seller:

Re: Chapter 93A Demand Letter for Defective Toyota Corolla

I am writing to you to request relief under the provisions of Massachusetts General Laws, Chapter 93A, §9 of the Consumer Protection Act.

On or about *August 3, 2005,* the following unfair or deceptive act(s) or practice(s) occurred: *I purchased an automobile from Joe's Used Auto Sales located at 2345 Chamberlain St., Worcester, MA 01613.* I specifically told the salesperson, Joe Amesbury, that I needed a reliable vehicle with good gas mileage for my daughter.

After testing several vehicles, my daughter and I purchased a 2002 Toyota Corolla for $6,500. The vehicle had sixty thousand miles and was described as "slightly used" by Mr. Amesbury. Mr. Amesbury told us his mechanic had cleared the vehicle for use, the car used 24–27 miles per gallon, and that with routine maintenance the car was going to last "right through college."

The Corolla I purchased from you broke down two weeks after I purchased the car. My daughter was on the way to college when her car suddenly lurched to a stop, leaving her stranded on the breakdown lane of Route 93 because of a faulty alternator. Mr. Amesbury agreed to refund the repair cost of $285, which he has not done. The car was in the shop for four days. Two days later the car stalled again, this time due to low transmission fluid, which is a standard procedure in any tune-up. Several days later, the car stalled again. The transmission needed to be completely replaced after this problem arose. The cost of the rebuilt transmission and labor was $1,600. I sent Mr. Amesbury a complaint letter requesting a return or replacement vehicle. To date, Mr. Amesbury has not responded to my complaint. Due to lack of an alternative, my daughter continued to drive the Corolla, and after the repaired transmission and within her first 450 miles of use, the brakes began to squeak when compressed and the tires would vibrate. The cost of new front and rear brakes as well as rotors was $475. To date, we have spent $2,360 for repairs on a car that originally cost only $6,500.

I believe Section 2 of Chapter 93A, which declares unfair methods of competition and unfair or deceptive acts or practices in the conduct of any trade or commerce unlawful, declares the acts or practices unlawful.

I have suffered injury or loss of money or property *(in the amount of or, as follows): $6,500 spent for a lemon automobile and $2,360 in repairs to a vehicle that did not meet the express or implied warranties offered by the seller.*

This letter serves as my demand for a refund of: *$8,860.00* to settle my legitimate claims against you under the provisions of Section 9 Chapter 93A. I am providing you with the opportunity to make a written offer of settlement of this claim within thirty (30) days. If you fail to make a good faith offer of settlement in response to this request within 30 days, I will institute legal action and a court may award me double or triple damages, attorney's fees, and costs if the court finds in my favor.

I may be reached at the address and phone number below. I look forward to hearing from you.

Sincerely yours,

Carla Consumer
Address, Telephone
Email Address[5]

Here is an example of a demand letter regarding the purchase of a defective television.

March 3, 2007
Name (person with authority)
Company Name
Address
City, State, Zip Code

Dear Seller:

On January 27, 2007, I purchased an XYZ 32" High Definition television (HDTV), Model #1234567, for $1099.99 from your Big Store in South Burlington, Vermont. Since the purchase of my HDTV, I have experienced ongoing problems with periodic color shifting, and the picture periodically bounces. When I attempted to return the HDTV, the clerk told me that the

HDTV warranty was covered for thirty days from the date of purchase. I next took the television to your local service representative for repair, but they were unable to resolve the color shifting and picture bouncing problems. Enclosed is a copy of the receipt. The warranty booklet (copy enclosed) states that the warranty period for the HDTV is one year. I want to exchange my television for a new model or receive a complete refund.

I hope we can solve this problem in a mutually agreeable way. Please respond by April 7, 2007. If I have no response by then, I will have no alternative but to pursue my legal rights and remedies.

Sincerely,

Carl Consumer
Address
Telephone
Email Address

Example: Filing an FTC Complaint. Though the FTC cannot file an individual action on your behalf, the commission's staff investigates consumer complaints and enjoins unfair acts. The FTC is increasingly taking the role of sheriff in cyberspace investigation, Internet-related fraud, fraudulent or unfair telemarketing, identity theft, and other fraud-related complaints. The FTC compiles data on consumer fraud in its Consumer Sentinel database, shared with state or federal law enforcement. To file a consumer complaint, you can complete an easy-to-use online form at www.ftc.gov. You can also speak with an FTC staff member at 1-877-FTC-HELP (1-877-382-4357); TTY: 1-866-653-4261. You may contact the FTC by mail at Consumer Response Center, Federal Trade Commission, Washington, DC 20580.

The FTC filed a number of cases against Internet sites to enforce their promises in privacy statements, including promises about the security of consumers' personal information. The FTC settled a 2002 case with Quicken Loans, an Internet website that failed to comply with the statutory requirements of the Fair Credit Reporting Act. In a 2006 case, CardSystems Solutions settled a case with the FTC due to inadequate computer security of credit card information that led to millions of dollars of fraudulent purchases. The FTC filed charges that the credit card company engaged in unfair acts by failing to take reasonable steps to protect the personal information of millions of consumers. The FTC has received over 100,000 complaints of identity theft since 1998.

How State Attorneys General Can Help You

In our system of federalism, states play a critical role in protecting the consumers. The mission of a state's attorney general, or functionally equivalent agencies such as the New York State Consumer Protection Board (CPB), is to protect, educate, and represent consumers injured by unfair or deceptive practices. You can research your state's specific consumer laws online or at your local community library. New York's Consumer Fraud and Protection Bureau in the attorney general's office is one of the most respected prosecutors of businesses and individuals engaged in false, misleading, or deceptive acts or trade practices.

State attorneys general are the chief legal officers of the states and frequently the chief enforcers of the state law of consumer protection. State attorneys general are empowered to institute civil lawsuits and criminal proceedings against companies that defraud consumers. Every state attorney general plays a role in enforcing antitrust laws against monopolies, oligopolies, and other concentrations of power. The vast majority of state attorneys general enforce general as well as specific consumer protection law. Every state has a general purpose statute to enjoin, punish, or deter unfair and deceptive trade practices. Appendix A to this book provides the legal citations for these "Little FTC" statutes, which punish defendants engaged in unfair or deceptive acts or practices. An attorney general will file a state deceptive trade practices action when three elements are present:

1. A business is engaged in trade or commerce.
2. The business has committed unfair *or* deceptive acts or practices in the trade or commerce in which they are engaged.
3. The consumer proves the financial injury they are seeking damages for was caused by the defendant's unfair or deceptive acts or practices.

The phrase "unfair or deceptive acts or practices" is flexible enough to encompass a wide range of sharp practices in the marketplace. If a business violates some consumer protection law, the Uniform Commercial Code, or other government regulation, it may be deemed unfair. The concept of unfair or deceptive trade practices always involves an assessment of the ethics of a particular practice in the marketplace. The attorney general is far more likely to take action if a given act or practice causes substantial injuries to many consumers. In addition to the state's little FTC statute, state attorneys general have jurisdiction to enforce consumer protection statutes. State attorneys general also benefit consumers by handling criminal prosecutions against fraudulent business enterprises, intervening in public utility rate cases, and joining with other states' attorneys general in class actions against companies injuring the public interest (such as the billion dollar tobacco settlement). A state attorney general, for example, can file a criminal as well as a civil action against a fraudulent home improvement contractor. A state attorney general has the authority to impose a corporate death penalty by revoking the charter of a business engaging in systematic fraud and oppression of consumers. Their offices have won settlements on behalf of large classes of individuals, but keep in mind that they have no statutory authority to file suit on an individual consumer's behalf.

Notes

1. *FTC v. Pac. First Benefit, LLC*, 361 F. Supp. 2d 751 (N.D. Ill. 2005).

2. Bruce Mohl, "To Avoid Fees, Customer Has to Know Enough to Ask," *Boston Globe*, October 1, 2006, 1.

3. The doctrine of laches means that the plaintiff is barred from a remedy because they have slept on their rights. The doctrine of laches is as follows: "1) Unreasonable delay in pursuing a right or claim—almost always in equity—in a way that prejudices the party against whom relief is sought; 2) The equitable doctrine by which the court denies relief to a claimant who has unreasonably delayed asserting the claim, when the delay has prejudiced the party against whom relief is sought" (*Black's Law Dictionary* 406, 3d pocket ed., 1996).

4. This practice pointer was authored by John Martin, a third-year law student at Suffolk University Law School. During the summers of 2006 and 2007, Martin served as Rustad's research assistant.

5. This sample letter closely tracks the sample letter recommended by the Massachusetts Attorney General's office; that model letter is available at http:www .mass.gov.

3
Small Claims Courts

Suppose your landlord withholds your security deposit on your vacated apartment when you did not damage the apartment beyond ordinary wear and tear. A property owner is not permitted to take your security deposit for routine maintenance such as painting or carpet cleaning. This chapter explains the mechanics of filing your small claims—to recoup your security deposit and other diverse consumer claims—in clear understandable language, using many examples. Topics include:

- Drafting your complaint
- Filing a statement of claim
- Naming the plaintiff and defendant
- Subpoenas, witnesses, and evidence
- Claims, counterclaims, and third parties
- Changing your court date and transfer actions
- Mediation
- Problems of proof
- Preparing for trial
- Conduct of trials
- Defendant's claim of appeal for trial by a judge or before a jury
- Appealing the judgment
- Default judgment
- Collecting the judgment
- Recovering costs and interest

Every state has procedures governing small claims acts that are designed to facilitate the just, quick, and inexpensive determination of claims. Small claims courts allow you to take direct action to get your security deposit back. They are informal tribunals where you can represent yourself in non-criminal matters in which the money damages are only a few hundred or thousand dollars. Every state has detailed rules on the cap on small claims damages. For example, California's small claims procedure states:

> An individual cannot ask for more than $7,500 in a claim. Corporations and other entities (like, government entities) cannot ask for more than $5,000. You can file as many claims as you want for up to $2,500 each. But you can only file 2 claims in a calendar year that ask for more than $2,500.
>
> You can only sue a guarantor for up to $4,000 ($2,500 if they don't charge for the guarantee). But, if you are a natural person filing against the Registrar of the Contractors' State License Board, you can sue a guarantor for up to $7500. A "guarantor" is a person who promises to be responsible for what another person owes.[1]

Small claims courts are an ideal forum for resolving a broad range of simple cases. For many consumers, small claims are the keys to the courtroom door for important consumer rights cases in which the money damages are too low to justify hiring a lawyer. In Massachusetts, the most common small claims include:

1. *Home improvement contractor claims:* Homeowners, as well as contractors, make these claims. Contractors sue for damages on unpaid invoices, and homeowners file claims for property damages caused by negligent repair or failure to complete a contract.

2. *Tenant security deposit:* These are residential tenants' claims for return of their security deposit. Issues frequently include termination of the tenancy, housing code violations, rent withholding, and treble damages.

3. *PIP claim:* PIP is short for the "personal injury protection" benefit that your automobile insurer must promptly pay for reasonable medical expenses and lost wages that you and your passengers incur, irrespective of negligence. Each state has a PIP limit, which may be as high as $25,000, as in New York. The typical PIP claim filed in small claims court is for a physical therapist or chiropractor who has not been paid.

4. *Motor vehicle negligence torts:* These are property damage claims resulting from a motor vehicle collision.

5. *Used motor vehicle warranty claims:* These cases arise out of the sale of used cars by dealers where the car fails to function shortly after the sale.

6. *Damage to personal property:* These small claims are typically against car repairers or car dealers for negligent repair of motor vehicles.

7. *Consumer collection:* These small claims are filed by credit card companies or debt collectors. In many instances, the debt has been assigned to a collection agency. If a consumer defaults on a credit card, utility bill, or a school loan, the collection agency will use the small claims court to collect the unpaid judgment.
8. *Check cashiers:* These cases tend to occur in low-income areas where consumers do not have checking accounts and rely on businesses to cash checks for a fee. Issues frequently involve fraud or misrepresentation in check collection.
9. *Loans versus gifts:* These small claims arise when relationships break-up and often present difficult issues for proof as to whether the plaintiff loaned money or gave the defendant a gift.
10. *Quantum meruit:* The term *quantum meruit* means that a benefit has been conferred for which the plaintiff is entitled to the amount merited. *Quantum meruit* claims frequently arise out of the parties' failure to put in writing the terms for work that is to be performed.[2]

What Is a Small Claims Complaint?

A small claims complaint is a paper filed in court and delivered to the party that you are suing. Small claims begin with a simple statement of claim and notice form in most jurisdictions. Print clearly or, better yet, word process your claim in concise language, but be as particular and comprehensive as possible. In many jurisdictions, the plaintiff can request assistance in completing the form. In small claims courts, a claim will not be dismissed because of the failure to allege all the elements of a prima facie case. In contrast, in a court of general jurisdiction, a complaint not alleging all the elements of a tort or contract *will be* dismissed.

Nevertheless, the clerk magistrate or small claims court should minimally be able to determine the nature of your claim, whether it is a tort or contract claim. A magistrate or assistant clerk magistrate hearing your case may or may not be an attorney. The presiding magistrate or judge can be qualified because of their training as well as their education. In small claims court, the plaintiff is the person suing, and is sometimes called the claimant. The person or company you are suing is called the defendant. If there is more than one defendant, you can file claims against multiple parties. If the defendant asserts a counterclaim, the small claims plaintiff is a defendant for purposes of the counterclaim.

Who May File a Complaint?
Example: Rental Car Complaint against Consumer. Rental Cars–R–Us of Big City files this claim for property damage to an automobile. On May 5, 2007, Carl Consumer rented a vehicle from the company. Consumer signed a rental agreement in which he agreed to assume responsibility for damage

to the vehicle. The vehicle was involved in an accident while being negligently operated by Mr. Consumer and sustained damages of $3,581.96.

Small claims courts have the popular image of "people's courts," where consumers seek redress from businesses or against their neighbors. Small claims courts were originally developed for individual consumers, not companies, but today, big companies like the rental car company are using small claims to collect debts or judgments. Small claims courts have evolved into inexpensive venues for debt collectors such as landlords, credit card companies, and other businesses to collect awards against consumers. Creditors use small claims courts as an efficient and inexpensive forum for debt collection, judging by the predominance of these cases on the docket. A few states have countered the trend toward creditors using informal courts as a method of debt collection. New York, for example, prohibits corporations, partnerships, associations, or their assignees from filing suit against consumers in small claims court. However, businesses can be sued in New York small claims courts. Commercial claims other than claims arising out of consumer transactions can be commenced by New York businesses, provided the claimant is a New York business.

Types of Small Claims

The states vary in what they consider a small claim. In general, small claims are for tort or contract cases with a statutorily set cap on the size of the award. The subject matter for small claims disputes is diverse. A small claims court, on a typical day, will consider neighborhood disputes, dog-bite cases, home improvement contracts, plumbing subcontracts, motor vehicle property damage cases, faulty transmission work, tenancy breaches, or negligently performed repair services. In Massachusetts, subrogation claims by insurers constitute a large segment of the document. Massachusetts classifies disputes where the amount in controversy is $2,000 or less as suitable for resolution in a small claims court. The statute provides: "Any individual, business, or corporation may bring a small claims suit for the recovery of money when the amount requested is $2,000 or less, except in cases involving property damage caused by a motor vehicle (where your claim can be higher). Even if you have a claim for a slightly greater amount, you may choose to voluntarily limit it to $2,000 to take advantage of the small claims court's streamlined procedure. Attorneys are allowed, but not required."[3]

Small claims courts are appropriate for claims based upon contract or the law of torts. Small claims courts have no jurisdiction to adjudicate medical malpractice, product liability, or other complex tort actions.

Every state's small claims division will exclude entire categories of cases from the jurisdiction of these informal tribunals. Many civil cases cannot be filed in a small claims court. Most small claims courts do not permit plaintiffs to file claims for libel, slander, or malicious prosecution. Similarly, you cannot contest a will or interpret a trust in a small claims court. In some jurisdictions, housing claims are filed in a special housing court.

Example: Automobile Repair. Paula Plaintiff hired Cars-R-Us to repair her vehicle. In court, she alleged that the defendant's work was unsatisfactory. Paula claimed that she allowed the defendant numerous attempts to repair the vehicle, but defendant was unable to do so. Defendant denied liability. In an actual case based upon these facts, the court entered judgment in favor of the plaintiff for $1,800 plus court costs.

Example: Billing Dispute. Patricia Plaintiff called for a repair to her leaky fireplace. A representative of the Fireplace Repairs–R–Us called upon her, and in two trips, the leaks were fixed. The bill for the work was $243.20 but the plaintiff elected not to pay it, contending that the defendant had over-stated their time. The plaintiff's housekeeper recalled that the worker was only there a few minutes, whereas the bill reflected several hours. The repair company wanted their money and initiated the litigation by filing a small claims complaint against the plaintiff. The plaintiff protested the inflated bill and the "usurious" 2 percent service charge added to her bill. In the actual case, the Fireplace Repairs–R–Us prevailed by calling an expert who testi-fied that the $243 bill was reasonable.

Courts will generally permit property, contract, and tort claims that fit the damages cap. The following categories of claims that *cannot* be filed in Ari-zona's small claims division are those for (1) libel or slander, (2) prejudgment remedies, (3) injunctive relief, (4) specific performance, (5) class actions, (6) traffic violations, (7) criminal matters, (8) claims greater than $2,500, (9) forcible entry or detainer, (10) action against the state or any governmental unit, and (11) action against an officer or employee in an official capacity. Ev-ery other state will have similar categories of cases outside the scope of small claims jurisdiction. Before you file a small claim, determine whether your cause of action can be tried in that claim. This information can be obtained by consulting your state's attorney general's website.

You can check with the clerks at the Small Claims Court in your juris-diction or locate a copy of your state's small claims statute online to answer most questions relating to jurisdiction, venue, pleadings, or procedures. You cannot file claims for cases where the court has no subject matter jurisdic-tion, such as bankruptcy, antitrust, or intellectual property infringement. Your action will be dismissed for lack of subject matter jurisdiction. Simi-larly, your small claim will be dismissed where there is no personal jurisdic-tion. The problem of "minimum contacts" occurs when there is insufficient contact with the forum state where the small claim will be tried. The defen-dant must have enough contacts with the state to satisfy the state long arm statute or the Fourteenth Amendment due process clause. A Massachusetts district court dismissed a small claims case arising out of a Massachusetts resident filing suit against a private citizen for striking and damaging his rental car in Hawaii at a beach parking lot.

What to Include in Your Complaint

Your complaint or statement of claim must be able to explain the reason for the lawsuit, the amount you are claiming, and the correct name and address, including zip code, of the person or business that is being sued. If you are not sure of the correct name of the business, you should go to the county clerk's office in the county where the business is located and look up the certificate of doing business, photocopy the certificate, and bring it to the court. The complaint should explain the facts concisely and any statute that was violated, if applicable.

Example: Negligent Towing. Complaints should have a statement of facts and the application of law if there is a statute on point. A consumer suing a towing service for causing damages to a minicoach van engine will need to explain the basis for the claim. If a towing company neglected to disengage the van's drive shaft, it would cause severe damage to the van's transmission. A small claims court will need to be satisfied that the damage to the van could have been caused by the defendant's omission. The plaintiff's burden will be to convince the court that the defendant failed to disconnect the van's drive shaft. The complaint should tell the story of how the van developed problems consistent with the towing company's negligence.

Filing a Small Claim

Small claims are filed in person or by mail. A filing fee must accompany your claim, but the court may waive this charge if your income is so low that you are classifiable as an indigent. In most states, the fee is under $25. In Massachusetts, the fees are graduated. The filing fee is $30 for claims under $500 and increases to $40 for claims between $500 and $2,000. You will likely be required to pay the filing fee by cash, certified check, money order, or bank check. Some jurisdictions will not accept personal checks. You may also incur expenses in serving process to the other side, but the overall expense is far less than you would pay in a court of general jurisdiction.

After you file your claim, you will be provided with your own copy of the statement of claim and notice forms. The date of commencement of the small claims complaint is when the claim is filed. Many small claims courts encourage their personnel to provide procedural information and help consumers prepare the forms, especially if they have difficulties understanding the requirements of a well-pleaded complaint.

Thirty-Day Demand Letter Prior to Filing Lawsuit

Small claims courts are a last resort after all reasonable attempts to settle claims have been exhausted. Ninety percent or more of civil claims settle. Few people relish the prospect of going to court, ranking it slightly below a root canal in the hierarchy of unpleasant activities. Many small claims matters may be resolved amicably by contacting the customer service representatives of businesses. Most businesses would prefer a happy customer, and if you have a winning case in small claims court, the chances are good that the case will settle if you present your case to the company.

If you are filing a claim under most states' unfair and deceptive trade practices acts (UDTPA), you need to make a written demand to the defendant to settle the claim at least thirty days prior to filing a claim, whether it is in small claims court or in a court of general jurisdiction. Most states require you to show proof that you gave your written letter of demand at least thirty days before filing your small claim or other action. At a minimum, your demand letter should identify the facts supporting your claim that the defendant is liable for unfair or deceptive acts or practices. The demand letter should also document any injury or damages you suffered.

No Injunctive Relief or Restraining Orders

Remember that a small claims court has no power to enjoin the other party or issue injunctions or other equitable relief. If you are seeking an injunction or a restraining order, you should not be in small claims court, which is reserved for simple contract matters or personal property disputes. All jurisdictions have small claims courts to handle simple matters involving contracts, property, or the rescission of agreements. The states vary significantly in what they consider a small claim. In most of these courts, a judge hears your side, but in some jurisdictions, volunteer lawyers serve as arbitrators.

New York's small claims courts are often convened in town and village courts. In New York City, Nassau and Westchester Counties, the cities of Buffalo and Rochester, and some other locations, both judges and arbitrators are available to try cases. Small claims courts are informal courts with informal procedures because the consumers are representing themselves. In a small claims court, you need to support your complaint with documents or witnesses that are relevant, just as if your case was being tried in a court of general jurisdiction. Many small claims courts give consumers the option to arbitrate. Arbitration is a process in which an impartial attorney trained in arbitration, assistant clerk magistrate, or a retired judge decides your dispute, rather than a court. The downside of arbitration is that an arbitrator's decision is final and there is no right to a jury or an appeal.

Mediation is a process in which a third party attempts to help you and the merchant resolve your differences. Mediation is an informal discussion led by an impartial third party to facilitate the settlement of a lawsuit. The results of mediation are not binding unless the parties have signed a settlement agreement. Mediation, unlike arbitration, permits you to file a lawsuit if you are dissatisfied with the result.

Jurisdiction and Venue

Small claims courts, like any other court, require jurisdiction and venue. "Personal jurisdiction" refers to the court's power to compel an out-of-state defendant to appear in court. You are required to comply with your state's "long arm" statute when filing suit against defendants outside a state's boundaries. Consumers who suffer property damage in Alaska will find it all but impossible to find personal jurisdiction in North Dakota unless they can obtain a basis for personal jurisdiction. If the defendant resides in or is domiciled outside the forum state, it will be difficult to prove that the defendant has sufficient "minimum contacts" which would require the defendant to appear in court. Also, the alleged complaint must arise out of or relate to the defendant's "minimum contacts" with the forum. In the majority of small claims, jurisdiction will not be a problem because the defendant will either be physically present or doing business in the state where the claim is filed.

In addition to personal jurisdiction, courts must also have "subject matter jurisdiction," which is the court's authority to issue judgment on the case. The subject matter of small claims consists largely of small dollar contracts and torts claims. Most small claims courts have simple jurisdiction for matters not exceeding a few thousand dollars, though this amount may be capped at $10,000 in a few states. Every jurisdiction has a limit to what may be recovered in a small claims court. In Vermont, the limit is $3,500. Arizona's small claims courts cannot exceed $2,500.[4] Massachusetts recognizes an exception to the $2,000 damages cap for property damages arising out of motor vehicle collisions.

Venue refers to the location of the court, and a motion for a change in venue is simply a motion to change the location for the trial. For example, venue in a civil court action in Massachusetts occurs in Suffolk, Plymouth, or Middlesex Counties. In Maryland, you cannot file a small claim unless it is for $5,000 or less and your claim is for money damages rather than return of property or performance of a service. In most jurisdictions, there is no discovery (depositions, requests for documents, and the like) in small claims courts. In other words, if you need to conduct discovery, you should not file your claim in a small claims court. It is important to understand that the defendant must object to venue, as well as personal jurisdiction, shortly after receiving notice. If no objection is made, the court will assume that the defendant has consented to venue and personal jurisdiction, and the defendant will not be able to object, even on appeal.

Small claims cases are simple, and therefore, lawyers are not allowed in some states. In California, for example, lawyers cannot represent you in small claims court, though you can consult a lawyer to help you draft a complaint or speak with a lawyer before or after the court hearing. In other states, lawyers are not permitted unless the parties otherwise agree. Arizona, for example, has a form entitled "Stipulation for Use of Attorneys," which may be filed prior to the hearing. Of course, attorneys may appear in the small claims division if they are representing themselves in their capacity as a consumer. Either party may object to the proceedings being held in the small claims division. The request must be made in writing at least ten business days prior to the date of the hearing. The court will transfer the case out of the small claims division after the written request.

Two motions are commonly filed in small claims courts: *motions to change venue* and *motions to vacate judgments*. An action in a consumer case is a civil judicial proceeding whereby one party prosecutes another for a wrong done or for protection of a right or prevention of a wrong. If you file a consumer action in court, you will be required to give service of process on the adversary party or potentially adversary party. Small claims courts have less formal procedures, and service of process is informal, generally done by regular mail in most jurisdictions. Most small claims courts train their personnel to assist potential litigants in small claims procedures. If you are able to visit the small claims court in person or telephone the office, you can find helpful clerks who will give you valuable tips on how to comply with procedures. Court personnel will not typically give you information on substantive law or evaluate the merits of your claims. You may file your claim in person or by mail in every jurisdiction.

Preparing Your Small Claims Case

Where to File a Small Claim against an Individual
The plaintiff in a small claims case can sue the defendant where she lived when they allegedly made the agreement or her present domicile (where she lives now). For example, if the parties live in Kingston or Cohasset, Massachusetts, you must begin the lawsuit in Plymouth County. The other party has the right to ask your case to be dismissed if it is filed in the wrong court. If you receive such a notice of a complaint, you can request the claim be dismissed by writing to the court shown on the claim. The letter should briefly explain why you have grounds for a dismissal. To find the location of the small claims court in your county, do a simple Google search.

Where to Sue Corporations
In general, companies may be sued at the place where the contract was breached or broken. A corporation may also be sued where a person was hurt or property was damaged. Finally, you may sue a corporation at its principal place of business. If you are unsure where the principal place of business is, check with your state's secretary of state or other office that registers corporations doing business in your state. Also, you may sue a corporation in the state where it was incorporated.

Procedural Requirements for Filing Complaints

States vary on where and how to file small claims. Most states have procedures that are designed to be simple and informal. You can find the small claims court rules and standards online. In Massachusetts, small claims are governed by the Uniform Small Claims Rules and Standards. In New York City, filings are made in person, but New Yorkers living outside the City of New York may file claims by mail.

Setting a Hearing Date

The clerk of the small claims court will give you a date for the hearing and notify the other side. In many jurisdictions, small claims are held during regular hours. However, in New York State, small claims court hearings are usually held at 6:30 p.m. In most states, a hearing is set within one to two months of filing a complaint with the court. The defendant will receive notice of the hearing by certified mail or regular mail, depending upon the jurisdiction.

Notice to Defendant, Answer to Claim, and Summons

Many states have a form called the "notice, claim, and summons" that you fill out to begin an action. Filling out that form is parallel to filing a complaint in a court of general jurisdiction. States vary in how service is made to the other side. In Colorado, the clerk of the small claims court sends a certified letter to the other side. Be sure you have the correct name and address of the defendant. Also, when you draft the complaint, be sure you identify the registered agent of the corporation. You can find the agent's name and address by doing a search at your secretary of state's office, where the corporation or other company will be registered to do business in your state. In many states, you can call the secretary of state's office and get this information at no charge.

Service of process is made by first-class mail in nearly every jurisdiction. If the first class mail is returned undelivered, service of process is deficient since the plaintiff supplies addresses. The statement of the claim in every jurisdiction accompanies the notice of the claim. If the defendant is out-of-state, there may be different rules for service of process, depending upon the jurisdiction.

The notice sent to the defendants instructs them that they may submit a written answer to the plaintiff's claim, which may be in the form of a letter to the court. The defendants have an opportunity to present their side of the story, but an answer is not a requirement. In a court of general jurisdiction, the failure to answer a complaint may result in a default judgment, but in a small claims court, an answer is optional. As with the plaintiff's complaint, the defendant's answer should use clear, jargon-free language in explaining why the plaintiff should not prevail. A good answer addresses specific aspects of the plaintiff's complaint and gives the reasons why the plaintiff should not prevail. The defendant's answer must be sent to the plaintiff. If the plaintiff does not receive an answer, a clerk may grant a continuance. The continuance will give the plaintiff time to respond to the defendant's answer once it has been received.

Example: Claim and Defense to Neighborhood Dispute over Fallen Limb
    Plaintiff's Claim: On April 1, 2007, a section of a large limb fell onto our stockade fence in Big City, Massachusetts, causing $1,950 in damages. This large limb has remained on our property for seven months. The defendant told us that they would remove the limb but did not fulfill their promise. The estimate for the damaged stockade fence is enclosed, as well as the cost of removing the limb.

    Defendant's Answer: It is the defendant's position that they are not liable because in Massachusetts, a landowner does not owe a duty to protect an adjoining landowner's property from damages caused by the dropping of "leaves, branches, and sap from a healthy tree." *Ponte v. DaSilva*, 388 Mass. 1008 (1983) (copy attached). The plaintiffs have offered no proof that our tree was unhealthy and that we knew or should have known of the unhealthy condition.

    Defendant's Counterclaim: The defendant may assert a counterclaim in either his answer or in a separate writing. A counterclaim is a defendant's claim against the plaintiff. The defendant can assert as many counterclaims as he or she wants without incurring any filing fee or charge. Counterclaims arise out of the same facts constituting the plaintiff's complaint, and both claim and counterclaim are considered one case. Defendants must mail counterclaims to the plaintiff at least ten days in advance of the scheduled trial date in Massachusetts. Other states have similar notice requirements. Defendants can bring counterclaims in small claims court at any time, so long as they are in a signed, written document. The plaintiff is not required to answer the defendant's counterclaims.
    A plaintiff filing a small claims action may end up writing a check in favor of the defendant if the court rules in favor of the defendant's counterclaim. For example, if you sue a property owner for his failure to return your security deposit, the landlord may respond with a counterclaim for documented damages during your tenancy. The result may be that not only will you not receive your security deposit, but also that you may have to pay a counterclaim entered against you. Before you file a small claim, be sure you are in the right and do not have outstanding claims against you, which are the functional equivalent of a small claims court blowback.
    Statutes of limitations apply equally to small claims courts and to courts of general jurisdiction. You will have two or three years to file a personal injury claim, depending upon the jurisdiction. Most states give you six years

to file complaints for debts owed on written contracts. That is a general guide, so you must check your jurisdiction's relevant statutes of limitations.

Example: Counterclaim in Home Improvement Contract. In a Massachusetts case, the homeowner/defendant began a home improvement project to construct an enclosed three-season porch on his house. The plaintiff/contractor, who had a full-time day job doing construction work, agreed to help the defendant on weekends. The homeowner had records indicating that the plaintiff worked between seventy-two and eighty hours on the project. The contractor claimed that the homeowner owed damages of $1,350.00, which was the balance due on the work on the porch. The homeowner filed a counterclaim, alleging that the contractor was liable for damages to the home caused during the construction of the porch. Since the parties had no written contract covering the project, the clerk magistrate awarded damages on the reasonable value of services conferred. In that case, the contractor was awarded $3,200 for his labor as well as the value of a $450 nail gun the contractor had purchased to work on the project. The clerk magistrate ruled against the homeowner on his counterclaim that the contractor caused damage.

Third-Party Practice
Small claims courts also have procedures for a defendant to bring a claim against any third party who may be liable for all or part of the plaintiff's claim. However, one limitation is that the defendant's claim must be within the jurisdiction of the small claims court. The defendant incurs no charges or filing fees for bringing in third parties, and the procedure is similar to that of the assertion of a counterclaim.

Transfer to a Court of General Jurisdiction
The small claims court may transfer a claim to the regular civil docket at the request of a party or its own motion. A case may be transferred to a regular civil court because the small claims court does not have subject matter jurisdiction. A case involving First Amendment rights, for example, would not be properly adjudicated in small claims court and may be transferred to a civil docket. In Massachusetts, an action arising out of a tenancy may be transferred to the Housing Court. Any claim for medical malpractice must be referred to the medical malpractice tribunal in that state. Other states have similar mechanisms to permit the transfer of actions to the proper court.

Amendments, Discovery, and Pretrial Attachment of Property
Small claims may be amended at any time in most jurisdictions. Since small claims courts are intended to be speedy and efficient, no discovery is allowed. On rare occasions, a clerk magistrate can order good cause for discovering documents or exhibits in the possession of the defendant. Witnesses may be

summoned to court. Small claims courts have no provisions for attaching the property of the defendant, unlike civil courts of general jurisdiction.

Preparation for the Small Claims Court Hearing

A clerk magistrate or small claims judge has no discretion to accept disputes outside the court's jurisdiction, such as bankruptcy, family law, probate matters, or criminal matters. Either party may make a request to dismiss or transfer an action to a general court in writing prior to the time set for the hearing. Courts of general jurisdiction will permit you to re-file your action if it is outside the jurisdiction of the small claims tribunal.

If your case goes forward, a clerk magistrate or similar official sets a hearing date. Keep in mind that the small claims court is an informal tribunal where formal rules of evidence or civil procedure are not used. Although formal rules do not apply, you need to plan how you will try your case. First, think about what you are going to say. Second, prepare the documents (receipts and other evidence) you intend to use to prove or defend against a claim. Talk to witnesses and arrange for them to attend the hearing. You may also want to talk to the person you are suing or who is suing you. Going to court as a litigant is an unpleasant experience for most Americans. If you talk to the other side, you may be able to work out a settlement and avoid going to court.

Draft an opening argument based upon the facts you are asserting. Draft a timeline of the events, supported by documentation. Just as in the *People's Court* on television, you need to document your claim. Make copies of key documents, assemble all relevant evidence, including photographs, written agreements, itemized bills, and invoices marked "paid," or receipts. Even if a Statute of Fraud does not require writing, get everything in writing in the event there is a dispute.

Supply the court with two itemized written estimates of the cost of services or repairs that would be required to satisfy your claim. Bring everything of relevance to court, including canceled checks, receipts, and other evidence supporting your claim. If you purchased clothing, for example, bring the damaged item or article of clothing to court. If you sent a demand letter or gave the seller notice, bring in the letter or other written documents. If there are records that are not in your possession, you may wish to ask the other side to produce them. Document these requests and bring evidence of the request to court.

Prepare your witnesses, but be sure that you tell them that they are under oath and must be truthful. The testimony of a person who has special or expert knowledge and experience concerning the subject of your claim may be necessary for you to prove your case. For example, if your claim involves the quality of automobile repair or plumbing, you may want to bring a professional willing to testify to the work you received. If that person cannot appear in court, you may want to get a notarized statement.

The Days before Your Hearing

Be sure to visit the court where your small claims action will be tried so you can be in a comfort zone. You will be less likely to be nervous if you have a greater understanding of how proceedings work or the habits of the judge trying your case. If you know where you will be sitting when presenting your case and have a feel for the layout of the courtroom, you are more likely to be at your best on the day of the hearing. Organize a file with all your key exhibits marked for identification. Write out your argument and practice delivering it before families and friends. Think of the court proceedings as a conversation. You are telling a story backed by facts, not giving a speech. Small claims courts are no occasion to practice your best imitation of Perry Mason or Johnnie Cochran. Be prepared. The more you practice, the greater poise and confidence you will have the time of your hearing. Also, be sure to search online for the directions for the courthouse if you do not have the time to visit it ahead of time.

Dress professionally. Do not wear baseball caps backward. Cover all body art. Keep in mind that your average magistrate is middle-aged and will be judging you on your dress and demeanor. It is a good idea to arrive at least half an hour early at your proceeding. You never know what is going on in the courthouse that day, and every person must go through security clearances. Make sure you do not bring anything that can be considered a weapon with you, even if you have a license to carry a firearm, because most, if not all, jurisdictions have statutes that prohibit a civilian from bringing a weapon into any government building. The most common mistake people make is to have a Swiss Army knife or pair of scissors.

In big cities such as Boston or Philadelphia, small claims courts will have a crowded docket and the court proceedings will begin at the scheduled time. If you are late and your name is called, the court may dismiss your action or issue a default judgment against you, even if you are the plaintiff. Your only recourse will be to convince the clerk magistrate to set aside the default judgment.

Limitations of the Small Claims Court

The advantages of the small claims court are the low filing fees, simplified procedures, efficiency of process, and speed of the proceedings. There are, however, limitations that exist in the small claims court. For example, a plaintiff filing a small claims action is waiving his right to a civil jury trial. A defendant still has a Seventh Amendment right to have civil actions tried by a jury. If a plaintiff files an action in small claims court, a defendant can petition to have the action tried in a court of general jurisdiction. Two experienced Massachusetts clerk magistrates with decades of experience explain other limitations of the small claims procedure:

1. The matter may never be heard by a judge or jury;
2. A plaintiff who loses has no right of appeal;
3. If the plaintiff wins, the defendant may appeal to a District Court jury session;
4. There is no further right of appeal after the jury session;
5. There is no discovery unless specifically allowed;
6. Rules of evidence do not strictly apply;
7. The defendant may be permitted to transfer the case to the regular civil docket over the objection of the plaintiff; and
8. There is no pretrial attachment available.[5]

Small Claims Procedures

What happens when you appear in small claims court? Assume you are the claimant or plaintiff. A clerk magistrate or assistant clerk will call your case. If the defendant does not appear, procedures vary. In California, the claimant will go before the judge or arbitrator to present evidence to prove his or her case while the defendant's case is represented only by an empty chair. It may be possible for either party to reopen the case later, but they have a difficult burden of proving "good cause" for their failure to appear.

If both parties are present, the plaintiff's case is presented first after he or she is sworn in as a witness. If you are the plaintiff, it is your burden to prove that you have a good contract or tort cause of action. You must tell your story of how you were defrauded, injured, or suffered damages at the hands of the defendant. If you are the defendant, you will be given an opportunity to respond to the plaintiff's case. Your goal will be to present defenses to the plaintiff's claims and assert counterclaims if available. Be courteous and professional! Watch an episode or rerun of television programs such as *People's Court*, *Judge Judy*, *Judge Joe Brown*, or *Judge Maria Lopez*. Television judges, like real small claims court judges, will not take kindly to rudeness toward themselves or the other party. When the judge or magistrate asks you a question, wait for him or her to finish the question. Listen carefully and be sure that you answer the question asked.

Unlike Judge Judy or other television judges, it is unlikely that your small claims court clerk magistrate or presiding judge will berate you for bad parenting, mate choices, or careless decisionmaking. A small claims court judge will question you to satisfy questions he or she has about your claim. If you treat questions like a conversation and give polite responses, you will present your best case. Keep in mind that the role of the small claims judge or magistrate is that of a fact finder. You will not experience an inquisition or dramatic one-act play or the entertaining proceedings depicted in television small claims courts.

Be sure to have all documents, witnesses, and other evidence ready. State legislatures creating small claims courts seek to provide an inexpensive court for deciding lawsuits where damages are fairly low. Clerk magistrates or judges convening small claims have the broad discretion to admit evidence that sheds light on the plaintiff's claim or the defendant's defense. When the claimant has finished testifying, the judge, arbitrator, or the defendant may ask some questions to clarify matters. The judge or arbitrator or either party can also question all witnesses. The defendant then will be sworn in, tell his or her side of the story, and present evidence. The defendant also may present other witnesses. The claimant or the judge or arbitrator may ask questions of the defendant and the witnesses called by the defendant.

If you are suing a business, be certain to ask the defendant's witness the full and correct legal name of the business and the name of the person who owns the business. If the name of the business is different from the name you wrote in your notice of claim, correct your notice of claim.

After both sides and the witnesses have testified, the judge will render a decision. Sometimes the decision will be rendered the same day of the trial, and other times the decision will be rendered later. The decision will be mailed to the parties within a few days of the hearing.

Enforcing a Judgment

It is one thing to be awarded damages and another to collect them. Small claims courts will not collect your judgment for you. If you win a judgment, you are a *judgment creditor*. The person or business that owes you the judgment is known as the *judgment debtor*. The first thing you should do is ask the debtor to pay you while in court, immediately after the judgment is rendered. If this is not an option, write a letter requesting that the judgment be paid. Send your demand for payment by certified mail, return receipt requested. Be sure to caption your note with the civil action number and a copy of the judgment. Remind the losing party that you are entitled to post-judgment interest. The prevailing party automatically receives an award of the filing fee.

Conclude your demand letter by saying that full payment will release the other side from all claims and end the dispute. If the judgment debtor is unable to pay, offer a payment schedule. Be careful about accepting partial payment unless you are settling the claim for a lesser amount. An "accord and satisfaction" is an agreement between a debtor and creditor in which the creditor accepts a lesser amount. Do not cash a check for a partial amount if it states, "This check is payment in full and final satisfaction of all claims." If the check does not contain such a clause but is still in a lesser amount, write "Debt not paid in full, the right to collect the remaining balance is retained by the signor" on the endorsement line of the check. Clerk magistrates or assistant magistrates will often assist the parties in creating payment schedules. Once the parties agree to a payment schedule, it becomes a court order.

Jurisdictions vary in deciding when a small claims court judgment becomes final. In California, the small claims court judgment becomes final and enforceable thirty days after the small claims clerk has delivered or mailed the notice of entry of judgment. Jurisdictions also vary as to whether a judgment may be appealed. In California, the defendant may file a notice of motion to vacate judgment. If the defendant files an appeal and loses, the judgment becomes enforceable after transfer of the case back to the small claims court. If you are the defendant in a consumer case, you may be required to satisfy the judgment. Be sure to get the judgment creditor to complete and file an acknowledgment that the judgment has been satisfied.

States also differ in their procedures to help you collect small claims judgments. New Hampshire, for example, offers the following advice on collecting a small claims judgment:

1. After thirty days from the date of the written decision, you may request a "Motion for Periodic Payments" hearing. Complete the required form and mail with the $15.00 entry fee to the court. You must mail the pink copy of this form to the defendant.
2. The court will schedule a hearing on this request and return the paperwork to you to make service. Carefully follow the instructions that will accompany this form. If the defendant is not served with notice of the hearing, you will have to request rescheduling.
3. Some courts require your appearance. If you fail to appear, you cannot contest the defendant's statements with regard to his or her ability to make payments, and you cannot review the financial affidavit that the defendant filled out for the court.
4. The judge may order the defendant to pay you the lump sum, or make weekly or monthly payments, depending on the defendant's financial situation.
5. If the defendant fails to appear at this hearing and proper service has been made, you may request that a civil arrest warrant be prepared and forwarded to the sheriff's department for service.
6. Your judgment is good for twenty years, provided you seek periodic review of the matter by the court no less than every two years.[6]

You are unlikely to collect your judgment if the defendant has no resources or is out of state, beyond the reach of process. It is unlikely that you will collect a foreign or out-of-state judgment. The California Department of Consumer Affairs recommends the following steps for locating the judgment debtor and collecting your judgment. Many of these tips apply equally well to judgments obtained in a general jurisdiction court as well.

1. Read the Notice of Entry of Judgment (Form SC-130) that you have received from the small claims court. It tells you and the other party how the judge ruled. If you discover an error in the judgment, you may file a Re-

quest to Correct or Vacate Judgment (Form SC-108). Either a plaintiff or a defendant may file such a request.

2. If either of the parties was unable to attend the hearing for good cause, the party who did not appear may file a Notice of Motion to Vacate Judgment (Form SC-135) to request a new hearing in the small claims court.

3. Judgment debtor—If the other party asserted a claim against you, and you appeared at the hearing, and the judge decided against you, and there is good reason for you to believe that the judge made a mistake, you may file a Notice of Appeal (Form SC-140) to obtain a new hearing before a different judge.

4. Judgment debtor—You may comply with the judgment (for instance, by payment to the judgment creditor or the court). If you can only make weekly or monthly payments, the court probably will issue an installment payment order if you request it by filing a Request to Pay Judgment in Installments (Form SC-106).

5. Judgment debtor—If you haven't paid the judgment in full within 30 days after receipt of the Notice of Entry of Judgment (Form SC-130), complete the Judgment Debtor's Statement of Assets (Form SC-133) that accompanied the Notice of Entry of Judgment (Form SC-130) and send it to the judgment creditor.

6. Judgment debtor—After the judgment creditor has received full payment, make sure that the judgment creditor files an Acknowledgment of Satisfaction of Judgment (Form EJ-100) with the small claims court.

7. Judgment creditor—File an Acknowledgment of Satisfaction of Judgment (Form EJ-100) with the court when the judgment debt is paid, or take steps to collect the judgment.[7]

Conduct a Judgment Debtor's Examination. In every jurisdiction, you will need to take steps to collect your judgment. Visit your small claims court and talk to the clerk magistrate or her assistant about how to conduct an examination of a judgment debtor. Under this procedure, the judgment debtor is ordered to appear in court to answer your questions about the existence, location, and amount or value of the judgment debtor's salary, other income sources, bank accounts, tangible property, and anything else that could be used to generate proceeds to pay the judgment. You may be able to subpoena the debtor's bankbooks, property deeds, paycheck stubs, and similar documents and require the judgment debtor to bring them to the hearing. You may ask the judge to order the judgment debtor to turn over any assets in the judgment debtor's possession.

You will need to complete and pay a fee for an application and order for appearance and examination or its equivalent in other jurisdictions. You will need a small claims subpoena for personal appearance and production of documents at trial or hearing and declaration if you want the defendant to produce evidence at trial. The application and order for appearance and examination (and the subpoena if you want to serve that too) must be served on the debtor by the sheriff or a registered process server, or by a private person specially appointed by court order at the judgment creditor's request. In Massachusetts, the judgment debtor must reside or have a place of business within 150 miles of the court, but that requirement varies from state to state.

Suspend the Judgment Debtor's Driver's License. If you obtained a judgment for $750 or less in an auto accident case and the judgment is not paid within thirty days after the judgment becomes final, you may want to consider having the debtor's driver's license suspended for ninety days. You must complete DMV Form DL17, available from local offices of the Department of Motor Vehicles.[8] You can download online forms from other states by doing a simple online search for your jurisdiction's state court website.

Arbitrating Small Claims

A growing number of jurisdictions use volunteer arbitrators to hear and decide small claims. Postdispute arbitration is a popular way to resolve disputes. In New York, arbitrators are attorneys with at least five years of legal experience and training in arbitration procedures. The 1,800 small claims arbitrators in New York City try 95 percent of the small claims. Arbitration decisions are final and are not subject to reversal on appeal. Arbitrators, like umpires in baseball, do not reverse their decisions. Unlike umpires, a small claims court is not subject to review by a higher authority.

Mediation

You will also have an option to mediate your claim with the consent of the person or company you are suing. You still have the option to file a court action if mediation fails. You are not required to mediate the dispute, but it may be quicker to resolve your case without going to court. Mediators do not have the power to award court costs unless the parties have entered into a mediation agreement permitting such a remedy.

Many states administer mediation programs as an alternative to going to court. Maryland's District Court's Alternative Dispute Resolution Program gives consumers the opportunity to try to resolve disputes outside of court. To learn more about Maryland's mediation program, call the District Court's Alternative Dispute Resolution office at 1-410-260-1676. Mediation is generally free, but there may be a small charge in some jurisdictions. Most mediation lasts less than an hour, and if you cannot reach agreement, you can proceed to court. In California, you can mediate your complaint before or after filing a small claim.

The mediation session takes place outside the courtroom on the day scheduled for the trial. Both the plaintiff and defendant must agree to participate in the process. A mediator from the program will meet with you and the other party in your case. You do not need to make an appointment ahead of time to participate in mediation on the day of your hearing; however, you may call the program office ahead of time if you wish to try to resolve your small claims case prior to the hearing date.

If your case is resolved through mediation, you and the other party will sign a document that outlines what you both have agreed to do. The document will become part of the court file. If you are not able to resolve your case through mediation, you will go back into the courtroom, and a judicial officer will hear your case. Mediation will not delay your opportunity for a court hearing.[9]

Many states have mediation programs that apply to civil actions filed in general jurisdiction courts. In Oregon, as in many other states, the mediators are volunteers and may be lawyers, law students, court clerks, retired teachers, public officials, or businesspeople.

Filing an Appeal

In courts of general jurisdiction, you have a right to appeal a judge's decision. That is not the case if you filed the small claim. The plaintiff can not appeal the decision but the defendant has the option to appeal. A defendant's claim of appeal for trial by a judge or before a jury is made in writing. The defendant will be asked to specify whether he claims a trial by a judge or before a jury. The defendant is required to mail a copy of a claim of appeal to the defendant. Most states will schedule a hearing before a judge of the division of the trial court if the defendant's appeal is filed in a timely manner.

Relief from Judgment or Order

If you did not attend a small claims hearing for a good reason, you may be able to ask the court to cancel your judgment (called a "default judgment") and receive a new hearing. In California, you will need to file a form titled Notice of Motion to Vacate Judgment and Declaration (Small Claims). Other states have similar procedures for vacating judgments, but you must show good cause.

Self-Representation

You are proceeding *pro se* when you represent yourself in court. You should not proceed *pro se* in cases involving medical malpractice and products liability or other complex litigation. The ABA also suggests the possibility of retaining a lawyer for unfamiliar tasks. However, in simple consumer issues involving small claims court, proceeding *pro se* is more practical for economic reasons.

The ABA publishes an excellent guide on self-representation entitled *Consumers' Guide to Legal Help: Helping Yourself*. This guidebook may be found at the ABA's public service website: http://www.abanet.org/legalservices/find legalhelp/faq_selfhelp.cfm. The ABA does not endorse self-representation or hiring a lawyer for some tasks but not others. The judiciary in a number of states do not favor self-representation. In any case, whether you retain a lawyer or not, the principles stated in this book about consumer law will be good background for you in understanding your rights and remedies.

Notes

1. California Courts Self-Help Center, available at http://www.courtinfo.ca.gov/selfhelp/smallclaims/scbasics.htm#whatis (accessed March 25, 2007).

2. This top-ten list of Massachusetts small claims was prepared by William Farrell, an assistant clerk-magistrate in the Dorchester Court Division, Boston Municipal Court Department, drawing upon the 1,095 statements of small claims trials he heard from 1999 to 2007 in the Dorchester Court as well as in special assignments for Barnstable and New Bedford, Massachusetts (March 2, 2007).

3. Sherrie Bennett, Massachusetts Small Claims, available at http://research.lawyers.com/Massachusetts-Small-Claims.html (accessed October 8, 2006).

4. Nolo has published a fifty-state survey of the monetary caps on how much you can claim or recover in a small claims court, available at http://www.nolo.com/article.cfm/ObjectID/ADF1FA1B-C67D-4B95-AD615532C3AE0862/catID/D80CF756-DBF6-432D-B625E7D1A29183D0/104/308/273/ART.

5. Sean P. Coleman and Michael D. Prosser, *Pursuing a Case in Small Claims Court* (Boston: Massachusetts Continuing Legal Education, 2007), 33.

6. New Hampshire District Court, "How to File a Small Claim/Court Procedure," available at http://www.nh.gov/judiciary/district/claims.htm (accessed October 16, 2006).

7. California Department of Consumer Affairs, *The Small Claims Court: A Guide to Its Practical Use* (2007), http://www.dca.ca.gov/publications/small_claims/checklist.shtml (last visited May 25, 2007).

8. California Department of Consumer Affairs, "After the Judgment, Collecting or Satisfying the Judgment," http://www.dca.ca.gov/legal/small_claims/collect.html (accessed September 23, 2006).

9. Superior Court of California, "Small Claims Mediation Program," available at http://www.saccourt.com/smallclaims/mediation/mediation.asp (accessed October 15, 2006).

4

Choosing and Working with Your Own Lawyer

Consumer law has a bearing on almost everything you do, but you cannot possibly consult a lawyer for every consumer problem. Most consumer issues are typically handled by complaints to state or federal agencies. Common sense might dictate that you consult a lawyer before you enter into a consumer contract and sign away all warranties, remedies, your first-born son, and your American citizenship. In big-ticket decisions, you may want to consult an attorney to go over the contractual provisions. In many consumer cases, you can take direct action such as filing a claim in small claims court against a creditor, lender, seller, landlord, or other merchant. Lawsuits should only be filed when informal resolutions fail.

Consumers may be able to retain a legal aid society, an organization willing to take their case pro bono, or a private attorney. The term *pro bono publico* is Latin for "for the public good." Lawyers take pro bono work without payment because the case should be filed for the public good.

However, the majority of consumers are not able to receive funded legal services in routine consumer cases. If legal aid or a legal clinic is unable to take your case, you will need to hire a private attorney. In many ways, your choice of an attorney is the most important decision you will make in a high-stakes case where self-representation is not an option because of the complexity of the litigation. You do not need to choose your attorney from television advertisements, billboards, or the yellow pages. This chapter gives you better ways to find the right attorney for your case.

Finding and Hiring a Lawyer

The American Bar Association recommends that you do not select a lawyer before doing some due diligence. The ABA consumer website is found at http://www.abanet.org/legalservices/findlegalhelp/home.cfm. Consumers in Massachusetts can receive assistance obtaining a lawyer through local bar associations. The Middlesex County Bar Association, for example, provides referral services to consumers in Middlesex County. Consumers in Boston can find help through the Boston Bar Association at http://www.boston-bar.org/LRS. The National Association of Consumer Advocates (NACA) is an organization of 1,000 or more lawyers who specialize in the law of consumer protection. You can find an NACA lawyer in your area by clicking on "Find an Attorney" at http://www.naca.net/db.php3.

Before you retain a lawyer, you can check if he or she has good standing with the bar by first locating your jurisdiction's board of bar overseers or equivalent by visiting the ABA's website. The ABA has a listing for each jurisdiction at www.abanet.org/cpr/regulation/scpd/disciplinary.html. The ABA website retrieves information from Martindale-Hubbell, which is a directory of ratings and other information on attorneys throughout the United States. For example, my listing shows that I am a law faculty member as well as a lawyer in private practice in Boston, Massachusetts. You can use the Martindale lawyer locator service for no charge available at http://www.martindale.com/.

What You Should Demand from Your Lawyer

What you are looking for is a lawyer who has the expertise to protect your rights and help you avoid liability. If you have a problem with consumer credit, you will need a lawyer who has experience in that type of case. Similarly, if you have a landlord/tenant problem, find a lawyer that has expertise assisting tenants. The Massachusetts Bar Association recommends that at the first meeting with a prospective attorney, the consumer should be proactive and ask questions about what prior experience the lawyer has in resolving your specific issue. In addition, you may ask some of the following questions:

- Can I receive an outline of my causes of action?
- How will my case be handled?
- Who will staff my case?
- How long will it take to litigate my case?
- Do you have malpractice insurance, and if so, who is your insurance carrier?
- To what degree can I participate in my case?
- How will I be informed about the progress of my case?
- What information can you give me about your legal fees, expenses, and billing?
- What is your hourly fee (if applicable)?
- Can you give an estimate of your total fee?[1]

Legal Resources for Consumers

Many Americans simply cannot afford to hire a lawyer for most problems and can only muster the resources to hire a lawyer on the rare occasion when they are faced with big decisions such as consumer bankruptcy, property transfers, divorce, and estate planning. Unfortunately, consumers who need legal help are frequently unaware of the availability of legal services.

Consumer law benefits all Americans in their capacity as consumers. However, much of the consumer law of the 1960s and 1970s targeted distinct populations. Senior citizens, low-income families, military personnel, and new immigrants have special vulnerabilities in the consumer marketplace. These vulnerable populations need legal representation.

In the American legal system, a consumer is generally responsible for paying their own legal fees despite the outcome of the case. The problem in most consumer credit cases is that the amount in controversy can be as little as $100. To make it affordable for the average American to file a lawsuit, many federal and state statutes award attorney's fees and costs to a prevailing plaintiff. Federal and state statutes that award attorney's fees and costs to the prevailing plaintiff are called "fee-shifting" statutes; they make it cost-effective for a plaintiff to file suit where otherwise the case would be dismissed as a "no damages" case. This is different than the traditional American rule for business litigants where each party is responsible for their own legal expenses.

Legal aid organizations give free legal representation for low-income populations typically underserved by lawyers. In addition, private organizations such as law schools represent groups frequently targeted by predators in the consumer marketplace. All states have state and federally funded programs that may be able to provide consumers with free legal assistance. For example, the Massachusetts Bar Association (MBA) has a service that provides legal representation at low cost to consumers. Contact the Legal Advocacy and Resource Center at www.larcma.org/. The MBA Lawyer Referral Service may be reached at 1-617-654-0400 or 1-866-627-7577. However, these agencies tend to be underfunded and are unable to represent many low-income consumers in civil matters.

Legal Services Corporation

Congress created the Legal Services Corporation (LSC) in 1974 to provide low-income Americans with equal access to the legal system. At the time the LSC was created, low-income Americans had no legal assistance or only token assistance in many states. Legal services are offered through local legal programs funded by grants from the LSC. The corporation itself does not offer legal aid directly. However, an LSC program in your area may be able to provide you with some assistance. You can easily locate your local legal services office by going to the LSC website at www.lsc.gov and finding your state on the map.

Few LSC offices are willing to take consumer cases in recent years because of the lack of resources. Many Americans who seek legal help on consumer issues from LSC-funded providers are turned away because of the lack of LSC sufficient resources.[2]

In 2005, roughly two million consumers sought legal help; LSC-affiliated organizations turn away one client for every client that can be helped. LSC attorneys are rejecting an estimated one million cases per year because they simply lack resources. As a result, self-help or help through a law school or other privately funded legal services will typically be the only alternative.

Law School Legal Aid Clinics

Wisconsin's Consumer Law Litigation Clinic. The University of Wisconsin Law School created a clinic to help low- and moderate-income consumers by representing them in state and federal courts. The Consumer Law Litigation Clinic litigates a variety of consumer cases against the perpetrators of consumer fraud, credit scams, the bad faith denial of insurance claims, antitrust violations, unfair debt collection practices, and "fringe banking" abuses by rent-to-own and payday loan companies. The clinic, for example, initiated a nationwide class action on behalf of elderly consumers who use Hytrin, a high-blood-pressure medication, against a pharmaceutical company that used unfair tactics to keep low-cost generics off the market. The clinic also filed the following lawsuits:

- A lawsuit claiming bad faith by a health maintenance organization (HMO) that refused to cover treatments for a three-year-old boy suffering from brain cancer;
- Numerous lawsuits filed on behalf of consumers whose cars were unlawfully repossessed;
- A lawsuit filed on behalf of several Latino consumers in Dane County victimized by a California company fraudulently promising careers as licensed auto mechanics;
- A lawsuit filed on behalf of an elderly widow challenging false advertising and fraudulent marketing tactics by a credit card company;
- A class action on behalf of consumers who entered into "payday loan" contracts with interest rates exceeding 500 percent;
- An antitrust class action on behalf of purchasers of physician services from a large medical clinic and HMO in northern Wisconsin;
- A statewide class action challenging a variety of false and deceptive practices by a company that sells timeshares in the Wisconsin Dells; and
- Representation of a mentally disabled man whose home was threatened with foreclosure after a bank convinced him to take out a line of credit whose payments he could not afford on his fixed income.[3]

Suffolk Law School's Housing and Consumer Protection Clinic. In Boston, Suffolk University Law School's highly acclaimed Housing and Consumer Protection Clinic specializes in assisting consumers with housing-related problems. Under the supervision of seasoned practitioners, Suffolk University law students have represented the interests of consumers in a number of high-profile housing cases in the city of Boston and surrounding towns. Suffolk's consumer law clinic focuses on housing, evictions, and landlord/tenant issues cognizable under the Massachusetts Consumer Protection Act.

In recent years, the Suffolk clinic has branched out, bringing actions in various courts as a way to address clients' needs. For example, the clinic handled a high-profile case in which tenants were forced to leave their apartment in the middle of the winter when the City of Chelsea condemned the building because it was a fire hazard due to the plumbing and electrical work the property owner performed without a permit. The Suffolk Housing and Consumer Protection Clinic also filed suit against a property owner who took a deposit from a prospective tenant on an apartment, retaining the deposit even though no apartment was offered to the consumer to rent. In another case, the law school clinic sued a landlord who converted hundreds of dollars worth of personal property from a tenant she evicted.

The Suffolk Housing and Consumer Protection Clinic also filed a suit against a storage company that specialized in handling the personal property of evicted tenants. In that case, the tenant was evicted from public housing after being less than $200 behind in rent. The housing authority hired a storage company to remove the tenant's belongings. While the storage company was removing her belongings, the tenant was required to sign a document that stated that the storage company had a "right to charge a three-month minimum no matter how long we have goods." The statute governing post-eviction storage did not allow a storage facility to charge a three-month minimum, but rather allowed such a facility to charge a "reasonable storage fee" (M.G.L.A. c. 239, §4 [amended 2004]).

Two days later, the tenant contacted the storage company to inquire about removing her property. She was informed that the storage fee was $1,800 (not including the cost of moving the property). The clinic brought a consumer protection action against the storage company in Superior Court, alleging that the storage company's actions and fee structure were unfair and deceptive. The case was settled, and the storage company returned the tenant's property.

The Suffolk Housing and Consumer Protection Clinic then joined forces with advocates from a variety of groups, including clinical programs, legal services entities, and private practitioners, to draft an amendment to the post-eviction storage law. The Massachusetts legislature enacted the amendment in 2004. A newly minted Massachusetts statute requires fees to be commercially reasonable and to be filed with the Massachusetts Department of Public

Safety. The amended statute also contains provisions requiring notice to tenants of the whereabouts of their property, an inventory of the property, and a one-time right of access to the property to retrieve items of sentimental value (M.G.L.A. c. 239, §4 [2004]). In October 2006, a justice of the Massachusetts Superior Court permanently enjoined the owners of that storage company from engaging in the business of storing the property of evicted tenants. The Office of the Attorney General brought the case after the Suffolk Housing and Consumer Protection Clinic brought these abuses to their attention.

Harvard's Predatory Lending/Consumer Protection Clinic. Harvard University Law School's Predatory Lending/Consumer Protection Clinic also represents Massachusetts consumers who have been victimized by unfair and deceptive subprime loans. Predatory lenders use unfair or deceptive marketing practices to convince consumers to agree to exorbitant fees and high-interest rates. Consumers induced to enter these one-sided loans are far more likely to be the victims of foreclosure. Harvard's clinic seeks to protect the equity of low- and moderate-income homeowners and ensure equal and fair access to markets. The clinic, funded in part by the Boston law firm of Hale and Dorr, represents homeowners seeking to defend against foreclosure, while also litigating against banking institutions, subprime lenders, home improvement contractors, brokers, and "foreclosure rescue scam artists." To learn more about the activities and the mission of Harvard University Law School's Clinic, you can find information at the clinic's website at http://www.law.harvard.edu/academics/clinical/lsc/clinics/predatory.htm.

Penn State Elder Law Clinic. Penn State/Dickinson School of Law's Elder Law and Consumer Protection Clinic represents elderly consumers in a variety of matters, including Social Security, bankruptcy, housing, health care advance directives, and nursing home neglect and abuse. The clinic represents elderly consumers in the Harrisburg, Pennsylvania, vicinity.

Resources for Attorneys Representing Low-Income Consumers

The National Consumer Law Center. Lawyers representing low-income consumers can often find help by contacting organizations dedicated to consumer protection such as the National Consumer Law Center (NCLC), http://www.consumerlaw.org/. The NCLC's website states that it is a "consumer advocacy group providing research assistance to consumer attorneys, writing manuals on law, and working with lawmakers to adopt laws and regulations which benefit and protect consumers." The NCLC cannot represent clients directly but is broadly supportive of attorneys trying cases. It has received grants that make it possible for staff attorneys to assist or consult with lawyers representing consumers. NCLC staff attorneys have assisted pro bono and legal aid lawyers in California, Massachusetts, and Washington, chiefly in cases involving low-income clients or the elderly.

You may suggest to your attorney to contact NCLC's intake attorney at 1-617-542-8010 if your case fits into either of these categories.[4]

Other Organizations for Lawyers. Attorneys representing consumers may also find resources through other public interest groups such as the Consumer's Union, Consumer Action, the Consumer Federation of America, the Consumer Law Center of the South, the National Association of Consumer Advocates, Trial Lawyers for Public Justice, the National Consumers League, and the U.S. Public Interest Research Group. Consumer class actions, in particular, are often complex and require consultative services with organizations having specialized knowledge of the statutes and remedies.

Contingency Fee Representation

Contingency fee agreements are the principal means of securing representation for torts victims. If injury victims were required to pay an hourly rate or retainer, few could afford to vindicate their rights. The meaning of "contingency" here is that the lawyer's fee is contingent upon her success with her case. The lawyer is paid nothing in the event of a defense verdict. However, if there is a verdict in the plaintiff's favor or a pretrial settlement, the lawyer is paid out of that sum after all litigation fees have been paid. Contingency fees vary, but the typical case gives the lawyer one-third of the recovery after expenses. The attorney will generally receive this amount, but there are jurisdictions in which the lawyer's share may be as high as 40 percent.

A few states have adopted mandatory sliding scales that base the fee on the size of the judgment or settlement among other factors. The Model Rules of Professional Conduct prohibit unreasonably large contingency fees. Reasonableness is determined by factors such as the complexity of your case, the time and labor involved, the novelty of the case, the fees customarily charged for similar cases, and the experience, reputation, and ability of the lawyer. When you interview prospective attorneys, you are entitled to an explanation of how expenses are computed and alternatives to the contingency fee arrangement.

When hiring a contingency fee lawyer, you will be looking for a specialist in cases like yours with the experience, reputation, and the ability to represent you. The contingency fee lawyer is paid in full for all expenses such as retaining witnesses, depositions, and the costs of trying your case before the remaining fees are divided between you and your lawyer. A deposition is sworn testimony of a witness answering questions by the other side's attorney. A tort victim's best option in redressing injuries is to enter into a contingency fee agreement with a lawyer who has dealt with similar cases. If you have suffered injuries as the result of abuse or neglect in a long-term care facility, you should seek representation from an attorney experienced in litigating these often complex cases. Similarly, if you suffer an injury at the hands of a medical provider, you will need a specialist with experience trying medical malpractice cases.

The contingency fee system is under attack by corporate America, medical professionals, and the insurance industry. The negative portrayal of the contingency fee system is part of a larger "tort reform" movement manifest in the efforts of insurance companies, the tobacco industry, and corporate-funded think-tanks and advocacy groups to mislead the public about our civil justice system.[5] The tort reformers ply reporters and the public with "fictitious or badly misleading stories about the contingency fee system purporting to show that the nation suffers from a crisis of frivolous litigation."[6]

Tort horror stories are disseminated by a corporate-funded "outrage industry" whose long-term goal is to limit the rights of consumers. The contemporary campaign against tort reform arose as a response to the expansion of consumer rights in the post–World War II era. Corporate America has been waging a war against the contingency fee system since the 1950s to return to the "good old days" when consumers had very limited rights. The natural tendency of most Americans is to be sympathetic to the plight of injured consumers and to the grief of the victims of product liability or medical malpractice. The outrage industry's concerted effort is to push the jury away from its natural moorings by portraying the corporation as the true victim of a contingency fee system gone amuck.[7] The constant onslaught against the contingency fee system poisons juries, making it more difficult for injured consumers to get a fair trial.

The contingency fee system is a uniquely democratic institution that gives Americans equal access to the civil justice system. Without the contingency fee system, most consumers would be unable to secure legal representation. The contingency fee system does not, however, guarantee that you can find an attorney willing to take your case. Attorneys working on the contingency fee system receive no compensation unless they win. Plaintiff's counsel may spend tens of thousands on expert witnesses, as well as other out-of-pocket expenses, to bring a case to the point it can be either settled or tried. Plaintiff's lawyers need to be convinced that the potential payout in your lawsuit justifies them taking the risk that they will not recoup their considerable expenses.

When you interview a potential attorney to represent you in a consumer action, keep in mind that you are also being interviewed. Contingency fee attorneys will incur costs and only be paid if your case is successful. Attorneys need to make a decision to take your case or turn it away based upon the likelihood and amount of the potential damages. Nursing home neglect and abuses cases did not develop until states began enacting statutes awarding punitive damages and attorneys fees in the 1980s and 1990s. Prior to that time, nursing home cases were generally turned away because they were regarded as "no damages" cases. Even if you do have a good cause of action, you will not find representation if the damages are too low to make the case worthwhile for an attorney who may incur tens of thousands of dollars in expenses for your case.

For example, you will find it all but impossible to find representation in Equal Credit Opportunity Act actions because the total payout cannot exceed $1,000. Thus, the costs of filing the lawsuit and conducting discovery will frequently exceed the potential jury award. Even with the possibility of attorneys' fees and costs, this relatively small potential award is not likely to be great enough to warrant undertaking the case. If you have a disorganized personal life, a history of drug or alcohol addiction, a criminal record, weak family ties, and other unattractive qualities, you will find it difficult to find representation because these personal qualities will not play well to a jury. Even if your personal qualities have nothing to do with the harm you suffered, jurors will often superimpose their ethic of personal responsibility. Plaintiffs' attorneys are skilled at knowing what cases are winnable and whether a plaintiff is worthy of representation. If you cannot find an attorney willing to take your case, your only other option is direct action.

Keep in mind that finding a lawyer in a consumer or products liability action is partially an exercise in impression management. The entire world is a stage, and you are a player on that stage who must make a good impression. Contingency fee lawyers are assessing how *you* will play before a jury. Success is how well you present yourself to an attorney. Wear a suit or your best Sunday clothes to an interview with an attorney. If you wear your baseball hat backward and show visible body art, you will be less likely to find a lawyer willing to take your case, no matter what the merits. Law, as well as life, is largely about impression management skills. Be polite, professional, and businesslike, and you will maximize your chances of retaining a contingency fee attorney. Your appearance, demeanor, and credibility as a plaintiff are key factors, almost as important as the damages or injuries you have suffered.

If you were driving drunk, it will be all but impossible to convince a jury that the manufacturer was at fault even though your vehicle caught on fire due to a design defect after being struck from behind at low speed. Attorneys will, for example, screen out many cases in which the injured consumer has contributed significantly to his injury or used illegal drugs or alcohol at the time of an accident. Keep in mind that contingency fee lawyers have overhead and office expenses that often foreclose the possibility of taking an undesirable case.

Attorneys interviewing you about your case are judging you as a potential witness before a jury. The better documented your case and the clearer the causation, the more likely you will find presentation of self and personal qualities are key factors in determining whether you can find an attorney willing to take your case. If you are seeking representation for your aged parent in a nursing home neglect case, it is desirable if you have strong family ties and made frequent visits to the home. On the other hand, you will find it difficult to obtain representation if you and other family members had an estranged relationship with the nursing home resident. Juries evaluate your personality and character and it is always a factor in every case.

Filing a Complaint against a Lawyer

You have a right to be fully informed about your case and can ask your lawyers anything about your case. Discuss the problem you're having candidly and openly with your lawyer before filing a complaint. Clients may become dissatisfied with their lawyers for many reasons, but discipline will not be imposed unless there is a violation of professional ethics.

Every state has some mechanism for registering a complaint about a lawyer's breach of ethics or lack of professionalism. Filing a complaint against a lawyer or another professional is a serious matter and should be undertaken carefully. Avoid filing a complaint simply because you did not win your case. The fact that you lost your case does not mean that your attorney violated a canon of professional responsibility.

In Massachusetts, for example, you can register a written complaint about your lawyer with the Board of Bar Overseers, but this organization does not accept email complaints. Every state has an equivalent agency or entity that oversees the organized bar. New York, like Massachusetts, also requires a written complaint. The Massachusetts Board of Bar Overseers gives the following advice that I adapt for filing complaints in other jurisdictions.[8]

What Your Complaint Should Contain
Document your claim and draft a concise description of what happened. It will be necessary to provide as many facts and as much documentation as possible. Although you may feel certain that the acts complained of constitute misconduct, a simple statement that misconduct has occurred is not enough. Include dates, the nature of the legal matter, and specific information about what you feel the lawyer did wrong. If you have documents, including a fee agreement, court papers, letters or notes that you think are helpful to understand the complaint, send copies.

What Happens When You File a Complaint
This section is based on the Massachusetts Board of Bar Overseers procedures, but many of the principles apply equally well in other states. A staff attorney will likely review your complaint that your lawyer violated a rule of professional conduct. A number of states have enacted the Model Rules of Professional Responsibility. It is a violation of the Rules of Professional Conduct if a lawyer misappropriates property belonging to clients.[9] Lawyers owe a fiduciary duty to their clients and must not reveal confidential information given to them by their client without their consent.[10] Similarly, a lawyer must disclose conflicts of interest and not engage in business

inimical to his client's interests.[11] If there is a basis for a complaint that your lawyer violated a professional conduct rule, the Office of the Bar Counsel will conduct an investigation.

If the Bar Counsel determines that your complaint does not involve the Rules of Professional Conduct, your complaint will be dismissed and your case closed. You may request review of this decision by a member of the Board of Bar Overseers. However, there is no appeal from a decision by the board not to bring disciplinary charges against an attorney. If a lawyer is found to have committed a relatively minor infraction of the rules, your lawyer will receive an admonition. However, misconduct that is more serious will be referred to a local Hearing Committee appointed by the board.

The Hearing Committee will hear from you, as well as your attorney, and all evidence will be considered. The Hearing Committee then submits a written report to the Board of Bar Overseers with its recommendation as to discipline. If the Bar Counsel and the lawyer reach agreement as to discipline, the recommendation may be submitted directly to the board without referral to a Hearing Committee. The board may accept or modify the recommendation for discipline. If the board feels it needs additional information, it may return the case to the Hearing Committee for further hearing or conduct hearings of its own before making a final determination.

What Sanctions Are Available

The Board of Bar Overseers has limited sanctions available. In Massachusetts, the following discipline may be imposed by the board:

- *Admonition*. It involves reprimanding the lawyer, but there is no public record.
- *Public reprimand*. In Massachusetts, public reprimands are published in *Massachusetts Lawyer's Weekly* and other publications and are compiled in the bound volumes of the *Massachusetts Attorney Discipline Reports*. Every jurisdiction will have a similar way of publicizing a reprimand.

  In Massachusetts, if the Board of Bar Overseers determines that more severe discipline is required, it will send the entire matter, together with its recommendation, to the Supreme Judicial Court. Massachusetts' highest court is the only panel that can impose the most serious sanctions, such as suspension or disbarment.
- *Suspension* signifies that your lawyer may not practice law, either for a specified term or an indefinite period. A lawyer suspended for an indefinite period may not apply for reinstatement for a period of five years.
- *Disbarment*, which means that the lawyer's license to practice is revoked, and the lawyer's name is stricken from the list of licensed lawyers.[12]

In addition to these serious sanctions, an attorney may receive the lesser sanction of probation or a reprimand. An attorney may also be permitted to resign from the bar rather than face disciplinary action, but only with the court's consent. Decisions of the board and the court with respect to public discipline are released for publication. Recently published decisions and orders are available on the Board of Bar Overseers website.

What to Expect

The Board of Bar Overseers offers these guidelines about its procedure, which are similar to guidelines followed in other states:

- A prompt reply from the Office of the Bar Counsel acknowledging receipt of your complaint.
- A fair and impartial investigation. The board's Bar Counsel conducts a hearing in which he or she considers all of the evidence and your side of the story, as well as your attorney's perspective. Bar Counsel will on occasion conduct its own independent fact finding by interviewing key parties or gathering documents.
- An investigation by the Board of Bar Overseers may be conducted for a period of a year or longer, though it may only take a month.
- The Bar Counsel may interview you. Cooperate with the counsel for the Board of Bar Overseers to ensure a complete fact finding in your case.
- The board recommends sanctions that are calibrated for the type of offense or violation of the Rules of Professional Conduct.
- Your complaint will be dismissed and closed if your complaint does not fall within the jurisdiction of the Board of Bar Overseers (or similar organizations in your state).
- Contact the Board of Bar Overseers to gain up-to-date information on the progress of their investigation into your complaint. You have a right to be notified of the final disposition of the complaint; that is the rule in every jurisdiction.
- You will incur no charges or other costs if you file a complaint with the Office of the Bar Counsel or the Board of Bar Overseers.

What Not to Expect

Neither the Office of the Bar Counsel nor the Board of Bar Overseers in Massachusetts or their counterparts can provide you with legal advice or legal services. Their role is to protect the public. You will not receive money damages or other individual remedies because of filing a complaint. You may have a cause of action for legal malpractice, which is a tort action if your attorney breaches a standard of care. It is a professional malpractice if a lawyer fails to appear at a hearing and summary judgment is entered against you. Similarly, a lawyer who prepares a will with insufficient attesting witnesses will be in malpractice. Lawyers are expected to apply the knowledge and expertise of their legal specialty when preparing your case.

You will need to retain a private attorney to get advice on whether you should file a legal malpractice case. The Board of Bar Overseers suggests that you contact the Massachusetts Bar Association Lawyer Referral Service at 1-617-654-0400 in Boston (or 1-866-627-7577), the Boston Bar Association Lawyer Referral Service at 1-617-742-0625, or similar organizations in other states to get the names and contact information for attorneys who could represent you in a private action. Remember that the bar counsel or bar overseers in all jurisdictions have a narrow role and that is to protect the public. No bar counsel for any states' bar overseers can represent you personally. In Massachusetts, as in many other states, the Board of Bar Overseers has no power to compel your attorney to refund money, release your cases, or return files. The board in Massachusetts and other states can only discipline attorneys or recommend discipline to the court.

Confidentiality

The Board of Bar Overseers and the Office of the Bar Counsel must treat complaints as confidential matters. Until the court has imposed public discipline, the board and bar counsel may not disclose that a complaint has been filed, except in certain cases as specified in the rules. You are immune from liability based upon your complaint. Many states have agencies for registering complaints about electricians, plumbers, and real estate brokers as well as doctors and lawyers. The guidelines described by the Board of Bar Overseers are functionally equivalent to the procedure used in New York and in many other states.[13]

Notes

1. These guidelines are drawn from questions developed by the Massachusetts Bar Association. See Mass Law Help, "Choosing a Lawyer," available at http://www.massbar.org/public-and-community-services/need-a-lawyer (accessed June 18, 2007).

2. See Legal Services Corporation, *Documenting the Justice Gap in America: A Report of the Legal Services Corporation* (Washington, D.C.: Legal Services Corporation, 2005).

3. To learn more about these cases serving the public interest, visit the University of Wisconsin Law School's Consumer Law Litigation Clinic's website at www.law.wisc.edu/fjr/eji/consumer/index.htm.

4. National Center for Consumer Law, Consumer Information, http://www.consumerlaw.org/advice/consumer_info.shtml (visited June 17, 2007).

5. Stephanie Mencimer, *Blocking the Courthouse Door: How the Republican Party and Its Corporate Allies Are Taking Away Your Right to Sue* (New York: Free Press, 2006).

6. Ibid., 22.

7. See generally, Thomas H. Koenig and Michael L. Rustad, *In Defense of Tort Law* (New York: New York University Press, 2001), pp. 72–77.

8. "How to File a Complaint," available at http://www.mass.gov/obcbbo/complaint.htm (last visited June 17, 2007).

9. Model Rules of Professional Responsibility, Rule 1.15 Safeguarding Property.

10. Model Rules of Professional Responsibility, Rule 1.6 Confidentiality of Information.

11. Model Rules of Professional Responsibility, Rule 1.8 Conflict of Interest: Current Clients, Specific Rules.

12. "What Sanctions Are Available," available at http://www.mass.gov/obcbbo/complaint.htm#happens (June 17, 2007).

13. See "How to File a Complaint—What to Expect," http://www.courts.state.ny.us/ad4/AG/Page2.howto.htm.

5

Mandatory Arbitration: What You Should Know

This chapter explains why you should be wary of mandatory arbitration agreements. The overwhelming trend is for companies to require consumers to submit disputes to arbitration even where the claims have yet to arise. Arbitration in consumer transactions in almost every industry is in the form of adhesion contracts with mandatory arbitration clauses. Adhesion contracts are "take it or leave it" contracts in which the consumer has no meaningful alternative but to "adhere" to the terms of the stronger party. Arbitration is far more expensive than small claims court and is often the equivalent of no remedy at all where the amount in controversy is small. Few plaintiffs, for example, will seek arbitration for improper credit card charges where the cost of the arbitration exceeds that of the potential payout. A growing number of nursing homes, consumer creditors, financial services companies, trade schools, hospitals, car rental companies, and countless other industries are requiring consumers to agree to binding arbitration as a precondition of doing business. Courts have enforced one-sided arbitration clauses that (1) required the loser to pay many arbitration costs, (2) precluded class actions by borrowers, and (3) excepted from arbitration foreclosure actions and actions involving less than $15,000. The practical effect is that many consumers will be unable to pay the arbitration fees and costs. Even if consumers were able to afford arbitration, the arbitration clause contained features such as caps on damages and a loser-pay provision that deters consumers from seeking to vindicate their rights.

Mandatory arbitration clauses are frequently buried in text using small typefaces. Some companies insert mandatory arbitration clauses in monthly bill-stuffers. Cingular's standard contract, for example, includes mandatory arbitration agreements in its service contracts. Moreover, Cingular's arbitration contract precludes the possibility of the customer participating in a class-action lawsuit over roaming charges or other fees. Arbitration is a popular forum for the business community because consumers will be unable to seek the full array of damages available in the court system. What are advantages for businesses will hamstring consumers' rights. This chapter gives you the information you need to know before you waive your rights by agreeing to arbitration.

Mandatory Predispute Arbitration

Arbitration is a form of alternative dispute resolution (ADR) in which the parties agree to waive their right to a court trial in favor of a private trial in which an arbitrator decides a dispute. These are private proceedings, with informal rules of evidence and no opportunity for an appeal.

Mandatory arbitration agreements typically mean that you are waiving your right to a jury or court trial before a dispute has arisen. Mandatory predispute arbitration should be distinguished from more fair-minded procedures such as postdispute arbitration. Arbitration in consumer transactions in which the parties do not have relatively equal bargaining power raises serious concerns.

Consider the case of Charles Smith, who signed a mandatory binding arbitration agreement as part of his admission to a long-term care facility. Charles Smith has no present memory that he signed an arbitration agreement as part of his admission to Sunny Valley Rest Home on January 1, 2006. That is not surprising since Charles Smith has Alzheimer's disease. Serving as the responsible party for his father, Ron Smith signed a twenty-five page admission contract that also has multiple addendums. When Ron consulted with a lawyer about the quality of care his father was getting at Sunny Valley, his attorney pointed out that any disputes were subject to an arbitration clause. Neither Ron nor his father remembered signing an arbitration clause. But sure enough, on page 22 of the nursing home admissions contract, there was a two-paragraph clause titled "Mandatory Arbitration." The arbitration clause stated:

> The Resident and/or Responsible Party understands, agrees to, and has received a copy of this Arbitration Agreement, and acknowledges that the terms have been explained to him/her, or his/her designee.
> The undersigned acknowledges that each of them has read the arbitration agreement and understands that by signing this arbitration agreement, each of them has waived his/her right to a trial, before a judge or jury, and that each of them voluntarily consents to all of the terms of the arbitration agreement."

Ron asked whether he had to agree to the arbitration clause and was told by a Sunny Valley social worker that every resident accepted at Sunny Valley in the past five years agreed to the clause. Ron Smith had no present memory that Sunny Valley Rest Home officials told him that he needed to sign the admissions agreement if his father was accepted to the skilled care unit. No official would come out and say that arbitration was a precondition to admissions. Ron Smith has no present memory of whether Sunny Valley's officials ever disclosed that he was signing an arbitration agreement. Sunny Valley did not have him separately sign the arbitration clause, nor did they ever point out the special significance of the clause. The nursing home claims a meeting discussing arbitration took place in an office with nobody else present.

The arbitration agreement signed by Smith and his son made mandatory arbitration applicable to all claims for violations of any rights granted to the nursing home resident by law or by the admission agreement. The arbitration contract specifically limited remedies like punitive damages, noneconomic damages, and attorney's fees.

The basis of Charles Smith's claims against the nursing home was breach of the contract of care and negligent care. Mr. Smith suffered from decubitus ulcers that led to the amputation of his left leg. Smith's pressure sores were caused by neglect, which was partly the result of the failure of Sunny Valley's minimum wage nursing home aides to turn Smith at regular intervals. Sunny Valley also altered medical records by recording care that Smith did not actually receive. On July 17, 2006, Ron Smith filed a lawsuit for personal injuries suffered by his father due to neglect at the nursing home. Sunny Valley moved for arbitration pursuant to the agreement. Charles's attorney conceded that arbitration agreements are generally enforceable but raised the defense of unconscionability. The trial court enforced Sunny Valley's motion to compel arbitration.

Most consumers would not understand that agreeing to mandatory arbitration meant that they were waiving their right to a jury trial and their right to have their dispute decided in a court of law. Mandatory arbitration provisions are especially troubling in the nursing home context, where the resident is not in a position to bargain with the nursing home. The responsible party is often afraid that by challenging the arbitration clause, they will lose their parent or loved one's place in a nursing home. Predispute mandatory arbitration clauses are widely enforced in consumer transactions.

These one-sided clauses are often now separately executed contracts or even called to the attention of the consumer. Predispute arbitration is included in standard form contracts such as purchase orders, terms of service agreements, and "clickwrap" licenses (where you must click yes to continue on a website; see p. 101). The big picture is that consumers are losing their Seventh Amendment right to jury trial through contract. These contracts, which often operate by stealth, are now routinely part of a growing number of transactions, including credit cards, home repair, homeowners' insurance, Internet service, department stores, theme parks, health clubs, auto rentals, tour operators, financial services, telephone service, HMOs, and nursing homes.

Consumers should be wary of submitting to mandatory arbitration. Arbitration is popular with the business community because consumers will be unable to seek the full array of damages available in the court system. Businesses choose arbitration to reduce the cost of litigation, which means that consumers are far less likely to obtain a full and fair recovery for their injuries or economic losses. In a high-stakes case such as a nursing home or medical malpractice case, you will need an attorney to represent you in opposing an order to arbitrate.

Attorneys have successfully challenged arbitration clauses because the elderly and infirm nursing home patient often did not have contractual capacity or their representative did not have the legal authority to bind the resident to arbitration. Arbitration agreements that are a condition of admission are particularly vulnerable to challenge. Arbitration is inappropriate for consumer transactions because consumers lack the understanding of the clauses and lack equal bargaining power.

In fact, a marked imbalance in knowledge and power more often characterizes consumer contracts. When the party with superior sophistication, knowledge, and financial resources inserts a mandatory arbitration clause into a form contract or unilaterally imposes such a significant new contract provision through a billing or statement insert, consumers usually are unaware of and have not consented to these terms. Moreover, merchants generally include an arbitration requirement as a condition of doing business.

Consumers typically do not understand the consequences of such a clause and, even when they do, will not have the option to negotiate its terms. Rather, consumers either must agree to the contract terms or lose the chance of obtaining the goods or services from the merchant. These circumstances are bad enough when the consumer actually has seen and signed an arbitration agreement. The consequences are exacerbated when the consumer has not signed an agreement and attests to not having seen the notice changing the account agreement to require arbitration.[1]

Arbitration agreements in the financial services industry have been successfully challenged on a variety of contractual grounds. The New Jersey Supreme Court recently ruled that a class action ban in an agreement to arbitrate disputes in a high-cost payday loan contract violated the public interest and was unconscionable and unenforceable.[2]

Federal Arbitration Act

The Federal Arbitration Act (FAA) (9 U.S.C. §1 et seq.) provides that an arbitration clause in a transaction involving commerce shall be valid, irrevocable, and enforceable, save upon such grounds as exist in law or in equity for the revocation of any contract (9 U.S.C. §2). The FAA establishes a liberal policy favoring arbitration agreements. Courts compel arbitration under the FAA if two tests can be satisfied: (1) Have the parties agreed to a valid, enforceable arbitration agreement? (2) Is the complaint at issue within the sphere of application of the parties' arbitration agreement? Courts are required to stay a consumer lawsuit if it is referable to arbitration under a written arbitration agreement (9 U.S.C. §3). Courts will order that the parties to a valid arbitration agreement should proceed to arbitration in accordance with the terms of the agreement (9 U.S.C. §4). Courts have interpreted the Federal Arbitration Act to dictate that arbitration agreements be broadly enforced: any doubts about whether a dispute is to be submitted to arbitration are resolved in favor of arbitration over litigation.

A fence at the top of the cliff is better than an ambulance waiting in the valley below when it comes to mandatory arbitration clauses. Consider not signing standard forms with mandatory arbitration provisions. If you have signed an agreement, you will face an uphill battle challenging the validity or enforceability of the agreement. Keep in mind that courts are not particularly sympathetic if you signed the agreement. Courts assert that a consumer has the right to refuse services or products and put the pen down without signing the form (*Branco v. Norwest Bank Minn.*, N.A., 381 F. Supp. 2d 1274, 1282 [D. Hi. 2005]).

The *Branco* court's tacit assumption is based upon "freedom of contract," yet consumers placing an aged parent in a nursing home have no real choice but agree to arbitration. In too many cases, consumers cannot put the pen down because the facility may be the only suitable one in the area. Similarly, a consumer suffocating under the weight of credit card bills may feel he or she has no choice but to submit to an arbitration agreement included in a standard form credit application.

What You Should Know about Consumer Arbitration

Companies describe arbitration to the consumer as cheaper, faster, and a fairer means of resolving disputes. Indeed, arbitration does tend to be a cheaper and fairer way of resolving disputes between businesses. In most business-to-business disputes, the parties have relatively equal resources. Arbitration has more informal procedural and evidentiary rules than the parties would encounter in court. That is both good news and bad news for the consumer.

The goods news is that the consumer's attorney will find it less expensive to conduct discovery in arbitration hearings. Discovery is the process by which both parties have the right to secure documents and testimony from the other side. Testimony may be broadly thought of as an oral declaration made by a witness or party under oath. The Federal Rules of Civil Procedure and state codes have adopted a policy of free and open discovery. The process of discovery is essential to the consumer and of less significance to the seller, merchant, creditor, or defendant who renders services. Discovery typically benefits a plaintiff seeking a "smoking gun" document. The engine of discovery makes it possible to learn that a product manufacturer has a history of consumer complaints about a defective product. For example, the attorneys in the Ford Pinto case learned that Ford was settling numerous cases and knew that their automobile had a tendency to explode even after relatively minor accidents. Discovery also revealed that Ford Motor Company not only knew about the defect but also made a concerted effort to settle each case rather than correct the defect.

The bad news is that there is no discovery in most consumer arbitrations; arbitration hamstrings plaintiffs because it is the company that has all of the key documents. In proceedings without discovery, the consumer's lawyer does not have a mechanism to obtain documents necessary to try their case effectively.

Advantage to Repeat Player
Most consumers have little or no understanding of arbitration beyond the self-serving statements of those benefiting from arbitration. Neither Congress nor the state requires the seller to explain the procedure underlying arbitration. Few industries even require a consumer to separately initial arbitration clauses, even though consumers are waiving important legal rights.

Consumers are kept in the dark about arbitration because the law imposes no obligation to disclose this procedure's anticonsumer features. In the vast majority of consumer contracts, arbitration agreements that waive your right to a jury trial are not even presented to the consumer as a separate document. Most arbitration agreements do not even define arbitration, let alone explain the costs or the benefits of this method of resolving disputes. Unlike disputes adjudicated in the courts, arbitration findings are kept confidential, or are not recorded at all, leaving attorneys clueless as to what precedents have been set and are followed by the arbiter.

Why Mandatory Arbitration Often Harms Consumers
Few arbitration agreements explain the rules of arbitration. Many do not even make mention of how arbitrators are chosen. Even fewer arbitration agreements give any estimates of the costs of arbitration. The reality of consumer arbitration is that consumers are at a profound disadvantage. Arbitration agreements that prohibit or cap punitive damages or impose other restrictions on recovery have a chilling impact on the ability of the consumer to obtain representation. The consumer is responsible for the high costs in arbitration not found in litigation. A consumer will typically be required to split the cost of filing fees as well as the payment of arbitrators.

Mandatory arbitration agreements have become so common that the National Consumer Center states: "No matter what type of consumer lawsuits you bring, odds are you will have to deal with the enforceability of a binding arbitration clause!"[3]

The legal effect of a mandatory arbitration clause is that the consumer gives up any right to go to court and have their case heard by a judge or jury. The company will typically delineate a number of claims excluded from arbitration. Lenders, for example, will reserve the right to seek a judicial order to foreclose your real property. Similarly, a nursing home will often reserve the right to collect unpaid fees from the resident. Many corporations will have blanket exclusions for claims of a certain monetary size. These exceptions are calculated to give companies a right to a jury trial, but exclude the consumer from a judicial forum. The mandatory agreements are drafted by company lawyers to the advantage of the corporation, not the consumer.

Mandatory arbitration agreements, for example, preclude the possibility of class actions. Consumer class actions are often the only way a case can be brought when actual compensatory damages are low. An arbitration agreement's restrictions on class actions have the result of depriving consumers of representation where damages are large, despite an egregious violation of consumer protection law. Arbitration agreements in consumer transactions are skyrocketing as companies seek to eliminate the risk of large jury awards.

Consumers have much to lose when it comes to legal rights and remedies when they agree to arbitration. All Americans have a Seventh Amendment right to a jury, but this is not the case where the consumer has waived that right in a binding arbitration agreement. Binding arbitration agreements require the consumer to waive their rights even before an injury occurs. At present, consumers waiving their right to a jury or full damages are not given adequate notice or disclosure of the rights they are giving up. Arbitration is not an open process in which errors are subject to review. Arbitration is a private, closed-door proceeding where consumers are at a significant disadvantage when compared to companies who understand how to select a favorable arbitral panel and how these private proceedings can be used to their advantage. The corporations using arbitration are repeat players, and it is only human nature that arbitrators will have an eye to repeat business.

Court proceedings are open proceedings with balanced rules of evidence and discovery procedures that are beneficial to plaintiffs as well as defendants. Arbitrations are private proceedings with rules skewed in favor of repeat players with no opportunity for an appeal. Arbitration provisions are enforceable across the board because of federal law. The federal government looks at arbitration agreements as positive because the agreements conserve resources and bring the parties together. However, many arbitration agreements cap the total recovery, prohibit punitive damages, limit noneconomic damages, and even reallocate the cost of the company's attorney's fees to the consumer. The consumer also gives up the right to a jury trial, all discovery, and appeal and the ability to check records for precedents, as arbitrations are generally not made public. Additionally, the majority of arbitration agreements give the company the right to choose the place of arbitration—thereby creating expensive travel costs for consumers—and even the rules for choosing arbitration.

Mandatory Arbitration and Mortgages

The financial services industry uses mandatory arbitration agreements for most disputes, as is the case in many other industries. Lenders present consumers with an "arbitration agreement" as a condition of obtaining a loan. The typical arbitration agreement not only covers breach of contract for the services being rendered but all contractual claims, fraud, misrepresentation, statutory rights, and even torts such as malpractice. Many agreements even purport to bind third parties who are not parties to the contract, such as the children of victims of nursing home neglect or abuse.

Courts have generally rejected the argument that mandatory arbitration agreements are unconscionable. In fact, the mortgage company uses its dominant position in pressuring homeowners to submit to arbitration in its standard form contracts. True, you can refuse the mortgage company's offer and use a different lender, but all but a few homeowners sign the standard form agreement.

Mandatory Arbitration Agreements and Employment

A growing number of companies are precluding the possibility of you filing a suit against them by asking you to sign a predispute mandatory arbitration agreement as part of their employment contract. What this means that if you are terminated for reasons that violate public policy, are discriminated against because of your age, race, or sex, or otherwise treated unlawfully by your employer, you will not have your day in court. Mandatory predispute arbitration means that you will not be able to file a legal claim against your employer. Your grievance against the company will be arbitrated, and you will lose your right to have your day in court. Arbitration agreements in the employment context may be challenged on the grounds of unconscionability where several of the following factors are found: (1) the bargaining power between the employer and applicant was grossly unequal; (2) the terms of the agreement were nonnegotiable and "clearly" weighed in favor of the employer; (3) the employer retained the unilateral right to modify rules governing arbitration without input or notice to the employee at any time; and (4) the applicant was likely unaware that she was signing the arbitration agreement with a third-party arbitration services company, and not with the employer itself. Accordingly, these factors demonstrate a flagrant disparity in bargaining power, lack of meaningful alternatives available to the applicant, and the omission of critical terms and conditions in the arbitration document (*Am. Gen. Life and Accident Ins. Co. v. Wood*, 429 F.3d 83 [4th Cir. 2005] [citing cases]).

Mandatory Arbitration Agreements in Health Care

A joint commission of the American Arbitration Association (AAA), American Bar Association, and American Medical Association (AMA) identified four different types of health care arbitration as (1) predispute, final, and binding arbitration; (2) predispute nonbinding arbitration; (3) postdispute final and binding arbitration; and (4) postdispute nonbinding arbitration (American Arbitration Association, American Bar Association, and American Medical Association, Commission on Health Care Dispute Resolution [Final Report, July 27, 1998], at 10).

The commission developed a due process protocol for resolution of health care disputes whose first principle was that all parties were entitled to a fundamentally fair process. In predispute, final, and binding arbitrations, the parties' agreement is entered into before a dispute has even arisen. Voluntary arbitration or nonbinding arbitration gives the parties true choices, whereas arbitration tends to be offered to the consumer on a "take it or leave it" basis.

The joint AAA, ABA, and AMA commission unanimously concluded "that in disputes involving patients and/or plan subscribers, binding arbitration should be used only where the parties agree to same after a dispute arises." Yet the typical long-term care (LTC) admissions contract requires subscribers and nursing home residents to agree to binding arbitration. LTC facilities are increasingly insisting that residents or their "responsible parties" sign detailed admission contracts with embedded, mandatory arbitration agreements, thus limiting their exposure to public court trials of claims of care neglect, negligence, or even abuse.

Challenges to Mandatory Arbitration Agreements

Predispute mandatory arbitration agreements are not usually considered unconscionable, even though they contain elements of unfair bargaining. You may be able to challenge mandatory arbitration agreements containing provisions that would bar you from utilizing two remedies—punitive damages and class action relief—or require you to pay the long-term care facilities attorneys' fees if you lost your case. Your argument would be that those two remedies are essential to the enforcement and effective vindication of the public purposes of consumer law. Prohibitions on punitive damages and class action relief arising from the purchase and financing agreement have been found to be unconscionable by a number of courts.

Even though the consumer gives up the right to a jury trial, an appeal, and damages limitations, courts have generally ignored these realities, ruling that arbitration agreements usually do not limit the obligations or liabilities of either party but only substitute an arbitral tribunal for a judge or jury. The American Arbitration Association's Consumer Due Process Protocol states that arbitration agreements should make it clear that consumers retain their right to file claims in small claims courts for claims within the jurisdiction of the agreement.

What to Do: Avoid Imbalanced Predispute Mandatory Arbitration

Before you agree to arbitration, study the terms. You may even want your legal services attorney, legal representative, or family member to review the terms of arbitration agreements before you sign them. The American Arbitration Association and the American Bar Association promulgated Consumer Due Process Protocol, which set guidelines for when consumer arbitration proceedings are evenhanded:

> Providers of goods or services should undertake reasonable measures to provide consumers with full and accurate information regarding Consumer ADR Programs. At the time the Consumer contracts for goods or services, such measures should include (1) clear and adequate notice regarding the ADR provisions, including a statement indicating whether participation in the ADR Program is mandatory or optional, and (2) reasonable means by which Consumers may obtain additional information regarding the ADR Program. After a dispute arises, Consumers should have access to all information necessary for effective participation in ADR.[4]

Mandatory arbitration agreements are too frequently presented to consumers without reasonable notice. In an empirical study of mandatory arbitration agreements I did with Katherine Pearson of the Pennsylvania State University Law School, we found that mandatory arbitration agreements governing nursing homes were frequently drafted with unfair terms and presented to consumers in a deceptive manner at the time the elderly, often infirm, resident is admitted to a facility. The average mandatory arbitration agreement is buried deep within the admissions agreement or presented as a separate writing without even an elementary explanation of what rights are lost by signing the agreement.

Self-help is not an option when resisting mandatory arbitration clauses. The National Consumer Law Center (NCLC) in Boston has expertise in mounting the most effective challenges to arbitration. The NCLC provides free consultative legal services to aid attorneys in California, Massachusetts, and Washington. Your attorney can contact the NCLC's intake attorney at 1-617-542-8010. The NCLC also consults on a per-fee basis with private attorneys resisting consumer arbitration cases.

Mandatory arbitration agreements may be challenged on a variety of diverse grounds. The high fees charged by arbitrators typically mean that the consumer has no remedy at all. Many arbitration agreements seek to apply limits on noneconomic damages, attorney's fees, and punitive damages, which arguably conflict with state or federal statutory rights. Some companies stuff arbitration agreements into billing statements, which creates a question of whether an agreement to arbitrate even exists.

The National Consumer Law Center states that the misuse and abuse of consumer arbitration agreements is the number one consumer problem of the new century. One problem is that the consumer and the corporation have very unequal bargaining power. Corporations are frequently repeat players with arbitration and often choose the arbitral forum that is favorable to them.

In a business-to-business arbitration, the parties are free to bargain about the forum, which is not an option in consumer transactions. The American Arbitration Association's Consumer Due Process Protocol's most fundamental principle is that arbitrators be neutral and disqualify themselves if they have a financial interest in the outcome of the proceedings.

Example: The Enforceability of Mandatory Arbitration Fees. In *Brower v. Gateway 2000* (676 N.Y.S. 2d 569 [N.Y. App. Div. 1998]) a New York court upheld a "clickwrap agreement" that required any dispute arising out of the plaintiff's purchase of a computer and software to be resolved by arbitration. Gateway shipped its personal computers in a box containing a printed warning stating that: "This document contains Gateway 2000's Standard Terms and Conditions." The license agreement also stated, "By keeping your Gateway 2000 computer system beyond thirty days after the date of delivery, you accept these terms and conditions." One of the clauses of the contract mandated that all controversies arising out of the computer contract were to be arbitrated in Chicago, Illinois, applying the "Rule of Conciliation and Arbitration of the International Chamber of Commerce."

The court upheld the arbitration clause, holding that it did not render the contract an unenforceable adhesion contract. The court stated that because "the consumer has affirmatively retained the merchandise for more than thirty days—within which the consumer has presumably examined and even used the product(s) and read the agreement . . . the contract has been effectuated." However, the court did find that the $4,000 fee to arbitrate a dispute was unconscionable and excessive "and surely serves to deter the individual consumer from invoking the process," leaving consumers "with no forum at all in which to resolve a dispute." The fee to arbitrate the dispute far exceeded the price of the software, depriving the consumer of any effective remedy. The court remanded the case to the trial court with instructions to appoint an arbitrator who would not charge excessive fees.

Enforceability of Mandatory Arbitration

Courts consider the following factors in deciding whether to enforce arbitration clauses: (1) unequal bargaining power; (2) whether the weaker party may opt out of arbitration; (3) the clarity with which the arbitration clause is drafted; (4) if there is an unfair home-court advantage in favor of the stronger party; (5) whether the weaker party had a meaningful opportunity to accept the arbitration agreement; and (6) if the stronger party used deceptive tactics. Consumers have largely been unsuccessful in challenges to arbitration agreements based on the grounds of unconscionability. At a minimum, an arbitration clause needs to be prominently displayed and clearly written so those consumers understand that they are waiving their right to a jury trial and the right to a full trial on the merits. One-sided arbitration agreements that take away many substantive rights without giving consumers meaningful remedies in return are challengeable. If a court strikes an exclusive arbitration clause, the consumer will have the full array of rights and remedies available under the UCC or common law.

Voluntary Postdispute Arbitration

Voluntary postdispute arbitration is often a good option for consumers, in contrast to compulsory arbitration. Consumers often benefit from new and used motor vehicle arbitration, for example. In Massachusetts the arbitrators are appointed by that state's director of consumer affairs and business regulation to conduct state-certified new and used car arbitrations (described more fully in Chapter 8). In these arbitration hearings, it is the consumer that requests arbitration.

What to Do: Protecting Your Rights in Arbitration Hearings

Once arbitration requests are in process, you will receive notification as to the scheduling of the arbitration hearings. The arbitrator has a duty to attempt to accommodate your needs. In general, either party will be able to reschedule hearings for good cause, and these requests should always be in writing. As with any other hearing (court, small claims, etc.), your failure to appear at a hearing will result in a default judgment against you. If a default judgment has been entered against you, you must show good cause for why the arbitrator should set aside the default judgment, and time is of the essence. In voluntary postarbitration cases, it may also be possible to withdraw your request for voluntary arbitration.

Arbitration hearings are conducted by persons who must not have a financial or personal interest in the outcome of your case. If there is good reason to believe that that is not the case, you can move to have the arbitrator disqualified. Arbitration hearings, like small claims court hearings, are informal with no formal rules of evidence. You will be giving your testimony under oath, and you will have the right to introduce any evidence that helps the arbitrator render her decision. The arbitrator has a great deal of discretion in excluding evidence that is not helpful. Prior to the arbitration hearing, do your homework.

In order to prepare for an arbitration, you need to know the rules of the game. Be sure to ask the arbitral organization for a copy of the rules governing the arbitration. The American Arbitration Association rules for conducting consumer arbitrations are available online, as are those of other tribunals as well. Massachusetts's rules for arbitrating state-certified used or new car arbitrations are available online. These consumer arbitrations are commenced by the consumer, who also presents her case first, followed by the dealer or manufacturer (201 CMR 11.00).

Prepare your arbitration case ahead of time, following the guidelines for preparing a small claims case described in Chapter 3. Assemble evidence about your car's condition or repair costs in advance. Obtain written estimates or evaluations by experts. In Massachusetts, all written testimony must be signed under oath by the witness making the statement that "his testimony is true" if this testimony will be introduced as evidence in the arbitral proceeding. In a motor vehicle arbitration case, you will likely be required to bring your vehicle to the hearing, unless it is unsafe to operate or will not run. The arbitrator may test-drive your vehicle to check out the veracity of your claims (201 CMR 11.10).

As in small claims courts, you should handle yourself in a courteous and professional manner. An arbitrator, like a judge, can terminate a hearing if you or your opponent is not civil, because the hearing may become unmanageable. The outcome of your arbitration will depend upon the facts of your case, but your skill in presenting credible evidence will also be determinative. Arbitrators will typically not render their decision the day of the hearing, but by a writing mailed to you and the arbitration firm. In some cases, the arbitrator may render an oral decision, which is not binding until they issue a written opinion spelling out the reasons for their ruling. Keep in mind that the arbitrator's decision is final. Some arbitration rules have provisions for making technical corrections in the arbitrator's decision. Some arbitration procedures permit dissatisfied consumers (or defendants) to appeal the decision through a court of civil procedure, but that is not the norm.

Notes

1. AARP Amicus Brief in *Sobremonte v. Hon. Ricado A. Torres*, No. B102106 (L.A. Superior Ct., February 15, 1997).

2. *Muhammad v. County Bank of Rehoboth Beach*, 189 N.J. 1, 912 A.2d 88, 2006 N.J. Lexis 1154 (2006).

3. National Consumer Law Center, *Consumer Arbitration Agreements* (Boston: National Consumer Law Center, 2004), p. 1.

4. American Arbitration Association and American Bar Association, "Code of Ethics: A Due Process Protocol for Mediation and Arbitration of Consumer Disputes" (1998), available at http://www.adr.org/sp.asp?id=22019&printable=true (last visited June 17, 2007).

Part II

Common Law's Consumer Protection

6

Protecting Your Rights in Consumer Contracts

As a consumer you have rights under the common law of contracts, as well as state or federal statutes, when a business has breached or violated the terms of an agreement. You may also find yourself a defendant in a breach of contract action when you fail to comply with one or more material terms of a contract.

The law of contracts, like death and taxes, is a certainty for every American consumer. Each year Americans spend billions of dollars on goods and services purchased on credit. Consider the daily routine of Sue Smith, who lives in Marshfield, Massachusetts, located on Boston's South Shore. Sue works for Boston Financial Services, which provides loans, mortgages, and retail financing for the consumer market. Sue is not only a loan officer but has loans of her own, including student loans and a mortgage for her condominium located near Ocean Street that was financed with a $270,000 loan at a favorable rate of interest. While Sue is eating breakfast, she tunes into CNN's early morning show. She is able to receive CNN because she has contracted for communications services with a digital high-speed cable provider.

Before leaving for work, Sue sends her mother a text message instructing her to pick up Sue's dog Max, who has been at a doggie daycare. She also checks her email on America Online (AOL). Sue has been a paid subscriber of AOL since 1998 and has recently learned that AOL will be offering its services for no charge. Even though Sue will not be paying a licensing fee, she will be entering into another contract called a terms of services agreement.

Next, Sue drives to work in her Audi Sport hatchback, which she leases. Leasing is a method of paying for the use of the Audi over three years. She chose to lease because no down payment was required and she will stay within the 15,000 miles per year limit. At the end of the lease, she will have an option to purchase the automobile. Sue's automobile lease is classified as a consumer lease under UCC Article 2A because she is leasing the car for her own personal, household, or family use.

Sue drives a few miles onto Route 3 onto a toll road, where she pays $1.25 to the turnpike authority for use of the highway. Shortly before she reaches the highway to Boston, she stops at Quik Stop and orders a coffee with cream to go. As she is driving along Route 3, she listens to the BBC on satellite radio that she purchased at Circuitcity.com, an Internet site. The traffic is heavy on the Southeast Expressway, and as she drives into the city, she notes a number of billboards advertising everything from Absolut Vodka to the *Boston Globe*. She then makes her way through the famous Big Dig Tunnel and finds a parking garage near Government Center.

Sue pays $400 a month for an unreserved parking spot, which is quite a bargain when compared to the $900 that New Yorkers often pay. Sue's workday consists of entering into consumer credit installment contracts with consumers. After work each day, she goes to Executive Health Club to use the machines and pool and have the services of a private trainer.

Our hypothetical "Sue Smith" enters into scores of contracts every day as a consumer. For example, take Sue's lease of her automobile. In this case, Audi Financial Services is the lessor, Sue is the lessee, and the automobile is the personal property being leased. The lessor is the entity who transfers the right to possess and use goods (UCC §2A-103[p]), whereas the lessee is the person who acquires the right to possession and use of goods under a lease (UCC §2A-103[n]). The subject of the lease is *tangible goods* such as boats, cars, or computers. A lease gives the lessee the right to use goods according to the terms of the lease agreement. A lease is a contract in which there has been "a transfer of the right to possession and use of goods for an agreed upon term in return for consideration" (UCC §2A-103[n]). With a true lease, the consumer lessee returns the goods to the seller while there is still economic life remaining in the product.

In addition, in her capacity as a loan officer, she is required to comply with federal and state laws governing consumer credit transactions, including the Truth in Lending Act and Massachusetts's regulations of consumer credit transactions. We can see that it is almost impossible for an average American like Sue to avoid the law of contracts.

This chapter is not only a primer on the law of consumer contracts but provides practical guidance on what to do if you purchased defective goods or services. It covers the basics of contract law generally applicable to all sales and services contracts. Consumers form contracts whenever they purchase goods or services, such as ordering a meal in a restaurant, leasing an automobile, hiring a company to landscape your lawn, or buying products on eBay. A consumer recently wrote about his experience purchasing electronics on eBay on the website Complaints.com: "I purchased a power pack and received the item in a timely manner. When I received it, it was missing the power cord (making the power pack useless). I thought maybe the seller made a mistake. I received a prompt reply from the seller that it was not listed in the item description (but shown in the picture of the item) and was not included in the eBay auction. She would, however, sell me the cord for an additional sum of money. What are my rights and remedies?"

The purchase of the power pack constitutes the sale of goods. Every state but Louisiana would regard this as a sale of goods governed by Article 2 of the Uniform Commercial Code. Article 2 is a federal statute that governs many common problems you are likely to encounter as a consumer buyer. In addition to Article 2, every state has a statute modeled on the Unfair and Deceptive Trade Practices Act (see, e.g., Illinois's Uniform Deceptive Trade Practices Act, 815 ILCS 510 [2007]) that may come into play if the eBay transaction has elements of fraud or constitutes an unfair trade practice. EBay, as a direct and practical result of the progress of consumer protection law, offers its own mediation policy and remedies for many instances in which a buyer may be dissatisfied. The use of mediation is frequently the best solution, and eBay's role is to assist parties in resolving their own disputes.

EBay's mediation program is an inexpensive and reasonable method of resolving many disputes where the parties have acted in good faith. Mediation is unlikely to result in an effective remedy in fraud cases in which an online seller has swindled the consumer. Mediation tacitly assumes that the parties are in good faith willing to redress disputes in a reasonable manner.

Freedom of Contract

Freedom of contract is a well-established value in American society. Consumers have the "freedom to choose." Contract is a mechanism that keeps prices low and quality higher in a well-functioning market economy. Contract law also protects settled expectations and brings stability to American society. The theory of freedom of contract assumes that businesses bargain with consumers. In reality, most consumer contracts are "adhesion contracts" in the sense that the consumer adheres to the terms of the stronger party. Nevertheless, the Internet helps to even the playing field by giving the consumer the opportunity for comparison shopping never before possible. In theory, consumers have the same power to choose which law applies to their contracts and may devise their own tailored remedies in the event of the breakdown of a sales contract. UCC §1-102 (3) assumes that the parties to a commercial contract have freedom of contract. UCC Article 2, for example, permits sellers to disclaim or limit warranties and remedies. Nearly every provision of the UCC may be bypassed or side-stepped by the parties' agreement.

Everyone has a warranty drawer, usually in your kitchen, where you keep every warranty you have received since you were in high school. See if you can find a single manufacturer that offers more than limited warranties. Few manufacturers are willing to stand behind their product and offer a full warranty. In fact, they often offer the opposite: disclaimers of all meaningful warranties and remedies. Manufacturers reallocate risk to the user community for all failures of performance. The consumer is offered the product or service on a "take it or leave it" basis. Many, even most, license agreements do not allow bargaining over any term or condition of service. The typical consumer contract binds the weaker party to the terms of powerful corporations without the possibility of negotiating key terms. If you read all the hundreds of shrinkwrap agreements, website agreements, or software license agreements, you are unlikely to find a single example of a software licensor willing to provide any warranty for its software. Licensors typically disclaim warranties, offering only the repair or replacement of the software disk or other media as the sole and exclusive remedy.

The United States is rapidly shifting its economic base from the production of durable goods to software engineering and other types of information production. Since the 1990s, the licensing of software has displaced the sale of goods as the linchpin of the American economy. The total revenue of the largest software companies is hundreds of billions of dollars, and mass market software continues to be a high-growth sector.

The typical "click through" website agreement requires end users to click on an icon labeled "I agree," which opens a contract that requires the user to agree to submit to all of the licensor's terms and conditions. For example, Dell's software agreement binds the consumer to all the terms of its license agreement when the preloaded software is used.

A license conditions access to and use of software on acceptance of the license's terms. A mass market agreement generally begins with a legal notice, disclaimer, or terms of use, stating that opening the package indicates the users' acceptance of the license terms. Licensors do not often draw attention to the fact that consumers are licensing rather than purchasing software. In many cases, the consumer's first notice of the license agreement is when they boot up the software. The merchant seldom conspicuously displays the terms of a license agreement in advertisements or product packaging. Most consumers are probably unaware that Microsoft does not sell software to them but only licenses it for restricted uses. Some licensors even seal the license inside the product's packaging, making it impossible to ascertain the terms prior to purchase. A pundit wryly observed that soon adhesion contracts will be written so that you waive your right to any remedy, your American citizenship, and your first-born child. A few courts have refused to enforce one-sided license agreements on diverse grounds such as lack of contract formation, unconscionability, or public policy reasons. Some courts have refused to enforce sole and exclusive remedies that fail in their essential purpose.

Parties' Choice of Law and Forum

In *Carnival Cruise Lines, Inc., v. Shute* (499 U.S. 583 [1991]), the U.S. Supreme Court enforced a forum selection clause on a cruise contract even though it specified that all disputes be litigated in Florida, a forum distant from the consumer's residence. Choice of forum clauses are generally enforceable unless "unreasonable and unjust." "Choice of forum" is a contractual provision that predetermines the judicial or arbitral forum in the event of a dispute arising out of an Internet or website agreement. For example, Disney requires all disputes to be decided in a state or federal court located in Los Angeles County, and Nokia requires disputes to be submitted to an arbitrator in Finland. In addition, America Online's forum selection clause for its members provides that "exclusive jurisdiction for any claim or dispute with AOL or relating in any way to your membership with or your use of AOL resides in the courts of Virginia."

Internet merchants use choice of law clauses to predetermine the legal remedies that apply for disputes involving the online contract. Dell Financial Services, for example, requires that the law of Texas govern all claims relating to its website. The Alturian GPS Software website applies the law of Belgium in the event of disputes. The licensing agreement of RealNetworks requires consumers to resolve all disputes in binding arbitration applying Washington state law. If a consumer, for example, violated the RealNetworks' license agreement by exceeding the scope of its use restrictions, the company could seek an injunction in federal court, a right not granted to consumers.

These regressive provisions have the effect of depriving you of a remedy because the costs of travel to a distant forum and paying an arbitrator exceed the amount that is at stake. American courts have been inclined to enforce Internet or software license agreements with terms inimical to consumer welfare, such as pro-vendor forum selection clauses. (The parties select where the trial should be held in the event the contract is breached. Forum selection clauses generally require the consumer to acquiesce to the stronger party's choice. For example, America Online requires consumers to litigate disputes in the Northern District of Virginia in its forum selection clause.) In general, courts have been willing to enforce forum selection clauses drafted by the stronger party as long as the consumer has an opportunity to review the terms of the contract and manifest assent to the license agreement. A few courts have been willing to strike down these oppressive forum selection clauses as unconscionable.

Assume that one of Big Computer Company's customers had a dispute over billing. Big Computer Company's choice of law clause requires consumers to litigate any disputes in South Dakota. A Vermont consumer would have no remedy at all if this clause was enforced. Requiring a consumer to file suit in a distant forum functions as an absolute immunity, in which the cost and inconvenience of filing a lawsuit far exceed what can be recovered if they prevail. You will need an attorney or legal services to challenge burdensome choice of forum clauses, which in effect are anti-remedies. A low-income consumer may be able to find legal services to challenge these clauses.

A Contract Defined

We all make many promises, but not all promises are contracts. What makes a contract? A contract is any promise that, when broken, will give the non-breaching party a remedy at law. Contracts for the sale of goods are governed by Article 2 of the Uniform Commercial Code, whereas most service contracts will be governed by common law. A breach of contract, whether a sales or services contract, occurs when a party does not perform its contractual obligations.

To discuss the basic attributes of an enforceable contract in more detail, consider the example of a power pack purchased by a consumer on eBay. If the consumer purchased the power pack from a business (versus another consumer), it would be classified as a business-to-consumer transaction (B2C). The full array of protections governing consumer contracts applies. The principal source of law is UCC Article 2 because it is a contract for the sale of goods. The most common type of contract is made between a seller, who agrees to sell goods, and the buyer, who agrees to pay money. The purchase of the power pack in the eBay example above is easily classifiable as an enforceable contract. A consumer successfully bidding on an eBay or other online auction will be contractually bound by eBay's rules as well as UCC Article 2. He was the highest bidder in an auction, and his bid was a promise to pay the agreed-upon price for the power pack. Additionally, a contract may be some promised performance that the law recognizes as a duty.

Consumer Contracts Defined

Contracts entered into for personal, family, or household purposes are consumer transactions subject to mandatory state and federal laws protecting the weaker party. Consumer law is largely about giving consumers special protections, disclosures, remedies, and mandatory provisions. Our hypothetical consumer, Sue Smith, enters into a large number of binding consumer contracts each day. When she uses her cell phone, she enters into an express as well as an implied promise to pay charges. When she fills her car with gasoline, there is an enforceable promise to pay. Not all promises that Sue makes are enforceable contracts. If Sue promises to take her niece to a New England Patriots game, it is not an enforceable agreement. If Sue promises her mother to stop smoking, that is not an enforceable agreement, though it is a promise. Sue's Uncle Sal pledged to give her $500,000 at his death: that is a promise, but not an enforceable one. A contract is a binding promise that the law will enforce. The courts are not prepared to enforce all promises, only promises where there is a manifestation of assent.

Suppose Sue agrees to have her driveway paved, and the contractor arrives with his equipment, ready to proceed. She will breach the contract to pave the driveway if she sends him packing, claiming that she does not feel like doing business with him. If she sends him away claiming she is not in the mood to have her driveway paved, she will be liable to the contractor for damages. Of course, there must be proof that Sue agreed to the paving of the driveway. Some contracts need to be in writing to be enforceable, though oral contracts are frequently enforceable. Modern contract law makes it possible to make agreements by any reasonable method, including the exchange of electronic records. Courts will enforce a contract even though it does not spell out every term, so long as there is a sufficient basis for granting a remedy.

The Elements of a Contract

A consumer contract is an enforceable agreement between a person and a business to purchase goods or services for personal, family, or household use. In our example, Sue can enter into contracts by her words, conduct, or the combination of words and conduct. Sue's contracts may be verbal or memorialized in writing.

In each contract that Sue entered into in our hypothetical example, three elements needed to be present in order for there to be contract formation: (1) offer, (2) acceptance, and (3) consideration. The entire process of mutual assent is termed the "process of offer and acceptance."

Offers

An offer is an expression of willingness to enter into a contract. In all (sales or services) contracts, the person (or entity) making the offer is the *offeror*. The person in receipt of an offer is the *offeree*. The offeror is the master of the offer, which means that he can revoke it any time before it is accepted. An offer is the manifestation of willingness to enter into a bargain. Offers may be made orally, in writing, or by contract. The emblem of a valid offer is that a reasonable person would believe that a contract was intended. A common law offer is a manifestation of intent to be bound and is effective when received by the other party. Solicitations or advertisements, such as a price tag on an article of clothing, are generally not valid offers, but simply invitations to accept an offer. In general, where the parties have not agreed on key terms, the parties are likely in the process of negotiation and have not made a contract.

Before you accept an offer, study all the details about the products or services. The key terms that you must master are (1) the total price, (2) the delivery time, (3) the refund and cancellation policies, (4) the terms of any warranty, and (5) the procedure for redressing problems. Do not agree to contract terms that you do not understand. Also, avoid one-sided contractual provisions such as mandatory arbitration. Many sales and services do the equivalent of requiring you to waive warranties and remedies. If you are required to waive your rights, choose another seller, vendor, or creditor when possible.

Acceptance

At common law, the offeror is master of the offer and can set the manner of acceptance. The *mirror image rule* requires that an offeree must accept an offer in the precise manner called for in the offer. Therefore, if the offer specified that the acceptance be mailed with a blue ribbon, there would be no manifestation of assent if the paper was wrapped with a pink ribbon. If the acceptance varies from the offer or has different or additional terms, it is regarded as a counteroffer, which has the legal effect of killing off the original offer. An acceptance is legally sufficient if it matches up to the offer and evidences mutual assent between the offeror and the offeree. Under the *mailbox rule*, an acceptance is effective when a letter is mailed or a telegram is sent, as opposed to when either means of communication is received. The same rule presumably applies to email.

Acceptance may be by words or conduct as long as there is a manifestation of an assent to an offer. A period for acceptance fixed by the offeror in a telegram or a letter begins to toll when the telegram is handed to the offeree.

Consideration

Consideration is sometimes described as the mutuality of obligations. It is the inducement to enter into a contract. In a sales contract, the seller promises to deliver goods in return for a promise by the buyer to pay for them. "Consideration" is either a benefit given or to be given to the person who makes the promise or some other person or a detriment experienced or to be experienced by the person to whom the promise is made or some other person. Where the contract provides for mutual promises, each promise is a consideration for the other promise.[1] Contracts are promises but courts will not enforce every promise. Only promises backed by consideration are legally enforceable. In most consumer transactions, the benefit will be goods or services conferred, and the detriment will be payment of the price, which means that the buyer has less money in her purse.

A promise of a gift, for example, is unenforceable for lack of consideration. If your uncle Bill promises you a new BMW when you turn twenty-one, the promise is not an enforceable contract because you have given your uncle Bill no benefit or detriment. Contracts may also be enforceable because of *detrimental reliance*, which is a substitute for consideration. Suppose your uncle Bill promises to give you a new BMW if you refrain from using tobacco or alcohol. If you fulfill these conditions, the contract is enforceable because you have detrimentally relied upon your uncle Bill's promise. Consideration is rarely a problem in consumer contracts because consideration comes in the form of a promise to pay money in return for goods or services.

Rejecting Offers and Counteroffers

Suppose Sue offers Sean $25 to mow her loan. If Sean rejects Sue's offer, he no longer has the power to accept the offer unless Sue is willing to make a new offer. Sean may reject Sue's offer orally or in writing or in conduct that Sue would understand as a rejection of the offer. Suppose Sue sent Sean a letter offering him $25 to mow her lawn. If Sean responded by saying that he will mow her lawn for $40, he would be making a counteroffer. The legal effect of Sean's counteroffer is to terminate Sue's original offer.

Option Contracts

Parties making offers (offerors) may revoke them at any time before the other party (offeree) accepts. If no time is stated, the offer is open for a reasonable period. The definition of *reasonable* depends on the product on offer. A common law offer is revocable until acceptance because the promise has not yet been supported by consideration, which is the final ingredient necessary for contract formation. Option contracts are a special kind of offer in which the offeror agrees to hold the offer open in return for consideration, usually a sum of money paid by the offeree. If Sue pays her neighbor Bill $100 to hold the offer open to sell his BMW, it is an option contract supported by consideration. The option contract must be supported by consideration and is irrevocable for the agreed-upon period. For option contracts not supported by consideration, use detrimental reliance to create a period of irrevocability.

Firm Offers

The *firm offer* rule of UCC §2-205 is an exception to the general contract doctrine that offers are freely revocable. The Uniform Commercial Code applies if a consumer transaction is for the sale of goods. A firm offer has these attributes:

1. A firm offer is for the *sale of goods*.
2. A firm offer must be in *writing*.
3. Firm offers are made by *merchants*. A merchant is "a person who deals in goods of the kind or otherwise by his occupation holds himself out as having knowledge or skill peculiar to the practices or goods involved in the transaction or to whom such knowledge or skill may be attributed."[2]
4. A firm offer assures the offeree that it will be held open for a reasonable period of time, *not to exceed three months*.

The firm offer is the functional equivalent of an option contract, but no consideration is required. Firm offers do not require consideration so long as there is a signed writing giving assurance by the merchant-seller that the contract will be held open.

Formation of Sales Contracts

UCC Article 2 abandons the concept of requiring that both parties must be aware of the moment at which a formal contract is created. Article 2 agreements "sufficient to constitute a contract for sale may be found even though the moment of its making is undetermined." Domestic sales contracts are enforceable even if the parties leave many terms open, so long as there is a reasonably certain basis for giving the aggrieved party an appropriate remedy.[3]

An Article 2 sales "agreement means the bargain of the parties in fact as found in their language or by implication from other circumstances including course of dealing or usage of trade or course of performance" (see UCC §1-201[3]). In UCC Article 2 contracts, the hierarchy of contract terms is ranked in the following order: *express terms of the contract* are ranked first, followed by *course of performance*, then *course of dealing*, and finally widespread *usages of trade*. Express terms are "expressed" in the written contract and understandably prevail over all the implied terms: course of performance, course of dealing, and usage of trade.

A course of performance is prior conduct in the contract at issue, whereas the course of dealing refers to mutual understandings that evolve out of prior contracts between the parties. A course of dealing is a sequence of previous conduct between the parties to a particular transaction that has established a common basis of understanding for interpreting their agreement. A trade usage would be a widespread norm in an industry. In Vermont, for example, farmers give thirteen ears of corn rather than a dozen, calling it a baker's dozen. This usage of trade is part of the contract unless the farmer provides otherwise.

In every contract, there is an implied duty to cooperate with the other party. That means that consumers have broad protection against sharp or dishonest practices. Nevertheless, the consumer is also subject to this covenant. If Sue contracted with Sean to mow her lawn, she would have to give him reasonable access to her property to complete his obligation. If a consumer violates that duty, then she is not entitled to sue for breach of contract.

The Importance of Getting It in Writing

Many people erroneously believe that because they did not sign a written document, there is no contract. However, if a customer walked into Dunkin Donuts and helped himself to a donut, there would be a contract to pay for the delectable snack, even though there was no writing. You should always get important contracts in writing, even if the law does not require that formality. The Statute of Frauds, which is a UCC doctrine, requires that a writing signed by the party against whom enforcement is sought proves that the parties made a contract.[4] By having a signed agreement, you have proof there was a contract and often evidence of the terms, such as price, place of delivery, time of delivery, and other key terms. Oral contracts may be enforceable, but you will need to prove the terms, a feat which can prove difficult at times.

Note that for the sale of goods, the UCC requires a writing signed by the party against whom enforcement is sought if the price is $500 or greater (see

UCC §2-201). If you agree to purchase shares of stock, convertible debentures, or other securities, you will need a signed writing to enforce the agreement (see UCC §8-319). Article 9 of the UCC, governing secured transactions, requires a writing signed by the debtor to create a security interest in personal property or fixtures. A signed writing is also required for service contracts that cannot be performed within a year or for sales of land, to name a few exceptions outside sales law. A signed writing in all states must memorialize a number of other categories of contracts:

A. A contract of an executor or administrator to answer for a duty of his decedent;
B. A contract to answer for the duty of another;
C. A contract made upon consideration of marriage;
D. A contract for the sale of an interest in land;
E. A contract that is not to be performed within one year from the making thereof. (Rest. 2d Contracts, §110)

Contracts generally can be written, using formal or informal terms, or entirely verbal. The most important thing about contract law for a consumer is that if the other side "breaches" or fails to live up to its promise, there are remedies available to the aggrieved party.

Parol Evidence, Integration Clauses, and Exceptions

Parol evidence is evidence other than the "four corners" of the written contract where a court might look to determine a party's intent. The parol evidence rule requires courts to first examine whether the written agreement was intended by the parties as a final expression of their agreement with respect to such terms included in the writing. At common law, the "final expression" is a *partially integrated agreement*. A partially integrated writing simply means that the agreement is final only to some of the terms in the final writing. Either party was free to introduce additional terms so long as they did not contradict terms in the final writing. For partially integrated agreements, it is possible to admit evidence of additional terms so long as they do not contradict final terms in the writing. Either party is free to bring in documents or testimony explaining *ambiguous* terms.

In contrast, a *completely integrated* writing means that the writing contains all the final terms. A completely integrated writing is the complete and exclusive statement of all of the terms of the contract. In other words, the writing contains all the terms, and this means that the parol evidence rule excludes additional terms as well as contradictory terms. The parol evidence rule is often used by the seller to keep out oral statements made by the sales staff about warranties or remedies. It is the courts' role to determine whether a writing is a final expression of the parties agreement (partial integration) or a complete and exclusive statement of the terms of the agreement (complete integration).

Similarly, under UCC Article 2, parol evidence will typically take the form of prior negotiations, earlier writings, and oral statements by the parties. If a sales contract is a final agreement, parol evidence may explain or supplement a final writing. However, additional terms are excluded if the sales contract is "complete and exclusive." Written contracts may be explained or supplemented by course of dealing or usage of trade or by course of performance even if they are "complete and exclusive."[5]

Courts generally look to a contract's integration clause as a key factor in determining whether the agreement is partially or completely integrated. A contract's *integration clause* is a contractual clause that seeks to exclude or limit parol evidence: "This Agreement constitutes the entire understanding of the parties with respect to the subject matter." This agreement is the "complete and exclusive" agreement of the parties. The legal significance of this clause is to protect the finalized writing against claims by parties that inconsistent terms were part of the contract.

UCC §2-202 governs the parol evidence rule for the sale of goods, whereas UCC §2A-202 applies to the leases of goods. Under both of these sections, if the integration clause states that the written agreement is the parties' "complete and exclusive" agreement, neither party will be able to introduce evidence of either additional or contradictory terms from prior or contemporaneous agreements. If the parties merely use the phrase *final agreement*, the parties may introduce additional, consistent terms, but not contradictory terms. A consumer buyer will frequently want to introduce evidence of the salesperson's representations about products or services that were made prior or contemporaneous to the agreement. The integration clause serves as a gatekeeper, barring this evidence from court. Consumers can protect themselves by requiring the sales representatives to place any key representations in a separate writing or, better yet, the final integrated agreement. Even if the parties use an airtight integration clause, the parol evidence rule recognizes exceptions for fraud and conditions of contracts.

Modification of Contracts

The parties to a contract will frequently agree to a clause that all modifications must be in writing to be valid. The language will typically read that "no alteration, change or modification of this contract shall be binding or effective unless executed in writing and signed by both parties." The purpose of this clause is to emphasize that the parties to a contract may modify its terms only upon mutual agreement. It is unreasonable for a consumer to rely on an oral modification by a sales representative where the contract expressly calls for modifications to be in writing in order to be effective.

In a sale of goods, no new consideration is required to modify a contract. This is different than the common law pre-existing duty rule that required new consideration to modify a contract. UCC Article 2 requires that modifications be in writing and be signed by the representatives of the buyer and the seller.

Physical Duress That Deprives the Contracting Party of Free Will

Duress is a defense to contract formation where acts or threats of violence deprive the weaker party of free will. Contracts are not legally binding if contractual consent was a product of gunpoint. The classic example of duress is where a party signed a contract while being threatened by a moral monster brandishing a gun. Suppose a brutal bully threatened to beat his wife to a pulp unless she agreed to cosign a promissory note to purchase a new deer rifle. The test of duress is whether the person entering into the contract is able to exercise free will. Courts are not receptive to the argument that a party signed a contract because of economic duress.

Minority of Contracting Parties

Most jurisdictions define minors as natural persons under the age of eighteen. If you are a minor, you will have the right to cancel many contracts. Mississippi courts treat minors with disabilities as persons incapable of entering into contracts. In Oklahoma, a minor may not contract for real property or personal property not in his control. The state of Washington binds minors to contracts unless they disaffirm them. Consult the Juvenile Law Center's state survey on minority and the capacity to contract to determine the rule in your jurisdiction.[6] Every state has a statute addressing the issue of what contracts may be disaffirmed, whether minors are competent to enter into contracts, and exceptions. Married minors are competent to contract in a number of jurisdictions in New Hampshire. Iowa, too, defines majority legal status to include persons over the age of eighteen *or* upon marriage. Persons under the age of eighteen may contract for necessities such as food and shelter. After a person reaches the age of majority, she may also ratify contracts.

Void and Voidable Contracts

Consumers may seek a declaratory judgment that a loan or other consumer contract is *void* or *voidable* as an illegal contract against public policy. Void contracts may not be enforced, and they should be distinguished from voidable contracts, which are valid unless one of the parties chooses to void the contract. Void contracts are invalid from the inception, whereas voidable contracts may be valid if one of the parties does not disaffirm them. A person with diminished mental capacity due to insanity may disaffirm a contract, which is usually done through a guardian. If the parties lack contractual capacity, the contract is void. If the weaker party lacks the mental capacity to understand the true purpose of a contract, and the stronger party acted fairly, the contract is merely voidable. In sum, a contract is valid unless disavowed by the party who lacks contractual capacity or her legal representative.

Contracts entered into by minors are typically voidable unless they were for necessities. A seller who contracts with a minor does so at his peril and has no recourse if the minor opts out of the contract because it is *voidable* at her option. If a seller agrees to sell a Porsche to your sixteen-year-old daughter and you have no knowledge of this agreement, the contract is voidable. The contract is voidable because the young girl is under eighteen, and states have a minimum age for entering into contracts.

Unless the buyer damages the product, the seller is bound to the terms of the contract, but the minor is free to back out with impunity. A seller may be able to recover for the reasonable value of goods classifiable as necessities or if the minor destroys the items.

Unconscionable Contracts

Policing Unconscionable License Agreements

Unconscionability is a form of redress available when one party abuses a strong bargaining position to take advantage of the other party's weakness, ignorance, or distress. UCC §2-302 gives courts the power to strike down unconscionable contracts or terms, but the courts evaluate these matters strictly. A court may find a sales or lease contract with hidden terms to be unconscionable, especially if the price is unfairly high. The basic test is whether the contract term or entire agreement is "so one-sided as to be unconscionable under the circumstances existing at the time of the making of the contract."[7]

The essence of procedural unconscionably revolves around a showing of two factors—oppression and surprise. *Oppression* arises from inequality of bargaining power that results in no real negotiation and an absence of meaningful choice. *Surprise* involves the extent to which the supposedly agreed-upon terms of the bargain are hidden in the "prolix printed form drafted by the party seeking to enforce the disputed terms."[8]A court will also consider whether the buyer is a consumer and whether there was deception in hiding unfair terms. A court has a wide arsenal of remedies when finding evidence of an unfair bargaining process and unfair terms.[9]

Courts may refuse to enforce the contract as a whole if it is permeated by unconscionability, or it may strike any single term or group of terms in a contract, whether it be a sales, lease, or license agreement. A court has the power to enforce the contract, it may enforce the remainder of the contract without the unconscionable term or terms, or it may interpret the contract to avoid an unconscionable result.

UCC Article 2 gives the courts the power to review contracts to determine whether they were unconscionable *at the time made* (UCC §2-302). The idea of unconscionability is that the person has entered into a contract that no sane person would make. A judge has the discretion to strike down a sale's entire contract or a given contractual clause if it is so one-sided as to be unconscionable. A contract may be struck down as unconscionable if it is unfair both in the bargaining process (procedural unconscionability) and in the bargain arrived at (substantive unconscionability). An example of procedural unconscionability would be a used car sales representative who took advantage of a new immigrant with limited education and command of the English language. If Fast Frankie, a used car sales clerk, sold a defective car to a new immigrant at four or five times its market value, the bargain would be so one-sided that no sane person would enter into the contract. Courts will not strike down contractual clauses as being unconscionable unless the bargaining process is unfair and the substantive bargain is oppressive, one-sided, and extremely unfavorable to the consumer.

Illegal Contracts

The law does not permit consumers to enter into illegal contracts, which are void at their inception. The movie *The Contract* is a thriller about a legally unenforceable contract with a hired killer. A contract to sell your kidney, your American citizenship, or your first-born son would not be enforceable for public policy reasons. Few of the contracts entered into by characters on *The Sopranos* are enforceable because they are for an illegal purpose. Consumers purchasing doctored marijuana from a drug cartel would have no recourse because of the illegal product. Similarly, a consumer dissatisfied with a hit man's work will not be able to obtain a remedy at law.

Equitable Remedies

In most consumer contracts, money damages are at issue. However, in rare instances, a consumer may seek injunctive relief. For the sale of goods, it is appropriate to seek *specific performance.* Specific performance is an equitable remedy in contrast to a remedy for monetary damages ordered by the court in extraordinary circumstances. The classic justification for specific performance is that money damages are inadequate. Courts have considerable discretion in whether to order specific performance — to deliver goods that are unique (see UCC, §2-716). In the estate of a former U.S. president or famous movie star, many of the items sold at auction would be considered to be unique. The former First Lady Jackie Kennedy's inexpensive pearl necklace would be unique in light of the mystique of the Kennedy family. Similarly, the belongings of Princess Diana of Wales could be the subject of an order for specific performance. If a court orders specific performance, it will typically require the buyer to pay the price in advance.

Rescission is another example of an equitable remedy in which the plaintiff seeks to "unmake" the contract. In some consumer contracts, there will be a remedy for the reasonable value of services under the doctrine of *quantum meruit. Quantum meruit* is the amount merited or the reasonable value of services rendered. It is an equitable remedy because the damages are based upon services rendered or materials used as opposed to a written, enforceable contract.

Federal Truth in Mileage Act of 1986

Automobile sales are an example of a heavily regulated contract. The federal Truth in Mileage Act of 1986 developed the ground rules for odometer disclosure. That law requires a transferor to disclose the odometer mileage "in writing on the title or on the document being used to reassign the title." Turning back an odometer to conceal the condition of a vehicle is treated as common law fraud as well. The actual damages will be the market value of your automobile with more mileage. It is likely you will also receive treble damages as well as attorneys' fees.

Types of Consumer Contracts

Contracts come in multiple flavors, but it is the substance that counts, rather than the label used by the parties. As mentioned above some contracts are written, whereas others are oral. Contracts may be as simple as an IOU or a complex security agreement financing heavy equipment. Contracts are formed in diverse settings by fax, telephone, or email; on horseback; at the picnic table; or at company headquarters. Contracts may be formed on trains, planes, and automobiles.

Consumer contracts may also take a wide variety of forms. Sales, leases, and licenses are three common forms of consumer agreements. In a sales contract, the seller conveys title to conforming goods for a price. A lease, in contrast, gives the consumers the use of goods for a term. Licensing is one of the fastest-growing means of contracts. License agreements are found at every website offering software for download. Consumers are given a limited license to use software if they agree to the terms and conditions of the license agreement.

Licensing of Information

Many consumer contracts do not involve any real bargaining. It is rare for a consumer to be able to bargain with a multinational corporation such as Microsoft or Verizon. Contracts in which the consumer must adhere to the terms of the stronger party are known as *adhesion contracts.* A contract of adhesion is one in which one party uses its superior market power to force the other party into a one-sided contract on a "take it or leave it" basis.

Mass market license agreements that accompany software are classic examples of adhesion contracts, in which the licensor routinely disclaims all meaningful warranties and remedies, and the manufacturer reallocates the risk of loss to the user community for all failures of performance. Many, even most, license agreements do not allow bargaining over any term or condition of service. The trend is for courts to enforce these adhesion contracts so long as the consumer has an opportunity to review the terms and manifest assent by clicking on the "I agree" button.

Intangible intellectual property gives software its value, not the physical medium, such as the CD-ROM on which information is embedded. To appreciate the distinction between licensing information and the sale of goods, think of the difference between the price paid at Coconuts record store for a blank compact disc or the Super Mario Brothers theme by Kojo Kondo or the latest release of the Pussycat Dolls. The information embedded upon a CD-ROM constitutes the value sought, rather than the CD-ROM as a physical medium. The furor over downloading music from the Internet makes it clear that the physical medium is only incidental to the transfer of information. Downloading music from the Internet does not involve a physical medium at all.

Bad Software Lawsuits

The licensing of downloadable software shares little common ground with the traditional attributes of a sale of goods. If software does not perform according to its specifications or as advertised, the consumer will have an action for breach of warranties because courts are likely to extend UCC Article 2 rights and remedies to licensing agreements. With the sale of goods, title passes from seller to buyer when the buyer accepts and pays in accordance with the contract, and it is marked by physical delivery of tangible goods. In contrast to the sale of goods, no title passes with the licensing of software. Location and use restrictions are necessary for software developers to realize their investment in developing intangible information assets.

Licensees are not permitted to resell licensed software. The licensor retains title to software or other information and imposes restriction on use. Licensing is a useful and necessary legal invention to permit software developers to have an unlimited inventory to realize their investment. If you retain counsel in a bad software case, your counsel will argue that you should be entitled to the same rights and remedies including warranty protection as if software were classified as goods. If the software does not perform according to specifications in advertisements or packaging, you may have an action based on an express warranty. If you are purchasing consumer software, the maker may not be able to disclaim all implied warranties of merchantability because it is arguable that the Magnuson-Moss Warranty Act applies. That law does not permit a seller to eliminate all implied warranties. It is arguable that the Magnuson-Moss Warranty Act should extend to software, though the federal warranty act applies to consumer goods.

What to Do: Avoiding Unfair or Deceptive Downloads. The National Consumer League's Internet Fraud Watch urges consumers to be wary about downloading digital images, music, games, and other software because of the risk that they are unwittingly downloading viruses. Before you click agreement to the terms and services of a website, be careful that you are not waiving minimum rights and remedies. Be wary of "clickwrap" (click yes if you agree; click no to leave the website) agreements that disclaim all meaningful remedies and warranties and require you to litigate in a distant forum such as Belize or Iceland.

Bailment Contracts

A bailment is a rightful possession of property created by contract. A bailment contract is created when the owner (bailor) hands over property to another (bailee) for storing or safeguarding it. Bailments may be either contractual where you pay $30 a day to park your car or gratuitous. In general, contractual bailees have greater liability than ones who agree to safeguard your property for no charge. The bailee has a general obligation to redeliver the property back to the owner. However, the bailment contract will generally stipulate the time, place, and manner of delivery. Consumers typically encounter informal bailment contracts, such as when they leave their coat at the coat check at a museum or other public place. Similarly, a bailment contract is formed when a consumer leaves their car with a valet.

Consumers will frequently encounter disclaimers of liability in bailment contracts, which are subject to state laws. In particular, many states restrict disclaimers in bailments. Massachusetts, for example, does not permit the owner or operator of a publicly owned parking facility to disclaim, limit, or exclude legal liability (M.G.L.A. ch. 231, §85M). Maine enacted a statute governing bailments, common carriers, and hotel keepers that define the bailment agreement as supported by value. Under Maine law, if a bailment agreement is supported by consideration (contractual versus gratuitous), the bailee has the duty of ordinary care and will be liable for negligence. The bailor must prove a bailee's negligence, but that is not a difficult burden:

A. If a bailor can prove that the goods were delivered to the bailee and that the bailee failed to return the item undamaged;
B. Then the bailor has established a *prima facie* case of negligence by the bailee;
C. The bailee must then present facts that show the bailee's actions were consistent with due care; if not, the bailee will be found negligent. (Maine General Law §29.5)

The Maine statute, like the laws of many other states, applies to consumers when they park their car in commercial lots. Similarly, the law applies if you leave your coat with a checkroom attendant. However, the law is not applicable in Maine and other states if you simply hang your coat on a restaurant's coatrack. In every state, a hotel or motel owner or operator is a bailee also subject to the standard of reasonable care.

Canceling a Contract

Federal Rights to Cancel Contracts

Distance Sales. The procedure for canceling a distance sale (a sale at a "home show" or other exposition, at a seminar held in a hotel banquet room, or at a "sales party" in someone's home) is to sign and date one copy of the cancellation form provided by the seller or creditor. If you were not given a cancellation form, you can draft your own cancellation letter. You need not give reasons for canceling the contract; the statute gives you a right to withdraw from the contract for any reason or no reason.

Mail the cancellation form to the address given for cancellation. Be certain that the envelope is postmarked before midnight of the third business day after the contract date. (Saturday is considered a business day; Sundays and federal holidays are not.) It is a good idea to send the cancellation notice by certified mail so you have a return receipt to prove that you have given proper notification. You can also deliver the cancellation notice to the business directly so long as the cancellation notice is given before midnight of the third business day. Be sure to retain a copy of the cancellation form for your records.

Door-to-Door Sales. The FTC rule, entitled "Cooling Off Period for Door-to-Door Sales," as well as state laws governing door-to-door sales and home solicitations give you a "cooling off" period as well as other rights. In a home solicitation contract for sales of $25 or more, the salesperson must give you two copies of a cancellation form (one to keep and one to send) and a copy of your contract or receipt. The contract or receipt should be dated, show the name and address of the seller, and explain your right to cancel. The contract or receipt must be in the same language that is used in the sales presentation. The FTC's Door-to-Door Sales Rule concerning the cooling off period for door-to-door sales at residences and other locations apart from the usual place of business gives you until midnight of the third business day after a contract has been signed to cancel it.

Even if your state does not have its own home solicitation law, the federal three-day cooling off period applies to door-to-door sales for greater than $25 made anywhere other than the seller's usual place of business (16 C.F.R. 429.1). The cooling off rule applies to contracts entered into other than the "place of business of the seller (e.g., sales at the buyer's residence or at facilities rented on a temporary or short-term basis, such as hotel or motel rooms, convention centers, fairgrounds and restaurants, or sales at the buyer's workplace or in dormitory lounges)" (15 C.F.R. 429 [a]). Massachusetts, like many other states, has enacted a three-day buyer's remorse rule. Massachusetts's three-day cooling off period applies to consumer agreements consummated at places other than the seller's place of business

(M.G.L.A. Ch. 93A, §48). Check with your state attorney general's office to determine whether your jurisdiction has a similar rule.

The FTC regulations define the three business days to include Saturdays but not Sundays or legal public holidays. For example, if the events listed above take place on a Friday, you have until midnight on the next Tuesday to rescind. This federal cooling off period does not allow you to cancel sales made completely by mail or phone or real estate, insurance, or securities sales.

The right to cancel also does not apply if the goods or services are needed due to an emergency. The consumer buyer, however, may waive the cancellation right in a signed writing explaining the reasons. The FTC notes that its cooling off rule does not cover (1) sales that are under $25; (2) goods or services whose predominant purpose was personal, family, or household use; (3) sales made entirely by mail or telephone; (4) sales that were the result of prior negotiations at the seller's permanent business locations where the seller regularly sells goods; (5) goods needed to meet an emergency; and (6) sales made at your request to do repairs or maintenance on your personal property (purchases made beyond the maintenance or repair request are covered).

Keep in mind that there are a number of statutory exceptions to the FTC cooling off rule, including any sales that involve (1) real estate, insurance, or securities; (2) automobiles, vans, or motor vehicles sold at temporary locations; or (3) arts or crafts sold at fairs or locations such as shopping malls, civic centers, and schools. Assuming you give a timely notice, the seller has ten days to: (1) cancel and return any promissory instrument you signed; (2) refund all your money and tell you whether any product you still have will be picked up; and (3) return any trade-in. Within twenty days, the seller must either pick up the items left with you or reimburse you for mailing expenses, if you agree to send back the items. If you received any goods from the seller, you must make them available to the seller in as good a condition as when you received them. If you do not make the items available to the seller—or if you agree to return the items but fail to—you remain obligated under the contract.

The Truth in Lending Act's Three-Day Rule. The federal Truth in Lending Act (TILA) gives homeowners a three-day rescission right for home equity loans in which a security interest is taken on the consumer's primary residence (15 USC §1635). TILA requires all creditors to give disclosures. A creditor is defined as anyone who both (1) regularly extends, whether in connection with loans, sales of property or services, or otherwise, consumer credit that is payable in more than four installments or for which the payment of a finance charge is or may be required; and (2) is the person to whom the debt arising from the consumer credit transaction is initially payable on the face of the indebtedness, or by agreement (15 U.S.C. §1602[f]).

TILA's three-day cooling off period gives you the right to cancel the loan until midnight of the third business day. TILA's consumer credit disclosures apply to opening or increasing the credit limit for an open-ended credit plan in which a security interest is retained in your principal dwelling. A security interest is created by a security agreement that gives the creditor the right to take property offered as security if the loan is not paid. TILA also permits you to cancel a home improvement loan, second mortgage, or any other loan in which you are creating a security interest in your residence. There is no three-day cooling off period for your first mortgage.

The three-day cooling off period begins to toll after the last of the following three events occur: (1) you sign the credit contract; (2) you receive a truth in lending disclosure form containing certain key information about the credit contract, including the annual percentage rate, finance charge, amount financed, and payment schedule; and (3) you receive two copies of a truth in lending notice explaining your right to rescind.

If you are dealing with a home improvement contract, they may not begin work, deliver materials, or do any work until the rescission period expires. If you decide to rescind, you must notify the creditor in writing. You may not rescind by telephone or in a face-to-face conversation with the creditor. Your written notice must be mailed, filed for telegraphic transmission, or delivered if by other written means, before midnight of the third business day. Complaints against home improvement contractors should be first made with your state attorney general's consumer protection unit. You may also register a complaint with the Department of Housing and Urban Development at Home Improvement Branch, 451 Seventh St., SW, Room 9272, Washington, DC 20410, 202-708-2121, (fax) 202-708-4308, www.hud.gov/improvements.

Cooling Off Periods under State Law. A number of state laws also give consumers the right to a three-day cooling off period to rescind or cancel a retail contract made with a door-to-door sales representative. The state of Washington gives consumers three business days to cancel a retail installment contract made with a door-to-door salesperson, regardless of the amount. The tolling period for the retail installment plan cooling off period begins on the date the buyer signs the contract or credit agreement. The cooling off period ends at midnight of the third day (excluding Sundays and holidays) following the date the buyer signs the contract or charge agreement. The Washington act also applies to other distance contracts, made either in person or at a place other than the seller's business. Cash sales are not covered in the Washington statute. If the consumer rescinds the retail sales contract, she is entitled to a refund within ten days after the cancellation, which also includes any down payment. The buyer must return the goods in their original condition to the seller at the place where the seller delivered the goods (RCW 63.14.52).

Cooling Off Period for Timeshares. A growing number of states have time-share regulations that give the buyer the right to cancel the contract within seven days after signing the contract or seven days after receiving required disclosures about the timeshares. Washington's timeshare regulation applies to any kind of timeshare (RCW 64.36).

Jurisdiction-Specific Cooling Off Periods. Check your state attorney general's website to determine the applicable cooling off periods in your jurisdiction. New York, for example, gives consumers cooling off periods for a wide variety of contracts, including home food service plans, contracts with charitable organizations, prize award schemes, urea-formaldehyde foam insulation contracts, dating services, credit service business contracts with consumers, health club contracts, membership campground contracts, automobile broker business contracts, home improvement contracts, door-to-door sales contracts, telephone sales contracts, and sale or lease contracts for subdivided lands.

Contractual Waivers of Liability

Consumers are increasingly asked to waive their rights and remedies. If you have a school-age child, you will be asked to sign waivers of liability for field trips, extracurricular activities, and other special events. High school administrators frequently require parents to sign waivers of liability as a condition of their children participating in sports and other activities. If your child is injured in a sport, the defendant will argue that the waiver of liability form you signed absolved the school from liability, even if officials were negligent. In order for a clause to be enforceable, it must include an exculpatory clause that clearly states it releases the party from liability for its own negligence. The tendency is for courts to enforce waivers of liability in recreational activities. You are truly assuming the risk for you and your children when you agree, for example, to a waiver of liability to use a cycle park.

Courts broadly enforce waivers signed prior to participation that excuse the defendant and its employees from liability for personal injuries. In essence, the participant is agreeing that the business or other entity owes them no duty. A growing number of organizations use waivers that include indemnification clauses and "hold harmless" provisions to limit their liability. Suppose Sue, our hypothetical consumer, decides to go on vacation at a dude ranch in Montana. She will likely be asked to sign a release and hold harmless clause, as in the following:

> By signing this agreement, you are giving up certain legal rights, including the right to recover damages in case of injury, death, or property damage. Read

this agreement carefully before signing it. Your signature indicates your understanding of and agreement to its terms.

I, Sue Smith the undersigned, in consideration of the services of the City Slacker Dude Ranch Corp., its officers, agents or representatives (hereinafter referred to as "City Slacker Dude Ranch"), hereby agree to release and discharge City Slacker Dude Ranch, on behalf of myself, my heirs, assigns, personal representative and estate as follows:

1. I understand and acknowledge that the activity I am about to voluntarily engage in as a participant and/or volunteer bears certain known risks and unanticipated risks which could result in injury, death, illness or disease, physical or mental, or damage to myself, to my property or to spectators or other third parties. The following describes some, but not all, of those risks:

A horse may, without warning or any apparent cause, buck, stumble, fall, rear, bite, kick, run, make unpredictable movements, spook, jump obstacles, step on a person's feet, push or shove a person and saddles or bridles may loosen or break—all of which may cause the rider to fall or be jolted, resulting in serious injury or death.

2. I acknowledge that horseback riding is a dangerous activity and involves risks that may cause serious injury and in some cases death, because of the unpredictable nature and irrational behavior of horses, regardless of their training and past performance.

3. I voluntarily assume the risk and danger of injury or death inherent in the use of the horse, equipment and gear provided to me by City Slacker Dude Ranch.

4. I release, discharge, and promise not to sue City Slacker Dude Ranch doing business under its own name or any other name and/or any of its owners, officers, employees and agents (hereinafter referred to as "Releases"), for any loss, liability, damage, or cost whatsoever arising out of or related to any loss, damage, or injury (including death) to my person or property.

5. I release the Releases from any claim that such Releases are or may be negligent in connection with my riding experience or ability, including but not limited to training or selecting horses, maintenance, care, fit or adjustment of saddles or bridles, instruction on riding skills or leading and supervising riders.

6. I indemnify and save and hold harmless City Slacker Dude Ranch and its employees and agents against any loss, liability, damage or cost that may incur arising out of or in any way connected with either my use of the horse and any equipment or gear provided therewith or any acts or omissions of wranglers or other employees or agents.

7. The undersigned expressly agrees that the foregoing release and waiver of liability, assumption of risk, and indemnity agreement is governed by the State of California and is intended to be as broad and inclusive as permitted by California law, and that in the event any portion of this Agreement is determined to be invalid, illegal, or unenforceable, the validity, legality and enforceability of the balance of the Agreement shall not be affected or impaired in any way and shall continue in full legal force and effect.

8. I acknowledge that this document is a contract and agree that if a lawsuit is filed against City Slacker Dude Ranch or its owner, agents, employees, guides or wranglers for any injury or damage in breach of this contract, the

Undersigned will pay all attorney's fees and costs incurred by City Slacker Dude Ranch in defending such an action.

My signature below indicates that I have read this entire document, understand it completely, understand that it affects my legal rights, and agree to be bound by its terms. I understand it is a promise not to sue and is a release and indemnity for all claims.

Sue Smith

When Sue signed this waiver, she was contractually agreeing with City Slacker Dude Ranch that they owed her no duty to protect the plaintiff from an injury-causing risk. If Sue was injured because the City Slacker Dude Ranch directed her to ride into abnormally dangerous terrain, it is unclear whether the waiver would actually cover that particular risk. The release or waiver should only excuse liability for injuries that ordinarily and inevitably occur without fault.

Another issue for Sue is whether she knowingly and voluntarily entered into a contract in which she agreed to limit the dude ranch's liability. A consumer is free to contract with the proprietor of a recreational activity to relieve them of responsibility for damages or injuries because that is deemed to be a *primary assumption of risk*. In our example, Sue Smith is giving her *express* consent relieving City Slacker of an obligation to protect her from the known risks of horseback riding. In other words, if Sue is thrown from her horse, kicked by a stampeding horse, or paralyzed by a horse falling on her, City Slacker cannot be sued for negligence. Courts are willing to enforce these agreements because the plaintiff is agreeing by the contract to relieve the defendant of any duty to protect them from the hazards of a particular activity.

Nearly all courts will enforce exculpatory clauses releasing parties from liability for injury or damages resulting from hazardous recreational activities so long as the clause is not contrary to public policy. A university hospital in California, for example, cannot compel patients to waive their right to sue for medical negligence (*Tunkl v. Regents of University of California*, 383 P.2d 441 [Cal. 1963]). Attorneys, like other professionals, may not limit their malpractice liability by requiring clients to sign exculpatory clauses.

Releases are broadly enforceable unless the exculpatory clause is contrary to a well-recognized public policy. In deciding whether an exculpatory clause contravenes public policy, courts look to the nature of services to see if they are a necessity or not. In general, legal and medical professionals are not permitted to ask their client to waive their right to pursue actions for malpractice as a matter of public policy. Courts also consider whether the contract was drafted in clear and unambiguous language. Private recreational businesses such as the Dude Ranch in our example will not qualify as services demanding a special duty to the public. Riding a horse in rugged terrain is not a matter of practical necessity for Sue or any other member of the public. Courts, however, disagree as to the specific language necessary to bar liability for negligent acts. Some courts require the exculpatory clause to clearly express the intent to limit liability for negligence to be enforceable. Exculpatory clauses are commonly used for a wide variety of activities, including attending sporting events. The owners of major league baseball stadiums frequently post signs in the stadium stating that the team is not liable for injuries. A professional hockey team, for example, will not be liable to you if you are injured by a flying puck. A consumer can challenge an exculpatory clause, like any other contract, on grounds of unconscionability or other contract formation problems. A court will look at the exculpatory clause or waiver to determine whether the intent was to release the business from liability for negligence.

Even where contractual intent is found, a few courts will not enforce contractual clauses that purport to exclude or limit the liability of a party for causing physical injury to another party. Similarly, claims for gross negligence, recklessness, or willful misconduct cannot be waived by a release or exculpatory agreement. A few states will not enforce releases for ordinary negligence. The Vermont Supreme Court struck down a release from liability clause as void for public policy reasons in a case involving an injury at a Killington ski lodge. The lodge required all skiers to sign a form purporting to release the resort from all liability from negligence. The court struck down the release in a case where a skier collided with a negligently placed metal pole on a downhill trail.

In a Florida case, a five-year-old girl was riding a motorized bicycle on a Pee Wee Track at a cycle park, when she was struck in the neck by a raised cable and thrown from the motorcycle. The little girl's attorney contended that the park owner allowed a dangerous condition to exist on the premises, which caused injury to the plaintiff. The park owner's defense was that liability waivers signed by the plaintiff's parents barred their lawsuit to recover tort damages.

The park owner argued that in addition to a release and waiver of liability signed by the plaintiffs prior to using the track, the parents also signed a release indemnifying the defendants for any loss, liability, damage, or cost incurred as a result of the minor plaintiff's participation at the track and taking full responsibility and risk for any bodily injury sustained by the participant.

The Florida court held that this one-sided release agreement signed by the girl's parents was a binding contract that clearly and unambiguously released the defendants from claims for bodily injury, even if caused by the cycle park owner. In that case, the court entered a summary judgment in favor of the park owner, which resulted in the dismissal of the case (*Gonzalez v. Defendants*, No. 03-2055-CAG [Marian Cty. (Fla.), April 26, 2005]). The lesson of this case is to be wary of signing releases of liability unless you really want to take the risk that you will receive no redress for negligently inflicted injury. Florida is in the majority of states upholding such releases for consumer services of all kinds. Courts will enforce these participation waivers if the release was freely and fairly entered into by parties with equal bargaining power, and no social interest overrides the contract. Contractual assumption of risk focuses on three questions: (1) Did the parties agree? (2) What risks were included in the agreement? What is the scope of the plaintiff's consent? (3) Are there are any public policy reasons or contract defenses that preclude enforcement?

Arguments against Waivers. In a Maryland case, a member of a health club was walking near a whirlpool at the club when she stepped on a skimmer plate covering a filter. The plate, which was not screwed down, popped up and the plaintiff fell into the hole. The consumer filed suit, arguing that the health club created a hazard and owed her a high duty as a business invitee. The defendant contended that that the plaintiff signed a waiver of liability when she became a member and she was therefore barred from pursuing this claim. This case was settled at arbitration after a judge ruled that the waiver of liability clause was invalidated by the defendant's violations of safety regulations.

Consumer Rights for the Sale of Goods

Every state save Louisiana has enacted UCC Article 2, which governs the sale of goods. UCC Article 2 is entitled "Sales" but has a broader scope because it provides laws applicable to "transactions in goods." Goods are defined in UCC §2-105 to mean tangible products that are movable at the time they are identified by the seller as what will be conveyed to the buyer. Many courts stretch UCC Article 2 to cover intangibles such as the licensing of software. Goods include future goods, specially manufactured goods, and the unborn young of animals, growing crops, and other identified things attached to realty. The term *goods* excludes transfers of electronic information, "the money in which the price is to be paid, investment securities under Article 8, the subject matter of foreign exchange transactions, and chose in action." A *chose in action* is an intangible right such as an insurance contract or a right of proceeds under a trademark license agreement.

The Law of Retail Sales

The law of retail sales is based largely upon contract law, though most states and some local authorities regulate the sales of goods. Many states, for example, require that a store's return policy be prominently posted. Many stores have policies that give you rights beyond those required by state or federal law. Special rights given by the store are enforceable contractual rights.

Mandatory Rights and Remedies in Consumer Contracts

Unsolicited Merchandise

Nearly all consumer regulations are mandatory in the sense that a seller cannot require you to waive your rights. Mandatory consumer terms are created by federal and state statutes rather than by the parties' contract. The federal and state rules governing the sending of unsolicited merchandise are mandatory provisions. Federal and state law treats unsolicited merchandise sent to you as an unconditional gift to the recipient, who may use it in any manner without any obligation to the sender. Of course, that does not apply to mis-delivered merchandise or merchandise offered as a good faith substitution for unsatisfactory products. You can treat unsolicited merchandise you receive as a gift; any attempt by the sender to treat it as a debt will be an unfair or deceptive trade practice under Section 5(a) of the Federal Trade Commission Act and every state's UDTPA.

Example: 9/11 Freedom Towers Coin Scam. A New York court enjoined the promoters of the "9/11 Freedom Tower" coin fraud to pay nearly $370,000 in penalties as well as to refund consumers $25,000 for its deceptive marketing and sale of its "Freedom Tower" Silver Dollar. The mint, located in the Northern Marianas Islands, a U.S. territory, promoted its "Freedom Tower" coin as a "legally authorized government issue silver dollar" on its website, in magazines, and in television advertisements. The coins were not a U.S. government-issued silver dollar at all, but were instead manufactured and issued by a private company and were not even legal tender.

The ads also stated the coins were made of pure silver from silver bars recovered at Ground Zero, but in fact, they were made of an inexpensive metal alloy minted with 1.4 cents worth of silver. There was no evidence that any came from the Ground Zero recovery operations. The unsolicited merchandise claim arose out of the mint's marketing practice of sending customers unordered items and then threatening collection actions for the unpaid items.

The Pennsylvania attorney general filed suit, alleging violations of Pennsylvania's UDTPA, the FTC's Regulation Rule Concerning Mail or Telephone Order Merchandise, the FTC Rule Concerning Prenotification Negative Option Plans, the Federal Truth in Lending Regulation Z, and other state and federal acts pertaining to the mailing of unordered or unsolicited merchandise.[10] An attempt to institute a collection effort for unordered merchandise can also constitute mail fraud (18 U.S.C. §1341).

The mint continues to sell the coins in the United States. However, the current advertisements for the coins make it clear that the coins are not issued by a governmental authority.

What to Do: Stopping Collection Efforts for Unordered Merchandise. Send a letter explaining why you consider unordered merchandise to be an unconditional gift. Cite your state's little FTC or UDTPA Act, the FTC's Regulation Rule Concerning Mail or Telephone Order Merchandise, and the federal Mail Fraud Act (18 U.S.C. §1341). You might also attempt to settle the claim by sending a thirty-day demand letter.

Example: Unordered Merchandise Letter

Name of Merchant
Address

Dear Customer Service:

Re: Unordered Necktie, Chapter 93A Demand
   Sometime around July 1, 2006, I sent a card to your company to get a free necktie. Before sending the card, I checked to see whether ordering the free Santa tie would result in any other obligation. In August 2006, I received a second necktie after receiving my free Santa tie. On December 1, 2006, I received notice that my payment was overdue and was being referred for collection.
   Your demand for payment is a violation of the Federal Trade Commission's Rule Concerning Mail or Telephone Order Merchandise. The FTC Rule on unordered merchandise treats the second tie as an unconditional gift. It may also constitute a violation of the federal Mail Fraud Act (see 18 U.S.C. §1341). The demand for payment of the unordered second necktie also is a violation of Chapter 93A of the Massachusetts General Law [Substitute your state's UDTPA or Little FTC citation found in Appendix A.] This letter is also a demand under Chapter 93A that you settle this claim by dropping your demand for payment for the second necktie.
   You have thirty days to drop your collection efforts, or I will take further action under state and federal law. Your company must not take further steps to attempt to collect this claim, as it is a violation of state and federal law on debt collection. I also expect that you will confirm that you have eliminated any claim and collection efforts. You have thirty days to take this step before I take further action by contacting the Massachusetts' State Attorney General's Consumer Protection Division, the Federal Trade Commission, and the United States Postal Service's Inspection Division.
   I look forward to hearing from you at a suitable time to clear up this misunderstanding.

Sincerely,

Carla Consumer

What to Do When Goods Are Out of Stock. Many states have regulations governing advertised specials in which the demand exceeds the supply. In Massachusetts, sellers are required to have enough of advertised items available to meet reasonably anticipated demand. It is not false advertising if a store runs out of an advertised item and any one of the following is true: (1) the store had a reasonable quantity, but demand was extraordinary; (2) the advertisement disclosed that quantities were limited and no rain checks were available; (3) the seller offered a rain check; (4) the seller offered a comparable substitute item; or (5) the seller can prove shipping delays. If a store runs out of an advertised item, ask for a rain check, if one is offered, allowing you to purchase the item at the advertised price at a later date. The store must then notify you when the item is back in stock if it sells for $25 or more. Also, the rain check must be honored within sixty days.

Store Return Policy

A store's return policy is a matter of contract law, though retailers will typically have duties under UCC Article 2 if the goods fail to live up to warranty or performance standards or otherwise fail to conform to the contract (see UCC, §2-601's "perfect tender" rule). A retailer can have any type of return policy it wants—"all sales final," "merchandise credit only," or "full cash refunds within thirty days"—so long as the customer has been given conspicuous notice of the policy. A seller's refund, return, or cancellation policy must be disclosed to the buyer clearly and conspicuously before the transaction is completed. Usually, it is done by means of a sign at the point of purchase. Printing the store's return policy only on a cash register sales slip does not comply. A seller cannot misrepresent its refund, return, or cancellation policy, or fail to honor any promises about it. Also, you may return goods within a reasonable period of time if no return policy was disclosed.

Stores vary significantly in return policies if there is nothing wrong with the goods, but you have merely changed your mind, do not like the color, or have decided to return the product for some other reason. State law may govern return policies.

If there is nothing wrong with the goods, the store's policy on returning goods, refunds, and other limitations is contractually based. Save all receipts, warranties, and instruction booklets for any products that you buy or receive as gifts. Retain the packaging, including tags or labels. The key is that the store must disclose its refund policy to you before you make the purchase. If a retail store has violated its own policy or refuses to give a refund for goods that are defective, you will have a cause of action. If you have already accepted goods, you can revoke that acceptance. Revocation of acceptance must occur within a reasonable time after you discover or should have discovered the grounds for it and before any substantial change occurs in the condition of the goods that is not caused by their own defects.

If the goods are not fit for their environment of use, you may have an action under your state's uniform commercial code for the implied warranty of merchantability. Goods must be at least fair average, which means that they must at least be in the middle range, to be merchantable. Goods must also be adequately contained and packaged. If the goods you purchased do not stand up to the test of merchantability or there is a breach of an express warranty, you have a right to return or refund under your state's UCC Article 2 (unless you live in Louisiana, which has not adopted the UCC). If goods are defective or breach an express or implied warranty, the store's return policy is irrelevant since the cause of action is based on the UCC.

If you have an issue with a store's return policy, start with the customer service representative of the store where you purchased the goods. Bring in your receipts, the goods, the original packaging, and the store bag you were given. National stores are beginning to revise their return policies because of the prevalence of consumer return swindles. These fortified return policies sometimes have a chilling effect on your good faith efforts to return merchandise. If you are not satisfied with the way a store handled your return, ask to speak with the store manager. Most national companies have consumer complaint departments at the regional and national levels. If none of these avenues is effective, you can contact the Better Business Bureau in your city. If all these informal methods fail, you may consider complaining to your state attorney general's consumer protection unit. If a store violates its own policy, it is likely a violation of your state's Unfair and Deceptive Trade Practices Act. Purchasing goods with a credit card gives you the right to exercise your charge back rights, so long as you act within sixty days.

Gift Certificates and Merchandise Credits

States vary as to whether they have statutes governing gift certificates. In Massachusetts, gift certificates are good for seven years from the date of issuance. The seller must clearly indicate the date of issuance and expiration date, either on the face of the certificate or, if it is an electronic card with a banked dollar value, on the sales receipt or by means of an Internet site or toll-free number. If the expiration date is not on the gift certificate, it is to be redeemable in perpetuity. The same principle exists for an electronic card, in which the expiration date must be made available on the receipt or through an Internet site or toll-free number.

Gift certificates issued but not yet redeemed as of April 1, 2003, are also to be good for seven years from the date they were issued. Once a gift certificate has been redeemed for 90 percent of its value or more, a consumer may elect to receive the balance of the value remaining in cash. The law of gift certificates is not applicable to prepaid phone cards.

What to Do: Redeeming a Merchandise Credit. A merchandise credit can be redeemed for a period that varies from state to state. Massachusetts permits sellers to establish a period of redeemability of between five and seven years. A number of other states have statutes governing the period of redeemability. If no statute applies, you can use a contract argument based upon the "usage of trade." The usage of trade is that the period for redeeming merchandise credit should be no less than five years unless special circumstances otherwise apply.

What to Do: When Can You Return Goods? Article 2 of the UCC does not address a store's return policy, which is generally a matter of simple contract law. Consumers simply do not have a statutory right to return merchandise for any reason. Before buying goods, consumers should request a copy of a store's return policy. Many stores have a liberal return policy, but with many exceptions and conditions. For example, Wal-Mart's return policy requires customers to take the item, invoice, original packaging, and accessories to any customer service desk at their local Wal-Mart. All merchandise from Wal-mart.com must be returned to a store or mailed within ninety days of receipt.

Associates will issue an immediate credit to the original payment method or provide a store credit for the cost of the item and sales tax, in those states with sales tax. Wal-Mart has a number of exceptions to and special conditions on its return policy. Some examples of special conditions are that shoes, apparel, or accessories must be returned unworn, with tickets attached, and in the original package. Video games, CD-ROMs, and software must be returned unopened; computer hardware must be returned within fifteen days of receipt along with any software; diabetic supplies may not be returned; and all sales of clearance merchandise are final.

A store's return policy should be regarded as an enforceable contract subject to the terms and conditions of the store's specific policy, as in the case of Wal-Mart. However, if conditions are not reasonable, they may be challenged. For example, the condition that a music CD not be opened may be overcome if it is proved that the CD sold was defective. Similarly, if the shoes you purchased from Wal-Mart evaporated in the rain, the condition would not be enforceable. The return policy is only enforceable if the goods generally conform to the contract.

The Consumer's Right of Rejection

When you encounter a problem with a financial product or service, you should first complain to the firm you think is responsible. In most cases, the firm will be able to resolve the issue. If merchandise does not perform to the salesperson's representations, is dangerously defective, or fails to function, buyers will have rights irrespective of the store's return policy. Even if a store says nothing about the performance of its products, consumer buyers may still have a right to reject or revoke acceptance of the merchandise. Many states require stores to post their return policy. Article 2 of the UCC gives consumers various remedies in addition to state law. Under UCC Article 2, you can "reject" merchandise if it fails to conform to the contract in any respect (see UCC §2-601). However, your right to reject goods is subject to a seller's right to cure (see UCC §2-508). A cure is nothing more than a second chance for the seller to get it right by replacement, repair, or refund. You must give notice to the seller that you are rejecting goods or you foreclose the possibility of obtaining a remedy.

Example: Hypothetical Ford Fiesta Fiasco. A consumer purchased a Ford Fiesta in 2005 from Cars-R-Us, a used car dealer. The Fiesta was manufactured in June 2004 and had covered 18,000 miles. Carla Consumer requested a test drive but was told it was not possible for insurance reasons. She purchased it anyway and was initially happy, but after only 24 hours, the clutch had to be replaced at a cost of $350. The car's sales invoice states: "I hereby understand that I have fully inspected this vehicle and have accepted it in its present condition. Cars-R-Us cannot accept any responsibility whatsoever once the vehicle has left the lot." Assuming that Carla Consumer never rode the clutch or misused the car's clutch, is there a claim against the dealer?

Carla Consumer will have rights under UCC Article 2, since Cars-R-Us did not follow the appropriate methodology in limiting or excluding the implied warranty of merchantability. Here, the clutch failed in a day's time, which is evidence that the used car was not fit for its ordinary purpose. UCC Article 2 applies to used goods, though the standard is lower than for new goods. A used car's clutch should not fail within a day's time; that it did so constitutes a violation of the implied warranty of merchantability. Moreover, Cars-R-Us did not disclaim the warranty despite its statement that it was not responsible for defects.

A seller would have to use a phrase like "as is" or "with all faults" or mention merchantability to effectively disclaim that warranty. Since it is a consumer transaction, Carla can use the fact that the seller did not disclaim warranty to obtain relief under the federal Magnuson-Moss Warranty Act. Cars-R-Us did not describe the warranty using the phrases *limited warranty* or *full warranty*. The seller will be liable for failing to adequately disclose the warranty and the disclaimer, be subject to statutory remedies, and may be liable for paying Carla's attorney's fees and costs.

What Is a Seller's Warranty?

UCC Article 2 recognizes three distinct types of warranties that have to do with the performance of goods: (1) express statements made by sellers that go to the basis of the bargain (UCC §2-313); (2) the implied warranty of merchantability that goods are fit for their ordinary purpose and are at least fair, average, and have other reasonable performance standards (UCC, §2-314); and (3) the implied warranty of fitness for a particular purpose that goods conform to the promise made by a seller that they will fulfill a particular purpose made known to the seller (UCC §2-315).

UCC Article 2 provides you with rights and remedies as consumers, whether for big-ticket items such as cars or items you purchase from a dollar store. Consumer law encompasses the daily purchase of household goods. I recently purchased a pair of "Gold Medal Hosiery" from the Good Sox Store for the pricey sum of $4.00. The socks were advertised as fine English ribbed cotton with a "comfort top"; however, I was greatly disappointed to find a large hole at the top of one sock once I removed the "gold medal tags." The defective socks were not very thin, but they drooped. In the end, I was entitled to a refund because the socks did not conform to minimum quality standards. The store cheerfully gave me the choice of a new pair of socks or a refund.

Every day we enter into transactions qualifying as sales of goods under Article 2 of the Uniform Commercial Code, which governs consumer and commercial sales. The seemingly trivial Gold Medal socks transaction raises consumer issues. For example, statements made by the seller about the socks' qualities constituted express warranties. An express warranty is a legal concept in which sellers must stand behind any statements made about their goods that go to the "basis of the bargain." A seller is liable for any statement going to the basis of the bargain.

Express warranties by the seller of the "Gold Medal" socks were created by the description of the socks being made of the finest English ribbed cotton. Because the socks had been made out of inferior cotton, I had a breach of express warranty action against the seller. An express warranty is breached when a product fails to exhibit the properties, characteristics, or qualities specifically attributed to it by its warrantor and therefore fails to conform to the warrantor's representations.

Even if the seller of the socks had made no express warranties, he may be subject to liability for breaching Article 2's implied warranty of merchantability. Every sales contract implies a warranty that the goods sold are merchantable, that is, that the socks will be suitable for their ordinary purposes. Even if the seller makes no express warranties about goods, they must minimally be of fair, average quality and fit for their ordinary purpose. The socks were fit only for the rag bin and thus were not suitable for ordinary use. Education about consumer laws is a key tool to prevent unfair and deceptive trade practices. In the bad socks case, it is quite likely that a merchant would provide a replacement pair of socks or refund without resort to the law. If a merchant balked at providing a replacement, the consumer could remind them of the law of warranties.

The defective socks transaction is a mundane example of an everyday transaction governed by consumer law. The perceptive socks buyer could likely resolve the consumer problem by contacting the seller directly. If the socks were purchased from a store and it was in easy driving distance, you could speak with either the salesperson or the customer service representative. If a replacement or refund is not offered, you can ask to speak with the supervisor. If that does not work, you can go higher by contacting the national headquarters of the seller. Many manufacturers of goods have toll-free numbers for customer relations. In many instances, a polite letter or call to the company will get you a refund. Toll-free numbers can be found by visiting a company's website or by dialing the directory of toll-free numbers at 1-800-555-1212.

How Are Express Warranties Created?

Express warranties are statements made by the seller that go to the basis of the bargain. Any affirmation of fact or promise made by the seller in any manner, including in a medium for communication to the public such as advertising or in product literature, becomes part of the basis of the bargain. If the seller provides information related to the performance of the product or goods, it is likely an enforceable express warranty that the goods conform to the affirmation or promise. UCC Article 2 does not require the seller to use any particular language of guarantee to create express warranties. Express warranties are, in effect, promises created by a seller's representative, advertising, and any other descriptions of goods. A seller's model, sample, or a picture in a catalogue can create an express warranty.

Express warranties must be distinguished from mere seller's talk. A statement that an overcoat for men is of very unusual excellence is puffery. Similarly, to say that B&O table syrup adds joy to eating is also empty seller's talk. However, seller's talk that includes information about the product is more likely to be an enforceable warranty rather than puffery. The statement, for example, that gloves are of sewed capeskin in slate color constitutes a number of express warranties. An advertisement for an antique restored Kupmobile that states that the car has a long stroke motor, three-speed sliding gears, and a Bosch magneto are advertisements that are definite enough to be express warranties. Contrast this with the statement that the car has a "rakish design." This is an example of seller's talk.

Big Sales Company, for example, creates express warranties in any description of goods in a catalogue because samples, models, or demonstrations create express warranties. Statements made on an online banner advertisement for Big Sales Company's website may constitute an express warranty if they are sufficiently definite to form the basis of the bargain. Technical specifications for a computer system posted on a website will also likely constitute an express warranty. For example, if a computer depicted on an advertisement has a DVD drive, that picture creates an express warranty. If the actual computer delivered has no DVD drive, you will have a variety of remedies under UCC Article 2. You are entitled to the difference between what was promised and what was delivered. You may go out into the marketplace, return the computer, and purchase a new one with a DVD drive, in which case you will be entitled to recover the difference between the cover price (substitute transaction) and the contract price plus any incidental or consequential damages.[11]

How Are Implied Warranties Created?

Implied warranties are unspoken, unwritten promises created as a matter of federal as well as state law after the enactment of the 1975 Magnuson-Moss Warranty Act. The seller does not have to say something specific to activate implied warranties. UCC Article 2 recognizes two implied warranties of quality that run with consumer products: the *implied warranty of merchantability* and the *implied warranty of fitness for a particular purpose.*

The Implied Warranty of Merchantability. To satisfy the implied warranty of merchantability, the product need not be the best, but it cannot be absolutely unfit for its purpose. It must fulfill general industry standards for performance. Steak knives must be sharp enough to cut a steak. Cars must have four wheels that turn. Air conditioners must cool the air. A computer must be fit for the ordinary purpose for which such computers are used. The implied warranty requires that goods be adequately packaged and labeled and of even kind, quality, and quantity within each unit. In other words, an implied warranty of merchantability is an implied promise by a merchant that the goods will function as goods of that kind are supposed to function.

The Implied Warranty of Fitness for a Particular Purpose. The implied warranty of fitness for a particular purpose arises when a consumer-buyer relies upon the seller's expertise in selecting a product for a specific purpose. Suppose Wolfgang Puck is the seller of turkey pans, and the buyer asks him for his recommendation for a pan that will accommodate a 25-pound turkey. If Wolfgang, as the seller's representative, recommends a particular pan and that pan is not suitable for basting and roasting such a large turkey, the consumer will have a cause of action. In this example, the law of sales says that the seller has made a warranty of fitness for a particular purpose.

What Warranties Do and Do Not Cover

Implied warranties do not last a lifetime. The length of time an implied warranty lasts depends upon the product. The time for an implied warranty for ice cream is shorter than for iron bars. Warranties are not available when the user has misused products or goods. A consumer injured while attempting to trim a hedge with a lawnmower is misusing the product and will not be able to collect damages for personal injury under UCC Article 2 or any other theory of product liability. Even if a product is defective, a manufacturer should not be responsible for bizarre or unforeseeable misuses of goods.

Disclaimers for Consumer Warranties

UCC Article 2 permits the parties to disclaim or modify all implied warranties by words or conduct (see UCC §2-316). UCC Article 2 validates the universal practice of disclaiming implied warranties and selling goods on an "as is" basis, without warranties. The software industry routinely disclaims all implied warranties. Microsoft, for example, disclaims all express or implied warranties for its software products, as in the following clause: "The software product and any related documentation is [*sic*] provided 'as is' without warranty of any kind, either express or implied, including, without limitation, the implied warranties or merchantability, fitness for a particular purpose, or noninfringement. The entire risk arising out of use or performance of the software product remains with you."

Microsoft is attempting to disclaim its implied warranties in the above clause. An Article 2 written disclaimer of the implied warranty of merchantability must mention "merchantability" or "quality." The term "as is" or "with all faults" means that the seller is not giving you a warranty. To disclaim the warranty of fitness, the exclusion must be made by a written and conspicuous statement. Warranty disclaimers and liability limitations are subject to state and federal consumer law, common law, and equitable doctrines such as the covenant of good faith, fair dealing, and unconscionability. Many websites will place a notice that they seek disclaimers "to the full extent permissible by applicable law." Website disclaimers may not alter consumer protection statutes that preclude the disclaiming of implied warranties in consumer transactions.[12]

Sellers routinely disclaim all the implied warranties in written warranties, though the Magnuson-Moss Warranty Act and many state consumer protection regulations prohibit this practice. The Magnuson-Moss Warranty Act, for example, precludes suppliers of goods from disclaiming the implied warranty of merchantability completely.

Magnuson-Moss Warranty Act

The goal of the Magnuson-Moss Warranty Act is to educate consumers about warranty coverage so that they can pursue remedies if a consumer product fails to live up to reasonable expectations. The FTC's Rule on Pre-Sale Availability of Written Warranty Terms does not require that a seller provide a written warranty, but if they do, it must be made available to consumers prior to purchase if the goods cost more than $15.[13] The titling requirement that sellers label warranties as full or limited applies to consumer products costing more than $10 and defined as goods for personal, household, or family use. Additionally, the federal consumer warranty statute applies only if a seller gives a "written warranty" about these consumer goods (16 U.S.C. §700.1 [2000]). The act does not apply if the seller makes only oral warranties. Sellers are not required to provide written warranties or warrant their products for any specific length of time. If, however, a written warranty is offered, full disclosure is required, and the warranty information must be made available to consumers before the product is sold.

The federal consumer warranties statute applies to suppliers, defined as anyone engaged in the "business of making a consumer product" (15 U.S.C. §2301 [4]). It also applies to warrantors or those who give written warranties or who may be obligated under implied warranties. In addition, the Magnuson-Moss Warranty Act applies to written warranties that pertain to either the material or workmanship of goods. The act requires all written consumer warranties to be labeled as either "full" or "limited." The warranty caption *full warranty* signifies that the seller provides all federal warranties, such as a right to a refund if a seller is unable to correct defects. In contrast, the term *limited* means that the written warranty does not meet the federal minimum standards. Few sellers have offered a "full warranty" in the history of the Magnuson-Moss Warranty Act.

The FTC has adopted three major rules to implement the federal consumer warranty statute: "(1) the *Rule on Disclosure of Written Consumer Product Warranty Terms and Conditions* (the Disclosure Rule), (2) the *Rule on Presale Availability of Written Warranty Terms* (the Presale Availability Rule), and (3) the *Rule on Informal Dispute Settlement Procedures* (the Dispute Resolution Rule)."[14] In addition, the FTC has issued an interpretive rule that clarifies certain terms and explains some of the provisions of the act.

The Cross pen company is one of the few suppliers willing to make "full warranties." Cross pens, which are high-quality writing instruments, come with a "full warranty" as products costing greater than $10. If a seller provides written warranties, they must be given to the consumer prior to purchase for consumer goods greater than $15. This broad language applies to written warranties for consumer products sold over the Internet.

If a manufacturer of computer hardware has not corrected or cured problems in its computer system after a reasonable number of attempts, the consumer must receive a refund or replacement without charge, plus reasonable expenses. The Magnuson-Moss Warranty Act provides a remedy to consumers in cases in which there are "repeated failures to pass agree acceptance tests," as well as failures to provide deliverables such as source codes that caused the licensee to withhold payment. If the Magnuson-Moss Warranty Act were extended to Internet-related licenses, the implied warranty of merchantability would be nondisclaimable in consumer transactions.

The FTC's Rule against Tie-ins
The Magnuson-Moss Warranty Act not only governs warranties but also prohibits unfair practices such as "tie-in sales." A tie-in may be broadly defined as the illegal practice of requiring a consumer to purchase services in order for warranties to be given. A warranty cannot require that a product be upgraded by paying for new equipment in order for that warranty to continue. Under the act, an electronics manufacturer may not condition warranty coverage on using a certain brand of batteries in a digital camera. Similarly, Honda Motor Company cannot condition its vehicle warranty on the use of a given brand of stereo system, security system, or satellite radio.

Warranty of Title
When you purchase goods, the seller implies, by offering them for sale, that they have good title and that the goods are free from any liens or encumbrances of any kind. In other words, you are entitled to quiet enjoyment of the goods as a buyer. Buyers have no interest in pursuing a lawsuit over ownership of goods. Whenever you purchase goods, you will have a warranty of good title. Sellers also warrant that the goods you purchased do not infringe the intellectual property rights of third parties. The warranty of ti-

tle covers (1) good title; and (2) rightfulness of transfer and freedom from any security interest, lien, or encumbrance of which the buyer has no knowledge. A lien is nothing more than a claim against property to compel payment of a debt.

If the merchant-seller delivers goods that infringe a trademark, copyright, or patent, the buyer will have a remedy as long as she gives notice to the seller of the infringement prior to filing the lawsuit. Do not purchase goods if the seller disclaims good title, unless you are willing to assume the risk of a lawsuit over ownership of the goods.

Performance of the Sales Contract

You can learn about your rights and remedies for the performance of the contract by consulting your state's UCC Article 2. In general, the seller must deliver goods that conform in every respect to the contract. You have accepted goods if one of three things has happened: (1) you have expressed acceptance; (2) you failed to make an effective rejection; or (3) you did anything with the software or information inconsistent with the licensor's ownership. You have a right to inspect goods before payment or acceptance. You have no choice but to accept goods if they conform to the agreement and are delivered in a timely manner. In other words, you have no three-day cooling off period to cancel a contract for the sale of goods unless a special distance contract or home solicitation rule applied. Once conforming goods are delivered to you, you must either reject or accept the goods. If you accept the goods, the seller is entitled to receive payment. To exercise your right to reject, you must give a notice to the seller specifying the reasons for rejection.

Even if you reject goods, the seller must be given an opportunity to cure, which is a second chance to get things right (UCC §2-508). If, however, you have already accepted the goods and a problem arises, you may be able to revoke acceptance. Revocation must occur within a reasonable time after discovering the material nonconformities. You must notify the seller promptly of the problem that caused your revocation of previously accepted goods, just as you must specify the problem when you reject goods (that is, when you do not accept goods upon delivery). If a buyer fails to give prompt notice that he is revoking acceptance of goods, he loses any remedy he might have under UCC Article 2. Your failure to notify the other party of breach has the legal consequence of waiver of all remedies for the breach (UCC §2-607[3]).

Failure of Essential Purpose

Sellers seek to limit not only warranties but also remedies. Courts may strike down limitations on remedies if an exclusive remedy fails of its essential purpose. If the seller or lessor offers a consumer-buyer a limited remedy that deprives him of the benefit of the bargain, it will be unenforceable

(UCC §2-719[2]). A consumer challenging a limited remedy will need to show that the seller's exclusive or limited remedy fails of its essential purpose. For example, if a seller gives a consumer ten days to return a sweater, that remedy may fail of its essential remedy if the problem with the sweater appears only after laundering the garment (i.e., the colors run after laundering). In that case, ten days would be an unreasonably short period, and the court would strike it down.

If a court finds a remedy to fail of its essential purpose, the aggrieved consumer should have the full range of UCC remedies at their disposal. UCC §2-719(2) is one of the most powerful consumer rights tools and has frequently been used by buyers to strike down one-sided remedy limitations (UCC §2-719, O.C. #1). The official comment on §2-719 by the UCC drafters explains that the purpose of the failure of the essential purpose rule is to guarantee buyers a minimum adequate remedy if the sole or exclusive remedy fails.

Sellers generally attempt to limit remedies of buyers, a practice endorsed by UCC Article 2 (see UCC §2-719[1]). Many sellers will attempt to substitute a limited remedy to consumers for the remedies otherwise available under UCC Article 2. If the seller does not make it clear that its limited remedy is sole and exclusive, the consumer will have the right to all remedies, including the seller's limited remedy. If the seller states that a given remedy is "sole and exclusive," the buyer will lose all other remedies under UCC Article 2. Many sellers will attempt to limit the buyer's remedy to a repair or replacement. However, a buyer may suffer consequential damages as the result of the seller's breach. Assume, for example, a homeowner entered into a contract with Tools-R-Us to purchase a saw for cutting tile in a home improvement project. The seller's breach might cause a homeowner to suffer consequential damages if her goal was to place her home on the market. The delay in finishing the tiling could force the homeowner to cancel home showings.

If the seller makes it clear that the limited remedy is the sole and exclusive remedy, the consumer will not have the usual UCC Article 2 remedies. Sellers may not disclaim consequential damages such as personal injuries caused by defective goods—that would be prima facie unconscionable.

In a breach of contract action, the plaintiff must establish that the other party breached. In sales contracts, a seller breaches a contract by delivering goods that do not conform to the contract in any respect (UCC §2-601). However, the consumer must give the seller notice that she is rejecting goods and give the seller a right to cure (UCC §2-508). If the buyer has accepted the goods and then learns of a substantial problem, she may revoke acceptance (UCC §2-608). In a common law contract, the standard for breach is "material breach." A service contract such as for construction requires that the contractor perform all work in a reasonably skillful or workmanlike manner.

Anticipatory Breach or Repudiation

A party may suspend his own performance if the other party makes it clear that he is not intending to perform (UCC §2-610). However, a consumer may not refuse to perform a contract anticipating that the other party will not perform. The best course is to place the other party in breach by getting a writing that he will not perform.

Contract Remedies

If a seller or renderer of services breaches a contract, the nonbreaching party will typically have a wide array of remedies. In the common law, a material breach occurs when there is a substantial failure that goes to the gist of the contract. If there is a material breach, the nonbreaching party need not perform and may file a lawsuit for damages. In a common law action, there may also be an action for rescission. UCC Article 2 spells out the remedies available for all purchasers of goods. A nonbreaching consumer buyer will be able to elect from an array of UCC Article remedies. The buyer can *cover* by seeking a substitute transaction or file suit for contract damages based on the difference between the contract price and the market price. Suppose a consumer elects to cover after a car seller reneges on the deal. The consumer cannot cover by purchasing a Mercedes in a deal for a Ford Fiesta. In other words, the consumer must cover by buying a reasonable substitute. A consumer should consider covering if she expects to suffer consequential damages. Suppose a consumer enters into a contract with Tents R Us to supply a tent for a wedding. If Tents R Us repudiates the contract, the seller should attempt to cover by finding another person willing to supply a tent. If the consumer makes no attempt to cover, they will be unable to collect damages for consequential damages, which in this case could be considerable. If a wedding could not be held due to rain and no tent, there could be potentially tens of thousands in consequential damages.

UCC Article 2 also permits the recovery of consequential damages (as long as they are reasonably foreseeable), as well as incidental damages. The seller's remedies are provided for in part 7 of your state's Article 2 of the UCC §§2-703 to 2-710. Buyer's remedies are spelled out in UCC §2-711 to §2-717. In addition, the parties may specify liquidated damages at the formation stage where damages are difficult to compute, but they must not be unreasonably large (UCC §2-718).

In common law contracts, there are similar principles, but the general rule is that the plaintiff is entitled to the benefit of the bargain. Nonbreaching parties may also be entitled to general or consequential damages. Different remedies may be available, depending upon the type of contract. In real estate contracts, the typical remedy will be the difference between market price and contract price. If a dentist negligently constructs a dental prosthesis that causes the patient to lose all of their front teeth, the patient will have consequential damages such as medical bills, lost earnings, and general damages such as pain and suffering. This contract would be governed by law of negligence rather than UCC Article 2 since the contract is predominantly for services rather than a sale of goods. In professional services contracts where professional services are rendered, the standard is one based upon negligence rather than UCC Article 2.

All contract law is bound by the covenant of good faith and fair dealing as well as the standard of reasonableness, which are nondisclaimable standards applicable in every consumer contract. In a home improvement contract, the recovery will be the reasonable market price of completing the work. Consumers, like all other contracting parties, have a duty to mitigate losses. In the case of a home improvement contract not completed, the homeowner may mitigate damages by taking prompt remedial steps to avoid unnecessary loss. The rule that a plaintiff not unreasonably run up damages is known in tort law as the *rule of avoidable consequences*. Some jurisdictions treat a plaintiff's failure to mitigate damages in tort law as comparative negligence. The duty to mitigate applies to both personal injury and property damages in contract law and tort law.

Statute of Limitations

The statute of limitations is the period following a sale within which a lawsuit must be filed in order to avoid loss of the claim. UCC Article 2 adopts a complicated statute of limitations that combines a discovery rule with a rule of repose. In general, there is a four-year statute of limitation for the sale of goods. The parties to a sales contract may agree to reduce the period of limitations, but not to less than a year after the cause of action accrues.

What to Do to Resolve Sales Disputes Informally. Save your receipt and the original packaging and document the problems you have with consumer goods. The first rule of dispute resolution is to give the seller notice of problems. Be dispassionate and avoid emotionally charged language. Do not make gratuitous insults, which will only lower the probability that you can resolve a problem amicably. Be sure that you keep a record that demonstrates that you have given notice of problems with the goods to the seller. Letters to sellers should be professional and specifically explain why you are not satisfied with products. Be sure to notify the seller of the specific reasons you are rejecting or revoking acceptance of goods. If you are rejecting goods, specify the particular problems with the goods you are rejecting. At a minimum, you need to describe the serial or model number, location of the seller, when you made the purchase, and what you paid. In your initial letter, you should be clear about what remedy you seek. That is, are you seeking a refund, repair, replacement, or some other remedy? Be sure to provide your name, address, email address, and telephone number to make it easy for a seller to contact you.

Notes

1. *MHC Inv. Co. v. Racom Corp.*, 209 F.R.D. 431, 437 (S.D. Iowa 2002) (citing Iowa Civil Jury Instructions 2400.4.

2. UCC §2-104.

3. See UCC §2-204 (3).

4. Most contracts are not subject to the Statute of Frauds.

5. UCC §2-202.

6. Juvenile Law Center, "Contracts," available at http://www.jlc.org/index.php/agerequirements/contracts (accessed October 8, 2006).

7. *Maxwell v. Fidelity Financial Services, Inc.*, 184 Ariz. 82, 88, 907 P.2d 51, 57 (2000).

8. *A & M Produce v. FMC Corp.* 135 Cal.App.3d 473, 486 (1992).

9. *Branco v. Norwest Bank Minn., N.A.*, 381 F. Supp. 2d 1274, 1282 (D. Hi. 2005).

10. This example is drawn from a press release from the Pennsylvania attorney general's office, "'Freedom Towers' and 'American Mint' Coin Scams Halted," available at http://www.consumeraffairs.com/news04/2005/coin_scams.html (accessed October 1, 2006).

11. UCC §2-712.

12. See, for example, M.G.L.A., ch. 106, §2-316A (2000) (prohibiting sellers from disclaiming the implied warranty of merchantability in consumer transactions, including sales and services).

13. Federal Trade Commission, "Making Warranties Available Prior to Sale," available at http://www.ftc.gov/bcp/conline/pubs/buspubs/warranty.shtm (last visited June 18, 2007).

14. Federal Trade Commission, *A Businessperson's Guide to Federal Warranty Law*, available at http://www.ftc.gov/bcp/conline/pubs/buspubs/warranty.htm#Magnuson-Moss (accessed June 17, 2007).

7

Redressing Civil Wrongs: Torts and Defective Products

Hollywood films such as *Silkwood, A Civil Action,* and *Erin Brockovich* portray ordinary citizens courageously taking steps to expose corporate wrongdoers. In those films, private citizens armed with tort remedies uncovered risky environmental conditions. The films accurately reflect the role of tort law as an institution of social control to punish and deter companies that endanger the safety of all Americans. Tort law, like sunlight, acts as a disinfectant by exposing hidden threats to the public welfare not detected by public authorities.

Lawyers on behalf of the estate of Karen Silkwood convinced an Oklahoma jury to award $10 million in punitive damages to punish and deter the reckless handling of plutonium at Kerr-McGee's Oklahoma processing plant. Kerr-McGee was unable to account for 4.4 kilograms of plutonium, which has the potential of precipitating a mass disaster. Karen Silkwood's mysterious death after exposing this wrongdoing became the basis for the movie *Silkwood.* The punitive damages mentioned above were properly imposed because of substantial, credible evidence that workers "knew of a variety of ways to remove large amounts of plutonium from the facility without detection" and were recklessly indifferent to the extreme hazards posed by one of the most lethal substances in existence.[1]

The actual legal case that inspired the best-selling book and movie *A Civil Action* could not have been brought without tort law remedies. *A Civil Action* was based upon a Massachusetts federal district case, *Anderson v. W. R. Grace.*[2] In *Anderson,* eight Massachusetts families sued W. R. Grace and Beatrice Foods as successor corporations of the polluters that contaminated the Woburn groundwater with toxic chemicals, including trichloroethylene and tetrachloroethylene. A cluster of child leukemia cases was found in close proximity to a field where tanning chemicals were dumped; the contaminated area was eventually designated a Superfund site in 1983. Sixteen of the twenty-eight living plaintiffs were relatives of the children who died of cancer. Three of the claimants suffered from leukemia and were being treated for the disease. The other plaintiffs alleged that the contaminated water caused a variety of other illnesses and damages. The testimony of several experts was necessary to establish that these illnesses were more likely than not to have resulted from drinking water tainted with hazardous chemicals.

Tort law is a branch of consumer law in which individuals file lawsuits to redress civil wrongs. For example, American consumers have filed suit against physicians for medical malpractice lawsuits for leaving surgical sponges and instruments in them after a surgery. After these lawsuits were settled, U.S. hospitals instituted measures to prevent this from ever happening again. Additionally, elderly and disabled residents of nursing homes have benefited from the contingency fee system, which allows them to have the means to obtain legal representation to redress neglect and substandard treatment by profit-seeking corporate chains.

The contingency fee system is used almost exclusively for consumer cases, chiefly in personal injury and malpractice cases. The contingency fee system is a method for paying for legal services where the attorney receives a fixed percentage (usually one third) of an award or settlement after expenses are taken out. The contingency is that the lawyer only gets paid if she wins. If there is a settlement in favor of the plaintiff, the lawyer deducts her fee as a percentage of the settlement, but in case of a loss, the plaintiff pays nothing. All Americans are safer as the result of the direct action taken by American consumers in diverse fields of law.

Torts Defined

William Prosser, a leading torts scholar, acknowledges that a satisfactory definition for torts has not been found. Think of torts as a branch of the common law in which private litigants seek redress for injuries, usually in the form of money damages. Tort actions are about personal accountability and responsibility for injuries as diverse as the human experience, such as toxic spills, trucking accidents, nursing home neglect and abuse, online stalking, fraudulent sales and services, medical malpractice, slip and fall accidents, automobile accidents, dog bites, and many other causes of action. Before there was consumer protection law, torts addressed those economic injuries. In fact, tort law was the earliest and often the only way to redress consumer injuries before Congress and the state enacted specific statutes addressing harmful medical products, unfair credit terms, or redress for dangerously defective consumer products.

Types of Tort Damages

A consumer seeking relief in tort may receive the following damages: *compensatory, special,* and *punitive* damages. Compensatory damages consist of economic and noneconomic damages. Economic damages compensate the plaintiff for injuries to his person or property and may include medical bills, past and future earnings, and other direct economic expenses. Noneconomic damages, often referred to as "pain and suffering" damages, are a second category of compensatory damages. The loss of consortium is a type of noneconomic damages. To prevail on a claim of loss of consortium, a plaintiff must show, among other things, that one spouse suffered an injury, which deprived the other spouse of some benefit that formerly existed in the marriage. Pain and suffering awards include compensation for disfigurement, infertility, or reproductive injuries.

Special damages typically encompass measurable economic losses that are direct, reasonable, and expectable items of loss from an injury. Tort damages are capped in small claims cases. In a conversion case in which a neighbor destroyed the plaintiff's dog, the market value of the dog is recoverable. If a motor vehicle is damaged while being parked in a parking lot, the plaintiff must produce evidence of the damage to tires or the vehicle. Evidence may be in the form of an estimate to make the repair. Special damage or out of pocket expenses are generally proven by producing documents such as bills, cancelled checks, or estimates.

In contrast to compensatory damages, *punitive damages* punish and deter extremely aggravated misconduct by the defendant. Louisiana, Massachusetts, Nebraska, New Hampshire, and Washington State do not recognize the tort remedy of punitive damages, unless it is specially provided for in a statute. Punitive damages will not be a component of damages in a small claims court, absent a statutorily mandated punitive damages provision, such as unfair and deceptive trade practices acts.

Punitive damages fulfill the latent function of sending a message to the entire community that "Torts do not pay!" Punitive damages are frequently awarded in intentional tort cases where there is aggravated misconduct deserving of punishment. O. J. Simpson was assessed $25 million in punitive damages by a civil jury for the aggravated circumstances surrounding the murder of Nicole Simpson and Michael Goldman. The size of the verdict was calibrated to have the proper punitive effect in light of O. J. Simpson's wealth and imputed future earnings.

The Law of Torts

The Three Branches of Tort Law

The three branches of tort law are (1) intentional torts; (2) negligence; and (3) strict liability. Intentional torts, such as assault, battery, and false imprisonment, require a finding that the defendant desired to cause the consequences or the results were substantially certain to occur.

Many of the intentional torts against the person or property have parallels on the criminal side of the law. Assault and battery are both criminal actions and torts. In the O. J. Simpson case, the defendant was acquitted of criminal homicide but found liable for the tort of battery and assessed $25 million in punitive damages. Similarly, the torts of conversion or trespass to chattels have parallel in crimes punishing theft. The torts of false imprisonment and false arrest are also prosecuted on the criminal side of the ledger. Trespass is both a tort and a crime.

In contrast, negligence occurs when a defendant has breached a standard of care and an injury was reasonably foreseeable. Strict liability is the imposition of near absolute liability on the defendant because the undertaken activity is abnormally dangerous. A defendant is strictly liable, for example, for injuries to others caused by harboring a wild animal. Similarly, a defendant engaged in ultra-hazardous activities that harm others will be strictly liable.

Tort law assigns responsibility for injuries to the wrongdoer by requiring the payment of compensation. In all tort cases, the actor is liable because his conduct (a) was intended to cause harm, (b) was negligent, or (c) created extra-hazardous risks to others. The branches of tort law turn on the defendant's state of mind. A plaintiff proving torts cases must prove every element. The plaintiff has the burden of proof as well as the burden of persuasion when claiming tort actions, and the defendant has the burden of proof and persuasion for defenses to tort actions.

Intentional Torts Defined

The "intent" in intentional torts refers to the state of mind of the defendant. The definition of intent is that the defendant consciously desires to cause the consequences of his act or he believes that the consequences are substantially certain to occur. Malice is not necessary for intent—all one needs is intent to affect the other party, not necessarily the intent to commit harm. Intentional torts are in turn subdivided into torts against the person, torts against property, or business torts. The tort of fraud or misrepresentation is the most important consumer-related tort against property, though other torts may be asserted in a consumer law case. Common law fraud is actionable when a consumer reasonably relies upon a misrepresentation of fact or omission to her detriment.

The tort of intentional infliction of emotional distress, often called the tort of outrage, allows recovery if a defendant intentionally subjects the plaintiff to serious mental distress. The key question is whether the defendant acted in a manner that may be characterized as extreme or outrageous. "Mere insults, indignities, threats, annoyances, petty oppressions or other trivialities" do not rise to the level of the outrageous conduct essential to the plaintiff's right of recovery (Rest. 2d Torts §46, cmt. d). The tort of outrage is only actionable when the distress is extreme and the conduct so out of bounds with community norms that it causes the clerk to exclaim: "That is outrageous!" The tort of outrage, for example, may apply when a neighbor deliberately poisons your dog by offering your beloved pet a drink of deadly antifreeze that is certain to shut down his kidneys.

Torts against the person typically focus on damages for physical harm caused by assault, battery, false imprisonment, and the intentional infliction of emotional distress. Intentional torts against property include trespass to land, trespass to chattels, and conversion. A plaintiff will generally try to recover monetary damages for property-based torts. Finally, there are intentional torts frequently used in consumer cases (such as fraud or misrepresentation), privacy-based torts (such as intrusion upon seclusion, false light, public disclosure of private facts, and the right of publicity), and abuse or misuse of legal process or malicious prosecution.

A company may be liable for the tort of deceit for products and services it sells online. Fraudulently representing goods or services on the Internet subjects the seller to liability for the pecuniary losses of those who relied on the misrepresentations.[3] A person selling a baseball bat autographed by Ted Williams or golf clubs purportedly used by President John F. Kennedy, for example, is liable for any misrepresentations made about goods sold in an online auction. Misrepresentation in an online transaction may occur with the sale, licensing, lease, exchange of goods, or rendering of services.

A consumer suing a bank for violation of such federal consumer protection statutes as the Fair Debt Collection Practices Act (FDCPA), the Truth in Lending Act (TILA), the Retail Installment Sales Act (RISA), and for violation of state consumer sales acts such as the Uniform Deceptive Trade Practices Act may also have a claim for the personal property torts of trespass to chattels or conversion, if the lender wrongfully repossessed her automobile. Torts were once the sole remedy for consumers, but today they supplement state and federal consumer protection law. Finally, there are intentional torts filed against businesses, such as fraud, the intentional interference with contract, or prospective advantage.

Intentional or Negligent Misrepresentation. The independent tort of fraud or misrepresentation is perhaps the most versatile and widely used tort in consumer cases. The law of torts recognizes two fraud-related causes of action: intentional misrepresentation and negligent misrepresentation. A seller committing fraud is not shielded by the parol evidence rule, which in the common law of contracts normally restricts the parties to the rights and remedies under their contract or agreement.

Parol evidence, for example, may consist of seller's statements about goods made by a seller prior to the parties signing the agreement. Additional terms may be used to explain or supplement writing. However, a finalized writing that is "complete and exclusive" triggers a rule of admissibility that is even more stringent under UCC §2-202. The purpose of any parol evidence rule is to protect the integrity of writings but exclude evidence of prior or contemporaneous agreements, negotiations, or other evidence.

To establish a *prima facie* case of intentional misrepresentation or fraudulent concealment, a consumer must show the following: (1) a false representation, or deliberate concealment, of a material fact, by the defendant; (2) the defendant acted with *scienter,* or foreknowledge, with (3) an intent to induce plaintiff's reliance on the misrepresentation or concealment; (4) causation; and (5) damage resulting from the misrepresentation or concealment.

Negligence Defined

The law of torts is largely about negligence. In consumer cases, the most frequent category of negligence is automobile accident law. According to the U.S. Department of Justice during 1996, in the nation's seventy-five largest counties, automobile accident cases accounted for 49 percent of all tort trials in courts of general jurisdiction.[4] Negligence is conduct that falls below the standard of care established by the law for the protection of others against unreasonable risks of harm. It is important to remember that whether a plaintiff's complaint seeks monetary damages or injunctive relief, torts based on negligence contain four elements: (1) duty, (2) breach of duty, (3) damages, and (4) causation.[5] Ninety percent or more of all tort cases are based upon negligence. Automobile negligence, in turn, constitutes about 40 percent of all tort claims. Suppose a car accident was caused by a negligently designed brake system. A claim of the manufacturer's negligence requires proof of the following elements: (1) a duty of care owed by the manufacturer to the consumer, (2) the automobile was designed in a substandard manner not meeting industry standards, (3) an injury or loss, (4) cause in fact, and (5) proximate or legal cause. Once a merchant, seller, or other party owes you a reasonable standard of conduct, the question is whether the duty has been breached.

Negligence is conduct that departs from the reasonable standard of care imposed by law for the protection of others. Ordinary care means that degree of care that would be used by a person of ordinary prudence under the same or similar circumstances. It is frequently easy to prove breach of the standard of care when a commercial driver causes you to suffer personal or property damage by violating a rule of the road. Every state has "rules of the road" statutes that govern such matters as driving vehicles in a single lane, riding and passing, the use of ways upon the approach of emergency vehicles, right-of-way at intersections, and traffic control signs and devices.

When a defendant violates a rule of the road, the statutory violation is at least some evidence of negligence and, in many cases, presumptive or conclusive of negligence. Negligence is largely about excessive preventable dangers that could be reduced or eliminated by safety steps. Courts often employ a risk versus utility test in determining whether a given act or practice is negligent. If a practice has low social utility (like shooting off fireworks in a crowded neighborhood), the probability of harm is substantial, and the potential for injuries is great, such a practice will most likely be considered to be a negligent activity. The idea underlying negligence is that excessive harm or risks may be eliminated by precautions or by not doing the activity.

Through negligence-based tort lawsuits, private litigants advance the public interest by encouraging corporations to adopt policies that reduce or eliminate unreasonable danger from products or practices by implementing an efficient level of precaution.

Example: Negligent Securing of Cargo. On July 9, 2007, Paula Plaintiff was struck by cast iron ductile pipe while traveling in a pickup truck on Busy Street in Big City, Massachusetts. At the time of the accident, Paula Plaintiff was the operator of the vehicle and her daughter was a passenger. The cast iron pipe fell from a tractor-trailer owned by Dan Defendant. Dan Defendant will be liable for negligently securing its cargo. Massachusetts, like many other states, has a statute requiring commercial truck drivers to secure their cargo. The truck driver's violation of the statute would be strong evidence that the defendant was not acting as a reasonable person in the circumstances, which is the legal liability standard (*Medeiros v. Whitcraft*, 931 F. Supp. 68 [D. Mass 1996]).

Example: Negligent Business Practice. Peter Plaintiff, who is age thirteen, attended a bar mitzvah at Gillette stadium. The entertainment was Big Bill the Magic Man. Peter and other guests at the party were instructed by Big Bill to dance on their partner's backs. Dick became unhappy with Peter climbing on his back and threw him off. Unfortunately, Peter fell flat on his face on the turf near the fifty-yard line and knocked out his favorite front tooth. The cost of dental surgery is $1,500.

In this case, Peter and his parents will have a claim of negligent supervision against Big Bill the Magic Man if this activity breaches the standard of reasonable care in the circumstances. Big Bill has a duty to provide reasonable entertainment for adolescents. It is quite likely that a court would find having teenagers dance on each other's backs to be an unreasonably dangerous activity. "Back dancing" is not customary like a game of touch football and it involves excessive preventable dangers. In this case, Big Bill took few precautionary measures, such as placing mats in the event a dancer fell, nor did he provide warnings or disclosures of the potential danger. A court would likely find that the utility of "adolescent back dancing" was low and that no precaution would eliminate the excessive preventable dangers of such an activity. When Dick threw Peter off his back, he may have potential liability for the intentional tort of battery, though it is arguable that he may be privileged because he was acting in self-defense. This defense would be available only if Dick's self-defense was proportional to the peril.

Professional Malpractice

The common law imposes a higher duty of care upon professionals such as doctors or lawyers. In the field of medical malpractice, courts determine whether physicians exercised the care and skill of the average qualified practitioner. If the patient dies because of medical malpractice, there is no liability absent breach of the standard of care. Doctors, lawyers, accountants, and other established professionals do not guarantee results. Even though many fields label their practitioners as professionals, the term *professional malpractice* is restricted to a few well-established fields.

No court, for example, has held a software company liable for failing to meet professional computer security standards. Courts have also been reluctant to recognize the tort of computer malpractice for negligent design of hardware or software. Software engineering is a relatively new field without the well-established professional standards that are found in more developed professions such as law and medicine. For example, medical specialists must pass far more stringent board certifications than the optional certification examinations provided by various computer services vendors. Courts have uniformly rejected attempts to apply a professional standard of care to software engineers, designers, or consultants, despite the fact that software designers and computer engineers have professional organizations that set standards.

The central inquiry will be to determine whether a defendant complied with a professional standard of care, calibrated to the standards of care followed in the specific profession. Self-help is not an option in pursuing a claim against a professional because of the complexity of this kind of litigation. A mechanic is negligent unless she uses the due care of a reasonable mechanic. Mechanics must repair engines consistent with the practices in the auto repair industry. A carpenter who constructs a new porch that collapses from the weight of a single person will be liable for negligent construction. An architect's work must comply with the standards in the profession. For nonprofessionals, the issue is whether the defendant complied with best practices in the industry. In industries in which customs are weak or ill-formed, it is possible for defendants to be negligent even if they comply with industry standards.

The cost of pursuing a medical or legal malpractice case is often tens of thousands of dollars because expert testimony is required to prove that the defendant has breached a professional standard of care. You will need to find an attorney experienced in professional malpractice cases in order to have any likelihood of success in such matters. Consult your local bar association's referral service to find an attorney with a strong record in professional negligence cases.

What to Do: Recognizing a Premises Liability Lawsuit

Businesses are increasingly liable for criminal attacks by third parties on customers, a new field of tort law called "premises liability." The essential element of a tort is the legal duty the defendant owes the plaintiff. Under common law, a property owner had no duty to protect tenants from a third party's crimes. In the early 1970s, however, courts began to hold property owners liable for the failure to provide reasonable security for their tenants. The property owner's duty to minimize the risk of crimes to tenants has served as a viable legal theory for other consumer cases. The owners and operators of shopping malls, for example, are liable for failing to provide adequate security to prevent third-party criminal attacks on shoppers. For example, a Springfield, Massachusetts, bus terminal was found liable for inadequate security in the stabbing death of a passenger waiting to board one of its buses.[6] In premises liability cases, courts balance the foreseeability (likelihood) of harm and the gravity of harm against the burden of precaution.

A common carrier such as a bus company or railroad, for example, cannot prevent all attacks on passengers, but it can provide reasonable security. Courts are concerned that if they impose too much of a burden of precaution, it will drive businesses into bankruptcy. The owner of a retail establishment could theoretically be liable for the reasonably foreseeable harm caused by third parties who injure customers if the attacks could have been prevented with security. A court will generally not impose a duty of reasonable security unless there have been "prior similar" attacks on customers. Other courts look at the totality of the circumstances in determining the duty to maintain security. The most important relevant circumstances include the number, nature, location, and response to prior crimes or security incidents.

Contributory Negligence. The defense of contributory negligence bars recovery entirely if the plaintiff's own negligence contributed to the injury. A website, for example, could defend against a claim for Internet security because plaintiffs contributed to their injuries by losing their passwords. Plaintiffs who contribute to their own injuries are precluded from any recovery in a contributory negligence jurisdiction.

Comparative Negligence. Most U.S. jurisdictions have adopted some form of comparative negligence. In a comparative negligence jurisdiction, the negligence of the defendant is compared to that of the plaintiff. The plaintiff's recovery is diminished by the degree of her negligence, as compared to a contributory negligence regime, in which the plaintiff's fault relieves the defendant entirely from liability.[7] Comparative negligence jurisdictions may be classified as "modified" or "pure" comparative negligence systems. In a modified system, negligent plaintiffs may recover, provided their negligence is neither equal to nor greater than that of the defendant. In a pure comparative negligence regime, the plaintiff's recovery is diminished by their degree of negligence, even if their negligence is greater than or equal to that of the defendant's. A plaintiff's failure to use standard antiviral software might constitute comparative negligence in a lawsuit over the transmission of software containing a virus.

Assumption of Risk. If plaintiffs voluntarily assume a known risk, they cannot recover for harm, even if the defendant is at fault. The plaintiff must have voluntarily known of and appreciated the specific risk. If Paula Plaintiff falls off a water raft and is struck by another raft, she likely assumes the risk of injury. The contractual assumption of risk, in which the parties entered into an agreement relieving the defendant of liability, was discussed in Chapter 6.

Strict Liability Defined

The expansion of strict product liability is one of the most dramatic consumer protection developments since World War II. Strict liability is a branch of tort law in which the defendant may be found liable for your injuries without the necessity of proving that he was at fault.

The underlying policy rationale for the doctrine of strict liability is that the manufacturer, rather than the consumer, is in the best position to avoid the peril through better design and fortified warnings. A company may be held strictly liable if it transports a hazardous substance that ends up contaminating the soil, even though the corporation exercised the utmost care in its handling of the pollutant. The mercury polluters of a state waterway, for example, are strictly liable to others for the harms caused by toxic wastes stored on their property. The actual cases inspiring *A Civil Action*, *Silkwood*, and *Erin Brockovich* were strict liability actions in tort.

Example: Toxic Torts Case. Homeowners brought a toxic torts case against an exterminating company that used chlordane in a compound to kill termites. The plaintiffs' theory of the case was that they were not given adequate warnings regarding the dangers of exposure to the chemicals. The plaintiffs relied in part upon testimony from an occupational medicine expert that the levels of chlordane in the house after installation by the defendant were dangerously high and, as such, posed a health hazard to the plaintiffs. The plaintiffs additionally contended that the defendant failed to provide warnings regarding the health risks associated with exposure to the product. The plaintiffs' occupational medicine expert contended that the medical literature on chlordane was consistent with the plaintiffs' injuries. His expert opinion was that the plaintiffs' respiratory problems and immune deficiency were caused by a chemical hypersensitivity. The consumers received a verdict of $625,000, which included $75,000 for loss of consortium.

Product Liability

Product Liability Defined

The term *product liability* refers to the branch of civil law in which manufacturers and anyone else in the distribution chain are liable for injuries or deaths caused by exploding television sets or any other dangerously defective product. Product liability is a branch of law that has tort and contract elements. A tort is simply a civil wrong that gives the injured party the right to recover monetary damages for losses sustained. A plaintiff in a product liability lawsuit must prove that her injury was caused by some condition of the product that was unreasonably dangerous. The injured plaintiff must also prove that the defect or dangerous condition existed at the time the product was in the manufacturer's control.

Overview of Product Liability

The National Commission on Product Safety's 1967 report on ordinary consumer product hazards raised the national consciousness about shoddy products that posed risks to life and limb and the need to reform the design process to create better quality control. This valuable study demonstrated that consumer products were involved in most household accidents. Annually, those accidents killed 30,000 people, permanently disabled 110,000, and hospitalized 585,000 more. The commission's report described "cribs that strangle, tip-over steam vaporizers that scalded, rotary power mowers that clipped off fingers and toes, gas-fired floor furnaces that seared the unwitting with waffle-like patterns, thousands of TV fires caused by poorly insulated wires, wringer washing machines that crushed the young and unwary, thousands of glass doors that shattered[,] becoming makeshift shards and guillotines, high handlebar bicycles that broke cheekbones. A nightmare, yes, but this gruesome catalogue was no dream."[8]

A 1969 *Wall Street Journal* report noted, "Roofs leak. Shirts shrink. Toys maim. Toasters do not toast. Mowers do not mow. Kites do not fly. Radios emit no sounds, and television sets and cameras yield no pictures. Is not anything well made these days?"[9] The report asked, "Why are things so shoddy?"[10] The *Journal* reported that the finish on a $425 General Electric refrigerator peeled and that a $400 Admiral color TV set required a complete factory overhaul.[11] Not only did products fail to conform to their desired function, but also more seriously, product quality problems had the real potential of killing and maiming unsuspecting consumers.

Product quality has improved dramatically since the 1960s as the result of fortified state and federal consumer protection laws and the rise of the field of product liability to redress injuries or deaths caused by dangerously defective products. Product liability is a field of tort law that concerns the legal liability of manufacturers for injuries caused by defective products. Manufacturers, sellers, distributors, retailers, and others in the distribution chain are potentially liable if they market products to users or consumers that cause injury or death. Defective products can have deadly consequences, as evidenced by what happened to Valerie Lakey, a five-year-old North Carolina girl who was playing in a community wading pool. The pool's drain cover, which constrains the strong hydraulic vortex, was somehow displaced, and Valerie became lodged in the opening.[12] The pool's suction exerted a force from the uncovered drain that eviscerated the child. Seventy-five percent of her bowels were pulled out of her anus, and her life was saved only by the heroic efforts of the medical personnel at a North Carolina hospital.[13] The little girl ultimately survived but endured years of surgeries, hospital stays, and consultations with specialists.

Consumers injured by defective products or families of consumers who have been killed by them need to hire a lawyer who specializes in product liability. Relatively few attorneys are experts in trying product liability cases, and self-representation is not an option, nor is representation by a general practitioner. Valerie Lakey's parents hired John Edwards (later a U.S. senator and candidate for president), who is a product liability specialist. The Lakeys filed suit against Sta-Rite Industries, a Wisconsin pool equipment manufacturer, on behalf of their daughter.[14] Valerie Lakey's attorney used aggressive pretrial discovery to uncover what the manufacturer of the pool drain knew and whether there were prior similar incidents. In a dozen prior cases, children had suffered catastrophic injuries or near misses caused by broken or missing pool drain covers. What did the company do in the wake of this developing profile of dangers? Too little, too late. Only after the case was filed did the manufacturer change its warnings and instructions. The state of North Carolina also passed statutes requiring wading pool drain covers after the child's injury but before the case was tried.[15] An internal report discovered by the plaintiff's counsel stated that such "accidents were more common—the pressure from open drains tearing rectums and disemboweling small children. Without the grate, the suction is unimpeded and can exert considerable force." Valerie Lakey's lawyers were able to win a $25 million punitive damages settlement directly based on these "smoking gun" documents, which showed that Sta-Rite failed to take safety steps after learning that the suction from open drains could be deadly. Reports of the settlement led the entire swimming pool industry to recall its drain covers. The U.S. Consumer Product Safety Commission (CPSC) published extensive guidelines to help pool operators avoid similar entrapment injuries in the future.[16]

Product liability cases in which products have unexpected dangers bring to mind a short story by science fiction writer Philip K. Dick. In Dick's short story "The Colony," space travelers found an apparent utopia on a distant planet. The setting was like Hawaii before Captain Cook, a paradise without snakes, pollution, famine, pestilence, or other natural calamities. Everything was perfect, until one day the captain of the space expedition was showering, and as he reached for his towel, it nearly strangled him. Another space traveler was crushed by his belt, which transformed into a deadly, python-like creature. A scientist was nearly strangled by his microscope. Still another colonist was almost killed when his armchair closed around him. A young husband was nearly killed by a red-and-white scatter rug that wrapped around his legs. In shock, he explained, "The rug had been in my family for years. It was a gift from my wife. I trusted it completely." In the end, all the space travelers were killed off by deadly beings disguised as ordinary objects.

This science fiction short story, though absurd, makes a critical point. Psychologically, we have to trust our consumer products to function. We have to believe that when a firm learns of a developing danger, it will protect the consuming public. Consumers depend upon manufacturers reporting "substantial hazards" to the CPSC and undertaking prompt remedial action. Products of all kinds may cause serious injury or death because of hidden dangers. Consumers should have a reasonable expectation that products were thoroughly tested and designed for the foreseeable environment of use.

Example: Defective Smoke Alarms. After a smoke alarm failed and a fire killed three children and left a fourth child with devastating burns over 12 percent of her body, the representatives of the children filed suit in a Massachusetts federal court.[17] The product at issue in the case was a smoke detector sold by Sears Roebuck and manufactured by another company. The plaintiff argued that Sears and the manufacturer of the smoke alarm failed to provide adequate instructions advising the purchaser to wire the smoke detector onto its own separate electrical circuit. If this precaution was not taken, the alarm would simply not function in the event that a fuse was blown due to the malfunctioning of another appliance or cord wired into the same circuit. What happened in this tragic accident is that the smoke detector failed to operate when a defective extension cord short-circuited the electrical wire. This product defect set off a deadly chain of events that caused the smoke detector to malfunction and triggered the fire.

In product liability cases, the trial judge decides which causes of action can be considered by the jury. A judge may decide, for example, that there is not enough evidence for the jury to arrive at a correct result. In this case, the federal district judge refused to instruct the jury on the question of whether Sears was liable for selling a product with a design defect. The court did instruct the Massachusetts jury on a failure of warning. The Massachusetts jury awarded the plaintiffs $1,800,000, which included $350,000 for the death of each child and $750,000 to the child that sustained burns.

Types of Product Defects

Not every tragic accident caused by a product is actionable. Product sellers are liable only if they market products posing an unreasonable, preventable danger to the user. A person who has been injured using a product may be able to sue the manufacturer, wholesaler, retailer, or other commercial sellers who sold a defective product. Injured consumers can only prevail in product defects suits if they can prove that a company or other person selling or distributing a product sold it in an unreasonably dangerous condition. Lawsuits may be brought if the consumer's injury was caused by a product defect, but no product liability lawsuit may be filed unless there is proof of a defect.

A person who has been injured using a product may be able to sue the manufacturer, wholesaler, retailer, or other commercial sellers who sold a defective product. Injured consumers can file suit if they can prove that a company or other person selling or distributing a product sold it in an unreasonably dangerous condition. The plaintiff's attorney must collect the "smoking gun" evidence of the manufacturer's poor design decisions during discovery, which occurs before the trial. It is then up to the jury to decide whether the product is defective. The consumer does not get to trial without evidence supporting each element. Lawsuits may be brought if the consumer's injury was caused by a product defect, but no product liability lawsuit may be filed unless there is proof of a defect.

Manufacturing Defects

The design is not the problem in manufacturing defects; instead, something is wrong with the production process. The classic example of a manufacturing defect case is a foreign object appearing in food. A manufacturing defect means that something went wrong with the batch that caused foreign substances such as nails, wire, or glass to be embedded in food. A consumer who breaks a molar on an unexpected foreign substance, such as a penny nail in her pie, will likely have as good a cause of action for product liability as will someone who finds a decomposed rodent skeleton in his or her soda. Mice seem to drown in Coca-Cola versus Pepsi by a wide margin, judging by the law reporters from the 1940s and 1950s. Today, bad food cases are frequently settled because the liability of the manufacturer is absolute.

Both restaurants and distributors of food are liable for selling or marketing products containing food-borne contaminants or foreign objects. In *Heimsoth v. Falstaff Brewing Co.*,[18] a patron of a tavern drank a bottle of beer containing a used "rubber prophylactic contraceptive latex."[19] The plaintiff suffered "nausea, sustained a fixation neurosis, and had considerable loss in his business as a result of having consumed the bottle of beer with the latex prophylactic in it."[20] If a consumer encounters a foreign substance in food that was there when the product was injected into the stream of commerce, the manufacturer will be strictly liable for the consequences.

Prior to the advent of product liability, there were numerous lawsuits against manufacturers broadly known as "foreign object" cases. Even now, food-borne injuries continue to be frighteningly common. In October 2006, Foxy, one of the most popular sellers of California lettuce, recalled its lettuce on the heels of an *E. coli* crisis over bagged spinach that caused several deaths. That same week, an Iowa company recalled 5,200 pounds of ground beef suspected of containing *E. coli*. If food is contaminated with *E. coli*, it is likely to be a manufacturing defect. Food contaminated by microbial pathogens subjects companies to product liability. Food-borne illnesses should be treated no differently than "foreign object" cases.

Courts have generally determined whether an unexpected object is a natural or foreign object. A consumer would, for example, expect to find bones in haddock or northern pike or walleye fillets. Similarly, bones, which are natural to meat, are not classified as foreign substances. A consumer who eats meat ought to expect bones but not nails or glass. Courts have traditionally had little difficulty finding warranty liability in cases in which the object is foreign and not naturally occurring. Conversely, courts have usually denied warranty liability in bad food cases in which the object was a natural substance, such as a pit in a cherry or a bone in a filet of cod.

The manufacturer is in the best position to take steps to ensure that foreign objects are screened out during the manufacturing process, rather than first discovered lodged in your throat. If your injury is rather minor in a food-borne case, contact the manufacturer for a remedy. Unless your injuries are significant (at least temporary partial disability), you will be unlikely to find a lawyer interested in taking your case. The severity of the injury and the manufacturer's culpability are the two most important variables in determining whether a product liability lawyer will take your case. Of course, you cannot recover, no matter how serious your injury, unless your attorney can prove that the product was defective.

Design Defects

The essence of a design defect is that the product is made as intended, but proves to have excessive preventable dangers. A poorly designed product, for example, may not contain a safety feature that would have prevented catastrophic injury. In *Greenman v. Yuba Power Products, Inc.*, a consumer was severely injured while using a Shopsmith, which was a home shop power tool that could serve as a saw, drill, and wood lathe.[21] The consumer saw a Shopsmith demonstrated by the retailer and studied a brochure prepared by the manufacturer. He decided he wanted a Shopsmith for his home workshop, and his wife bought and gave him one for Christmas.

Two years later, in 1957, he bought the necessary attachments to use the Shopsmith as a lathe for turning a large piece of wood he wished to make into a chalice. After he had worked on the piece of wood several times without difficulty, it suddenly flew out of the machine and struck him on the forehead, inflicting catastrophic head injuries. The court held that the machine used inadequate set screws to hold it together, which allowed for the parts to come loose during vibration under normal use, supporting a claim of negligent construction.

In modern times, there is a controversy over how product defects should be defined.[22] The Restatement (Second) of Torts adopted a "consumer expectation test," which provides: "One who sells any product in a defective condition unreasonably dangerous to the user or consumer or to his property is subject to liability for physical harm thereby caused to the ultimate user or consumer, or to his property."[23]

In *Gryc v. Dayton-Hudson Corporation,*[24] the manufacturers of cotton flannelette nightwear were found to be liable for incorporating flammable materials into the design of this unreasonably dangerous consumer product. Internal documents showed that the company knew that the flannelette could burst into flames because the fabric was inadequate for the environment of use. The company, knowing that the federal flammability standard was inadequate, marketed the pajamas with reckless disregard of the known risk. The *Gryc* court rejected the defendant's argument that no warning was necessary because the sleepwear fully complied with the U.S. government's flammability standards.

Product liability is a consumer remedy for recovering injuries caused by marketing unreasonably dangerous products to the consumer. In another design defect case, a toddler was horribly scarred by a common household drain cleaner. The drain cleaner contained a high concentration of hydrochloric acid. A television advertisement depicted the liquid drain cleaner as suitable for home use, with a housewife casually swishing her hand in a kitchen sink after using the drain cleaner. The advertisement became the "basis of the bargain" and was found to be enforceable.

In this case, a two-year-old girl was accidentally splashed with the caustic drain cleaner when she sat beside the bathroom sink that her father was unclogging with the drain cleaner. The father of the young girl took prompt remedial measures, flushing his daughter's face with cold water, but the water only accelerated the flesh-eating properties of the drain cleaner. The court found the express warranty to have been breached because the drain cleaner was a flesh-eater and not safe for contact on the skin. The product dissolved human tissue in a fraction of a second because it contained too high of a percentage of sodium hydroxide.

The essence of a design defect is that the risks exceed the benefits of a given design feature. It differs from a manufacturing defect, in which one product in a batch or an entire batch is defective due to quality problems. There are two different ways to measure a design defect: the relationship of risk to utility (that is, whether a safer alternative is available at a low cost) or the consumer expectation test. A product is defectively designed if a reasonable consumer would not appreciate the hidden danger of a particular design or feature.

Inadequate Warning or Failure to Warn
Manufacturers have a duty to provide adequate warnings to potential users of their products, especially if there is a hidden risk of injury created by the manufacturer's design. And even if a product is not unreasonably dangerous per se or flawed by a construction defect, it may still be an unreasonably dangerous product if the manufacturer fails to adequately warn about a danger associated with it.

The category of *failure to warn* applies to a product that may be designed in an optimally safe way, but bears a latent danger that would not be apparent to an ordinary consumer. As with all tort laws, the tort of failure to warn varies from state to state, what legal scholars refer to as "jurisdictional differences." In order to establish that a product is defective for failure to warn, for example, a plaintiff must demonstrate that a manufacturer (1) had actual or constructive knowledge of the alleged danger, (2) had no reason to believe that consumers would know of this danger, and (3) failed to exercise reasonable care to inform consumers of the danger.

Courts in most states apply a risk-to-utility to determine whether a design is defective. A court must first determine what risk, if any, the product created and then decide whether a reasonable person would conclude that the danger outweighs the utility of the product. That is a risk-to-utility analysis. A product is unreasonably dangerous because of an inadequate warning if, at the time the product left its manufacturer's control, the product possessed a characteristic that may cause damage and the manufacturer failed to use reasonable care to provide an adequate warning of such characteristic and its danger to users and handlers of the product. The manufacturer or distributor of a product has a duty to give adequate warnings of product features with potentially harmful consequences. Many asbestos manufacturers, for example, were found liable for failing to warn workers and consumers after they were aware of the dangers of asbestos. A product may be defective because it does not incorporate warnings or other safety features mandated by the government.

Proving Product Defect

Product liability is a term describing the legal liability of manufacturers for injuries caused by defective products. Knives cut, too much butter in the diet kills, and excessive consumption of whiskey causes liver or kidney failure. However, the manufacturer will not be liable for these consequences, since there is no product defect. In order to have product liability, a product must be defective. As noted above, the most common defects are manufacturing defects or design defects.

Manufacturing defect. To prove a manufacturing defect, one must show that there is a difference between the product's actual condition when it leaves the manufacturer's possession and its intended condition according to the manufacturer's plans for it.

Design defect. A design defect can be proved through one of two tests, depending on the jurisdiction: (1) consumer expectation or (2) risk to utility. The Restatement (Third) of Torts followed in a minority of jurisdictions eliminates the consumer expectation test and considers a defective design to occur "when the foreseeable risks of harm posed by the product could have been reduced or avoided by the adoption of a reasonable alternative design by the seller or other distributor, or a predecessor in the commercial chain of distribution, and the omission of the alternative design renders the product not reasonably safe."[25]

Texas, for example, requires the plaintiff to prove "that there is an economically and technologically feasible safer alternative design available at the time of manufacture in most product liability actions for defective design."[26] Most jurisdictions continue to permit consumers to prove design defects through consumer expectation as well as through risk-to-utility analyses. A risk-to-utility analysis balances the risks of the product against the costs of making the product safe.

In order for you to recover in a product liability case, your attorney will need to retain an expert to testify whether a product design was reasonable in light of its risks and benefits. Factors included in this analysis are (1) the product's usefulness and desirability as designed, (2) the likely occurrence and severity of injury, (3) the availability of a safe alternative design or product, (4) the manufacturer's ability to eliminate danger without impairing its usefulness or making it too expensive, (5) the user's ability to avoid the danger, (6) the user's anticipated awareness of the danger, and (7) the feasibility of the manufacturer's spreading the risk through insurance. The majority of jurisdictions do not require the plaintiff to prove a reasonable alternative design as part of their burden of proof and production. In most jurisdictions, your attorney can prove defect design through either a consumer expectation or risk-to-utility test (defined above).

What to Do If You Have Been Injured by a Defective Product

Self-help is not an option if you have been injured by a defective product. Instead, seek out a lawyer. If an attorney is willing to take your case, you will sign a contingency fee contract in which the attorney will receive a set percentage of the overall recovery. In addition, the attorney generally advances litigation costs and is compensated in full before the claimant recovers.

You must preserve the product causing the accident and photograph the accident scene. The product should be kept in the same condition it was in at the time of accident. Without the defective product, you may be left with no proof of the product's defect, and the possibility of a successful lawsuit will vanish for failure of proof.

A product liability lawsuit is the best remedy for consumers injured by unreasonably dangerous products. Product liability cases are difficult to litigate, and it is even more difficult to obtain a favorable jury verdict. Product liability is a specialty practiced well by only a handful of firms in most cities. I interviewed a large number of product liability attorneys when I conducted my study of punitive damages in product liability cases. Product liability cases are high-stakes cases and frequently cost $100,000 or more to litigate. The success rate of these cases is 40 percent or lower in many jurisdictions. As a result, it is frequently difficult to find a product liability attorney who will take your case unless you have a clear defect, serious injuries, and are free from fault in the product accident.

Who May Be Sued?

A lawsuit may be filed against the immediate seller, the remote manufacturer, and every other defendant in the chain of distribution. If the immediate seller is sued, they will frequently seek indemnification from the manufacturer or maker. In other words, the consumer may sue anyone in the line of distribution.

Keep in mind that product liability cases are complex and require lawyers with experience and expertise trying these cases. Product liability is expensive because of the need to hire experts to establish defect. Frequently, the pretrial process of discovery is also expensive. If you have a strong case, you will need a specialist to litigate your claim against the manufacturer or other parties in the chain of distribution. A product liability lawyer will gather evidence substantial enough to show that the product was indeed defective and present the evidence in court.

Defenses to Products Liability Actions

A seller is not liable under products liability if a product is misused. "If the injury results from abnormal handling, as where a bottled beverage is knocked against a radiator to remove the cap, or from abnormal preparation for use, as where too much salt is added to food, or from abnormal consumption, as where a child eats too much candy and is made ill, the seller is not liable."[27] A homeowner who uses a lawn mower to trim the hedges would be barred from recovery. In a negligence-based products liability action, the consumer will be barred from recovery for assumption of risk or contributory negligence. In jurisdictions that have adopted comparative negligence, the consumer's judgment will be reduced according to his negligence. In addition to conduct-based defenses, the consumer must file his lawsuit in a timely manner. In most states, the tort statute of limitation is two or three years in contrast to the four-year statute of limitation under UCC Article 2.

Privity of contract, a common law contract that restricts liability only to the parties specified in the contract, has been eliminated in negligence and strict liability actions and has been scaled back under UCC Article 2. In general, natural persons as well as commercial entities may be plaintiffs in product liability actions. A bystander injured by a product will also be able to file suit, even though she was not the purchaser.

What to Do: Complaints about Drugs

The FDA encourages consumers to register their complaints of their experiences with medical products or devices. Today the FDA "is responsible for ensuring that foods are safe, wholesome, and correctly labeled. It also oversees medicines, medical devices (from bandages to artificial hearts), blood products, vaccines, cosmetics, veterinary drugs, animal feed, and electronic products that emit radiation (such as microwave ovens and video monitors), ensuring that these products are safe and effective."[28]

What to Do: Consumer Product Safety Commission (CPSC)

Congress created the CPSC in 1972 to implement the Consumer Product Safety Act. The CPSC's mission is to "protect the public against unreasonable risks of injuries and deaths associated with consumer produ'   you are a gun manufacturer, the product you make is not subject to safety regulation by the Consumer Product Safety Commission. Toy guns are subject to safety regulation; water pistols are, but not real guns."[29]

The CPSC has jurisdiction over more than 15,000 types of consumer products. The CPSC has a strong interest in protecting children from the hazards of toys, cribs, power tools, cigarette lighters, and household chemicals. CPSC enforcement actions have "contributed significantly to the 30 percent decline in the rate of deaths and injuries associated with consumer products over the past 30 years."[30] Consumers injured by a consumer product or concerned about an unsafe product should report it to the CPSC to reduce the radius of the risk of product-related injuries or death. Consumers can file a CPSC complaint by email at hazard@cpsc.gov, by toll-free telephone at 1-800-638-2772, or by fax at 1-800-809-0924. Complaints may also be sent by regular mail to U.S. Consumer Product Safety Commission, Injury Report, Washington, D.C. 20207. CPSC consumer complaints are restricted to safety concerns, rather than the full range of warranty issues. The CPSC, like every other public consumer agency, has no jurisdiction or authority to represent you as an individual, but it will investigate your complaints. However, the CPSC is understaffed and underfunded. Each year the agency receives more than 10,000 reports of product-related injuries or death and can only investigate a small fraction of these serious concerns.

The Tort Reform Crying Game

Since the late 1970s, tort reform has become the rallying cry of powerful corporations who wish to shift costs back to the injured victim, the victim's family, and the taxpayer. Tort reformers have successfully conveyed the impression to policymakers, the press, and the public that juries frequently victimize corporations by awarding bizarrely large amounts of money to overly litigious plaintiffs. This corporate crying game uses tort horror stories such as the McDonald's hot coffee case as evidence that the civil litigation system is in need of reform. The facts behind the McDonald's coffee case reveal a completely different story. McDonald's had more than 700 complaints from burns suffered by purchasers of its superheated coffee. At the time, McDonald's served its coffee at a temperature of 180-190 degrees Fahrenheit, which has the potential of causing napalm-like burn injuries. The plaintiff, Stella Liebeck, suffered second- and third-degree burns on her thighs, buttocks, and groin when she spilled a cup of coffee on her lap, and the hot liquid remained in contact with her clothes for over a minute. She nearly died from her injuries, and had to undergo multiple skin graft operations. This could have been easily prevented if McDonald's had simply lowered the temperature at which it served its coffee. McDonald's had prior notice of a developing profile of danger from hundreds of complaints about injuries from its product. Yet, the media portrayed the case as an example of a greedy plaintiff seeking recovery in a frivolous lawsuit.

Tort reformers find it relatively difficult to concoct realistic-sounding tort horror stories when describing most toxic torts.[31] Although plaintiffs in product liability lawsuits can easily be accused of misusing the products that injure them, few victims of environmental torts know about the peril and, therefore, cannot evade it. The residents of Love Canal, for example, had no knowledge that a residential subdivision was built in close proximity to a chemical dump site. Even the most creative public relations expert would be hard-pressed to blame the victims of hidden toxic waste dumps for contributing to their long-term illnesses or deaths. Tort reformers argue that tort rights need to be scaled back and replaced with criminal sanctions. That is a disingenuous argument because the environmental regulatory agencies at the state and federal level are also being scaled back. Note that tort reform is always aimed at injured workers, consumers, and patients but is rarely proposed for lawsuits filed by businesses.

Notes

1. *Silkwood v. Kerr-McGee*, 485 F. Supp. 566, 591 (W.D. Okla. 1979).

2. 628 F. Supp. 219 (D. Mass. 1988).

3. *Restatement (Second) of Torts* §531 (1976).

4. U.S. Department of Justice, Office of Justice Programs, Bureau of Justice Statistics: Tort Trials and Verdicts in Large Counties, 1996, NCJ 179769. http://www.ojp.gov/bjs/pub/ascii/ttvl96.txt

5. "Proximate cause" means that cause which, in a natural and continuous sequence, produces an event, and without which cause such event would not have occurred. In order to be a proximate cause, the act or omission complained of must be such that a person using ordinary care would have foreseen that the event might occur. Proximate cause "has little to do with physical causation, emphasizing instead the continuity of the sequences that produces an event." Bryan A. Garner, *A Dictionary of Modern Legal Usage,* 2d ed. (New York: Oxford University Press, 1995), 211.

6. *Sharpe v. Peter Pan Bus Lines, Inc.*, 519 N.E.2d 1341 (Mass. 1988).

7. *Ballentine's Law Dictionary,* 3d ed. (1969), 252.

8. Ibid.

9. "Caveat Emptor: Many People Complain the Quality of Products Is Deteriorating Rapidly," *Wall Street Journal,* June 26, 1969, 1.

10. Ibid.

11. Ibid.

12. Anne Saker, "Child Hurt in Drain Accident Talks to Court," *Raleigh* (NC) *News and Observer*, December 14, 1996, B1.

13. Anne Saker, "Company Papers Reveal 13 Accidents Like Cary Girl's," *Raleigh* (NC) *News and Observer*, December 11, 1996, B3.

14. Ibid.

15. Ibid.

16. Ibid.

17. *Lappeari, Administrator v. Sears, Roebuck*, No. 79-2497-T (D. Mass. 1984) (available in LEXIS/NEXIS ALLVER Library).

18. 1 Ill. App. 2d 28, 116 N.E.2d 193 (1953).

19. Ibid., p. 196.

20. Ibid.

21. 59 *Cal. Rptr.* 697 (1963).

22. Mark A. Geistfeld, *Principles of Product Liability* (Mineola, N.Y.: Foundation Press, 2005), 26.

23. *Restatement (Second) of Torts* §402A (1965).

24. 297 N.W.2d 727 (Minn. 1980).

25. *Restatement (Third) of Torts: Product Liability* §2 (1998).

26. Texas imposed the reasonable alternative requirement in a product liability tort reform enacted in 1993. See American Tort Reform Association, *Product Liability Reforms*, available at http://www.atra.org/issues/index.php?issue=7341 (accessed March 17, 2006).

27. Ibid.

28. Food and Drug Administration, *How to Report Problems with Products Regulated by the FDA*, available at http://www.fda.gov/opacom/backgrounders/problem .html. (accessed August 2, 2006).

29. Michael Barnes Brainy Quote, available at http://www.brainyquote.com/quotes/quotes/m/michaeldb227312.html (accessed September 13, 2006).

30. Nancy Nord, "CPSC Overview," available at http://www.cpsc.gov/about/about.html (accessed August 12, 2006).

31. Jack B. Weinstein, *Individual Justice in Mass Tort Litigation: The Effect of Class Actions, Consolidations, and Other Multiparty Devices* (Evanston, Ill.: Northwestern University Press, 1995), 1 (noting that courts in the post–World War II period "held out the prospect of empowerment through the courts of the disadvantaged").

Part III

Specific Consumer Protection

8

Automobile Sales, Services, and Financing

This chapter tells you what you need to know about purchasing, leasing, or repairing motor vehicles before you go to a car dealer. The federal Truth in Mileage Act of 1986, for example, requires used car sellers to make odometer disclosures on a separate, signed document. The fraudulent turning back of an odometer is also classifiable as the tort of fraud and violates every jurisdiction's Unfair and Deceptive Trade Practices Acts.

I once had a Fiat that left me stranded on highways, *autobahns,* and *autostradas* throughout Europe. I ended up replacing every major part, but my lemon automobile was still in the repair shop on a weekly basis. I sometimes felt that I had joint custody of the car with my Italian mechanic. Once, I stopped for gas and ordered the attendant to "fill it up and put in a new motor!" The car was finally stolen in Naples, Italy. I hope that the car stranded the thief next to a police station. Repair swindles were common in southern Italy. When my car broke down, I was at the mercy of unscrupulous mechanics that often overcharged me and replaced unnecessary parts.

Buying a Used Car and the FTC's Used Car Rule

Used car salespersons earned their bad reputation through a long history of widespread consumer fraud. Their reputation was forged in an era when sellers repainted engine blocks to conceal defects. Today, many dealers have high standards thanks to vigilant public policing at the federal and state levels. Without government oversight, used car dealers could roll back the odometer with impunity. Today, consumer protection statutes regulate many terms and practices employed in used car sales.

The FTC's Used Motor Vehicle Trade Regulation Rule (Used Car Rule) requires used vehicle dealers to place a label on the side window of the car describing the condition of the car and whether there is a warranty or it is being sold on an "as is" basis. A used car is subject to the FTC regulation if it was driven for purposes other than moving it around the lot or test driving, even if it was not previously titled to another owner. The regulation applies to used vehicles, including light-duty vans, light-duty trucks, demonstrators, and program cars with a gross vehicle weight rating of less than 8,500 pounds, a curb weight of less than 6,000 pounds, and a frontal area of less than 46 square feet.

The Used Car Rule also prohibits the used vehicle dealer from making statements contrary to those on the label attached to the window. The FTC rule applies to dealers in all states except Utah and Wisconsin, which have similar regulations. It does not apply to businesses that sell vehicles to their employees or to lessors who lease a vehicle to a lessee.

The dealer must disclose the percentage of the repair costs it will pay under the warranty. The buyer's guide must also disclose that oral promises are difficult to enforce and purport the importance of getting all promises by the dealer in writing. It should disclose mechanical and electrical problems that a consumer should consider. The sticker must also disclose whether a service contract is available. The buyer's guide must be available for reference after the sale. Another disclosure that consumers must receive is advice to have a used car inspected by an independent mechanic. The FTC guide to the Used Car Rule requires dealers to post the buyer's guide prominently and conspicuously on or in a vehicle available for sale, on the rearview mirror, on the sideview mirror, or under the windshield wiper. Neither federal nor state law permits dealers to place the guide in the glove compartment or trunk, under the seat, or in another inconspicuous location.[1] If the dealer offers consumers a split cost warranty requiring them to pay a percentage of the repair cost for covered repairs, the dealer must include the following disclosures in the warranty document: the percentage of the total repairs the dealer will pay for, the percentage of the total repairs the buyer must pay for, and how the total cost of the repairs will be determined. For example, your warranty might state: "The total cost of a warranty repair will be the retail price ABC motors charges for the same job." As another example, your warranty might state: "The total cost of a warranty repair will be determined by adding the dealer's cost for parts to the labor cost. Labor will be billed at a rate of _____ per hour for the actual time required to complete the repair." As a final example, your warranty might state: "If the work is done by an outside repair shop, total cost of a repair will be the same price ABC Motors is charged by the outside shop. If the work is done by ABC Motors, the total cost of the repair will be the same price ABC Motors charges non-warranty customers for the same job.[2]

Every state has consumer protection rules governing used car sales, and some states have enacted used car lemon laws. A growing number of states prohibit "as is" used car sales. Massachusetts, for example, prohibits the sale of a used motor vehicle by a dealer unless it has an express warranty covering the full cost of both parts and labor to repair any defect that impairs the motor vehicle's safety or use. A consumer may not be required to pay more than $100 for the repair of any covered defect or combination of defects in the warranty period (M.G.L.A. ch. 90 §7N 1/4). Warranties may only be limited or disclaimed if the manufacturer's warranty is transferred to the customer and is enforceable. The duration of express warranties depends upon the age and mileage of the vehicle: For vehicles with less than 40,000 miles on the odometer, it is ninety days or 3,750 miles. Vehicles with 80,000 or more but less than 125,000 miles have a warranty duration of thirty days or 1,250 miles. Consult your state statutes governing express warranties by dealers of used motor vehicles by checking with your state attorney general.

State Used Car Laws That Permit the Voiding of Contracts of Sale

Massachusetts, like many other states, permits consumers to void or get out of contracts if the motor vehicle fails to pass inspection within seven days from the date of sale. However, a consumer may not void contracts for used cars when the damage resulted from an accident or abuse occurring after the date of the sale (M.G.L.A. ch. 90 §7N). In order to trigger this right, a Massachusetts consumer must notify the seller of his intention to void the contract within fourteen days of the day of sale, deliver the motor vehicle to the seller, and provide the seller with a written statement signed by the agent of the inspection station as to why the motor vehicle failed to pass safety and emissions inspection. The Massachusetts statute gives the buyer a refund of the purchase price unless the buyer and seller agree in writing that the seller will make the necessary repairs at its own cost and in a reasonable period of time. Most states have similar provisions. The mandatory consumer protection applies only to motor vehicles purchased for personal, family, or household use by the buyer.

What to Do: Exercise Caution When Buying a Used Car

Today the used car sales industry tends to be more even-handed. Still, there are questionable practices. Caution is the watchword whenever buying a used car. You should shop around for a dealer with a reputation for fairness. A car sales representative with three decades of automobile sales experience makes these observations:

> The things that I like least about the car business were technically legal practices that were unnecessary charges. Take the category of "documentation charges." In my experience, documentation charges were often random and inconsistent among car manufacturers and dealers. Take any number. Let's make it $149 or $179 or even a higher figure such as $249. All of the figures were legally tacked on in most states. Another widespread practice is what was known in the industry as ADP (additional dealer profit). ADP is a scam be-

cause it allows dealers to pretend to give more for a consumer's trade-in. This is a business where the squeaky wheel gets the grease.

Many people become disenchanted with these hidden costs and yet few complain. I worked for the XYZ Company, which has a reputation for integrity. Yet, we still treated people differently according to ability to negotiate the trade value. The XYZ Company usually did not venture from the price depicted on the side window. However, a new program or a price reevaluation might mysteriously appear the next day. A quick call to the customer usually resulted in an angry customer. Their complaint was: Why didn't you have that revised price for me yesterday when I looked at the car?

The entire used car system is designed so that the savvy buyer pays less than honest, trusting consumers. The trust is usually not well placed. Most car sales people do not determine their own numbers. The overseer watches the numbers closely. The overseer (desk manager) manages each deal in an effort to optimize the profit per car sale. The used car appraiser wants to buy the cars as cheap as possible so his acquisitions have decent gross profits. The whole profit picture lacks standardization and integrity.

As an individual salesperson, I tried to add a degree of integrity back into the process by offering information about the process that may have hinted at its lack of uniformity. Some clients just did not get it. Since I was working for the company, it was my job to make money. I realized that often my clients were paying hundreds more than they would have needed. Consumers could end up losing in dealerships with less integrity.[3]

When purchasing a new car, ask many questions and always visit the lot with another person, preferably a notary public. Get promises in writing. If you have particular requirements for the vehicle, ask the sales representative to recommend a model. If you are relying upon the seller's expertise in selecting a car for a particular purpose, you will have an implied warranty if the vehicle is not fit for that particular purpose. The implied warranty of fitness for a particular purpose described in UCC Article 2 is triggered when you rely upon a seller's expertise in selecting a vehicle. Please note that the seller's descriptions of their product must be substantive enough in nature to trigger such a warranty. A seller's subjective claims using colloquial language like "this is a great car" will not create an implied warranty for fitness for a particular purpose, but objective claims like "this car will definitely tow two thousand pounds" may create such a warranty, especially if the buyer sought the seller's advice on the matter, and a reasonable person in the buyer's shoes would have relied on such advice. In Massachusetts, Maryland, and a few other states, a seller may not disclaim the implied warranty of merchantability or fitness for a particular purpose. Ask the dealer whether the vehicle has been inspected and what (if any) defects were uncovered during the inspection. Be wary of dealers that attempt to disclaim all meaningful warranties for used cars. A growing number of jurisdictions restrict this unsavory practice.

You may also want to visit at least one other dealership to ensure that you are receiving quality care and pricing. If you need the car for a particular purpose such as off-road travel, ask the dealer whether the vehicle is suitable for that purpose. Ask if there is any manufacturer's warranty available for the vehicle. Ask the representative of the dealer whether this car was reconstructed, rebuilt, or salvaged. Do not buy a car from a dealer who does not have a complete buyer's guide for each used vehicle offered for sale. The FTC gives the following tips to purchasers of used cars:

- Check out the car's repair record, maintenance costs, and safety and mileage ratings in consumer magazines or online. Look up the "blue book" value, and be prepared to negotiate the price.
- Buying from a dealer? Look for the Buyer's Guide. It's required by a federal regulation called the Used Car Rule.
- Make sure all oral promises are written into the Buyer's Guide.
- You have the right to see a copy of the dealer's warranty before you buy.
- Warranties are included in the price of the product; service contracts cost extra and are sold separately.
- Ask for the car's maintenance record from the owner, dealer, or repair shop.
- Test drive the car on hills, highways, and in stop-and-go traffic.
- Have the car inspected by a mechanic you hire.
- Check out the dealer with local consumer protection officials.
- If you buy a car "as is," you will have to pay for anything that goes wrong after the sale.[4]

The Better Business Bureau (BBB) recommends that used car buyers undertake the same due diligence as new car buyers. *Consumer Reports* can be consulted about the cost of repairs for given models and makes of automobiles. If the cost of repairs is excessive for a Hummer, one might consider another choice. *Consumer Reports* is the best source for determining the overall reliability of models and makes. In addition, the BBB recommends the following due diligence research, available in many local libraries or online:

Terms for used auto loans at financial institutions change with the market and interest rates. You should spend some time researching the vehicles that you are interested in. Ask friends about their experiences and satisfaction with their older cars—would they buy the car again? Also, check auto and consumer books, such as *Edmund's Used Cars Prices and Ratings*, and magazines, such as *Consumer Reports*, for information on the reliability records of various models. In addition, the National Highway Traffic Safety Administration (NHTSA) operates a toll-free hotline (1-800-424-9393) and a page on the Internet (www.nhtsa.dot.gov), through which you can find out if a particular vehicle has ever been recalled for safety defects.

To help you investigate and compare prices, several publications provide general guidance on value for many models. Your local library, bookstore, bank, or insurance agent should have a copy of the monthly National Automotive Dealers Association (NADA) Official Used Car Guide (www.nada guides.org), monthly Kelley Blue Book (www.kbb.com), or *Edmund's* (www .edmunds.com) to estimate a car's resale value. Comparing prices of similar makes and models can give you an idea of which seller offers the best deals.[5]

Buying Used Cars from a Private Person

The FTC Used Car Rule does not apply to private sales unless the seller sells five or more automobiles in a year. Like a dealer, a private person selling a car is required to disclose all material facts concerning the product or service. Private parties have no immunities from truthfulness. If a consumer purchased the automobile from a private party, he or she too would be required to make such disclosures. Unlike a dealer, which has a higher duty to disclose material facts "up front," private persons do not have the same obligation to disclose material facts unless they are in response to a buyer's question or concern. If you buy a car from a private person, have your mechanic check out the car. You will not have protection from lemon laws if you do not purchase your car from a professional seller.

Commercial Car Advertisements

Many states have rules regulating the advertisement of automobiles. Massachusetts regulations, for example, are located at http://www.ago.state .ma.us. Advertisements for the sale of an automobile for a specified price that turns out to be different in person may be deemed to be a "bait and switch." The New Mexico attorney general explains how bait and switch works in a car sale. What happens typically is that the consumer sees an advertisement for the sale of a car (or other service) at an attractive price. When the consumer rushes to the business to snap up the offer, the offer is changed or the car or service offer is of a lower level than the original offer. "For example, if a V6 model vehicle is advertised at $20,000 and when you go into the dealership they say that the advertised price is only for the four-cylinder model, then that is bait and switch." For more information on bait and switch and other automobile sales gimmicks, visit the New Mexico attorney general's website at http://www.ago.state.nm.us/divs/cons/cons_ faqs_auto.htm.

Unless the advertisement clearly and conspicuously discloses that the equipment is not included, the advertised price is considered an unfair or deceptive trade practice when the price does not include certain standard equipment that the vehicles actually or ordinarily have. It may also be a deceptive and unfair practice if the advertisement that you specifically responded to did not clearly and conspicuously disclose the expiration date or any other conditions of the sale or promotion.

Spot Deliveries

Spot delivery is a type of car sales in which the dealer agrees to let the consumer take the vehicle home, even though the car loan has not yet been finalized. A common abuse in spot deliveries is for the dealer to add new charges and conditions at the closing. It is also common to present the consumer with a new, higher rate of interest at the time the loan is finalized. The consumer is under no obligation to accept a contract with different terms. According to the New Mexico attorney general's website, if a consumer signs a contract with a 7 percent finance rate, and the dealer calls and states that you can only qualify for a 15 percent rate, you are under no contractual obligation to accept the new rate. A consumer presented with new terms is under no obligation to accept new charges or conditions because that would be considered either a unilateral contract modification or a new contract requiring your agreement. Unilateral modifications by dealers may also be considered an unfair or deceptive trade practice under your state's act.

Automobile Repairs

State Unfair and Deceptive Trade Practices Acts frequently address consumer rights and remedies for unsatisfactory automobile repair.[6] Massachusetts has a state statute that mandates that any work not performed in a competent manner must be redone at no charge to the consumer.[7] State regulations also frequently require that the consumer be given a written repair estimate upon request. In Massachusetts, the automobile repair shop must get your permission before going ahead and doing the work if it is more than $10 above the estimate. Authorization may be by telephone or in person. However, if the mechanic has received no written or verbal authorization before going ahead with the higher-price repairs, the consumer is not required to pay for the unauthorized work.

If a repair shop represents to the consumer that certain repairs are necessary or desirable and that is not the case, the shop will be liable for unfair and deceptive trade practices. You have a right to get the old parts back from a repair shop. In California, consumers are entitled to a written estimate for repair work with no additional charges unless you approve, a detailed invoice of work done and parts supplied, and the return of replaced parts. California consumers can learn more about these remedies by calling the Bureau of Auto Repair at 1-800-952-5210.

Lemon Laws

My American experience with a lemon automobile occurred when I served as a clerk for a federal judge for the Tenth Circuit the U.S. Court of Appeals in

Denver. My defective car was always in the shop and was a textbook case of a lemon. I ended up taking a bus to the Denver federal court building each day because my car was so unreliable.

Virtually every state has a lemon law, and many of those statutes cover used cars as well as new cars. A lemon automobile is a vehicle with a substantial defect that the dealer cannot repair after a designated number of attempts. Lemon laws require dealers to perform a specific number of repairs (usually three or four) for the same substantial defect before the consumer is entitled to a refund or replacement vehicle. State lemon law statutes were enacted so that you receive a refund or replacement when repairing a vehicle is fruitless. Check your state's lemon laws to determine your rights and remedies.

Consumer Rights for Used Car Buyers

Every state has specific statutes protecting used car buyers, though your rights vary significantly by state. Massachusetts's Used Car Warranty Law (M.G.L. ch. 90 §7N1/4) gives consumers a wide array of remedies. As in many states, if the dealer does not refund or replace the vehicle, you have the right to arbitration.

The Right to a Refund for Used Cars

Under the Massachusetts Used Car Rule, consumers have a right to a refund if a defect that impairs safety or use of the vehicle arose during the warranty period and the defect continued to exist after either (1) three or more repair attempts were made for the same defect or (2) the vehicle was out of service for repair of any defect for a cumulative total of ten business days. Consumers are given thirty-, sixty-, or ninety-day warranties, depending upon the age of the vehicle and its mileage. Massachusetts extends the warranty period one day for each day your car is in the repair shop. In addition, the warranty is extended another thirty days after the completion of any repair attempt for any defect. No consumer wants to have joint custody of her car with her mechanic. The lemon law gives consumers recourse when the dealer cannot fix the problem.

Lemon Law Rights and Remedies

If the dealer does not issue you a refund, you can have your lemon automobile case decided by an arbitrator in many states. If your vehicle fails inspection within seven days and repair would cost more than 10 percent of the purchase price, you are entitled to a full refund so long as you return the vehicle to the dealer in fourteen days. Keep in mind that under the lemon law, you have the burden of showing that you have a right to a refund or replacement. In every state, the consumer has the burden of proof in demonstrating that substantial defects existed at the time of sale. A dealer is not responsible for defects caused by the consumer's own negligent maintenance or subsequent accidents. Most states allow a dealer a "reasonable number" of attempts to repair the defect within a limited time period before refunding the buyer's money. In Massachusetts, the limit is three repair attempts within a ten-business day interval.

No "As Is" Sales

Dealers cannot sell a car "as is," "with all faults," or with a "50-50" warranty in Massachusetts. The implied warranty of merchantability requires dealers to deliver cars that work for a reasonable time. If they do not comply with this implied warranty of being at least fair/average or not objectionable in the trade, you get your money back. You can learn about your state's provisions by consulting with your state attorney general. If you visit Autopedia's website, you will find an excellent summary of lemon law rights and remedies in your jurisdiction (http://autopedia.com/html/HotLinks_Lemon2.html). Used car warranty law information is provided at every state's website. If you do not have a computer, you can call the attorney general's consumer protection division. In Massachusetts, you can also call the Department of the Attorney General's Consumer Hotline at 1-617-727-8400.

Which Vehicles Are Covered?

In general, lemon laws cover vehicles used for "personal, family, or household purposes" but not vehicles that are agricultural implements. Many lemon laws do not apply to motorcycles, mopeds, all-terrain vehicles, or snowmobiles. Consult your jurisdiction's lemon laws to determine whether used vehicles are excluded. Florida's lemon law, for example, does not cover the following vehicles:

- Trucks weighing more than 10,000 pounds gross vehicle weight;
- Off-road vehicles;
- Vehicles purchased for purposes of resale;
- Motorcycles and mopeds; and
- The living facilities of recreational vehicles.

Dealer-owned vehicles and demonstrators may also be covered, as well as the portion of motor homes used for habitation. Most lemon laws cover leases as well as purchases. Lemon laws are generally for new cars, but a number of states—including Massachusetts—have separate statutes covering used vehicles.

How Long Does Lemon Law Coverage Last?

New car buyers are protected under the Massachusetts lemon law against serious defects in their new vehicle for one year or 15,000 miles, whichever comes first. State laws vary significantly, but usually a lemon law will apply for a minimum of a one-year period for new vehicles. The federal Magnuson-Moss Warranty Act and UCC Article 2 apply to all vehicles, so even if your state has no applicable lemon law remedy, you may find another remedy under federal or state statute.

Required Notice to Manufacturer or Dealer

Consumers who seek lemon law protection are required to notify the seller. Who is to be notified varies significantly from state to state. Most states require that notice be given either to the dealer or the manufacturer, although some states require that only the dealer be notified and others require notice to the manufacturer. Your lemon law notice (or manufacturer) must be in writing; some states require that notice be made by certified mail.

What Makes a Car a Lemon?

Most state lemon laws declare the vehicle a lemon after three or more major repairs, or if the vehicle has been out of service for more than thirty days. Idaho, for example, presumes that a car is a lemon if the nonconformity has been subjected to four or more repair attempts or at least one repair attempt if the defect is likely to cause serious injury. Idaho's lemon law also considers a car to be a lemon if it has been out of service thirty or more business days (Idaho Code §48.901). Ohio's lemon law gives the seller three attempts to repair the same substantial nonconformity or at least eight repairs of any nonconformity before requiring the seller to replace or refund the purchase price (Ohio Rev. Stat. Ann. §48.901). You will need to consult your state's lemon law to determine what makes a vehicle a lemon and how many chances a seller has to repair a substantial defect.

Remedies for Lemon Automobile Sales

New car dealers or manufacturers have the legal duty to repair, at no charge, any defect that substantially impairs the vehicle's use, market value, or safety. They must fix substantial defects within a reasonable time. All lemon laws give the consumer rights and remedies if all the required attempts fail. A number of lemon laws also give the dealer a last chance to cure defects. Massachusetts consumers are required to give the seller an additional seven-day window to fix the car. If the dealer or manufacturer fails to fix the car after that final chance, the consumer is entitled to a refund or replacement.

Most jurisdictions reimburse consumers for collateral and incidental charges minus a reasonable use allowance. About half of the lemon law statutes also hold out the possibility of attorney fees and costs. A number of states assess double or treble damages as statutory punitive damages for bad faith tactics such as stalling tactics, frivolous defenses, or unfair or deceptive practices.

Dealer's Defenses against Lemon Laws

The buyer has the evidentiary burden of proving that the manufacturer or dealer, rather than the buyer's own misuse or abuse, caused the substantial defects to the car. A dealer is not responsible for defects caused by an independent accident unrelated to any mechanical defect present at the time of the sale. Similarly, a dealer is not liable for damages caused by the consumer's accident, neglect, abuse, or modifications. Many lemon laws will not apply to problems caused by repairs or modifications made by unauthorized service agents.

Giving timely notice is a prerequisite for any remedy for breach of the sales contract for a new car. If the consumer does not give the dealer proper written notice, the consumer is barred from a remedy under Article 2 of the UCC, the Magnuson-Moss Warranty Act, and the state's lemon law. You will have no lemon law protection if you cannot show that your car's substantial mechanical problems were reported to the seller, dealer, or service agent during your state's lemon law rights period. You will most likely report substantial defects to the dealer, though you can also give notice to the manufacturer or its authorized service agent. The seller is entitled to notice under UCC Article 2 as well. Your notice should detail the number of repair attempts, the dates the car was out of service, and other details of the failure of repairs and be sent by certified mail to negate problems of proof. The Florida attorney general offers good advice for consumers desiring lemon law protection in any jurisdiction:

> Consumers should *keep records* of all repairs and maintenance. A written repair order should be obtained from the service agent (dealer) for each examination or repair under the warranty. The consumer should make note of the following: the date the vehicle was taken in for repair; the date that they were notified that work was completed; and, the odometer mileage when the vehicle was taken to the shop and when it was picked up after repair. Consumers should keep all receipts or invoices for payment of expenses related to the purchase/ lease of the vehicle and to any repair.[8]

Every state requires a consumer to give the dealership or manufacturer an opportunity to fix the defective vehicle. Pennsylvania consumers, for example, may recover for "any losses due to nonconformity of such vehicle as a result of the manufacturer's failure to comply with" that state's lemon law.[9]

Fraudulent Automobile Sales
Too many car sales involve fraud, deception, or unfair conduct. In Hurricane Katrina, more than half a million vehicles were damaged or destroyed.[10] Unscrupulous dealers sold these vehicles to consumers without notice that they had suffered water damage. Consumers are entitled to the full history of whether the car has been wrecked or salvaged or has a history of mechanical problems.

Auto Title Pawns
These transactions are recent phenomena in which the car owner pawns title to the car in exchange for a sum of cash. The effective interest rate of an auto title pawn can be astronomical (sometimes over 900 percent). If the

consumer falls behind on the monthly payments, the car will be at risk of re-possession, no matter how much has already been repaid on the loan.

What Is a Bill of Sale?

A bill of sale is a writing that provides evidence of a sale. Bills of sale are commonly used, and required, as evidence of the sale of big-ticket items such as automobiles. You need to check with your state's department of motor vehicles to see what the requirements are for a bill of sale. The Massachusetts Registry of Motor Vehicles, for example, requires proof of the sale between the buyer and the seller before an automobile, a truck, or any other vehicle may be registered.

In Massachusetts and many other states, the buyer will need a bill of sale to prove ownership if there is no registration title.[11] Massachusetts requires the following information in a bill of sale: (1) name(s), signature(s), and address of buyer(s); (2) name(s), signature(s), and address of seller(s); (3) date of purchase; (4) purchase price; and (5) identification information (vehicle identification number, or VIN, make, model, and year).

A VIN is analogous to a vehicle's fingerprints. Vehicles made from 1981 on are assigned a number composed of seventeen digits and letters. My blue 1990 Honda has this VIN: 1 HG037148LA042112. The first character in a VIN signifies the country of origin. The digit "1" means that the vehicle was manufactured in the United States. The second character is a unique identifier given to the automobile manufacturer. *H* stands for Honda. Each number or character in the seventeen-character sequence has a meaning. Vehicles built before 1980 will have a shorter VIN sequence.

The VIN can be found on the driver's side of the dashboard and is visible through the windshield. The dealership or car manufacturer can help you locate the VIN if it is in another location.[12] Before you purchase a used car, it is also good idea to get a vehicle history report. If the used automobile was involved in an accident or was flooded in a hurricane, there will be a notation in the history report. Carfax.com will do vehicle history reports to determine whether the car you are thinking of buying was a lemon, previously salvaged, flooded in a hurricane, rebuilt, involved in an accident, or previously leased or rented and a variety of other important historical facts. Mechanics are required by law to record the VINs for work done on a vehicle.

Below is an example of a bill of sale that will be legally sufficient in many states.

Example: Bill of Sale for an Automobile
State of Vermont
County of Chittenden

I, _____ (Seller), whose address is _____, in consideration of the payment of the sum of $3,000 agree to sell my blue 1990 Honda Accord,

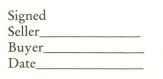

VIN 1HG037148LA042112 to _____ *(Buyer) whose address is*
_____.

Signed
Seller_____
Buyer_____
Date_____

Proving an Automobile Is a Lemon

Assuming your vehicle fits within your state's lemon law and you have
proper documentation, determine how many times your automobile has
been back to the service department for the same problem. Check your state
statute as to how many chances a service department has to solve the problem. If the lemon law is a three-strikes law, you have a remedy if the vehicle
is still not fixed for the same problem. You should first send a registered or
certified notice to the manufacturer. You can find the address for giving notice in the owner's manual that came with your vehicle.

The consumer's evidentiary burden also varies from state to state. A
Florida court held that a consumer-buyer need not establish the specific
cause of problems with a motor vehicle, only the existence of problems.[13]
California's lemon law provides for a refund if a car is repaired four times
for the same trouble or is in the repair shop for thirty days or more during
the first year of ownership.[14] New Jersey's lemon law defines a lemon vehicle as a "defect or condition, which substantially impairs the use, value or
safety of a motor vehicle."[15]

New Jersey courts have adopted the common law doctrine of "shaken
faith." Whether a defect rises to the level of an actionable nonconformity
depends on whether it "shakes the buyer's confidence" in the goods.[16] New
Jersey presumes that a defect is actionable if a manufacturer is unable to correct nonconformity within a reasonable time after the owner has made three
or more unsuccessful repair attempts or the vehicle "is out of service by reason of repair for one or more nonconformities for a total of twenty days."[17]
New Jersey claimants may recover a full refund of automobile plus finance
charges less a reasonable allowance for vehicle use.[18] Attorney's fees may
also be available to a successful lemon law claimant.[19] In one recent case, a
consumer sued the manufacturer after discovering that the frame was bent
on his "new" vehicle. The plaintiff was awarded a full refund, indemnification of his finance contract, costs, and attorney fees.[20]

Informal Dispute Resolution

Jurisdictions will sometimes require that the consumer submit to an informal
dispute settlement procedure by the manufacturer. The manufacturer's dispute resolution mechanism must comply with FTC regulations (16 C.F.R.
703). In many states, the manufacturer has ten days from the time the buyer
provides notice of their defective car to direct the consumer to a repair facil-

ity, and if the problem is not rectified in another ten-day period, the consumer will receive a purchase price refund or a replacement vehicle. Many states have arbitration programs if the manufacturer does not provide a refund or a replacement vehicle. Consumers in Florida may call the Lemon Law Hotline (1-800-321-5366); out-of-state consumers may call 1-850-488-2221. "State-certified" means the manufacturer's program meets certain state and federal requirements; it does *not* mean that the program is administered or sponsored by the state of Florida. In Massachusetts all dealers are required to participate in state-certified used car arbitration if requested by the consumer. A consumer, however, must assert his rights to repurchase within six months from the date of original delivery of a used vehicle. In Massachusetts, used car arbitrations are convened by professional arbitrators chosen by the secretary of consumer affairs and business regulation (M.G.L.A. ch. 90, §7N).

In Florida, if a manufacturer has no state-certified program, or if the manufacturer has a state-certified program but the program fails to make a decision in forty days or the consumer is not satisfied with the state-certified program's decision, the dispute must be submitted to the Florida New Motor Vehicle Arbitration Board, which is administered by the office of the attorney general. Florida consumers initiate the process by contacting the Lemon Law Hotline (mentioned in the previous paragraph) to obtain a request for arbitration form. If the arbitral board determines the vehicle is a lemon, the consumer is awarded either a replacement vehicle or a refund. Lemon laws frequently reduce the refund according to how long the consumer has used the vehicle. Minnesota permits car manufacturers to require consumers to submit to an informal dispute settlement mechanism before bringing an action in state court.[21]

Resale of a Lemon

Lemon laws require a full written disclosure and warranty for defects if an automobile was previously classified as a lemon. Illinois requires the seller to give a twelve-month or a 12,000-mile warranty on a resold lemon. Some states, such as Iowa, require that the title indicate the vehicle was previously returned as a lemon. Florida's lemon law requires any dealer ordered to buy back the vehicle to notify the office of the attorney general of the buyback and to have the vehicle's title branded "manufacturer buyback" by the Florida Department of Highway Safety and Motor Vehicles. Florida publishes a list of automobiles bought back under that state's lemon law. To see if any used car you purchased was a buyback, go to http://myfloridalegal.com/resale.nsf/VINLiabMan.

Variations in Used Car Lemon Law Coverage

States vary significantly in whether they give lemon law relief to the purchasers of used cars. Consumers in California and Virginia have rather limited lemon law protection for used vehicles.[22] New Mexico enacted lemon law protection for used cars in 2004. New Mexico, like New York, requires all used car dealers to give a warranty for any car they sell. New Mexico's statute covers the first 500 miles or fifteen days, whichever occurs first. Pennsylvania's lemon law covers leased automobiles. Check your state's lemon law to determine its sphere of application. Many states will have a separate lemon law statute governing used vehicles.

Massachusetts requires dealers selling vehicles for $700 or more to give a warranty for all parts and labor for use or safety defects according to the mileage on the odometer: (1) under 40,000 miles—ninety days or 3,750 miles; (2) 40,000–79,999 miles—sixty days or 2,500 miles; and (3) 80,000–124,999 miles—thirty days or 1,250 miles.[23] In Massachusetts, the consumer can get a refund only if they have given the dealer three repair attempts for the same defect or the car was out of service for eleven business days (M.G.L.A. 7N-1/4). The Massachusetts Lemon Aid Law gives the consumer a speedier refund if the car fails inspection within seven days of purchase and if inspection-related repairs are going to cost more than 10 percent of the purchase price. To obtain this protection, the consumer must return the car to the seller (dealer or private party) within fourteen days with a written repair estimate signed by the inspector and stating why the car failed inspection.

New York's Used Car Lemon Law provides a legal remedy for buyers or lessees of used cars that turn out to be lemons. The statute prohibits dealers from selling cars on an "as is" basis. At a minimum, used car dealers must give a written warranty guaranteeing that the dealer must repair, free of charge, any defects in covered parts or, at the dealer's option, reimburse the buyer for the reasonable costs of such repairs. As with the new car lemon laws, the consumer is entitled to a full refund if the dealer is unable to repair the car after a reasonable number of attempts.[24]

The Law of Car Repair

It is important to note that consumers who pay for repairs that do not fix the problem should not have to pay an additional amount to fix any shoddy repair work. In Massachusetts, for example, a state statute gives consumers a right to require the repair shop to do the repair correctly at no additional charge. States vary significantly in having special consumer protection governing repairs.

Warranties for Used Cars

Two kinds of warranties apply to used car sales, *warranties of title* and *warranties of performance*. A car seller, for example, makes a warranty that the title is clear. If you are arrested by a state trooper because you purchased a car with a defective title, you are entitled to damages (see UCC §2-312).

If you develop a problem with a used vehicle after purchase, it may be covered by a UCC Article 2 warranty governing performance (UCC

§2-313, §2-314, or §2-315). There are two kinds of performance warranties, *express* and *implied*. An express warranty is any affirmation, promise, or description of a car's qualities that goes to the "basis of the bargain." A car dealer does not need to use the word *guarantee* to be liable for express warranties. In contrast, an implied warranty is based on the idea that the car be at least able to pass without objection in the trade, be of fair, average quality, and conform to promises or affirmations of fact made about it (UCC §2-314). Finally, there is an implied warranty of fitness for a particular purpose, which only arises if the car seller "has reason to know any particular purpose" for which the car was to be used and the buyer relied on the seller's expertise in selecting the vehicle (UCC §2-315). Massachusetts, for example, does not permit used car dealers to sell cars "as is" or "with all faults." Any seller or manufacturer of goods and services is prohibited from excluding "any implied warranties of merchantability and fitness for a particular purpose or modify[ing] the consumer's remedies for breach of those warranties" (M.G.L.A. ch. 106, §2-316A).

A growing number of states are following Massachusetts's example in requiring dealers to give consumers minimum warranties for used cars. In Connecticut, for example, consumers receive an implied warranty on any used vehicle so long as it is less than seven years old and costs $3,000 or more. Keep in mind that this statutory protection is only available if you purchase a vehicle from a *dealer*, rather than from a private individual. The warranty period for vehicles costing between $3,000 and $5,000 is for 1,500 miles or thirty days. If the used vehicle costs $5,000 or greater, the warranty period is extended to sixty days or 3,000 miles, whichever comes first.

Connecticut's state statute governing used car warranties requires a dealer to pay for all repairs necessary to make a vehicle operational and safe; the consumer incurs no costs. Each day the car is in the shop, your warranty period increases by a day. Some dealers also provide for a longer warranty period. Whatever the period of warranty, the dealer must disclose it in writing on the buyer's guide window sticker. The window sticker rule is required by federal law rather than state consumer law.

What to Do: Choosing an Automobile Repair Shop

Consumers can best protect themselves by securing written estimates and choosing an automobile repair shop with a reputation for good faith and fair dealing. This section explains how to protect your rights when repairing vehicles, based on the guidelines developed by the Federal Trade Commission, the National Association of Attorneys General, and the American Automobile Association to help consumers in vehicle repairs:

- Ask for recommendations from friends, family, and other people you trust. Look for an auto repair shop before you need one to avoid being rushed into a last-minute decision.

- Shop around by telephone for the best deal and compare warranty policies on repairs.
- Ask to see current licenses if state or local law requires repair shops to be licensed or registered. In addition, your state attorney general's office or local consumer protection agency may know whether there is a record of complaints about a particular repair shop.
- Make sure the shop will honor your vehicle's warranty.

What to Do: Repair Charges

- Require the repair shop to give you an estimate of the costs of repair before you leave your car for work. Get written estimates of what the repairs will cost and how the shop prices each repair. Ask in advance whether there will be a charge for diagnostics to determine what is wrong with your car or truck. Ask whether the amount charged is the actual time spent on the repair or a standard published rate for a type of repair.
- When you pick up the car, go over the repairs with the service manager. Determine whether each repair is itemized and how much of the bill was allocated to parts versus labor.
- If you need expensive or complicated repairs, or if you have questions about recommended work, consider a second estimate.
- Be sure that the written estimate specifically addresses the parts to be replaced, the condition of the vehicle before you gave it to them, and the projected labor charge. Be sure to get a signed copy of the estimate for significant repairs, other than a minor tire repair and the like.
- Make it clear that the shop is to contact you before proceeding with work exceeding the written estimate. Most states impose this requirement by statute.
- Ask whether the amount charged reflects the actual time spent on the repair or a standard published rate for a type of repair.
- Ask in advance whether the repair shop is using new parts or reconditioned parts. The FTC Used Car Rule distinguishes between new, remanufactured, rebuilt, reconditioned, and salvaged parts:

    New—either the vehicle manufacturer or an independent company defines new parts as those made to original manufacturer's specifications. Your state may require repair shops to disclose to you if new parts are not used in the repair of your vehicle.

    Remanufactured, rebuilt, and reconditioned—These terms denote parts restored to a working order but not classifiable as new parts. Many manufacturers offer a warranty covering replacement parts, but not the labor to install them.

    Salvage—These are used parts taken from another vehicle without alteration. Salvage parts may be the only source for certain items, though their reliability is seldom guaranteed.

What to Do When You Pick Up Your Vehicle from the Repair Shop

- Go over the written repair order that describes each repair, the parts supplied, the cost of each part, labor charges, and the vehicle's odometer reading when you took your car in as well as the condition of the vehicle after the work was completed.
- Be sure that you receive the replaced part, which is a requirement in nearly every state. States enacted statutes about replaced parts because so many repair shops were untruthful about replacing parts or pretending to do work.

What to Do: Extended Warranties and Service Contracts

Many vehicle dealers and others sell optional contracts—service contracts issued by vehicle manufacturers or independent companies. Not all service contracts are the same; prices vary and usually are negotiable. To help decide whether to purchase a service contract, consider:

- The cost;
- The repairs to be covered;
- Whether coverage overlaps coverage provided by any other warranty;
- The deductible;
- Where the repairs are to be performed;
- Procedures required to file a claim, such as prior authorization for specific repairs or meeting required vehicle maintenance schedules;
- Whether repair costs are paid directly by the company to the repair shop or whether you will have to pay first and get reimbursed; and
- The reputation of the service contract company. Check it out with your state attorney general's office or local consumer protection agency.

What to Do: Resolving a Dispute Regarding Billing, Quality of Repairs, or Warranties

- Document all transactions as well as dates, times, expenses, and the names of people you dealt with.
- Talk to the shop manager or owner first. If that does not work, contact your attorney general or local consumer protection agency for help. These offices may have information on alternative dispute resolution programs in your community. Another option is to file a claim in small claims court. You do not need an attorney to do this.[25]

If a repair shop tells you that parts used in the repair of your automobile were new when actually they were reconditioned or used, you will have a cause of action for fraud. This misrepresentation will also constitute a violation of your state's UDTPA (see Appendix A). As a result, you may recover reasonable attorney's fees. Treble damages are also recoverable in such egregious circumstances.

What to Do: Filing an NHTSA Complaint

If you purchased an automobile with a safety defect, you may file a complaint with the National Highway Transportation Safety Agency (NHTSA) of the U.S. Department of Transportation (DOT). Congress gave NHTSA the authority to investigate unsafe vehicles. You can contact NHTSA's DOT Vehicle Safety Hotline at 1-888-327-4236. A representative from NHTSA will record your complaint; these data are useful in determining whether there is a design defect.

NHTSA will have its own engineers do testing. If they determine there is a serious safety-related defect, the agency will ask the car or vehicle manufacturer to recall the vehicles. In many cases, the manufacturer will order a recall prior to a demand by the government. As with the FTC and the CPSC, the NHTSA has no jurisdiction to investigate individual complaints or institute actions for a consumer harmed by a defective vehicle. If a remedy is ordered, it is for all buyers of a particular line of vehicles. For further information, you can email NHTSA at webmaster@nhtsa.dot.gov. You need to provide basic information such as the year, make, and model of the vehicle and the nature of the complaint.

Leasing a Car

Consumer lessors are required to give you Truth in Lending Act disclosures if you lease an automobile or other vehicle. The statutory purpose of TILA was to improve consumers' awareness of credit terms. Congress sought to reduce the uninformed use of credit and protect consumers against unfair credit billing and credit card practices.[26] The federal Consumer Leasing Act (CLA) also empowers the consumer by providing her with mandatory disclosures about the costs and terms of a vehicle lease.

A simple lease consists of an agreement between a lessor and a lessee. The lessor must give disclosures to the consumer lessee. If there are multiple lessors, each lessor is required make the disclosures. The primary obligor is the consumer-lessee who receives the disclosures from the lessor. Lessors (such as dealers) must make mandatory disclosures *prior* to the consummation of a consumer lease. Lessors are required to make easy-to-understand disclosures as to (1) the total amount of the initial payment; (2) the number and amounts of monthly payments; (3) all fees charged, including license fees and taxes; and (4) the charges for default or late payments. A lessor who does not give adequate disclosures or sends faulty notices of repossession is liable for actual and punitive damages as well as attorneys' fees.

Regulation M of the CLA, issued by the board of governors of the Federal Reserve System, implements the consumer leasing provisions of TILA (12 C.F.R. Part 213). Congress enacted the CLA to ensure that consumer lessees receive meaningful disclosures enabling them to do comparison shopping. Among other things, Congress sought to limit the amount of balloon payments in consumer transactions. Consumer leases are classifiable as either open-ended or closed. An open-ended lease determines the lessee's liability by measuring the difference between the residual and realized value of the leased property at the end of the lease term. Any lease not classifiable as an open-ended lease is treated as a closed lease (see Regulation M, 12 C.F.R. §213[d] and §213[j]).

Regulation M requires vehicle lessors to provide consumer lessees with a series of mandatory disclosures prior to entering into a lease agreement and dictates the form of the disclosures. The disclosures must be given either in a separate statement or in the contract or other document evidencing the lease. The lessor must provide you, the consumer, with "Federal Consumer Leasing Act Disclosures" on page 1 of the leasing agreement or form. Other disclosures, called "nonsegregated disclosures," may occur in other places on the lease agreement. The purpose of these disclosures is to enable you to compare lease offers and negotiate a lease that best fits your needs, budget, and driving patterns. The Federal Reserve Board has a good explanation of the mandatory disclosures required by Regulation M on its website. The lessor is required to explain mandatory disclosures in a user-friendly format, in context.[27]

Example: Unreasonable Fees Imposed in Renting a Vehicle. In a 2005 Connecticut case, a car rental company installed global positioning system (GPS) devices in its rental cars. When a vehicle exceeded 79 mph for more than two minutes, the device would emit a signal generating a fax report indicating the vehicle, time, location, and duration of the occurrence. Consumers were charged $150 for each two-minute occurrence that the vehicle was driven 80 mph or more. The rental company would assess a fee of $150 and immediately charge it to the customer's credit or debit card. A number of consumers testified that they were not given prior notice that the company used the GPS to assess speeding charges on their debit or charge cards. The consumer's first notice of the surcharge was when they discovered the rental company's automatic charges after reaching the spending limit on their credit cards.

Connecticut's Commissioner of Consumer Protection filed suit under that state's UDTPA. The commissioner found that the car rental company committed unfair trade practices by applying excessive fees, which were illegal penalties. Moreover, the commissioner found that the car company failed to give consumers adequate notice of its means of penalizing them for exceeding the speed limit. The Connecticut Supreme Court upheld the finding in the commissioner's original administrative hearing that the $150 was a penalty because, even assuming the worst-case scenario, the added wear and tear on the vehicle would be approximately 37 cents. The car rental company was ordered to refund consumers for the amounts charged and to cease and desist using this means of enforcing the speed limit restrictions

(*American Car Rental Inc. v. Commissioner of Consumer Protection,* Case No. SC 17241 [Conn. Sup. Ct., 2005]).

Disclosure Requirements

The federal TILA requires that all disclosures be clearly and conspicuously displayed (see 15 U.S.C. §1632). Two terms, "annual percentage rate" and "finance charge," must be highlighted in some way to make them more conspicuous than other terms. Conspicuousness is generally met by using a contrasting font or boldface type to set off the text in a way that a reasonable consumer will notice. When negotiating consumer leases, as well as other consumer credit transactions governed by TILA, you must receive the following five mandatory disclosures:

Finance Charges. TILA dictates mandatory disclosures about the loan's finance charge that includes the sum of all charges, payable directly or indirectly by the person to whom the credit is extended, and imposed directly or indirectly by the creditor as an incident to the extension of credit.[28] The finance charge is defined as the cost of credit over the life of the loan, expressed as a dollar amount. Finance charges are expressed as an "annual percentage rate." The finance charge disclosure need not be made if the amount financed is less than $75 and the finance charge is not greater than $5. Alternatively, a disclosure about finance charge is required if the amount financed exceeds $75 and the finance charge exceeds $7.50.

Annual Percentage Rate. The annual percentage rate, also known as the APR, is simply the cost of credit expressed as a percentage, considering all the additional costs added to the loan. For example, a loan of $200,000 with $5,000 in closing costs at an interest rate of 7.5 percent would yield a monthly payment of $1,433.39. However, since only $200,000 is being paid off, the APR would be 7.75 percent. Another way to look at this is that the APR of a loan without any additional costs would be the same as the interest rate of the loan (see Regulation Z, 226.22).

The annual percentage yield is similar to the annual percentage rate; however, it is the rate at which you pay off the loan when compound interest is taken into effect.

Amount Financed. The amount financed is also expressed as a dollar amount. It is calculated by taking the principal amount of the loan and subtracting those amounts that are considered to be finance charges. For example, you take out a $100,000 note and deed of trust on your home. The 5 points ($5,000) charged on this loan are financed and are therefore included in the $100,000 principal on the note. However, since the five points are defined as part of the finance charge, they are subtracted from the $100,000 in determining the amount financed ($100,000 − $5,000 = $95,000).

Schedule of Payments. The schedule of payments tell you the day of the month, timing, number, and dollar amount of payments due over the entire course of the loan. For example, you are required to make one payment of $500 on January 5, 1996, and fifty payments of $100 on the fifth of each month, beginning on February 5, 1996.

Total of Payments. The total of payments is always expressed as a specific dollar amount. It represents the total dollar cost of the loan to you, assuming all payments are made on time. The total of payments is calculated by adding up all payments disclosed in the schedule of payments (see OSC 226.18 [h]).[29]

A lessee entering into a closed-end (installment) lending agreement has a number of procedural rights under TILA's consumer protections, which are in the form of disclosures about the key terms for consumer credit. Before you sign the agreement, the creditor must give you written disclosure of the five mandatory terms of the agreement discussed above. TILA requires that all disclosures be clearly and conspicuously displayed (see 15 U.S.C. §1632). If a lender violates TILA's requirements, you may be entitled to statutory damages and attorneys fees. You will certainly be entitled to statutory damages if these disclosures were not made *prior* to you entering into a credit contract governed by TILA.

Dealership Financing and Direct Lending

Automobile dealerships frequently enable consumers to purchase or lease automobiles through two means: (1) "direct lending" or (2) "dealership financing." In direct lending, the consumer first selects a vehicle and enters into a contract with a dealership; then she obtains a loan directly from a finance company, bank, or credit union. "Dealership financing" is a form of direct lending in which a buyer and the car dealership enter into a contract in which the buyer agrees to pay the amount financed, plus an agreed-upon finance charge, over a period of time. In many cases, the dealer will assign the contract to its closely connected finance company, a bank or credit union, which services the account and collects payments.

Financial institutions and companies extending credit are subject to TILA, which is a federal credit law that requires mandatory disclosures about the true interest charges and payment conditions of a loan. Section 106(a) of the Truth in Lending Act, classified as 15 U.S.C. §1605(a), defines the "finance charge" in consumer credit transactions to include all charges incident to the extension of credit, but to exclude charges of a type payable in a comparable cash transaction.

Consumers have three days to reconsider a signed credit agreement and cancel the loan without penalty. This "right to rescind" or "right to cancel" is guaranteed by TILA. Consumers have a right of rescission in any credit transactions in which a security interest is retained in property used as the consumer's principal dwelling (15 U.S.C. §1635; 12 C.F.R. Parts 226.15[b] 226.17[d]). You have a right to rescind for any reason, but only if you are using your principal residence—whether it is a condominium, mobile home, or houseboat—as collateral, not a vacation or second home, to guarantee repayment. In any action subject to rescission, the creditor must deliver to the lender two copies of the notice of right to cancel form (12 C.F.R. Part 226.23[b] [1]).

The lender must disclose the schedule of payments. The schedule must include the day of the month, timing, number, and dollar amount of payments due over the entire course of the loan. You will be entitled to monetary damages from the creditor if they have not made the mandatory disclosures.

Motor Vehicle Retail Sales Finance Act

Many states have enacted a Motor Vehicle Retail Sales Finance Act, which gives you rights and remedies if the dealer fails to (1) sign and provide you with a retail installment contract before you sign the lease on the car, (2) provide you with the purchase order containing all the essential provisions before the contract was signed, and (3) accurately reflect the agreed-on value of your trade-in vehicle. Violations of the Motor Vehicle Retail Sales Finance Act will also likely violate your state's Unfair and Deceptive Trade Practices Act. In addition, you may have a common law action for the tort of fraud if a dealer misrepresented the price of your vehicle, inflated the price of the vehicle, deflated the credit to be given for your trade-in, misrepresented the terms of the loan on the contract, or other unfair or deceptive acts. If the dealer sold you an unsafe car, you may have a cause of action for automobile products liability.

Automobile Products Liability

Automobiles are a leading source of deadly product defects. Ralph Nader shook up the automobile industry with his critical study of vehicle safety: "It is clear Detroit today is designing automobiles for style, cost, performance and calculated obsolescence, but not—despite the 5,000,000 reported accidents, nearly 40,000 fatalities, 110,000 permanent disabilities and 1,500,000 injuries yearly—for safety."[30] His 1965 book, *Unsafe at Any Speed: The Designed-in Dangers of the American Automobile,* charged General Motors with marketing dangerously defective Corvairs that had a tendency to tip over because of their back-loaded design. Each year, millions of Americans suffer disabling injuries, and tens of thousands lose their lives in motor vehicle accidents.[31] However, products liability lawsuits are filed only when those dangerously defective designs cause tragic accidents. Automobile products liability cases are no exception to the rule that you will need an experienced lawyer to pursue a claim against a seller. Automobile products cases typically involve complicated discovery requests, expensive depositions, and protracted litigation over expert testimony. Therefore, finding representation is imperative.

Example: Automobile Products Liability. In *Durrill v. Ford Motor Company*, Devary Durrill was driving her Ford Mustang II on a four-lane highway when she had car trouble.[32] After she pulled over to the shoulder of the road, her Mustang II was struck from behind, causing it to roll over and burst into flames. Her second- and third-degree burns, which covered 80 percent of her body, were so devastating that her rescuer was initially unable to determine whether she was male or female. The seventeen-year-old girl survived another week in excruciating pain, and then died. Her nurse described the girl's horrifying injuries: "Her hair had all been burned off, like she was bald-headed. You lose many fluids from the burns, and it would crust up on her face. It was kind of red, black, swollen, and horrible. Her arms, legs and chest were simply charred. Her kidneys shut down and her heart failed."

As early as 1968, more than fifteen years before the *Durrill* case, Ford was aware that hundreds of people had suffered fatal burns from postcollision fires in its vehicles. Thus, Ford Motor Company had prior knowledge that its entire line of vehicles was prone to fuel-fed fires. Moreover, Ford's vice president testified that his company expected their fuel tanks to rupture at closing speeds of only 25 miles per hour. Ford's Chassis Research Department had advocated inexpensive changes that would have substantially reduced the risk of a fire hazard: bladder tanks, flak suits, and breakaway filler pipes. Nevertheless, Ford's chief executive officer, Lee Iacocca, personally lobbied President Richard Nixon to convince him to roll back proposed safety regulations.

The evidence that Ford saved $200 million over a three-year period by delaying its implementation of modifications to its fuel integrity system demonstrated its indifference to public safety. Ford had essentially the same fuel integrity system in the Mustang II as in the Pinto, but Ford chose not to warn Mustang II owners at the time it was notifying Pinto owners of the danger. When a manufacturer's profits are attributable to its willingness to market a product with a known defect, then punitive damages are appropriate.

In a Texas case, a 1977 Ford LTD automobile self-shifted from park to reverse due to a defect in the transmission, killing a fifty-two-year-old homemaker who left the vehicle to close a gate behind the car.[33] Ford had definite knowledge of hundreds of prior complaints of its cars self-shifting from park to reverse due to vibration.[34] Eighty-nine prior similar self-shifting accidents resulted in serious injuries or death.[35] Punitive damages were awarded based upon interoffice communications showing that Ford received approximately six letters per month complaining about its defective transmissions, yet failed to take remedial steps to protect consumers.[36] The general principles of product liability discussed in Chapter 7 apply equally well in defective automobile cases. As in all product liability actions, you will need to retain a lawyer specializing in these cases.

Notes

1. Federal Trade Commission, "A Dealer's Guide to the Used Car Rule," available at http://www.ftc.gov/bcp/conline/pubs/buspubs/usedcarc.htm (accessed June 17, 2007).

2. Ibid.

3. Email interview with automobile salesman with three decades of experience selling used vehicles, August 7, 2006 (name of companies and dealers withheld at the request of the respondent).

4. Federal Trade Commission, "Buying a Used Car," available at http://www.ftc .gov/bcp/conline/pubs/autos/ucartip.htm (accessed August 13, 2006).

5. Better Business Bureau, "Buying a Used Car," available at http://www.bbb .org/alerts/article.asp?ID=432 (accessed June 17, 2007).

6. See, for example, M.G.L.A. ch. 93A (Massachusetts UDTPA).

7. Massachusetts Attorney General Regulations, 940 CMR 5.00.

8. Ibid.

9. 73 ATS. §1958.

10. Michigan Office of the Attorney General, http://www.michigan.gov/ag/ 0,1607,7-164—131983—,00.html

11. See Massachusetts RMV Bill of Sale, available at http://www.dmv.org/ma-massachusetts/bill-of-sale.phat (accessed June 17, 2007).

12. Autohopper, "What Are Vehicle Identification Numbers?" available at http:// www.autohopper.com/resources/articles/vehicle_identification_numbers.asat (accessed June 17, 2007).

13. *Mason v. Porsche Cars of North America, Inc.*, .688 So.2d 361 (Fla. Dist. Ct. App. 1997).

14. Frank Green, "Auto Lemon Law Needs Some Repairs, Rally Told," *San Diego Union-Tribune*, February 19, 1993, 1.

15. N.J.S.A. 56, sections 12–30.

16. See *Berrie v. Toyota Motor Sales, U.S.A., Inc.*, 267 N.J. Super. 152, 630 A.2d 1180, 1182 (N.J. Sup. Ct. App. Div. 1993).

17. N.J.S.A. 56, sections 12–33.

18. Ibid., 56, sections 12–32.

19. N.J.S.A. 56, sections 12–42, permitting claimant to recover attorneys fees and costs in court actions brought before the New Jersey Superior Court or in the Division of Consumer Affairs in the Department of Law and Public Safety.

20. "Trials and Settlements Quarterly," *Michigan Lawyers Weekly* (August 18, 1997): B4.

21. Ibid.

22. Robin Leonard, *Money Troubles: Legal Strategies to Cope with Your Debt* (Berkeley, Calif.: Nolo Press, 2004), 1.

23. M.G.L.A. ch. 7N-1/4.

24. A fuller description of New York's used car lemon law is found at New York State Attorney General Elliot Spitzer's website, available at http://www.oag.state.ny .us/consumer/cars/usedqa.html (accessed March 30, 2007).

25. The source for the information in this section and more information on car repair may be found at the Connecticut attorney general's website, available at http:// www.ct.gov/ag/cwp/view.asp?A=2066andQ=292356 (accessed October 1, 2006). These tips were jointly drafted by the Federal Trade Commission, the National Association of Attorneys General, and the American Automobile Association.

26. 15 U.S.C §1601(A) (2006).

27. This form was developed by the Federal Reserve Board in a publication titled *Federal Consumer Leasing Act Disclosures*, available at http://www.federalreserve .gov/pubs/leasing/formce/default.htm (accessed October 31, 2005).

28. 15 U.S.C. §1605(A) (2006).

29. Clark County, Nevada, "What Is the Truth in Lending Act?" available at http://clarkcountylegal.com/tila.htm (accessed October 1, 2006) (discussing Regulation Z governing TILA).

30. Ralph Nader, *Unsafe at Any Speed: The Designed-In Dangers of the American Automobile* (New York: Grossman, 1965).

31. National Safety Council, Accident Facts, 78.

32. 714 S.W.2d 329 (Texas Ct. of App. 1985).

33. *Nowak v. Ford Motor Co.*, 638 S.W.2d 583 (Tex. Ct. App. 1982).

34. Ibid., 593.

35. Ibid., 594.

36. See *Ford Motor Co. v. Bartholomew*, 297 S.E.2d 675, 680 (Va. 1982), which upheld large compensatory damages based on a hidden defect in Ford transmissions that caused automobiles to self-shift from park to reverse.

9

Obtaining Credit

Consumer credit and consumer debt has always been a prevalent social problem throughout American history. Historians blame the panic of 1857 on a mountain of consumer and business debt that today looks more like a molehill.[1] In 1858, America had a debt load of $1.5 billion, or approximately $39 a person.[2] A recent empirical study uncovered nearly $2 trillion worth of credit card transactions each year.[3] Consumer credit debt nearly quadrupled from 1990 to 2002, from $173 billion to $661 billion.[4] Home equity lending quadrupled from $261 billion in 1993 to $1 trillion in 2003.[5] On the surface, all of this credit is beneficial because it enables buyers to finance transactions without paying the full cost for merchandise or services at the time of the transaction. The downside of credit is that consumers are often subjected to predatory rates and hidden unfair terms. Today, state as well as federal consumer laws protect consumers from such practices.

> Americans are often reminded of a golden age where we lived within our means. However, that is yet another myth of lost virtue. In reality, debt is as American as baseball and the Fourth of July. In fact, installment selling began in the last decades of the nineteenth century and automobile installment sales in the first decades of the twentieth century.[6]

State Usury Laws

The definition of usury varies significantly from state to state and changes in each historical epoch. The Christian fathers regarded usury as a sin: the first civil ban on interest-bearing loans was enacted by Charlemagne in Visigoth Catalonia.[7] The traditional ban on usury began to unravel during the Reformation with the rise of John Calvin.[8] Interest-bearing loans were first legitimated during the Age of the Enlightenment (1650–1800) through the influence of thinkers such as Jeremy Bentham and Adam Smith.[9] From the colonial period, consumer credit became emblematic of American society.[10]

Today, every U.S. jurisdiction has enacted a usury law that prohibits loans with interest rates beyond a certain level. However, those rates vary greatly from state to state, and some states have no usury limit at all. Colorado and Connecticut, for example, prohibit lenders from charging consumers an interest rate exceeding 12 percent annually on an unpaid balance. Maryland does not permit lenders to charge more than 16 percent per annum on the unpaid balance, whereas Indiana permits lenders to charge 21 percent.[11] For a complete list of usury interest maximums, see www.lectlaw.com/files/ban02.htm and www.debthelp-usa.info/reference/state-interest-rates.html.

Example: Violation of State Usury Law. In *Pyant v. Charles Todd, Inc.*, a consumer in Georgia contracted with a lender for a $3,100 second mortgage on the family's home at an annual interest rate of 60 percent. The mortgage provided for eighty-one payments of $158 and a smaller final payment for a total payback of $9,736. The consumer missed several payments and, as a result, the bank foreclosed the home and sold it for $4,700. The consumers charged the lender with implementing an interest rate that was usurious, violating the federal Truth in Lending Act (TILA) as well as the federal Fair Debt Collection Practices Act, and making a wrongful foreclosure of their home. The jury awarded the consumer $119,375, including $90,000 in punitive damages for the lender's unfair and deceptive credit practices.

Federal Regulation of Consumer Credit

I begin this chapter with an overview of the FTC's preeminent role in patrolling the consumer marketplace. I focus on practical, prescriptive advice on how to enlist the assistance of federal regulators and enforcement in vindicating your rights. My emphasis will be on what practical steps you can take as consumers complaining to agencies or filing private actions to supplement public consumer law enforcement.

I describe how consumers may recover damages against creditors that do not comply with the strict disclosure requirements of the Truth in Lending Act or Regulation Z (see 12 C.F.R.22 Part 6.1 et seq.). I also examine consumer rights in obtaining fair disclosures under both TILA and state law and how consumers can rescind consumer credit transactions as well as consumer leases if the statutorily mandated disclosures are not given.

Congress armed the Federal Trade Commission and other federal agencies with the jurisdiction to protect the consumer marketplace. The FTC is authorized to investigate "the organization, business, conduct, practices, and management of any person, partnership, or corporation engaged in or whose business affects commerce" (15 U.S.C. 46[a]). Consumer law has both a public and private component, as best illustrated by a recent U.S. Department of Justice (USDOJ) probe into the activities of a fraudulent lender. The USDOJ recently filed suit against a lender that discriminated based on national origin in one of its credit card programs. In that case, the lender required Spanish-language applicants to have a higher credit score than applicants applying on an English-language form. The lender also discriminated against Hispanics by offering lower credit limits and refusing to offer favorable credit promotions to Spanish-language account holders.

The FTC and the Department of Housing and Urban Development (HUD) also filed a complaint under the Equal Credit Opportunity Act. The ECOA prohibits discrimination in credit decisions based on "race, color, religion, national origin, sex or marital status, or age" (12 C.F.R. 202.6). Shortly after Citigroup acquired the lender, the FTC and HUD brokered a settlement in which the lender agreed to pay $1.5 million to several hundred consumers. The USDOJ prosecution and the FTC and HUD complaints are examples of public consumer law. The government was able to obtain recovery for individual consumers in this exceptional case. In most cases, the public regulator is unable to get your money back. In fact, Congress accorded no authority for federal agencies to file individual actions on your behalf.

To paraphrase Woody Allen, 80 percent of success is showing up. Filing your complaint with federal agencies is your first line of defense in protecting your rights as a consumer. Direct action is important in calling problems to the attention of federal regulators and prosecutors in every jurisdiction.

The Consumer Credit Protection Act and the Truth in Lending Act

Congress enacted TILA in 1969, as part of the Consumer Credit Protection Act (CCPA)[12] in order to "assure a meaningful disclosure of credit terms so that the consumer will be able to compare more readily the various credit terms available to him and avoid the uninformed use of credit."[13] TILA provides consumers with more uniform and accurate disclosures to make them more perceptive consumers of credit.[14] "Prior to TILA, there were no generally required definitions of loan terms so that consumers were unable to compare interest rates and other loan costs. Scams and fraud were pervasive."[15] It was all but impossible to discern the meaning of credit terms because lenders did not have a common vocabulary or even definitions of basic terms. TILA sought to give consumers the information they needed to make informed choices. Congress also hoped that TILA would create a credit market where lenders would compete to offer more favorable credit terms.

Congress amended TILA's civil liability provision in 1974 to permit aggrieved consumers to recover actual damages in addition to statutory damages and to provide separate statutory damages for class actions.[16]

TILA's Sphere of Application

TILA was enacted to address problems of consumer credit. TILA applies in four circumstances: (1) when credit is offered or extended to consumers; (2) when the offering or extension of credit is done regularly; (3) when the credit is subject to a finance charge or is payable by a written agreement in more than four installments; and (4) when the credit is primarily for personal, family, or household purposes.

What TILA Does Not Cover

- Credit transactions involving extensions of credit primarily for business, commercial, or agricultural purposes or to government.
- Transactions in securities or commodities accounts by a broker-dealer registered with the Securities and Exchange Commission.
- Credit transactions other than those in which a security interest is or will be acquired in real property, or in personal property used or expected to be used as the principal dwelling of the consumer, in which the total amount financed exceeds $25,000.
- Transactions under public utility tariffs, if the board determines that a state regulatory body regulates the charges for the public utility services involved, the charges for delayed payment, and any discount allowed for early payment.
- Transactions for which the board by rule determines that coverage under this subchapter is not necessary to carry out the purposes of this subchapter.
- Loans made, insured, or guaranteed pursuant to a program authorized by Title IV of the Higher Education Act of 1965 (see 15 U.S.C. §1603[2006]).

What Lenders Must Do to Comply with TILA

TILA requires a creditor to disclose information relating to the cost of credit, including finance charges, annual percentage rates, the amount financed, the schedule of payments, and total of payments.[17] The purpose of these five mandatory disclosures is to promote the informed use of consumer credit. The theory is that if consumers have adequate disclosures, they will be able to more readily make educated comparisons about the various credit terms available and avoid the uninformed use of credit.

The Remedies Consumers Have for TILA Violations

If a loan made in a consumer credit transaction is secured by the borrower's principal dwelling, the borrower has a right to rescind the loan agreement when the terms are not delivered or disclosed accurately.[18] In credit transactions covered by TILA, a consumer who has made a deposit on a home has the right to rescind that transaction within three business days. For property, consumers have a right of rescission that does not expire until three years after the loan closes or the real property is sold, whichever date is earlier (see 15 U.S.C. §1635[f]).

Any creditor who fails to provide TILA disclosures is liable for twice the amount of the finance charge, "except that liability under this paragraph shall not be less than $100 or greater than $1,000" (15 U.S.C. §1640). The amounts are raised to no less than $200 or greater than $2,000 for credit transactions not under an open-ended credit plan secured by real property or a dwelling. In a 2004 case, the U.S. Supreme Court found that the 1995 TILA amendment left intact the $100/$1,000 limits prescribed for TILA violations involving personal property loans.[19]

Disclosure Requirements for Creditors

A TILA "creditor" is defined as a lender offering loans with more than four installments or the payment of a finance charge. TILA requires creditors to highlight the cost of credit as a dollar amount over the life of the loan (the finance charge) and as an annual percentage rate (the APR). TILA requires additional disclosures for a loan secured by a consumer's home and permits consumers to rescind certain transactions that involve their principal dwelling. TILA's mandatory disclosure regime calibrates what is disclosed based upon the type of credit being offered to consumers. TILA requires each creditor to make disclosures (see 15 U.S.C. §1602[f]).

Homeowners, for example, have a right to rescind second mortgages. The homeowner may rescind home equity loans and home improvement loans. TILA requires that the homeowner be given notice of their right to rescind. Consumers may rescind loans against creditors until the later of (1) three days after the consummation of the transaction, or (2) once the creditor has delivered the information, two copies of the notice form, and the material disclosures required by TILA (15 U.S.C. §§1635, 1639[j]).

If the lender does not give you two copies of the notice, your right to rescind the loan expires three years after the consummation of the transaction, or once the property is sold, whichever occurs first (15 U.S.C. §1635[f]). TILA also has detailed regulations on whether the credit disclosures are given in an understandable manner. The consumer's written acknowledgment of receipt of the disclosures or documents mandated by the Truth in Lending Act creates a presumption of the delivery of such items (15 U.S.C. §1635[c]). In order to rebut this presumption, borrowers must present evidence to the contrary.

Consumer Rights under Regulation Z

Isolated transactions are not covered by Regulation Z. The credit must be offered on a regular basis. In other words, the creditor must be in the business of offering loans. Regulation Z also applies if there is a finance charge that must be paid in greater than four installments pursuant to a written loan agreement. Regulation Z gives consumers important rights, such as the right to cancel certain credit transactions that involve a lien on a consumer's principal dwelling. Regulation Z also regulates certain credit card practices and provides a means for fair and timely resolution of credit billing disputes. Regulation Z does not address what expenses may be charged for consumer credit, although it does require the lender to state the maximum interest rate in any variable-rate contracts secured by the consumer's dwelling. It also imposes limitations on home equity plans and places limits on loans secured by the consumer's principal dwelling.

What to Do: Complaining about Creditors

The Federal Reserve is the first stop for information about consumer credit. Its publication, "Consumer Handbook to Credit Protection Laws," can be found online.[20] Its website is an excellent source of information on how to file a complaint about a bank or other financial institution. It explains how one of the twelve Federal Reserve Banks investigates complaints.

The Federal Reserve Board is one of five federal banking agencies responsible for administering the federal laws that protect consumers in their dealings with financial institutions. The Federal Reserve banks investigate consumer complaints against its state member banks, which are privately owned corporations that typically trade their stocks publicly. The Board of Governors of the Federal Reserve Bank System works with the twelve Federal Reserve Banks (FRB) to ensure that state member banks comply with federal consumer protection rules.

Your first line of defense is to settle the problem directly with your bank. That may involve contacting senior bank management or the bank's customer service representative. If you cannot resolve the problem with your bank, you may want to file a complaint with the appropriate federal regulator. If you cannot identify the federal regulator, contact the FRB, and the staff there will forward your complaint to the appropriate agency. For complaints about state member banks, you can file a written complaint with the FRB. Be sure to sign and date your letter, and send it to the Board of Governors of the Federal Reserve System, Division of Consumer and Community Affairs, 20th and C Streets, NW, Stop 801, Washington, DC 20551, telephone: 1-202-452-3693.

Closed-End Credit

Closed-end credit (closed credit) is generally a single transaction. Sellers who finance the products they sell are engaged in closed credit transactions with consumers. "Closed ended credit transactions involve borrowing a sum certain [specific amount of money] and paying it back over a certain period of time."[21] Perhaps the best example of closed-end credit is a one-time loan for a specific period, such as for the purchase of an automobile. If a consumer purchases a car, she will receive a closed credit bank loan for a fixed amount with a given payment schedule. In that kind of transaction, credit approval is needed for each loan, and a down payment usually reflects creditworthiness. Regulation Z requires that disclosures must be presented in a specific manner for closed-end credit transactions.

Closed Installment Loans

Credit is defined as the right to defer payment of debt or to incur debt and defer its payment (12 C.F.R. Part 226.2[a] [14]). Closed credit is usually a single extension of credit in which the consumer's payment causes a steady decline in the amount of a debt. It is normally one transaction that is extended for a specific period. The number of payments, total amounts, and due dates are generally agreed upon by the creditor and the customer at the time of the transaction. An automobile loan is an example of a closed loan because it is a one-time as opposed to a repeat loan. Home mortgage loans are also closed installment loans. "Material disclosures" required under TILA are as follows:

- Annual percentage rate
- Method of determining the finance charge
- Balance upon which a finance charge will be imposed
- Amount of the finance charge
- Amount to be financed
- Total of payments
- Number and amount of payments
- Due dates or periods of payments scheduled to repay the indebtedness
- Disclosures required by TILA

Open-Ended Revolving Loans

In contrast, open-ended credit is defined as consumer credit extended by a creditor under a plan in which there will be repeat transactions, such as the credit card transactions covered in Chapters 10 and 11. The consumer may repay the debt either in full or in installments, and as the consumer reduces the debt, additional credit is made available. For this reason, open-ended credit is often referred to as revolving credit. With open-ended credit plans, the creditor reasonably contemplates repeated transactions.

Open-ended loans charge a finance charge, which may be computed from time to time on the outstanding unpaid balance. Let us say you have a credit card that charges you 1.5 percent per month, or 18 percent each year. The 18 percent is the APR of the credit card. However, because of the nature of compounding (if you only made the minimum payment, the next month's 1.5 percent would effectively be charging interest on interest), the average percentage yield (APY) figure would be 19.56 percent.

With open-ended credit, disclosures made at the outset include APR, annual fee, and conditions under which finance charges are applied, such as grace periods between the time of purchase and the time the finance charges begin to accrue. If the line of credit is backed by a security vehicle (mortgage assets used as collateral), the security line must be disclosed. Additionally, the lender must provide annual disclosures and renewal disclosures to comply with state and federal regulations.

The Rights of Cosigners

Cosigners also have rights to accurate disclosures under the FTC's Credit Practices Rule. If you are a surety (a person who agrees to be responsible for the debt or obligation of another), you cosign for another party's debt. Sureties agree to pay if the primary borrower does not pay their loan. If you cosign for your son's car loan, you will be regarded as a surety. Below is the statutorily mandated language that lenders must use:

> *Notice to Cosigner.*
> You are being asked to guarantee this debt. Think carefully before you do. If the borrower does not pay the debt, you will have to. Be sure you can afford to pay if you have to, and that you want to accept this responsibility.
> You may have to pay up to the full amount of the debt if the borrower does not pay. You may also have to pay late fees or collection costs, which increase this amount. The creditor can collect this debt from you without first trying to collect from the borrower. The creditor can use the same collection methods against you that can be used against the borrower, such as suing you, garnishing your wages or your property. If this debt is ever in default, that fact may become a part of your credit record. This notice is not the contract that makes you liable for the debt.[22]

Cosigning a promissory note is a serious undertaking. You are, in effect, promising to pay if the person you are signing for does not pay. Uncompensated sureties or cosigners also have a number of defenses under state law. If, for example, the lender extends the time for repayment, the uncompensated surety is released from the debt. In effect, any change to the original note has the effect of eliminating the surety or cosigner's liability. If you are a compensated surety, many of these defenses do not apply.

Loan Sharks

A loan shark is anyone who loans money at an extortionate rate of interest. Loan sharking is to organized crime as fireworks are to the Fourth of July. The 1995 film *Get Shorty* features Chili Palmer (John Travolta), a Miami loan shark who's been sent to Los Angeles to use self-help measures to collect the proceeds of a high-interest loan from Harry Zimm (Gene Hackman), the producer of a string of terrible movies. Loan sharks are also prominently featured in many episodes of HBO's hit series about an organized crime family. *The Sopranos'* principal character, Tony Soprano (James Gandolfini), promoted Bobby Bacala to head up the family's loan shark business.

The CCPA was designed to drive organized crime's loan-sharking enterprises out of business. However, extortionate extensions of credit continue to be a widespread problem despite the CCPA. An example of a loan shark transaction would be a loan of money with the agreement that any delay or failure to repay the loan will result in violence or other criminal self-help measures.

The CCPA considers loans indicative of loan sharking as those that are civilly unenforceable (illegal) or that have interest rates exceeding 45 percent. In addition, if these features are present, a court may also consider the creditor's reputation for unsavory collection practices, even if direct evidence of the debtor's actual belief as to these practices is not available (15 U.S.C. §892[c]). The following activities are prohibited by loan-sharking statute:

- Repayment would be unenforceable through civil process against the debtor;
- The rate of interest on the loan was in excess of 45 percent per annum;
- The debtor reasonably believed either that the creditor had collected or attempted to collect one or more debts by extortionate means or had a reputation for doing so; and
- The debtor owed the creditor more than $100, including interest, upon the making of the loan. (15 U.S.C. §892[c])

A consumer may prove that there has been an extortionate threat by evidence that other persons were threatened, that the loan shark collected or attempted to collect one or more loans by extortionate means, or that the loan shark punished nonrepayment by extortionate means (18 U.S.C. §894[b]). It is also considered to be a federal crime to threaten or use violence, even if the loan itself is not illegal or extortionate.

Credit Insurance

When you take out a second mortgage or other loan, you will be offered credit insurance. *Credit life insurance* pays off your loan should you die. The typical application for insurance will require you to answer questions about whether you have been treated for or diagnosed with cancer or other serious diseases. Many insurers will not offer you credit life insurance if you have been treated for alcoholism or substance abuse. If you qualify for this product, the insurer will pay the outstanding balance of the loan at your death.

Credit disability insurance is a second type of credit insurance that pays off your loan should you become disabled and unable to work. To qualify for this product you cannot have a pre-existing condition. Some policies will have a waiting period delaying the effective date of the insurance for six months or more. If you purchase this product, ask about the waiting period.

Involuntary unemployment insurance is a policy by which your loan is paid should you be laid off or be unemployed for a reason not of your making. *Credit property insurance* protects personal property used to secure your loan. If, for example, a thief stole your car or vandals destroyed your mobile home, it would be covered. Credit property insurance protects against theft, accident, or natural disasters.[23] The FTC advises consumers to be vigilant about the premiums and to ask questions such as the amount of the premium and whether the premium will be financed as part of the loan. The FTC advises caution when it comes to credit insurance because of the prevalence of unfair, fraudulent, and deceptive practices in this industry. Consider life or disability insurance as an alternative to credit insurance.

Notes

1. Lendol Calder, *Financing the American Dream: A Cultural History of Consumer Credit* (Princeton, N.J.: Princeton University Press, 1999), 39.

2. Ibid.

3. Jim McWhinney, "Consumer Credit Report: What's on It?" December 22, 2004, available at http://www.investopedia.com/articles/04/122304.asat (accessed October 16, 2005).

4. Ibid.

5. Ibid.

6. Calder, *Financing the American Dream*, 23.

7. Ibid., 22.

8. Ibid., 59.

9. Ibid., 73.

10. Ibid., 105.

11. Robert D. Manning, *Credit Card Nation: The Consequences of America's Addiction to Credit* (2003), 203.

12. 15 U.S.C. §1601 et seq. (2006).

13. 15 U.S.C. §1601(A) (2006) (quoting Section 102 of the CCPA).

14. 15 U.S.C. §1600 et seq. (2006).

15. Washoe County Legal Services, "What Is the Truth in Lending Act?" available at http://www.washoelegalservices.org/truth.htm#what (accessed December 18, 2005).

16. 15 U.S.C. §1640(A) (2006).

17. 15 U.S.C. §1601 et seq. (2006).

18. 15 U.S.C. §1635(f).

19. Ibid.

20. Federal Reserve Board, "Filing a Credit Complaint," available at http://www.federalreserve.gov/Pubs/consumerhdbk/complaint.htm (accessed August 10, 2006).

21. Ibid.

22. Federal Trade Commission Credit Practices Rule, 16 CFR Pt. §443.

23. Federal Trade Commission, "Is Credit Insurance for You?" available at http://www.ftc.gov/bcp/conline/pubs/alerts/credinsalrt.shtm (visited June 17, 2007).

10
Banking, Credit Cards, and Debit Cards

In 1949, Diner's Club launched the first charge card company based upon open credit. Increasingly, department stores, gas stations, and other institutions push open-ended credit. In this chapter I examine your rights and remedies in the use of credit and ATM cards. An open-ended credit plan is one in which the creditor expects to permit the consumer to make a series of transactions. Contrary to its name, an open-ended credit arrangement does not allow a consumer free access to an "open," or unlimited, amount of credit, but instead allows a consumer to purchase items on credit up to a fixed ceiling. Consumers are expected to pay the outstanding balance, usually with significant interest, each month. For example, you or your spouse may have a department store account on which you can charge up to $1,000. You receive a monthly bill with your balance and a minimum payment. The Truth in Lending Act has distinct rules for two categories of consumer credit: open-ended (revolving) credit plans, such as credit card accounts and other lines of credit; and closed-end (installment) transactions. Your automobile loan or purchase of a boat or mobile home is an example of a closed-end transaction. The FTC also has jurisdiction to enforce TILA and the portion of Regulation Z that apply to credit cards.

The total volume of consumer credit, including credit cards, auto loans, and other nonmortgage debt, doubled between 1990 and 2000 to $1.7 trillion.[1] The Federal Reserve Board estimates that the average American household owes $2,200 on their credit cards, which is two times the average indebtedness in 1992. A recent empirical study uncovered nearly $2 trillion worth of credit card transactions each year.[2]

Three things determine the consumer's cost of using a credit card: (1) interest rates, (2) minimum payments, and (3) penalty fees and interest. Interest rates vary significantly, depending upon the consumer and the type of transaction. In the present consumer marketplace, lenders present potential customers with a bewildering array of credit card terms, interest rates, and penalty schedules. Many credit card companies are marketing cards with different rates for cash advances and purchases.

TILA's Credit Card Regulations

The Truth in Lending Act is the chief federal statute governing credit cards as well as ATM cards. TILA's underlying jurisprudence is to provide consumers with uniform disclosure of costs and other terms so that they can know the true cost of credit. TILA provides you with a variety of protections in your use of credit (and debit) cards. It protects you, for example, against inaccurate and unfair credit billing and credit card practices. Promotional rates and deferred interest plans for limited periods are commonly layered onto these basic features. However, under some credit card agreements, paying late or exceeding a credit limit may trigger significant fees and a penalty rate that is applied to the entire outstanding balance, and may trigger higher rates on other credit card accounts. Moreover, the amount of consumers' payments, how creditors allocate those payments to outstanding balances, and how the balances are calculated all affect consumers' overall cost of credit under open-ended plans.

Federal Reserve Bank Regulations on Credit Cards

The principal law governing credit cards is a federal statute called the Fair Credit Billing Act (FCBA), which was a 1974 amendment to TILA. The FCBA defines credit as "the right granted by a creditor to a debtor to defer payment of debt or to incur debt and defer its payment" (15 U.S.C. §1602[e]). Two elements must therefore be present in every instance of "consumer credit." First, the credit must be issued to a natural person, and second, the credit must be received primarily for personal, family, household, or agricultural purposes. The federal regulations define *credit card* to mean "any card, plate, coupon book, or other single credit device that may be used from time to time to obtain credit. *Charge card* means a credit card on an account for which no periodic rate is used to compute finance charges" (12 C.F.R. §226.2).

Credit Card Disclosures

TILA requires the credit card issuer to disclose finance charges, which includes any charges incident to the extension of credit, as well as interest. The finance charge is broadly defined as the dollar amount you pay to use credit and turns on how much you owe on your outstanding balance and the annual percentage rate.

   In addition, a consumer must receive disclosures about "other charges," such as late payment fees. An annual fee is the charge the consumer pays for having a card and is now becoming less common as credit card issuers impose a number of other charges summarized by the Federal Reserve in the list below.

- *Cash advance fee.* Charged when you use the card for a cash advance; may be a flat fee (for example, $3.00) or a percentage of the cash advance (for example, 3%).
- *Balance-transfer fee.* Charged when you transfer a balance from another credit card. (Your credit card company may send you "checks" to pay off the other card. The balance is transferred when you use one of these checks to pay the amount due on the other card.)
- *Late-payment fee.* Charged if your payment is received after the due date.
- *Over-the-credit-limit fee.* Charged if you go over your credit limit.
- *Credit-limit-increase fee.* Charged if you ask for an increase in your credit limit.
- *Set-up fee.* Charged when a new credit card account is opened.
- *Return-item fee.* Charged if you pay your bill by check and the check is returned for non-sufficient funds (that is, your check bounces).
- *Other fees.* Some credit card companies charge a fee if you pay by telephone (that is, if you arrange by phone for payment to be transferred from your bank to the company) or to cover the costs of reporting to credit bureaus, reviewing your account, or providing other customer services. Read the information in your credit card agreement to see if there are other fees and charges.[3]

TILA mandates adequate notice to a cardholder, which means a printed notice that explains rights clearly and conspicuously. The term *clear and conspicuous*, as in countless other consumer protection statutes, means that a reasonable person would have noticed and understood the meaning of the term. Such notice may be given to a cardholder by printing the notice on any credit card, on each periodic statement of account issued to the cardholder, or by any other means reasonably assuring the receipt thereof by the cardholder. The Federal Reserve mandates that the lender present disclosures in a disclosure box, such as the one depicted in Table 10.1.

Explanations for Each Disclosure
- APR for purchases: The annual percentage rate you'll be charged if you carry over a balance from month to month. TILA requires the issuer to disclose both the introductory rate and the rate after the introductory rate expires.
- Other APRs: The amount you are charged for such services as a cash advance, a balance transfer from another card, or a late payment.

Table 10.1   The Federal Reserve Board's Mandatory Disclosure Boxes

Required Disclosures	Examples
I. Annual percentage rate (APR) for purchases	2.9% until 11/1/07 after that, 14.9%
II. Other APRs	Cash-advance APR: 15.9% Balance-transfer APR: 15.9% Penalty rate: 23.9%*
III. Variable rate information	Your APR for purchase transactions may vary. The rate is determined monthly by adding 5.9% to the prime rate.**
IV. Grace period for repayment of balances for purchases	Twenty-five days on average
V. Method of computing the balance for purchases	Average daily balance (excluding new purchases)
VI. Annual fees	None
VII. Minimum finance charge	$.50
VIII. Transaction fee for cash advances	3% of the amount advanced
IX. Balance transfer fee	3% of the amount transferred
X. Late payment fee	$25
XI. Over-the-credit-limit fee	$25

* If your payment arrives more than ten days late two times within a six-month period, the penalty rate will apply.
** The prime rate used to determine your APR is the rate published in the *Wall Street Journal* on the tenth day of the prior month.

- Variable rate information: The initial interest rate for your card and how much it will increase.
- Grace period for repayment of balances for purchases: The number of days you have to pay your credit card bill in full without triggering a finance charge.
- Method of computing the balance for purchases: The method used to calculate your outstanding balance, if you carry over a balance and will pay a finance charge.
- Annual fees: The amount you'll be charged each twelve-month period for simply having the card.
- Minimum finance charge: The minimum, or fixed, finance charge that a creditor imposes during a billing cycle. A minimum finance charge usually applies only when a finance charge is imposed, that is, when you carry over a balance.

- Transaction fee for cash advances: The charge that will be imposed each time you use the card for a cash advance.
- Balance transfer fee: The fee that will be imposed each time you transfer a balance from another card.
- Late payment fee: The fee that will be imposed when your payment is late.
- Over the credit limit fee: The fee that will be imposed if your charges exceed the credit limit set for your card.[4]

Unauthorized Use of a Credit Card

The FCBA caps your total liability for unauthorized charges on your credit card at $50 per card (15 U.S.C. §1666). The statute does not define what is meant by an unauthorized use, so state law is often used to determine whether you "authorized" the use of the card. If your credit card was stolen or lost, you will not have a difficult time proving that the use was unauthorized. You need take no step other than giving a written notification of unauthorized use to the credit card issuer. An unauthorized charge may also be raised as a billing error, or a claim that the goods paid for on a credit card never arrived or were defective.

If you report the loss of your card before your credit cards are used, the FCBA says the card issuer cannot hold you responsible for any unauthorized charges (15 U.S.C. §1643). If the loss involves your credit card number but not the card itself, you have no liability for unauthorized use. Most credit card companies will have the toll-free number published on the card, but you can easily find the number on the Internet or your credit card billing statements. To minimize your liability, report the loss of your card as soon as possible. Use the toll-free number on your statement and then follow up this telephone notice with a letter, which is a requirement of the statute.

Rights of Consumers Using Credit Cards

You can find a summary of your rights as a holder of a credit card by reviewing the summary of rights on each bill the issuer sends you.

Prompt Credit for Payment

The Fair Credit Billing Act requires a creditor to post payments promptly, pursuant to TILA's federal regulations (Section 15 U.S.C. §1666c). If your account is not credited on the date your payment is received, it is a violation of the provisions of TILA and Regulation Z (12 C.F.R. Part 226), unless you made a mistake regarding how to make payments or the delay did not result in a charge to you.

Refunds of Credit Balances

When you return merchandise or pay more than you owe, you can have the refund amount placed back on your account or request a cash refund (15 U.S.C. §1666d). To obtain a refund, you must write to the card issuer. The issuer is required by TILA to send you a refund within seven days after receipt of your request.

Credit Card Billing Errors

Billing errors are broadly defined as statements of an extension of credit that was either not made to you or not made in the amount listed on the statement you received. Moreover, billing errors include goods or services not accepted by you or not delivered in accordance with the agreement you made at the time of the transaction. Billing errors also include computation errors or similar errors of an accounting nature (15 U.S.C. §1666[b]).

TILA prescribes procedures a creditor must follow for the correction of billing errors concerning a statement of account "in connection with an extension of consumer credit" (15 U.S.C. §1666[a]). If the creditor fails to comply with the TILA obligations for correcting billing errors, it forfeits its right to collect the first $50 of the dispute amount, including finance charges (15 U.S.C. §1666[e]). The Fair Credit Billing Act provides that whenever a creditor sends you a statement of your account and the statement contains a billing error, you may send the credit card issuer a written notice. If the creditor receives this notice within sixty days of transmitting the statement of account, the creditor has two obligations. First, the creditor must send a written acknowledgment that it has received the notice. Second, within ninety days or two complete billing cycles (whichever is shorter), the creditor must investigate the matter and either make appropriate corrections in your account or send a written explanation of its belief that the original statement it sent you was correct. The creditor must send its explanation before attempting to collect the disputed amount.

Credit card issuers are required to give you a statement of their procedures for correcting billing errors when you open your credit card account. Issuers must also give you a statement of the procedure at least once a year. Most issuers print a summary of your rights on each bill they send you. For more information on what to do about billing errors, see the FTC's website on Fair Credit Billing.

What to Do: Resolving a Dispute with a Credit Card Company

Consumers may have a dispute with a merchant that results in a billing error. A merchant may, for example, charge your card for the wrong amount. To resolve the problem with a merchant, you must report the problem in writing to the merchant. In order to get the charge reversed, you must serve the merchant with a written complaint within the sixty-day window given by the Fair Credit Billing Act.

Suppose that you have been hunting on eBay for the perfect butterfly collection. You submit the winning bid and consider yourself lucky. You pay by credit card, and the eBay seller tells you to expect the prized collection in three weeks.

The exotic butterflies never arrive. What steps can you take to reverse the charge on your credit card with the eBay seller? The first thing you should do is to contact the credit card issuer. You will need to send a letter. In the letter, be sure to include your account number and a brief description of why you think that the charge is incorrect. Also, "Be sure to include a copy of your monthly statement and highlight or underline the charge you believe is incorrect," says Robert Patrick, a Federal Deposits Insurance Corporation (FDIC) attorney in Washington. "This will help the creditor identify the transaction quickly and otherwise speed up the process." Send your note to the address designated by the creditor for handling errors. Do not send it in the same envelope with your payment. Be aware that you are still expected to pay the rest of your bill that is not in dispute. You have only a sixty-day window to report errors, which begins to toll after the creditor sends you the statement.

A consumer has no liability for unauthorized charges for a credit card that was never received or used. The letter below is an example of a step you can take when an issuer attempts to collect charges for which you are not liable.

Example: Letter to Credit Card Company

XYZ Stores
Attn: Customer Service
1234 Main Street
New York City, NY

Dear Customer Service:

I am writing to you to demand that you cease and desist collecting unauthorized charges on an XYZ Credit Card, which I applied for but never received and it was never used by me. I applied for the card in March 2006 but never received a notice from your company that the card had been approved (or declined). The first I knew of any issue with the card is when I received a demand from your investigator to pay more than $400 in charges, which I did not incur. I have no liability for charges on a credit card that I have never used. The Fair Credit Billing Act (FCBA) states the card issuer cannot hold me responsible for a card I did not receive. The law is clear. A consumer that has not used a card or received it is not liable for the charges. If you continue to attempt to collect on a credit card never used, you are in clear violation of the FCBA. You are also violating section 5 of the Federal Trade Commission Act, as it is an unfair and deceptive trade practice to attempt to collect an obligation that I do not have. Your attempts to collect a bill not owed are also a violation of ____ state's unfair and deceptive trade practices act.

Please consider this letter your thirty-day demand letter to resolve this matter. I expect a written release from all further collection efforts. If this is not forthcoming within thirty days (30 days), I will consider taking further action.

Sincerely,
Carla Consumer

Credit Card Chargeback

"Chargeback," or your right to reverse charges on your credit card, is one of the most important consumer protection rights ever enacted. The FCBA gives you the right to chargeback for goods or services not delivered or not conforming to the contract you signed. Chargeback makes the card issuer subject to all claims (except tort claims) and defenses of any transaction in which the credit card is used as a method of payment (15 U.S.C. §1666i). You have a right to chargeback, for example, if (1) the same transaction appears multiple times on your statement; (2) an incorrect account number was captured, resulting in a transaction being posted to the wrong account; or (3) a transaction was processed for an incorrect amount. Chargeback is also appropriate when goods are not delivered or do not conform to the contract. Nondelivery of goods also gives the buyer UCC Article 2 remedies. A seller is not entitled to the purchase price unless conforming goods are delivered. Similarly, if you use your credit card to purchase an electronic product that malfunctions, you have rights to warranty damages.

If you have a problem with merchandise or services charged your credit card, you must first make a good faith effort to work out the problem with the seller. Typically, you will be dealing with customer service representatives, managers, or regional representatives. If the seller allows return of merchandise that was purchased with a credit card, he must promptly inform the credit card issuer that the consumer is entitled to a credit for the amount of the transaction (15 U.S.C. §1666e).

If informal settlement efforts fail, you have the right to withhold payment from the credit card issuer. You can withhold up to the amount of credit outstanding for the purchase, plus finance or related charges (15 U.S.C. §1666i [a]). However, you have no right to stop payment on your credit charges altogether.

What to Do: Protecting Your Rights Regarding ATM Cards

A federal statute called the Electronic Funds Transfers Act (EFTA) governs ATM cards. If a financial institution does not follow the provisions of EFTA, the consumer will have an action for actual damages. In egregious cases in which the financial institution refuses to correct an error or reaccredit an account, the consumer may recover three times actual damages, plus punitive damages of not less than $100 or more than $1,000. EFTA also permits prevailing plaintiffs to recover court costs as well as attorney's fees. If an institution fails to make an electronic fund transfer or to stop payment of a preauthorized transfer when properly instructed by you to do so, you may sue for all damages that result from the failure.

As with every federal statute, there is an implementing regulation. Regulation E covers a variety of electronic fund transfers involving consumers, such as ATM transactions. EFTA caps the total liability of consumers for the unauthorized use of a lost or stolen card to a sum between $50 and $500, depending on how quickly the wrongdoing is reported. If you report a stolen ATM card within two days, your exposure is limited to $50. If you report the loss after two days but before sixty days, your total exposure is $500. After sixty days, you risk losing all of the money in your account.

Avoid ATM cards with large fees. Use direct deposit to avoid ATM charges for deposits. Protect your passwords. Keep a copy of your financial institution's name, its customer service phone number, and your account number in a place apart from your wallet. If you lose your Visa ATM card in the United States, call 1-800-847-2911. If you lose your Visa ATM card (or credit card) in another country, you can easily locate the toll-free number by visiting http://corporate.visa.com/pd/consumer_services/lost_card .jsp.

If you lose your MasterCard within the United States, call 1-800-MC-ASSIST (1-800-622-7747) (for Spanish-speaking services, use 1-800-633-4466). The TDD/TYY number for the hearing-impaired is 1-636-722-3725. If you lose your ATM MasterCard (or credit card) outside the United States, you can find the toll-free number for the country you are visiting online at http://www.mastercard.com/cgi-bin/emergserv.cgi. You can also call Visa or MasterCard for issues including (1) emergency replacement cards; (2) emergency cash advances; (3) the location of an ATM that accepts MasterCard, Maestro, and Cirrus cards; (4) access to account-related information; and (5) access to any applicable card benefits.

Fiduciary Duties Owed by Bank/Trustees

The bank-customer relationship is based on contract. However, banks will sometimes owe a higher fiduciary duty that is based on equitable principles. A bank administering a trust has a fiduciary relationship with the lifetime and residuary beneficiaries of certain inter vivos (living) and testamentary trusts administered by the defendant bank in its capacity as trustee. A bank may be sued for breaching its fiduciary duty if it mishandles the trust assets. A trustee owes the beneficiary a duty of loyalty and cannot use the corpus of the trust for its own benefit. In a breach of fiduciary duty case, a consumer may be awarded losses in the value of the trust due to the trustee's negligence or neglect.

GAO Study of Credit Cards

A 2006 Government Accountability Office (GAO) study of credit cards of the six largest issuers uncovered credit cards with interest rates of 30 percent or more and penalties for late payment as high as $39 for a single occurrence.[5] The study found that late penalty fees have skyrocketed from $13 in 1995 to $34 a decade later. Credit card issuers reported that 35 percent of cardholders were assessed late fees in 2005, and 15 percent were over the limit during that year. The GAO also found that credit card issuers are devising a range of new fees for such actions as cash advances, balance transfers, foreign transactions, returned convenience checks, stop payments, telephone payments, duplicate copies of account records, and the rush delivery of credit cards. Three in four credit card companies charged annual fees in 2005, but the decreased emphasis on annual fees has been displaced by increased consumer costs for penalty fees and special services.

The GAO credit card study criticized the credit card issuers for giving inadequate disclosures about penalties and called for the Federal Reserve to strengthen TILA disclosures given to consumers. The GAO concluded that weaknesses in credit card disclosures hindered consumers' understandings of when penalties could be imposed for late payment and the like. The GAO study concluded that most issuers fail the Federal Reserve test of disclosures because the disclosures were not understandable by the average eighth grader.

The Law of Credit Cards

Many of the concepts discussed in Chapter 6, on consumer contracts, apply equally well to credit cards since they are contracts between credit card issuer and the consumer. A credit card is essentially a contract in which the card issuer (credit card company) enters into a contract with you (the cardholder) to advance you open-ended credit. Open-ended credit grants you funds to buy now and pay later. The contract you have with the credit card company then sets limits for what is extended while charging a high rate of interest, up to 30 percent or more, until the payments are made. Credit card companies offer their contracts with many different products that often turn on your creditworthiness. In the past few years, issuers offer multiple interest rates for a single account, making it difficult to determine the true cost of credit.

In recent years, credit cards companies across the industry have dramatically increased penalty fees. The GAO cited a study demonstrating that penalty fees increased 115 percent from 1995 to 2005. Consumer Action, an advocacy group, found that costs have increased 119 percent during the same decade.[6] This empirical study confirms the necessity of paying off your balance and not reaching your limits.

If you have not paid off the entire balance on your credit card, your payment includes interest for one month based on the outstanding balance or average daily balance.[7] No statute prevents a credit card from calculating interest charges at the time of the purchase, nor do regulations (other than usury laws) govern the rate of interest. Other credit cards will charge no interest until a balance remains in the new billing cycle.

In addition to basic contract law, credit card issuers must comply with federal disclosure rules. The Federal Reserve has primary jurisdiction over issuers that are chartered as state banks. Mandatory arbitration clauses are frequently made part of take it or leave it clauses in credit card agreement. Consumers are at a great disadvantage in these proceedings because arbitrators are likely to be pro-defense.[8]

Credit Card Terms
The key terms to check when choosing a credit card are the annual percentage rate, periodic rate, annual fee, grace period, finance charge, and other fees. Do comparison shopping and pick the most favorable terms. You should not use a card unless you have studied the credit card disclosures required by the Fair Credit Billing Act.

Credit Card Insurance
Credit card insurance is invariably a fraud and certainly an unnecessary expenditure because your total exposure, if you promptly report a lost or stolen credit card, is only $50. Credit card insurance should be treated as an unfair or deceptive trade practice since it is insuring a liability you do not have.

Debit Cards

A debit card is a plastic card that looks similar to a credit card but that consumers may use at an ATM or to make purchases, withdrawals, or other types of electronic fund transfers.

Debit Card Disclosures
The Electronic Fund Transfers Act requires the issuer to disclose to you the following information about your rights and responsibilities with regard to debit cards:

- A notice of your liability in case the card is lost or stolen;
- A telephone number for reporting loss or theft of the card or an unauthorized transfer;
- A description of its error resolution procedures;
- The kinds of electronic fund transfers you may make and any limits on the frequency or dollar amounts of such transfers;
- Any charge by the institution for using EFT services;
- Your right to receive records of electronic fund transfers;

- How to stop payment of a preauthorized transfer;
- The financial institution's liability to you for any failure to make or to stop transfers; and
- The conditions under which a financial institution will give information to third parties about your account.

Debit Scams

Since the early 1990s, fraudulent telemarketers have been calling consumers, claiming that the consumer has won a sweepstakes or contest. Then the caller will typically request your checking account number or other information printed on your check in order to deposit funds in your account. This is a ploy. Do not give out checking account information over the phone unless you initiate the call or are familiar with the company. In one version of the swindle, you get a postcard, telephone call, or email that says you have won a free prize. If you respond to the offer, the telemarketer often asks you right away, "Do you have a checking account?" If you say "Yes," the telemarketer then goes on to explain the offer, making it sound too good to pass up. Nevertheless, do just that: take a pass.

Using a Dual Credit/Debit Card

When you make a purchase with a dual card, request that you use the credit card so that you exercise your chargeback rights in the event of a dispute. Banks sometimes charge customers a fee for purchasing goods with debit cards.

Stolen or Lost Debit Cards

Call your bank or issuer if your debit card is lost or stolen. You can find a toll-free number to report a lost or stolen card. Look on your bank statement. The Electronic Funds Transfer Act (EFTA) (FRB Regulation E) governs debit cards. A consumer's liability for unauthorized use of their ATM or debit cards depends on whether timely notice was given. If you report an ATM or debit card missing before it's used without your permission, the EFTA says the card issuer cannot hold you responsible for any unauthorized transfers.[9] If unauthorized use occurs before you report it, your liability under federal law depends on how quickly you report the loss. If you notify the financial institution within two days, you are liable for the lesser of $50 or the amount of the unauthorized transfer occurring before notice.[10] Thereafter, your liability is limited to $500 or the lesser of the amount of unauthorized transfers that occur after two business days and before notice to the financial institution. However, even then the financial institution must prove that the theft would not have occurred if you had given notice within the two day period. You must report an unauthorized use of debit card within sixty days after your periodic bank statement is mailed or you are liable for all the losses. Thus, prompt reporting is a must in the event of lost or stolen debit or ATM cards.

Notes

1. Liz Pulliam Weston, *Your Credit Score: How to Fix, Improve, and Protect the 3-Digit Number That Shapes Your Financial Future* (Englewood Cliffs, N.J.: Prentice-Hall, 2004), 7.

2. Jim McWhinney, "Consumer Credit Report: What's on It?" December 22, 2004, available at http://www.investopedia.com/articles/04/122304.asat (accessed October 16, 2005).

3. Federal Reserve Board, available at http://www.federalreserve.gov/Pubs/shop/#calculate.

4. See Federal Reserve Board, "Choosing a Credit Card," available at http://www.federalreserve.gov/Pubs/shop/#purchases (last visited June 17, 2007).

5. U.S. Government Accountability Office, "Credit Cards: Increased Complexity in Rates and Fees Heightens Needs for More Effective Disclosure to Consumers," available at http://www.gao.gov/new.items/d06929.pdf (accessed June 17, 2007).

6. Consumer Action, "New GAO Credit Card Study Highlights Anti-Consumer Practices," available at: http://www.consumer-action.org/press/articles/new_gao_credit_card_study_highlights_anti_consumer_practices/ (last visited June 17, 2007).

7. Washoe County (Nev.) Legal Services, "What Is the Truth in Lending Act?" available at http://www.washoelegalservices.org/truth.htm#what (accessed June 17, 2007).

8. Testimony of Paul Bland, Jr., Staff Attorney for Public Justice, House Judiciary Committee Hearing on "Mandatory Arbitration Agreements," Congressional Testimony, June 12, 2007.

9. 12 CFR Pt. 205.6 (b) (2007).

10. 12 CFR Pt. 205.6(b)(2).

11

Credit Reports and Discrimination in Lending

Consumer credit issues are at the top of every list of consumer complaints. This chapter examines how credit reports, discrimination in lending, and loan products tend to prey on low-income consumers.

Credit Reports

The Fair Credit Reporting Act requires each of the nationwide consumer reporting companies—Equifax, Experian, and TransUnion—to provide you with a free copy of your credit report, at your request, once every twelve months. Consumers are also allowed copies of their credit reports if their application for credit, employment, or insurance is denied. You can get a copy of your credit report (free in some cases, but no more than $9 under current law) by contacting any of the three major credit bureaus: Equifax (call 1-800-685-1111 or go to www.equifax.com on the Internet); Experian (call 1-866-200-6020 or go to www.experian.com); and TransUnion (call 1-800-888-4213 or go to www.transunion.com). Experts suggest that you review your credit reports from all three bureaus because not all lenders report information to all three of these credit bureaus, and your credit reports may therefore vary significantly.

You can also receive your credit report, annually, either online at http://www.annualcreditreport.com, or by calling 1-877-322-8228. This is the easiest way to obtain your credit report.[1] When you order your annual credit report, provide your name, address, Social Security number, and date of birth. To verify your identity, the credit reporting agency may request other information, such as the amount of your monthly mortgage payment.

Be cautious about using any of the numerous credit reporting services online that offer your credit report for a fee. Online services offering free

credit reports are usually fraudulent if the offer originates with an unsolicited email. Be aware that some of these emails are transmitted by criminals masquerading as people providing free services. The FTC warns that
they will not actually give you free credit reports, but may use your disclosure of personally identifiable information for nefarious purposes. The act
of "phishing" is a fraud that uses spam or fraudulent websites to deceive
consumers into disclosing their credit card numbers, bank account information, Social Security numbers, passwords, and other sensitive information.
Be wary of any unsolicited email inquiries purporting to be from legitimate
businesses. No legitimate business sends an unsolicited email asking for personally identifiable information.

Do not respond to unsolicited email offers for free credit reports. Only
the http://www.annualcreditreport.com website listed above is authorized
by law with the cooperation of the credit bureaus to provide consumers
with a free copy of their annual credit report. Other companies that claim to
offer any other services, such as "free credit" or "credit monitoring," may
end up charging your credit card and ruining your credit.

A lender's approval or denial of credit is based on your credit score,
which is affected by a number of factors. The three-digit credit score is used
to predict whether you will pay your bills on a timely basis. Just as the SAT
is used by college admissions to predict success in college, the credit score is
critical to determining whether to extend or decline credit. Credit scores
also make a huge difference as to the interest rate charged by lenders.

What to Do about Bad Credit Scores

Once a potentially negative credit reference appears in your credit report, it
typically remains on your credit report for seven years beyond the date of
the negative credit incident. While the sting of a potentially negative credit
reference does fade over time (and factors less toward your credit score with
each successive billing cycle where you do make timely payments), the point
is to avoid the situation in the first place. Even if you have been denied credit
in the past, there are still measures you can take to improve your credit
score.[2] Credit scores are based on a number of factors, and the actual figures
used to compute a person's credit score remain a mystery to all but a few.

- *Do not "max out" your credit cards:* Even if you pay off the entire balance each month, maxing out your credit card tells companies that you
  cannot handle credit and the more credit they give you, the more
  likely the chance that you will max it out too.
- *Make timely payments:* Most companies offer you a grace period in
  which they will not report you to the agencies (or when they begin
  charging late fees, etc.). However, you should always strive to make
  payments on time. One simple way is to have the funds debited from
  your bank account, or, should you not want the company to have your

banking information, you may be able to send payments from your on-line bank account to your bill using their bill pay services.

- *Avoid applying for too many credit cards:* Having too many credit cards is just as bad as maxing out your credit cards. If you have more than two (not including a debit card), that is probably too many. However, all is not lost. First, look at which cards charge you a fee and which cards offer you the highest credit limit. You should keep one card with the highest credit limit (for emergencies). Pay off the balance and then keep the card somewhere, as long as it is not in your wallet.

  Of the remaining cards, pay off all the balances, even if it means consolidating them onto one card. You should then work to pay off that one card. An easy way to pay it off faster is by totaling up the payments you were making each month to all the cards and writing one check for the consolidated amount. The cards you have left with no balances should be kept in a safe place and left unused or closed.

- *Get a copy of your credit report:* An understatement about getting your credit report is that you will be able to see exactly what is on it. Only you know what the report should say, so you are in the position of ver-ifying all the information on the report. You are entitled to a free credit report annually. Remember to obtain one from all three companies to avoid any discrepancies.

- *Request goodwill:* In the interest of goodwill, a lender may remove a po-tentially negative reference from your credit score if you request it in writing. Lenders will weigh such factors as the type of the negative ref-erence, how many successive pay periods without incident you have had since the potentially negative reference, and your overall improved financial condition.

Fair Credit Reporting Act

Congress passed the Fair Credit Reporting Act (FCRA) as a new section of the Consumer Credit Protection Act (CCPA) in 1971 (15 U.S.C. §1681([b]). FCRA's statutory purpose was to rein in the unfair and deceptive practices of third parties abusing consumer credit reports. The FCRA also addresses what information can be collected and transmitted in the decision whether to extend credit or insurance in consumer transactions. The FCRA has a duty to enact reasonable procedures to protect the confidentiality and accuracy of consumer credit information (15 U.S.C. §1683[e]). The U.S. Congress made the following legislative findings when it enacted the FCRA:

- The banking system is dependent upon fair and accurate credit report-ing. Inaccurate credit reports directly impair the efficiency of the banking system, and unfair credit reporting methods undermine the public confidence that is essential to the continued functioning of the banking system.

- An elaborate mechanism has been developed for investigating and evaluating the creditworthiness, credit standing, credit capacity, character, and general reputation of consumers.
- Consumer reporting agencies have assumed a vital role in assembling and evaluating consumer credit and other information on consumers.
- There is a need to ensure that consumer reporting agencies exercise their grave responsibilities with fairness, impartiality, and a respect for the consumer's right to privacy (15 U.S.C. §1681).

You have an action against the credit reporting agency if you suffered actual damages from any of the following misuses or abuses of your credit report: (1) furnishing a consumer report for impermissible purposes; (2) not following reasonable procedures to ensure maximum possible accuracy; (3) reporting obsolete information, as defined by the Fair Credit Reporting Act; (4) failing to make mandatory disclosures; (5) failing to conduct mandatory reinvestigation; (6) failing to correct inaccurate or incomplete information; and (7) failing to comply with the requirements relating to reinsertion of disputed credit information into the consumer's file. Again, you are entitled to actual damages, plus punitive damages that the court may allow if the violation is proved to have been intentional. In any successful lawsuit, you will also be awarded court costs and attorney's fees. A person who obtains a credit report without proper authorization or an employee of a credit reporting agency who gives a credit report to unauthorized persons may be fined up to $5,000 or imprisoned for one year or both.

What to Do: Opting Out of Prescreened Credit Offers

Consumers have a right to opt out of the screening process for new credit cards. To opt out, you need to contact each agency: (1) Equifax, P.O. Box 740123, Atlanta, Georgia 30374-0123, telephone 1-888-567-8688; (2) Experian, P.O. Box 919, Allen, Texas 75012, 1-800-353-0809; and (3) TransUnion, P.O. Box 97328, Jackson, Mississippi 39288, 1-800-680-7293. Consumers who exercise the opt-out right must be kept off the credit reporting list for two years. If you want your name and address permanently removed from the mailing lists obtained from the main consumer credit reporting agencies, visit www.optoutprescreen.com or call 1-888-5OPTOUT (1-888-567-8688). You can also locate their mailing addresses online and send a request by mail. Include the following information with your request:

- First, middle, and last names (including Jr., Sr., III);
- Current address;
- Previous address (if you have moved in the last six months);
- Social Security number;
- Date of birth; and
- Your signature.

In addition, consumers may opt out of solicitations by the members of the Direct Marketing Association (DMA) using the database of the credit report agencies. Once you opt out, you will stop receiving offers from companies that market from the agencies. Keep in mind that you will need to identify other direct marketers using nonagency consumer databases. To opt out of mailers who do not use agency lists, contact the DMA at Direct Marketing Association, Mail Preference Service, P.O. Box 643, Carmel, NY 10512; or Direct Marketing Association, Telephone Preference Service, P.O. Box 1559, Carmel, NY 10512. The DMA will require you to provide the following information to comply with your opt-out request:

- First, middle, and last names (including Jr., Sr., III);
- Current address; and
- Home area code and telephone number (only for Telephone Preference Service).

Equal Credit Opportunity Act

The federal Equal Credit Opportunity Act (ECOA) protects consumers who apply for loans to purchase a home or an automobile. ECOA makes it unlawful for any creditor to discriminate against an applicant who is seeking credit. ECOA is not limited to discrimination in just granting credit. Section 701 expressly covers discrimination in "any aspect of a credit transaction." ECOA applies to a consumer attempting to secure not only personal, household, or family loans but also business loans. ECOA covers credit card companies, banks, small loan and finance companies, retail and department stores, credit card companies, and credit unions. Real estate brokers and others who arrange financing must comply with the statute. Essentially, the act states that when a consumer applies for credit, a creditor may not discourage him from applying for a loan on the basis of (1) race, (2) color, (3) religion, (4) national origin, (5) sex, (6) marital status, (7) age (providing that the applicant is of the age to have the capacity to contract), or (8) part or all of your income being derived from a public assistance program (15 U.S.C. §§1601 et seq.).

Discriminatory Loans

Racial Discrimination

The U.S. Department of Justice (DOJ) filed an action based on racial discrimination against Delta Funding Corporation, a New York subprime mortgage lender, doing business primarily in Brooklyn and Queens, New York. The complaint arose out of a joint investigation between the Department of Justice, the U.S. Attorney's Office for the Eastern District of New York, Housing and Urban Development, and the FTC. The USDOJ complaint alleged that Delta violated the Fair Housing Act and Equal Credit Opportunity Act by making loans to African American females with higher broker fees than those for white males. The DOJ also alleged, on behalf of HUD, that Delta violated the Real Estate Settlement Practices Act by allowing unreasonable broker fees, and, on behalf of the FTC, that Delta violated the Home Ownership and Equity Protection Act by engaging in asset-based lending, in which the borrower pledges in collateral certain assets as a security interest. In the subprime lending context, asset-based lending occurs when the lender engages in the practice of "equity-stripping." The lender bases the loan on the value of the property with little regard for the lender's ability to repay the loan. In these loans, the borrower has a high risk of defaulting and losing their home through foreclosure.

The settlement agreement, which applies to the lender's operations nationwide, required Delta to refuse to fund loans with discriminatory or unearned broker fees and to ensure that loans are not made to persons who cannot afford the payments. The settlement included monetary relief of up to $12 million to be paid to victims under a previous agreement between Delta, the New York State Banking Department, and the New York state attorney general.

Marital Status

The Federal Trade Commission referred a case to the USDOJ in which a foreign bank with branch offices in the United States engaged in limited consumer installment and residential loans to its employees. The foreign bank required the employee's nonapplicant spouse to become personally obligated on mortgage notes, even when the employee was individually qualified. The FTC entered into a settlement agreement that required the bank to immediately change this policy and release spouses from all loans made in the previous year. Although this FTC action did not result in any money damages to the consumers, they would have also had standing to file individual lawsuits because of the lender's ECOA violation. *Standing* means that you have the right to make a legal claim, or to seek judicial enforcement of a duty or a right against a creditor, seller, or lender.

Section 701 of the ECOA requires the creditor to act promptly on a consumer's application for credit. The lender must notify the applicant of its decision to extend or not extend credit within thirty days after receipt of a completed application for credit. You are entitled to money damages if the lender fails to provide you with notification within thirty days of filing a complete application.

If credit is denied, you are entitled to a statement of the specific reasons for the adverse decision within sixty days after receiving it. The notice may be given orally, but you do have a right to have the statement of reasons confirmed in writing, on your written request. If you demand the notice in writing, the lender is in violation of ECOA if it does not give the specific reasons for the adverse action taken. The ECOA defines the term *adverse action* to mean a denial or revocation of credit, a change in the terms of an existing credit arrangement, or a refusal to grant credit in substantially the amount or on substantially the terms requested. The adverse decision does not extend to the lender's decision not to give additional credit under an existing credit arrangement in which the applicant is delinquent or otherwise in default. Acceptable reasons include: "Your income was low," or "You haven't been employed long enough." Unacceptable reasons are: "You didn't meet our minimum standards," or "You didn't receive enough points on our credit-scoring system." Indefinite and vague reasons are illegal, so ask the creditor to be specific.[3]

What to Do: Discrimination in the Denial of Credit

The following sequence of steps can be taken to vindicate your rights concerning discriminatory credit decisions:

Step 1: Self-Help. Write a formal letter of complaint to the creditor. Make it known you are aware that state and federal law prohibits them from discriminating against you. Self-help remedies will sometimes result in the creditor making things right and reversing the arbitrary, capricious, or discriminatory decision. Your letter should state the facts briefly and explain why the decision violates federal or state law. If you cannot get the lender to reverse its discriminatory decision, you have other options, namely complaints to public regulators and the possibility of a private lawsuit exercising your rights as a "private attorney general."

Step 2: File a Complaint with a Federal Regulatory Agency. If a retail store, department store, small loan and finance company, mortgage company, oil company, public utility, state credit union, government lending program, or travel and expense credit card company is involved, contact the Consumer Response Center, Federal Trade Commission, Washington, DC 20580.

The FTC and HUD referred a case against Action Loan, a subprime lender, to the Department of Justice in 2000. The subprime lender and its president were charged with the misrepresentation of fees, improper disclosures, and a violation of ECOA. The FTC and HUD negotiated a settlement for $400,000 in consumer redress. However, even when an FTC complaint results in recovery of money damages, the commission does not intervene in individual disputes. In many cases, the settlement will not provide you with restitution, and if you are seeking monetary damages, you will need to file your own lawsuit. If you file a complaint with the FTC, it must be concise, accurate, and well-documented. Provide your name and contact information or the agency may not refer, respond to, or investigate your complaint or request. The FTC has a general consumer complaint file downloadable at https://rn.ftc.gov/pls/dod/wsolcq$.startup?Z_ORG_CODE=PU01. You may also file an ECOA complaint by writing to Consumer Response Center, Federal Trade Commission, Washington, DC 20580.

Keep in mind that the FTC has no authority to sue on your individual behalf, and therefore will not be able to secure you an individual remedy. However, your complaint may lead to an agency action against the lender. For further information, see the FTC's website at http://www.ftc.gov/bcp/conline/pubs/credit/ecoa.htm.

If your complaint concerns a nationally chartered bank (National or N.A. will be part of the name), write to the Comptroller of the Currency, Compliance Management, Mail Stop 7-5, Washington, DC 20219. If your complaint concerns a state-chartered bank that is insured by the Federal Deposit Insurance Corporation (FDIC) but is not a member of the Federal Reserve System, write to the Federal Deposit Insurance Corporation, Consumer Affairs Division, Washington, DC 20429. If your complaint concerns a federally chartered or federally insured savings and loan association, write to the Office of Thrift Supervision, Consumer Affairs Program, Washington, DC 20552. If your complaint concerns a federally chartered credit union, write to the National Credit Union Administration, Consumer Affairs Division, Washington, DC 20456. Complaints against all kinds of creditors can be referred to the Department of Justice, Civil Rights Division, Washington, DC 20530.

Step 3: State Attorney General's Office. Most states have Consumer Protection Divisions within the state attorney general's office. Contact that office to initiate a complaint if you suspect that you have been discriminated against on statutorily impermissible grounds such as race, color, gender, or age. Many states have a special department devoted to enforcement of state consumer law. Connecticut's Department of Consumer Protection, for example, is charged with consumer education, complaint mediation and investigation, written comments to state and federal agencies, and litigation under various state and federal laws, with a major reliance on the Connecticut Unfair Trade Practices Act (CUTPA). Every state has a functionally equivalent statute to deter unfair and deceptive trade practices. These statutes are cited in Appendix A. In addition, every state attorney general is charged with enforcing countless specific consumer protection statutes. The states frequently have enacted statutes that parallel federal statutes governing lending, and an aggrieved consumer may have statutory protection under both state and federal law. Your complaint can refer to both the state and federal statutes. Your state attorney general's consumer protection division will then investigate whether the creditor violated state equal credit opportunity laws. Your state may decide to prosecute the creditor or assess civil penalties. If the state prosecutes the creditor or takes an enforcement action, you can use this evidence in a lawsuit in either state or federal district court.

Step 4: Seek an Attorney; File a Case in Federal District Court. Consult a private attorney or legal services attorney. Your attorney can help you make a decision about whether you should bring a lawsuit in federal district court. If you are a prevailing plaintiff, you may recover damages up to $1,000. You can also obtain compensation for attorney's fees and court costs. An attorney can advise you on how to proceed and whether you should join with other consumers in a class action lawsuit. As previously mentioned, one of the difficulties of an individual action is that the damages are so low that many attorneys will not take your case. It may be possible for you to be a representative plaintiff in a class action if there is a class of aggrieved consumers with a similar complaint. In a class action verdict, a court may award damages for the class up to $500,000 or one percent of the creditor's net worth, whichever is less (15 U.S.C. §1640[a] [2]).

Payday Loans

The Federal Insurance Deposit Corporation defines payday loans as unsecured loans for small dollar amounts that are repaid out of the consumer's next paycheck. These loans are characterized by very high initial interest rates that rapidly compound and are paid back on payday. The typical annual percentage rate will be 364 to 550 percent.[4] The best available empirical research reveals that the average interest rate is 474 percent.[5] One study found that the average payday loan customer took more than ten loans per year per customer.[6] Many payday lenders fail to comply with TILA statutes and state licensing requirements, and many systematically mislead consumers by masking the true cost of credit and loan products.[7]

Payday lending, like other forms of lending, is also susceptible to discriminatory practices. The ECOA prohibits a bank from having both payday and other short-term lending programs with substantially different interest rate or pricing structures. The FDIC instructs its examiners to closely examine payday loan products to ensure compliance with federal regulations. FDIC examiners are to determine to whom the products are marketed, how the rates or fees for each program are set, and whether there is evidence of potential discrimination. Acts of discrimination include discouraging applications, requesting prohibited information, or evaluating applications on a prohibited basis. If the lender requires that a borrower have income from a job and does not consider income from other sources, such as Social Security or veterans benefits, it is liable for illegal discrimination under the ECOA.

The ECOA and Regulation B, which implements the act, also preclude lenders from refusing to grant an individual account to a creditworthy applicant based on race, sex, marital status, or any other prohibited basis. Regulation B requires creditors to notify applicants of adverse actions taken in connection with an application for credit. Notices of adverse action taken must be provided within specified periods and in specified forms. State nonmember banks involved in payday lending must ensure that such notices are given in an accurate and timely manner. An empirical study shows clear and convincing evidence that predatory lenders are targeting military personnel for unfair and deceptive payday loans. The study concluded that payday lenders are aggressively targeting U.S. military bases.[8] In the twenty states studied, payday lenders have a greater concentration near military populations.[9]

Subprime Loans

TILA regulates disclosures about loans but does nothing to affect the interest rate and other substantive terms. TILA is solely a disclosure statute requiring lenders to make accurate disclosures to customers. Regulation Z requires, for example, that a bank must disclose finance charges and annual percentage rates for payday loans. Regulation Z also requires banks to advertise their loan products in accordance with their provisions. A bank must accurately disclose specific credit terms. If an advertisement states a finance charge, it must state the rate as an APR, using that term. If the APR may be increased after the initial origination date, the advertisement must say so. Additional disclosures may also be required in the bank's advertisements.

What to Do: Credit Unions

If you qualify to join a credit union, you are more likely to find loans with reasonable rates and interest rates there than at other financial institutions. Credit unions were originally a European financial institution; the first credit union in the United States was formed in Manchester, New Hampshire in 1909. The National Credit Union Administration (NCUA) regulates federal credit unions and is responsible for most of the 10,000 credit unions, which have more than $480 billion in assets and serve more than 79 million consumers. Federal credit unions are nonprofit, cooperative financial institutions owned and run by their members. Credit unions, unlike banks, have a mission of providing their members with a safe place to save and borrow at reasonable rates. The credit union motto is: *Not for profit, not for charity, but for service.* Low-income consumers may join specialized credit unions serving distressed and financially underserved areas.

NCUA, for example, has a revolving loan fund and provides technical assistance to Opportunities Credit Union, a nontraditional credit union in Burlington, Vermont. Opportunities, like other credit unions, is nonprofit, member-owned, and federally insured. It gives loans and offers services to Vermonters underserved by traditional banking institutions. Its mission is to serve "working families, women, immigrants, small businesses, students, seniors, and ordinary Vermonters." Opportunities Credit Union promotes "grassroots community development in Vermont through home ownership, small business development, reliable transportation, financial stability, and economic literacy."

If you are a person of low or moderate income, you should become a member of a credit union. You can find similar credit unions in your jurisdiction by visiting the National Credit Union Association website at http://www.ncua.gov.

Notes

1. Please note that the free annual credit report does not include your credit score. You can obtain your credit score through fee-based membership from the three credit bureaus directly, or through fee-based programs at your local bank or mortgage lender. Be wary of "free credit report" and "free credit score" email solicitations and websites!

2. This consumer law practice pointer was drafted by David Cormier, a Suffolk University Law student who was Professor Rustad's research assistant in the summer of 2006. The practice pointer was updated by John Gillis, who served as Professor Rustad's research assistant in the summer of 2007.

3. Federal Trade Commission, Equal Credit Opportunity available at http://www.ftc.gov/bcp/conline/pubs/credit/ecoa.shtm (last visited June 17, 2007),

4. Steven M. Graves and Christopher L. Peterson, "Predatory Lending and the Military: The Law and Geography of 'Payday' Loans in Military Towns," *Ohio State Law Journal* 66 (2005): 653.

5. Ibid., 659.

6. Ibid., 664.

7. Ibid.

8. Ibid.

9. Ibid., 669.

12

Your Debtor's Rights and Remedies

Creditors have a right to contact you if you are behind in your student loan payments, credit card payments, home mortgage, car loan, or other loans or debts. Congress enacted the Fair Debt Collection Practices Act (FDCPA) to prevent unfair debt collection practices, such as threats, harassment, and deceptive communications (15 U.S.C. §1692[e]). The federal law, for example, makes it illegal for creditors to contact you at your workplace once you have notified them that you may not be contacted there. It is considered to be an unfair act if a creditor (1) collects any amount greater than your debt, unless your state law permits such a charge; (2) deposits a postdated check prematurely; (3) uses deception to make you accept collect calls or pay for telegrams; (4) takes or threatens to take your property unless it can be done legally; or (5) contacts you by postcard.

The FDCPA does not apply to your brother-in-law who lent you money, but only to persons who regularly collect debts owed to others. The statute covers attorneys who collect debts on a regular basis. Consumers who have acquired debts for personal, household, or family purposes are protected by the FDCPA. The federal act prohibits any debt collector communicating with any person other than the consumer from stating that such consumer owes any debt (15 U.S.C. §1692[b] [2]). Collectors may not contact your family members or employer to collect a debt unless they have a final court judgment entered against you. The FDCPA applies to independent or third-party debt collectors, not generally to the actual creditor (15 U.S.C. §1692[a] [6]). The FDCPA protects debtors from misleading and abusive debt collection practices (15 U.S.C. §1692[e]).

FDCPA Rules Concerning Debt Collection

Acquisition of Location Information

The FDCPA prohibits creditors from contacting persons other than the debtor for any purpose other than location information (15 U.S.C. §1692b, 1692c [b]). Debt collectors may not, for example, tell the other person that the consumer owes a debt (§1692[b] [2]). Debt collectors are not permitted to communicate with a person other than the consumer more than once, unless the earlier response about the location of the debtor was erroneous or incomplete (§1692[b] [3]). The debt collector may only identify himself by stating that "he is confirming or correcting location information about the consumer" (§1692[b] [1]). The debt collector communicating with any person other than the consumer may not even reveal that he is a "debt collect or is in the debt collection business or that the communication relates to the collection of a debt" (§1692[b] [5]). Debt collectors may not use any language or symbol on any envelope or in the contents of any communication affected by the mails or telegram that indicates that the debt collector is in the debt collection business or that the communication relates to the collection of a debt (§1692[5]).

If you have retained an attorney, the debt collector must contact the attorney, rather than you. If you do not have an attorney, a collector may contact other people, but only to find out where you live, what your phone number is, and where you work. Collectors usually are prohibited from contacting such third parties more than once. In most cases, the collector may not tell anyone other than you and your attorney that you owe money (§1692[5] [6]).

The federal statute prohibits contacting the debtor at his or her place of employment if the collector has reason to know the employer objects, contacting the debtor at unreasonable times or places, contacting third parties about the debt, harassing the debtor, or other oppressive practices. The FDCPA does not permit debt collectors to communicate with third parties to collect location information on the debtor without the prior consent of the court or the consumer (§1692[c] [b]). The key provisions governing a debt collector's contacts with persons other than the consumer are set forth below:

Any debt collector communicating with any person other than the consumer for acquiring location information about the consumer shall

(1) identify himself, state that he is confirming or correcting location information concerning the consumer, and, only if expressly requested, identify his employer;
(2) not state that such consumer owes any debt;
(3) not communicate with any such person more than once unless requested to do so by such person or unless the debt collector reasonably believes

that the earlier response of such person is erroneous or incomplete and that such person now has correct or complete location information;

(4) not communicate by postcard;

(5) not use any language or symbol on any envelope or in the contents of any communication effected by the mails or telegram that indicates that the debt collector is in the debt collection business or that the communication relates to the collection of a debt; and

(6) after the debt collector knows the consumer is represented by an attorney with regard to the subject debt and has knowledge of, or can readily ascertain, such attorney's name and address, not communicate with any person other than that attorney, unless the attorney fails to respond within a reasonable period of time to the communication from the debt collector.[1]

Permissible Actions in Communicating with Debtors

The FDCPA was enacted to punish and deter widespread problems of creditors using unfair tactics such as profane language, threats of physical violence, threats to ruin credit ratings, and repetitive telephone calls late at night and in the early morning. A collector may contact you in person or by mail, telephone, telegram, or fax. However, a debt collector may not contact you at inconvenient times or places, such as before 8 a.m. or after 9 p.m., unless you agree. A debt collector also may not contact you at work if the collector knows that your employer disapproves of such contacts.

Some creditors have even threatened to embarrass debtors by publicly humiliating them in the larger community. Congress and many state legislatures responded to this unfair practice by enacting statutes providing for civil penalties as well as injunctions against predatory credit collection. Contacts with debtors are governed by the following rules:

Communication with the consumer generally:
    Without the prior consent of the consumer given directly to the debt collector or the express permission of a court of competent jurisdiction, a debt collector may not communicate with a consumer in connection with the collection of any debt

(1) at any unusual time or place or a time or place known or which should be known to be inconvenient to the consumer. In the absence of knowledge of circumstances to the contrary, a debt collector shall assume that the convenient time for communicating with a consumer is after 8 o'clock antemeridian and before 9 o'clock postmeridian, local time at the consumer's location;

(2) if the debt collector knows the consumer is represented by an attorney with respect to such debt and has knowledge of, or can readily ascertain, such attorney's name and address, unless the attorney fails to respond within a reasonable period of time to a communication from the debt collector or unless the attorney consents to direct communication with the consumer; or

(3) at the consumer's place of employment if the debt collector knows or has reason to know that the consumer's employer prohibits the consumer from receiving such communication.[2]

Ceasing Communications

If you notify a debt collector in writing that you refuse to pay the debt and demand the debt collector cease further communication with you, the persistent debt collector will be liable to you for further collection efforts. Additionally, if you notify a debt collector in writing that you are refusing to pay a debt and inform them not to have further communications with you and she persists, the debt collector is subject to TILA damages.

> If a consumer notifies a debt collector in writing that the consumer refuses to pay a debt or that the consumer wishes the debt collector to cease further communication with the consumer, the debt collector shall not communicate further with the consumer with respect to such debt, except
>
> (1) to advise the consumer that the debt collector's further efforts are being terminated;
> (2) to notify the consumer that the debt collector or creditor may invoke specified remedies which are ordinarily invoked by such debt collector or creditor; or
> (3) where applicable, to notify the consumer that the debt collector or creditor intends to invoke a specified remedy.
>   If such notice from the consumer is made by mail, notification shall be complete upon receipt.
> (4) For the purpose of this section, the term "consumer" includes the consumer's spouse, parent (if the consumer is a minor), guardian, executor, or administrator.[3]

Debt collection agencies must send you a written notice containing the amount of the debt, the name of the creditor, and a summary of what action you should take if you believe you do not owe the money. You can stop collection efforts by writing a letter telling the agency to stop. However, the debt collector can restart collection activities if she sends you proof of the debt, such as the copy of your bill.

Debt Collection Abuses

Regulation M addresses debt collection abuses. The general standard is that debt collectors may not harass, oppress, or abuse you in the collection of a debt. Regulation M gives guidance as to what kind of conduct constitutes harassment or abuse, but the broad standard encompasses many other abuses. Regulation M gives the following examples of harassment, oppression, and abuse:

(1) The use or threat of use of violence or other criminal means to harm the physical person, reputation, or property of any person.
(2) The use of obscene or profane language or language the natural consequence of which is to abuse the hearer or reader.
(3) The publication of a list of consumers who allegedly refuse to pay debts, except to a consumer reporting agency or to persons meeting the requirements of section 603(f) or 604(3) of this Act.
(4) The advertisement for sale of any debt to coerce payment of the debt.
(5) Causing a telephone to ring or engaging any person in telephone conversation repeatedly or continuously with intent to annoy, abuse, or harass any person at the called number.
(6) Except as provided in section 804, the placement of telephone calls without meaningful disclosure of the caller's identity.[4]

A debt collector must send you a written notice of what is owed, the name of the creditor to whom you owe the money; and what action to take if you believe you do not owe the money within five days of being first contacted. Debt collectors may not use any false or misleading statements when collecting a debt or falsely imply that

- They are attorneys or government representatives;
- You have committed a crime by not paying a debt;
- They are operating or working for a credit bureau;
- The amount of your debt is different from what it is; and
- The documents they are sending you are legal forms, when they are not.

Debt collectors are subject to monetary damages for using obscene, profane, or other abusive language (§1692[d] [2]). Collection agencies and creditors are prohibited from causing your telephone to ring incessantly or calling with the intent to annoy or harass you (§1692[d] [2]). It is a violation of the FDCPA to contact the debtor at that person's place of employment if the debt collector knows or has reason to know that the consumer's employer does not allow this kind of communication (§1692c [a] [3]).

It is a violation of federal law for the creditor to threaten to file suit or use other high-pressure tactics in an attempt to collect a debt. Debt collectors may be liable to consumers for engaging in unfair, deceptive, or abusive practices, regardless of whether a valid debt actually exists. State as well as federal law prohibits abusive credit collection and unfair collection tactics. The debt collector must cease and desist from contacting you after you refuse to pay the debt. You must state unequivocally that the debt collector must cease communicating with you (§1692[c]).

Fraud or Misrepresentation

The FDCPA sanctions creditors who falsely misrepresent the amount of the debt that you owe. The creditor has a general obligation not to lie about the legal status of a debt (§1692e [2] [A]). A creditor may not masquerade as an attorney or wrongly imply that communication with you is from a lawyer (§1692[e] [3]). Both a debt collector and a creditor cannot represent that nonpayment of the debt will result in your arrest or imprisonment. The creditor cannot tell you that your wages will be garnished or personal property will be attached or levied unless the action is lawful and the creditor actually intends to take these steps (§1692[e] [4]). Furthermore, a debt collector may not threaten to communication credit information that is false to harass you (§1692e [8]). Finally, the creditor is not permitted to use fraud, artifice, or other deceptive methods to collect your debt (§1692e [10]).

Private Enforcement of the FDCPA

You may recover money for any damages caused by creditors' unfair or deceptive debt collection practices, plus an additional amount up to $1,000 in TILA statutory damages. If you prevail in any TILA actions, you can recoup your attorney's fees as well as costs in the appropriate case. In a class action, your TILA recovery is capped at the lesser of $500,000 or 1 percent of the debt collector's net worth. As with an individual action, the prevailing plaintiffs may recover reasonable attorney's fees and costs. In a class action, the size of the FDCPA award may be calibrated on the nature of the offense, persistence by the debt collector, the nature of such noncompliance, the resources of the debt collector, the number of persons adversely affected, and the extent to which the debt collector's noncompliance was intentional. If a court finds that you or a plaintiff class filed a bad faith FDCPA lawsuit, you may end up paying the creditor or debt collector's reasonable attorney's fees and costs (15 U.S.C. §1692k). In individual cases, the debt collector may calibrate FDCPA damages on the frequency and persistence of noncompliance.

Defenses against FDCPA Actions

A debt collector can defend an action by showing that the violation was not intentional and resulted from a bona fide error, despite having procedures to avoid such errors. The statute of limitation for an FDCPA action is one year from the date of the violation.

FTC Administrative Enforcement

The FTC has the power to prosecute FDCPA violations as unfair or deceptive acts or practices in violation of the Federal Trade Commission Act. The FTC can use all its powers to enforce compliance with the act, even if there is no showing that the debtor was acting in interstate commerce (15 U.S.C.

§1692*l*). In addition, the member banks of the Federal Reserve System have jurisdiction to enforce the act, as well as the comptroller of the currency.

State Regulations on Debt Collection

Federal debt collection is governed by the Truth in Lending Act. Every state has functionally equivalent statutes governing truth in lending, as well as statutes governing debt collection, both of which protect you. Virginia's state statute provides that every lender subject to TILA shall also be subject to state penalties (see Va. Code Ann. §6.1-330.79). If a creditor fails to comply with TILA and its regulations in the offering or extending of consumer credit, you can file claims under both state and federal law, though you will only receive one award.

State law in many jurisdictions regulates debt collection agencies and businesses. Unfair debt collection is governed as well by state Little FTC Acts or Unfair and Deceptive Trade Practices Acts. It is considered to be a violation of UDTPA to make false or misleading statements to collect a consumer debt. It is a violation of state and federal debt collection laws and UDTPA whenever a collector harasses consumer debtors. You can receive treble damages or other remedies under state UDTPAs when a collector requests more than basic location information about the debtor from another person. Additionally, an employer or others cannot be told that you owe a debt, with one exception: If the creditor is garnisheeing your wages, it is therefore necessary to make that disclosure.

Defending Debt Collection in Small Claims Court

A growing number of creditors are filing lawsuits against debtors in small claims court. Small claims court is a forum with informal procedures and rules of evidence that encourages self-representation, but creditors will often have attorneys representing them. If you are sued in a small claims court, you will receive a *summons*, which is a written notice, in a specific form, delivered to the parties being sued. If you receive a summons, you must answer the plaintiff's attached complaint within a specific time and appear in court or a judgment will be entered against you. An *answer* is a paper filed in court and sent to the plaintiff by the defendant, either admitting or denying the statements in the plaintiff's complaint and briefly explaining why the plaintiff's claims are wrong and why the defendant is not responsible for the plaintiff's injury or loss.

Small claims courts were originally organized to help consumers, but the majority of small claims contract actions are filed by large corporations against consumers. If you have sufficient economic resources and a good cause of action, hire a lawyer. If your creditor files suit in small claims court (or in a state general jurisdiction court), it may be able to attach your home, wages, or other assets to secure payment if it wins the lawsuit.

What to Do: Stop Debt Collectors

The Fair Debt Collection Practices Act allows you to stop debt collectors from contacting you by requesting in writing that they stop. Congress enacted the FDCPA because of clear and convincing evidence of abusive, deceptive, and unfair debt collection practices by many debt collectors. Congress found that abusive debt collection practices contributed significantly to the number of personal bankruptcies, marital instability, loss of jobs, and to invasions of individual privacy. The FDCPA defines the term *debt collector* as "any person who uses any instrumentality of interstate commerce or the mails in any business the principal purpose of which is the collection of any debts, or who regularly collects or attempts to collect, directly or indirectly, debts owed or due or asserted to be owed or due another" (15 USC 1692a).

Once the collector receives your letter, they may not contact you again except to say there will be no further contact or to notify you that the debt collector or the creditor intends to take some specific action. The letter only stops collection efforts. The debt collector or your original creditor may still sue you for collection of the debt.

What to Do: Filing FDCPA Complaints

You can file an FDCPA lawsuit against a debt collector in either state or federal courts, so long as the action is filed within one year from the date of the violation. Another option is to complain to the state attorney general's consumer protection division. The chances are good that your jurisdiction will have state regulations governing debt collection. You can also file a complaint against a debt collector at the FTC's website at www.ftc.gov. Consumer complaints are shared with other agencies on FTC's Consumer Sentinel. You can also register your complaint by calling the FTC toll-free at 1-877-FTC-HELP (1-877-382-4357).

Enforcing Judgments against You

The term *judgment* refers to the final decision of the court. A judgment is a determination of the rights and obligations of the parties. In a given lawsuit, a judgment may direct a dismissal of the lawsuit, order payment of a money amount or direct one or more of the parties to do an act. The term *income execution* refers to the enforcement of judgment. Income execution means the legal process of enforcing a judgment. To do so, creditors will seek a court order to receive the appropriate authority to seize your property. *Garnishment* refers to the seizure of part of your wages or personal property. The garnishment of wages requires your employer to withhold a portion of your wages to satisfy the judgment. For that to occur, a judgment creditor (the party who is entitled to a judgment against you) must complete and file a wage garnishment order.

State law determines what portion of your wages or other property can be held in an amount to satisfy the judgment. The taking of property into legal custody by an enforcement officer is the process of *attachment*. The term *seizure* refers to the legal process by which a person authorized under the law takes custody of your personal or real property to satisfy a judgment. In addition, the seized property may be held to guarantee a judgment or be sold to satisfy a judgment. The term *replevin* is an action brought for the owner of items to recover possession of personal property, when those items were wrongfully taken or are being wrongfully kept by a creditor or other person.

Restrictions on Garnishment

Garnishment is a state law remedy that permits creditors to seize a portion of the debtor's wages as well as other assets. Federal law limits garnishment to 25 percent of the debtor's after-tax earnings, up to a maximum amount. In a recently published opinion, the Michigan Court of Appeals held that pursuant to 42 USC §407(a), Social Security benefits are not subject to garnishment, even after the recipient receives and deposits the money in a bank account.

Bankruptcy Filing and Credit Counseling

Credit cards are a high-profit financial service product with little in the way of consumer protection. The largest increase in consumer credit card debt is occurring among households with a reported income of less than $10,000.[5] Credit card marketing campaigns are aggressively recruiting new customers to take on greater debt levels.[6] Robert D. Manning of the Rochester Institute of Technology describes the rise of mailed solicitations that occurred in the period between 1997 and 2001: "66.7 percent: 1997 (3.0 billion), 1998 (3.4 billion), 1999 (2.9 billion), 2000 (3.5 billion) and 2001 (5.0 billion)."[7] The credit card debt incurred by senior citizens (over sixty-four years old) tripled from $1,497 in 1989 to $3,607 in 1998.[8] The most aggressive credit card marketing is to college students, who use the cards for everything from pizza to paying the rent. Consumers are left unprotected from the widespread availability of unsecured "revolving" credit. The true cost of borrowing on bank credit cards more than doubled from 1983 to 1992, when escalating penalty and user fees are taken into account.[9] The revenue earned by credit card companies from late fees increased from $1.7 billion in 1996 to $7.3 billion in 2001.[10]

Consumer bankruptcy is the running partner of liberal consumer credit. The U.S. Trustee Program of the U.S. Department of Justice protects the integrity of the nation's bankruptcy system by overseeing case administration and litigating to enforce bankruptcy laws. In 2005, the lending community successfully lobbied Congress to make it more onerous to file for bankruptcy protection. The Bankruptcy Abuse Prevention and Consumer

Protection Act of 2005 was enacted by Congress and signed into law by President George W. Bush on April 20, 2005. The federal statute has the words *consumer protection* in the name of the statute, but it is anything but a consumer's friend.

The law places new barriers in front of consumers who wish to file for bankruptcy. It requires a "means test" to determine whether a debtor is eligible for Chapter 7 (liquidation) or must file under Chapter 13 (wage-earner repayment plan). Additionally, the law gives the U.S. trustee new responsibilities and powers. The U.S. trustee's office certifies entities that provide mandatory financial education to debtors before they receive a discharge under bankruptcy. As of October 17, 2005, consumers are now required to seek credit counseling from one of those government-approved organizations within six months before filing for either Chapter 7 or Chapter 13 bankruptcy protection. The trustee's office supervises random audits for those consumers filing Chapter 7 documents to determine whether the disclosures are accurate. Consumers filing inaccurate disclosures are subject to criminal as well as civil liability. The trustee's office is also now required to provide greater oversight over small businesses in Chapter 11 reorganization bankruptcy.

It should also be noted that filing for bankruptcy will not alleviate all your debts. Student loans, alimony and child support, and court judgments, to name a few, are still largely the responsibility of the debtor, even if bankruptcy proceedings are successful. Bankruptcy courts will sometimes excuse debts in these categories if the debtor is suffering from severe mental illness, but the court's discretion is quite limited.

Consumers considering bankruptcy can locate a state-by-state list of government-approved credit counseling organizations at www.usdoj.gov/ust, which is the U.S. Department of Justice's website for the U.S. Trustee Program. Credit counseling involves general advice on money management, developing a budget, and managing debt. The consumer can comply with the federal bankruptcy act's credit counseling requirement by completing credit counseling in person, by telephone, or online.

The compulsory credit counseling session will last approximately ninety minutes and requires you to pay a fee. Credit counseling organizations on the U.S. trustee's list must waive the fee for anyone who is unable to pay the fee, which will generally be in the range of $50 but could be higher, depending on services offered or the area of the country. In order to comply with the requirement, the consumer must receive a certificate as proof.

Chapter 7 Liquidation Bankruptcy for Consumers
The federal bankruptcy code has a number of articles defining different types of bankruptcy. Chapter 7 is the article of bankruptcy that applies to "liquidation bankruptcies" for both consumers and businesses, also referred to as "total bankruptcy." A consumer filing a Chapter 7 bankruptcy will list all the

debts owed, and the bankruptcy judge will discharge many of them. Consumers without medical insurance, for example, may have thousands of dollars worth of medical bills that are discharged under Chapter 7. However, the downside of a Chapter 7 bankruptcy is that the consumer will be required to turn over his or her assets for distribution to the creditors, which usually includes one's home. For more information on Chapter 7 bankruptcy, see http://www.uscourts.gov/bankruptcycourts/bankruptcybasics/chapter7.html.

One of the great advantages of bankruptcy is that you get a "fresh start." Many of your debts, including credit cards bills, are discharged. Once a Chapter 7 bankruptcy is filed, the federal bankruptcy court imposes an automatic stay that has the effect of preventing creditors from continuing to demand payment of debts. Any relief that the creditors receive must be in petitions for relief of the automatic stay; they are not permitted to enforce debts after the bankruptcy petition has been filed. Pursuing collection contacts, lawsuits, garnishments, or repossessions despite the bankruptcy stay or discharge is a violation of federal law. If a debtor contacts you to collect debts after you file for bankruptcy, you may have an action for punitive as well as actual damages and attorney fees. The automatic stay requires that creditors cease and desist all collection efforts.

Chapter 13 Reorganization Bankruptcy for Consumers
A Chapter 13 bankruptcy involves a plan to adjust or reduce debts for a debtor with a regular source of income. It provides the ground rules for debtors to pay back their creditors, albeit at a reduced amount, pursuant to a plan in which the consumer makes payments over a period of time of up to five years. This process is completely supervised by the court. One of the advantages of a Chapter 13 bankruptcy is that debtors generally are allowed to keep their property. With the help of a bankruptcy trustee and in consultation with creditors, a plan is developed for repayment that must be approved by the bankruptcy judge. Once a Chapter 13 plan is approved by the bankruptcy court, the debtor begins to make payments within thirty to forty-five days. Creditors may be subject to punitive damages if they do not follow the terms of the repayment plan approved by the court. For more on Chapter 13 bankruptcy, see http://www.uscourts.gov/bankruptcycourts/bankruptcybasics/chapter13.html.

Exceptions to the Discharge in Bankruptcy
The federal bankruptcy law does not permit discharges for debtors in which any debt (money, property, services, credit, etc.) is obtained by fraud, false pretenses, or an intention to deceive (11 U.S.C. §523[a] [2] [A]). The creditor must prove that you obtained money through a material misrepresentation that at the time you knew was false or made with gross recklessness as to its truth. The creditor must also show that you had intent to deceive. Moreover, the creditor must prove that it reasonably relied on your false

representation and that its reliance was the proximate cause of loss. When a credit card company issues a credit card with no credit check of the applicant, it assumes the risk and cannot ask for a discharge in bankruptcy, even if there are mistakes on your credit card application.

Notes

1. 15 U.S.C. §1692(b).
2. 15 U.S.C. §1692(c).
3. Ibid.
4. 15 U.S.C. §1692(d).
5. Testimony of Dr. Robert D. Manning, Caroline Werner Gannett Professor of Humanities, Rochester Institute of Technology, hearing on "The Role of FRCRA in the Credit Granting Process," before the U.S. House of Representatives Subcommittee on Financial Institutions and Consumer Credit, June 12, 2003.
6. Ibid., 5.
7. Ibid.
8. Ibid., 6.
9. Ibid., 7.
10. Ibid.

13

Protecting Home Sweet Home

Buying a home is typically your most expensive consumer transaction. In the late twentieth century, housing prices skyrocketed in many areas of the United States. Like a candle, housing prices will burn themselves out during periods of economic slowdown. If home prices collapse, hundreds of thousands of consumers may lose their homes.

This chapter provides basic information on consumer protection rules governing housing. The FTC has the authority to enforce the Real Estate Settlement Procedures Act, Truth in Lending Act (TILA, implemented by Regulation Z), Fair Credit Reporting Act (FCRA), Fair Debt Collection Practices Act (FDCPA), and the Home Mortgage Disclosure Act (HMDA). The states will typically have the jurisdiction to regulate mortgage brokers or lenders. Massachusetts defines a mortgage broker broadly as any person who gains compensation from negotiating or assigning in the placement of mortgage loans on residential property for others (see M.G.L.A. ch. 255E). California, for example, issues finance lender's licenses as well as residential mortgage lender's licenses through the California Department of Corporations.

The Lease Contract

The relationship between property owners and their tenants is governed by the rental agreement, whether written or oral. The landlord-tenant agreement generally takes the form of a written lease agreement. If you do not have a written lease, you will be classified as a tenant at will. The two parties to the lease are the property owner, who holds the land, and the tenant, who pays rent as the quid pro quo for using and occupying the landlord's property. I rented an apartment in Lund, Sweden, in the summer of 2006 and found that the Swedish government dictated covenants, conditions, and conditional limitations in my lease agreement. I agreed, for example, not to paint the apartment without the property owner's consent. I was responsible for replacing batteries in fire alarms, but the property owner was responsible for the plumbing and other key infrastructure.

Renting Without a Lease

When the property owner and tenant enter into a contract without a written lease, it is called a month-to-month lease or tenancy. In the month-to-month tenancy, the tenant continues to maintain possession of the property for successive monthly periods, beginning on a specific calendar day. Either the property owner or the tenant may terminate a month-to-month lease as long as the terminating party gives one month's notice. If, however, notice of termination is given to the tenant less than one calendar month before the beginning of the next month-to-month period, the tenant may remain in the apartment for an additional month.

Landlord's Warranty of Habitability

In most states, the property owner must fulfill the *implied warranty of habitability* even if there is no written lease. Your landlord has a duty to maintain all apartments and buildings in a condition fit for living and not dangerous to the life, health, or safety of the tenant. Your landlord will be held liable for any violation of the warranty of habitability, even if the property owner did not cause the condition. Nevertheless, the property owner is not liable if you or your guest cause the condition breaching the warranty of habitability. If the property owner violated the implied warranty of habitability, you may withhold payment of rent until the condition is repaired or may take action to force the landlord to make needed repairs. If the property owner takes action against you, you can defend against any action with a counterclaim that the warranty of habitability was violated. If the conditions are so serious (no heat, electricity, infestation of rodents), you may claim "constructive eviction." You may leave the apartment or house, rescind the lease, and withhold payment until the landlord takes remedial actions correcting the condition.

Covenant of Quiet Enjoyment

Your rights as a tenant include the right to "quiet enjoyment." That term means that you have a right to enjoy the premises you rent. If your lease explicitly provides that the landlord perform a specific service for the tenant, such as providing utility services, the covenant prohibits the landlord from intentionally or willfully cutting off the service. A landlord may not interrupt utilities to a tenant unless the interruption results from bona fide repairs, construction, or an emergency. In New York, such action would also be a criminal offense. Because of the right to quiet enjoyment, the landlord cannot evict you without cause or otherwise disturb your right to live in peace and quiet.

Security Devices

All states have requirements as to the minimum features of an apartment. Texas state law, for example, requires that a house or apartment be equipped with security devices such as window latches, keyed deadbolts on exterior doors, sliding door pin locks and sliding door handle latches or sliding door security bars, and door viewers. The Texas attorney general requires that security devices be installed at the landlord's expense. If such devices are missing or are defective, you have the right to request their installation or repair. Texas state statutes are located in full-text format at http://www.oag.state.tx.us/AG_Publications/txts/tenant.shtml.

Security Deposits

You may be required by your landlord to pay a security deposit at the beginning of the lease to insure the landlord against potential damages and unpaid rent. The landlord may request up to one month's rent to be held in security during the term of the lease in most jurisdictions. Many states have statutes requiring the landlord to place your security deposit in a separate interest-bearing bank account.

Remedies for Breach of the Lease Agreement

You are responsible for paying the rent for the entire period of your lease. Even if you are evicted for failing to pay rent, you will be responsible for the rent remaining on the lease. However, the landlord must make attempts to find an alternative tenant. If the landlord made no attempts to obtain an alternative tenant and had, therefore, failed to mitigate damages, you will not be liable for repaying the landlord.

Tenant Rights: Failure to Give Notice of Eviction

Florida requires landlords to give a three-day notice to pay rent as well as initiation of the appropriate legal process for eviction. In Florida, the remedy for wrongful eviction is three times the monthly rate or actual damages, as well as attorney's fees. Nearly every state has a statute that requires the landlord to give you notice of eviction.

Constructive Eviction

If your apartment becomes uninhabitable due to rat infestation or other conditions, you will have the right to withhold rent. In a recent Maryland case, a landlord settled a claim for $95,000 for a family forced to destroy their belongings due to mold infestation. The family also suffered from flu-like symptoms, headaches, asthma, and respiratory problems from the mold and claimed $5,000 in medical expenses. In that case, the tenants complained about the mold over a nine-month period, and the property owner failed to take prompt remedial action (*Appollon v. Townley Associates*, No. CAL03-26744 [Prince George's Cty., Md., May 2005]).

Example: Wrongful Eviction. If the landlord removes your property or attempts to evict you for rent withholding due to hazardous conditions, you will have an action for wrongful eviction. In a 1990 Georgia case, a tenant paid one-half of one month's rent and did not pay rent the next month because of rat infestation. The property owner removed plaintiff's property from a storage area and the exterior doors from plaintiff's apartment and hauled away the tenant's possessions. A Georgia jury hearing about the landlord's callous actions imposed a $25,000 punitive damages award in addition to the actual damages of $5,650 (*Arnold v. Sycamore Drive Assoc.*, Case No. 89A-61191-2 [DeKalb Cty. Ga., Jan. 25, 1990]).

Landlord's Premises Liability

Premises liability is a relatively new legal development. At common law, the landlord had no liability for injuries caused by the condition of the premises once you were occupying the house or apartment. Today a landlord will have liability for injuries caused by dangerous defects in the premises in every jurisdiction. In a recent Michigan case, the tenant was sitting on the toilet when water run by plumbers leaked and caused the bathroom ceiling and walls to collapse onto him. In the process of escaping from the falling debris, the tenant jumped up and, while attempting to pull on his pants, he fell and struck his knee and head. In this unusual premises liability case, the plaintiff received $16,000 in compensatory damages.

A tenant can have a tort action against a landlord for dangerous conditions. If the landlord, for example, fails to keep the stairs in a safe condition for the tenants, the consumer will have an action for negligence. The property owner's general duty of care is to maintain the premises in a safe condition.

In a 2004 case, a Massachusetts tenant entered into a confidential settlement with the property owner who was charged with failing to comply with the federal government's standards for government-regulated lead paint removal requirements. The plaintiff in that case was a minor child whose claim was that her neuropsychological deficits were caused by lead paint. Once the leasehold began, it was the lessee's responsibility to correct unsafe conditions. Today, the landlord has liability for latent defects in the premises. If the stairwell collapses, the property owner's liability is clear, as is the landlord's duty to repair defects existing at the commencement of the tenancy. Property owners, for example, are responsible for lighting common areas. A property owner's tort liability may be based on violation of building codes, statutes, ordinances, or regulations.

In Colorado, for example, many communities require property owners to place fences around swimming pools. A property owner may also be responsible in a "slip and fall" case for failing to maintain sidewalks. A tenant slipping on an uneven or slippery walking surface would have a negligence-based cause of action.

Example: Negligent Maintenance of Apartment Parking Lot. A Massachusetts tenant received an $180,000 settlement arising out of a serious knee injury he suffered when he tripped and fell forward while he was walking in an apartment complex's parking lot. The tenant fell after his left foot became wedged between the slats of a drain grate located in the parking lot, causing his left leg to twist as he fell. The tenant filed a premises liability lawsuit contending that the property owner was liable for inadequate drainage, uneven pavement, and potholes developed in the spring because of frost heaves, which caused the pavement to break apart. The tenant had evidence that frost heaves caused uneven pavement in past years. The Massachusetts tenant also contended that the drain grate located in the parking lot did not conform to state codes because the slats were located too far apart, which allowed his foot to become lodged between the slats.

Common Areas

Many states have enacted the landlord-tenant statutes that require landlords to maintain leased premises in habitable condition and to maintain the common areas. A property owner, for example, will be liable for failing to keep common areas safe. A tenant injured when she fell on the apartment complex sidewalk may have an action against the property owner for failing to keep the sidewalk cleared.

Paint and Other Hazardous Conditions

A landlord will be liable to you for dangerous conditions such as lead paint or mold. If you move into a property and observe that there is flaking paint, take pictures. Be sure that you call the conditions to the attention of the landlord. If the landlord does not fix the condition, you should contact your local health department. The landlord-tenant relationship is governed by contract, and you can withhold rent until hazardous conditions are fixed. In addition, if you are injured by hazardous conditions, you need to retain an attorney and file a lawsuit based upon the property owner's negligence in failing to correct the condition. In most states, you will also be able to file suit for double or treble damages under a state UDTPA.

In a Maryland case, a two-year-old suffered brain damage from ingesting lead paint chips, and her mother prevailed under Maryland's Consumer Protection Act. In that case, the tenant took pictures of the conditions and contacted the landlord at the beginning of her tenancy. The jury awarded the injured tenant $1,500,000 for the damages caused by the toxic exposure (see *Byrd v. National Realty*, No. 94318092/CC188749 [Baltimore Cty. Circuit Ct., July 10, 1997]).

Negligent Security Liability

A growing number of states are recognizing that the landlord has a duty to maintain a secure environment. In 2004 a Fulton, Georgia, jury awarded a woman $9,000,000 in compensatory damages in a premises liability lawsuit against her apartment management and owners. In that case, two assailants put a gun to her back and pushed her into her apartment, where she was raped and robbed. The landlord was negligent in failing to properly maintain and secure the apartment complex and creating a nuisance by failing to remedy the dangerous condition. The plaintiff cited prior similar crimes in the immediate area, coupled with the landlord's knowledge of the problem as the basis of the duty to maintain greater security (*Anonymous Female v. EPT Management Co.*, No. 02VS034714 [Fulton Cty. Ga., Dec. 5, 2005]).

In order to win a negligent security lawsuit against your landlord, you must prove that the property owner had a duty to provide better security after having notice of prior similar issues. If there have been prior similar crimes such as rapes, robberies, or assault, the landlord has a duty to fortify security. Courts will typically examine factors such as (1) whether there have been prior similar crimes, (2) the cost of increased security measures, and (3) the degree to which security measures will detect or deter crimes. In the absence of a history of similar intrusions and security breaches, foreseeability is based on all facts and circumstances.

Any duty to protect consumers from third-party criminals is predicated on preventable risks. Courts are unlikely to be receptive to claims of premises liability where there has been no prior similar crime or the attack was a bizarre, unforeseeable event. Negligent security claims are premised upon the claim that the business failed to act in a reasonable way.

Buying a Home

Consider hiring an attorney to represent you when you purchase a home. Do not count on a real estate agent to represent your interests. The real estate agent's duty is to represent the seller of the home. Do comparison shopping on interest rates offered by lenders. The most important term is the annual percentage rate. The APR consists of the interest rate and other fees such as points, broker fees, and other credit charges. Be sure to determine whether the interest rate is fixed or adjustable. In late 2006, adjustable rate mortgages were raising payments hundreds of dollars per month. If the adjustable rate has a floor and ceiling, you will have more protection than if it can skyrocket.

The Real Estate Settlement Procedures Act
The Real Estate Settlement Procedures Act requires lenders to disclose closing costs, escrow account practices, and whether you can pay off your mortgage earlier. RESPA addresses unfair practices when interest rates at closings are different from what was promised. A second widespread problem was that lenders imposed additional costs not disclosed prior to the closing. Congress enacted RESPA to protect you from unreasonable and exorbitant real estate settlement costs.

RESPA suffers from the same disability as the other TILA provisions by focusing solely on disclosures. Congress assumed that consumers could protect themselves from exorbitant charges if they had accurate disclosures about the costs required to close a mortgage transaction. RESPA requires lenders to give you two important disclosures: (1) a good faith estimate of settlement costs, and (2) the settlement statement.

The good faith estimate provides you with an itemized estimate of the costs you are expected to pay at closing. RESPA's settlement cost disclosures (like all the other TILA disclosures) are expressed as the APR. The APR, as used in other TILA chapters, is expressed as an annual percentage rate that is functionally equivalent to an interest rate. The finance charge is expressed as the full dollar cost of borrowing over all years, whereas the APR is that dollar cost expressed as an annual percentage rate. Housing and Urban Development's Regulation X implements RESPA. Regulation X imposes other disclosure requirements in the mortgage servicing process, including initial and annual escrow account statements and notice of the transfer of loan servicing. RESPA prohibits kickbacks, referral fees, and unearned fees because these unsavory practices result in exorbitant costs for consumers. RESPA also limits the amounts creditors can collect for escrow accounts, prohibits sellers' requiring a purchaser/borrower to obtain title insurance from a particular title company, and provides rights for consumers when loan servicing is transferred. Mortgage lenders must also inform you if there is a possibility that your loan will be sold on the secondary market.

Home Ownership and Equity Protection Act

The Home Ownership and Equity Protection Act (HOEPA) amends TILA to cover certain high-rate home equity loans. You have the right to cancel home equity loans during the initial three-day period. In addition to notice of the right to cancel and other disclosures required by TILA, if a loan is covered under HOEPA, lenders must provide you with additional disclosures of the APR and monthly payment three days prior to closing.

These disclosures must also include provisions telling you that you are not required to sign the loan agreement simply because you received the disclosure statements. HOEPA also requires a disclosure that you may lose your home if you do not repay according to the terms of the loan. In addition to the disclosure requirements, HOEPA prohibits the inclusion of certain terms in the loan contract. Furthermore, if a refinancing or a home equity loan is classified as "high cost," the lender must provide key information about the loan three days before closing on the loan. The HOEPA also prohibits lenders from making a home equity loan without regard to a borrower's ability to repay.

A loan covered under HOEPA may not include the following: (1) a term that increases the interest rate in the event of default, (2) balloon payments in loans of less than five years' length, (3) negative amortization, (4) more than two prepaid payments, (5) extending credit to individuals without regard to their ability to repay the loan, and (6) disbursement of funds payable solely to a home improvement contractor instead of jointly or solely to the consumer. Most prepayment penalties are also prohibited. Violations of HOEPA's disclosure provisions and inclusion of prohibited contract terms will give rise to civil liability for actual damages, statutory damages, and attorney's fees and costs. In addition, there are special enhanced damages that include finance charges and fees paid by the consumer for material violations. HOEPA violations are also subject to the TILA's extended right to rescind.

If your loan is assigned (resold) to another lender, the company having a right to receive mortgage payments is the assignor, and the company obtaining the right to payment is called the assignee. When a loan company sells your mortgage, the assignee has the right to obtain payment from you. Assignees of loans covered under HOEPA are liable for all claims and defenses with respect to the assigned mortgage that the consumer could assert against the originator of the loan, except to the extent of certain limitations on damages. Because HOEPA is a chapter of the TILA, a plaintiff may seek rescission (cancellation of the loan agreement) or statutory or actual damages. Even where actual damages are not provable, TILA permits the recovery of statutory damages.

What to Do: Home Equity Loans
The FTC has the following advice on what to do and not do when it comes to equity loans. These FTC guidelines are also useful in avoiding being victimized by deceptive or unfair home lending practices:

Do Not:
1. Agree to a home equity loan if you do not have enough income to make the monthly payments.
2. Sign any document you haven't read or any document that has blank spaces to be filled in after you sign.
3. Let anyone pressure you into signing any document.
4. Agree to a loan that includes credit insurance or extra products you do not want.
5. Let the promise of extra cash or lower monthly payments get in the way of your good judgment about whether the cost you will pay for the loan is really worth it.
6. Deed your property to anyone. First consult an attorney, a knowledgeable family member, or someone else you trust.

Do:
1. Ask specifically if credit insurance is required as a condition of the loan. If it is not, and a charge is included in your loan and you do not want the insurance, ask that the charge be removed from the loan documents.

If you want the added security of credit insurance, shop around for the best rates.

2. Keep careful records of what you have paid, including billing statements and canceled checks. Challenge any charge you think is inaccurate.

3. Check contractors' references when it is time to have work done in your home.

4. Get more than one estimate before signing a home improvement contract.

5. Read all items carefully. If you need an explanation of any terms or conditions, talk to someone you can trust, such as a knowledgeable family member or an attorney.

6. Consider all the costs of financing before you agree to a loan.[1]

Mortgage Brokers

Mortgage brokers assist low- or moderate-income consumers in obtaining credit or a loan. Since the 1980s, mortgage brokers have evolved as a major player in home buying. The National Association of Mortgage Brokers (NAMB) has 16,000 members and forty-six state affiliates. Mortgage brokers account for nearly two in three contracts between American consumers and the mortgage industry. Four factors account for the rise of this new housing market player: interest rate volatility, widespread bank failure, capital market innovations, and information technology changes.[2]

Third-party mortgage brokers assist low-income and moderate-income clients through the application process with lenders. Many brokers, for example, assist consumers in resolving consumer problems. When the application has been accepted, the mortgage bank is responsible for communicating with consumers. A recent FTC study was critical of the compensation paid to brokers and concluded that consumers were more likely to obtain less expensive mortgages if they received information that encouraged comparison shopping on loan costs.

The NAMB is concerned with brokers that target low-income consumers incapable of paying back their loan. In recent Congressional testimony, the NAMB noted how abusive lending practices strip consumers of equity and destroy the dream of home ownership by foreclosure. Congress has been concerned with systematic abuses such as brokers who alter loan documents, misrepresent their client's ability to pay, and commit unfair and deceptive trade practices. Dishonest brokers will use false information to fraudulently induce lenders to loan more money to consumers than they would ordinarily qualify for by falsifying information such as down payments, the actual sales price of the property, and income information. By misrepresenting down payments, for example, the broker can then inflate his fees or commissions.

The FTC obtained a default judgment against a Colorado-based mortgage broker, enjoining him from making false claims about home mortgage financing services and ordering him to make redress to consumers. The FTC charged the broker with deceptively claiming he could refinance consumers' mortgages at the lowest available rates at no cost to consumers. In that case, the broker promised consumers "no-fee," low-interest home mortgages following a process of multiple refinances. This particular broker told consumers to apply for two loans, one at a competitive rate and one at a higher-than-market rate.

The lenders on the higher-than-market rate loans would then pay a premium to the mortgage broker that in turn would be used to pay fees associated with the lower-interest loan. The defendants allegedly claimed that the low-interest loan would then be used to pay the higher-interest loan, leaving the consumer with a low-interest, "no-fee" loan. What actually happened was that the consumer never received the low-interest loan and then only obtained approval for the high-interest loan. The broker often failed to pay appraisal fees, leaving many consumers with liens on their properties. The FTC action against this broker is available at http://www.ftc.gov/opa/2005/03/pwrprocessing.htm.

Brokers in Massachusetts were found to be systematically committing deceptive and unfair trade practices by offering mortgages that were unaffordable. All of them targeted low-income consumers in Boston and other cities. The Massachusetts commissioner of banks found three of the mortgage brokers to be unlicensed and drove all seven brokers from the Commonwealth of Massachusetts in September 2006.[3]

The NAMB favors prelicensure education and continuing education requirements for brokers. States vary significantly in their regulation of mortgage brokers. Alabama, Alaska, and Colorado, for example, have no state regulations governing mortgage brokers. Arizona, in contrast, requires brokers to be licensed and maintain a surety bond between $10,000 and $15,000. A surety bond is a contract by which a company is paid to step into the shoes of the mortgage broker if she fails to perform. The surety company, for example, is responsible to the consumer for fulfilling a contract if the mortgage broker defaults. Illinois requires that its mortgage brokers have a net worth of $35,000 and a surety bond of $20,000. Mortgage broker licensees must have three years' experience in real estate financing or attend mortgage lending classes. Massachusetts does not require its brokers to have any specific financial worth, but they must have a year's practice in selling real estate.

Refinancing a Mortgage

Be wary of lenders that encourage you to refinance. You should only refinance if you can get a rate at least 1 percentage point lower than your existing rate and if you plan to keep the new mortgage for several years. The extra fees incurred in refinancing are a concern if you treat your home as an ATM.

Reverse Mortgages

Reverse mortgages are marketed to American consumers age sixty-two or over. In a regular mortgage, you make monthly payments to the lender. In a "reverse" mortgage, the lender makes payments to you, and you do not pay anything so long as you live. The loan is repaid by selling your home after your death. The advantage of a "reverse" mortgage is that you can cash out the equity in your home and continue to live in your house. The proceeds of a reverse mortgage (without other features, like an annuity) are generally tax-free, and many reverse mortgages have no income restrictions. The FTC provides the following guidance before entering into a reverse mortgage:

- Lenders generally charge origination fees and other closing costs for a reverse mortgage. Lenders also may charge servicing fees during the term of the mortgage. The lender generally sets these fees and costs.
- The amount you owe on a reverse mortgage generally grows over time. Interest is charged on the outstanding balance and added to the amount you owe each month. That means your total debt increases over time as loan funds are advanced to you and interest accrues on the loan.
- Reverse mortgages may have fixed or variable rates. Most have variable rates that are tied to a financial index and will likely change according to market conditions.
- Reverse mortgages can use up all or some of the equity in your home, leaving fewer assets for you and your heirs. A "no recourse" clause, found in most reverse mortgages, prevents either you or your estate from owing more than the value of your home when the loan is repaid.
- Because you retain title to your home, you remain responsible for property taxes, insurance, utilities, fuel, maintenance, and other expenses. If you do not pay property taxes or maintain homeowner's insurance, for example, you risk the loan becoming due and payable.
- Interest on reverse mortgages is not deductible on income tax returns until the loan is paid off in part or whole.[4]

Federal Regulation of Home Lenders

The Fair Housing Act, the Equal Credit Opportunity Act, and the Truth in Lending Act as amended by the Home Ownership and Equity Protection Act and the Real Estate Settlement Procedures Act all provide consumers with disclosures for home loans. The Federal Land Sale Act is another potential source of protection for homeowners whose homes have been foreclosed.

Subprime Lending

Subprime loans offer loans with a higher rate of interest than prime loans to consumers with poor credit. HUD identifies three emblems of subprime lending:

1. Subprime lenders target home refinance loans far more often than do prime lenders;
2. Subprime lenders originate more of their loans in predominately black census tracts than prime lenders; and
3. The terms *consumer*, *finance*, and *acceptance* are frequently in the title of companies offering subprime loans (HUD, "Fair Housing and Equal Opportunity: Subprime Lending," 2006).

HUD found 183 subprime lenders in 2002, up from only fifty-one a decade earlier. HUD describes subprime loans as products offered to persons with blemished or limited credit histories who have a higher interest rate because of the greater credit risk. HUD documented empirical research confirming that upper-income African Americans were one-and-a-half times more likely to be offered subprime loans than their white counterparts.

The practice of *reverse redlining* involves targeting minority communities as a place to make high-interest, subprime loans. In neighborhoods where Hispanics comprise "at least 80 percent of the population, they were 1.5 times as likely as the nation as a whole to have a mortgage loan."[5] The implication of this finding is that Hispanics were targeted for subprime loans disproportionately even when they might have qualified for more favorable loans.

Predatory Lending

Predatory lending is the unsavory practice of using fraud or deception to take unfair advantage of less educated consumers. HUD and the U.S. Treasury describe predatory lending as unfair actions taken by "creditors, brokers, or even home improvement contractors," generally taking the form of aggressive sales tactics and often occurring in the "subprime mortgage market where most borrowers use the collateral in their homes for debt consolidation or other consumer credit purposes."[6]

Prime lending is reserved for borrowers who have a highly rated credit history. Prime loans are often called "A" credits. In contrast, subprime loans are extended to borrowers with troubled credit histories. Those who justify subprime lending note that the higher price of interest reflects risk-based pricing and serves borrowers who would not otherwise be able to obtain a loan in the prime market. Still, that is no answer to the well-documented abuses by subprime lenders throughout the United States.

Subprime loans are often called "A through D" credits."[7] The worry about subprime loans is that consumers will receive credit that they have little prospect of paying back. If you are a low-income consumer and believe that you have been victimized by a predatory lender, make an appointment to see your local legal services organization. Greater Boston Legal Services (GBLS) is an organization of nearly seventy lawyers funded in part by the Legal Services Corporation (LSC). GBLS's mission is to provide free legal services to families whose yearly income does not exceed 125 percent of federal poverty income guidelines ($24,188 for a family of four). Its elder law clinic assists persons age sixty or over on a variety of consumer-related issues, including evictions, long-term care issues, veterans' issues, and consumer protection. To locate legal services in your area, visit the website of the Legal Services Corporation at http://www.lsc.gov. Contact your local LSC-funded program by filling out a user-friendly intake form on the website. The Minnesota attorney general describes predatory lenders inducing consumers to enter into over-priced loans. Consumers vulnerable to these pitches are those with serious financial problems as the result of illness, injury, or natural disasters such as Hurricane Katrina. The chief warning sign of an overpriced loan is the price of the loan, given the credit score of the borrower and the security given for the loan. Abusive loans are enabled by a secondary market that buys loans, disregarding obvious signs that the loan is predatory. State and federal legislators could all but eliminate this unsavory practice by making liable the assignees (the financial services company who receives the right to receive the stream of payments from the consumer borrower).[8]

The Minnesota attorney general tells consumers to look out for the following red flags in loan offers: (1) high interest rates and fees; (2) small monthly payments with a huge balloon payment at the end of the loan; (3) a high loan-to-value ratio (i.e., a loan that exceeds the equity in the home), and (4) hidden fees and other charges (i.e., commitment fees).

HUD has also identified a number of red flags emblematic of predatory practices by lenders, appraisers, mortgage brokers, and home improvement contractors:

- Is the lender (or other responsible party) selling properties for much more than they are worth using false appraisals?
- Is the lender encouraging borrowers to misrepresent their income, expenses, or cash available for down payments in order to get a loan?
- Has the lender knowingly lent more money than a borrower can afford to repay? The term "knowingly" means actual awareness of the falsity, deception, or unfairness of the act or practice giving rise to the consumer's claim. Actual awareness may be inferred where objective manifestations indicate that a person acted with actual awareness.
- Does the lender charge excessive interest rates to borrowers based on their race or national origin and not on their credit history?
- Has the lender charged fees for unnecessary or nonexistent products and services?

- Has the lender pressured borrowers to accept higher-risk loans such as balloon loans, interest only payments, and steep prepayment penalties?
- Did the lender present cash-out refinance offers to vulnerable borrowers when she knew borrowers were in need of cash due to medical, unemployment, or debt problems?
- Did the lender "strip" the homeowners' equity from their homes?
- Does the lender encourage repeated refinancing when there is no benefit to the borrower? This practice is known as using the home as an ATM and indicates that the lender is engaged in flipping or refinancing a loan to a higher rate of interest.
- Does the lender use high-pressure sales tactics to sell home improvements and then finance them at high interest rates?[9]

The Federal Deposit Insurance Corporation provides this summary of common predatory lending schemes.

Bait-and-switch schemes. The lender may promise one type of loan or interest rate but, without good reason, gives you a different one. Sometimes a higher (and unaffordable) interest rate doesn't kick in until months after you have begun to pay on your loan.

Equity stripping. The lender encourages you to borrow heavily from the equity in your home (the amount you own free and clear of your mortgage) as an easy way to get additional money, consolidate debt, or fund home repairs, knowing that the fees and payments are so high you may not be able to make them. You dramatically reduce your equity and, in the worst case, the lender forecloses on the loan, takes possession of your home, and strips you of the equity.

Loan flipping. The lender encourages you to get additional cash by refinancing your mortgage again and again. This tactic significantly increases your debt because fees (often exorbitant) are tacked on to each loan transaction, and you may pay a higher interest rate than with your original loan. You become saddled with higher payments, higher debt, and the risk of losing your home.

Loan packing. The lender adds charges into the loan contract for overpriced items or items you don't need or didn't use, often totaling thousands of dollars. For example, the lender may pressure you into buying insurance you don't need or trick you into paying for phony services.

Home improvement scams. A contractor talks you into costly or unnecessary repairs, steers you to a high-cost mortgage lender to finance the job, and arranges for the loan proceeds to be sent directly to the contractor. All too often, the contractor performs shoddy or incomplete work, and the homeowner is stuck paying off a long-term loan on a house at risk.

Mortgage servicing scams. After getting the loan, you're told you owe additional money for bogus taxes, insurance, legal fees, or late fees. Or, if you try to pay off the loan, the lender provides inaccurate information that causes you to pay too much or discourages you from refinancing with another lender.[10]

The HUD–Treasury Task Force on Predatory Lending recommends four ways for governments to combat predatory lending practices:

1. *Improve Consumer Literacy and Disclosures:* Creditors should be required to recommend that high-cost loan applicants avail themselves of home mortgage counseling, disclose credit scores to all borrowers upon request, and give borrowers timelier and more accurate information as to loan costs and terms.
2. *Prohibit Harmful Sales Practices in the Mortgage Market:* Practices such as loan "flipping" and lending to borrowers without regard to their ability to repay the loan should be banned. New requirements should be imposed on mortgage brokers to document the appropriateness of a loan for high-cost loan applicants, and lenders who report to credit bureaus should be required to provide "full-file" payment history for their mortgage customers.
3. *Restrict Abusive Terms and Conditions on High-Cost Loans:* We recommend that Congress increase the number of borrowers in the subprime market covered by legislative protections; further restrict balloon payments on high-cost loans; restrict prepayment penalties and the financing of points and fees; prohibit mandatory arbitration agreements on high-cost loans; and ban lump-sum credit life insurance and similar products.
4. *Improve Market Structure:* Award Community Reinvestment Act (CRA) credit to banks and thrifts that promote borrowers from the subprime to prime mortgage market, and deny CRA credit to banks and thrifts for the origination or purchase of loans that violate applicable lending laws.[11]

The next section examines some of these predatory practices in more detail, giving you guidance on what to do to protect yourself against these unfair business practices.

Loan Flipping

Millions of American consumers are victimized by lenders overreaching, excessive interest rates, dishonest loan flipping, and rip-off second mortgages that suck the consumer into a whirlpool descending into bankruptcy. As

Woody Allen reminds us, "Money is better than poverty, if only for financial reasons." Because state usury laws apply to the various banking and financing entities differently, consumers would be well advised to consult with an attorney, should they feel that they are being charged an exorbitantly high rate of interest.

Loan flipping is characterized by frequent borrowing from the same lender. The typical pattern is for the borrower to begin with one loan and then take out loans to pay off the previous loans. In December 2003, the Massachusetts attorney general obtained refund checks for 11,000 Massachusetts consumers totaling $13.5 million in a settlement of a predatory lending lawsuit against Household Finance. The lender in that case was charged with misleading consumers into agreeing to home loans with different, unfavorable terms. Massachusetts consumers victimized by excessive loan points and unfair insurance credit products also received compensation.

The concept behind loan flipping involves getting the consumer locked into a loan product with unfavorable terms, resulting in higher fees for the lender. In some cases, the fraudulent scheme takes the form of false appraisals to jack up the value of the home. What happens is that the consumer takes out a loan to refinance debt. The lender then offers the consumer another loan. The consumer gets more cash by refinancing once again. The lender makes money on points and fees. The fraud involved in loan flipping occurs when a lender offers to refinance a borrower's existing loan on advantageous terms, concealing the fact that the terms are in fact highly unfavorable to the consumer. The FTC describes loan flipping as the unsavory practice of offering a homeowner a loan for reasonable terms and then, after a few payments, charging you high points and fees to refinance. Each time you refinance your interest rate goes up, and you end up paying a prepayment penalty each time you take out a loan. In other words, you have turned your home into an ATM that can easily be foreclosed upon because you cannot afford to pay the flipped loan with the high interest rates and fees.

Example: Loan Flipping. Loan flipping occurs when consumers, strapped for cash, repeatedly refinance their homes at higher and higher interest rates and points. Each time a consumer refinances they are given higher points, fees, and interest rates. This cycle repeats itself until finally the lender forecloses. The FTC notes the risks of loan flipping, resulting in a cycle of higher charges:

> You now have some extra money and a lot more debt, stretched out over a longer time. The extra cash you receive may be less than the additional costs and fees you were charged for the refinancing. And what's worse, you are now paying interest on those extra fees charged in each refinancing. Long story short? With each refinancing, you've increased your debt and probably are paying a very high price for some extra cash. After a while, if you get in over your head and can't pay, you could lose your home.[12]

Home Improvement and Repair

The home improvement industry is permeated with fraud and corruption in many states. In August 2006, government regulators in Miami, Florida, uncovered a widespread fraud in which hundreds of home repair contractors in Dade County bribed government officials to obtain fake licenses and final inspection certificates.[13]

Door-to-door sales for home improvement have defrauded countless consumers. Unscrupulous contractors raise the prices of a job after contracts are written and signed. In some cases, the contractor does not even begin work or completes it in shoddy fashion. Contracts between home improvement contractors and customers are near the top of consumer complaints in every state. In a 2005 Pennsylvania case, a home improvement contractor of windows and vinyl siding cashed the deposits of twenty-two homeowners but never completed the work. Vermont's General Assembly passed a 2003 law beefing up criminal penalties for those who commit home improvement fraud. Vermont's home improvement fraud statute criminalizes the following activities:

A person commits the offense of home improvement fraud when he or she knowingly enters into a contract or agreement, written or oral, for $500.00 or more, with an owner for home improvement, or into several contracts or agreements for $2,500.00 or more in the aggregate, with more than one owner for home improvement, and he or she knowingly:

- Promises performance that the contractor does not intend to perform or knows will not be performed, in whole or in part;
- Misrepresents a material fact relating to the terms of the contract or agreement or to the condition of any portion of the property involved;
- Uses or employs any unfair or deceptive act or practice in order to induce, encourage, or solicit such person to enter into any contract or agreement or to modify the terms of the original contract or agreement; or
- When there is a declared state of emergency (i.e., Ice Storm of 1997 [which was an unprecedented ice storm that caused massive property damages]), charges for goods or services related to the emergency a price that exceeds two times the average price for the goods or services and the increase is not attributable to the additional costs incurred in connection with providing those goods or services.

Vermont considers it a knowing violation of the statute if the person fails to perform the contract or agreement and, when the owner requests performance of the contract or agreement or a refund of payments made, the person fails to:

1. return the payments or deliver the materials or make and comply with a reasonable written repayment plan for the return of the payments; or

2. make and comply with a reasonable written plan for completion of the contract or agreement (13 V.S.A. §2029).

Vermont companies and individuals convicted of home improvement fraud must register with the Department of Public Safety. Consumers in Vermont and other states with registries can check online for contractors convicted of home improvement fraud. Those contractors convicted under the statute must post a surety bond (or irrevocable letter of credit) prior to engaging in future home improvement activities for compensation.

The General Services Administration (GSA) Federal Consumer Citizen Information Center suggests the following preventive law tips:

- Get recommendations and references.
- Get at least three written estimates.
- Check contractor complaint records with your state attorney general or Better Business Bureau.
- Make sure the contractor meets licensing and registration requirements.
- Get the names of suppliers of building materials and check to see if the contractor makes timely payments.
- Contract your local building inspection department to check for permit and inspection requirements.
- Be sure your contractor is insured.
- Get it in writing. Insist on a written contract that states what work will be done, what warranties are given, timetables, the name of subcontractors, the total price of the job, and the schedule of payments.
- Give a small down payment or limited down payment. Do not pay upfront.
- Don't make a final payment or sign a final release until you are satisfied.
- Pay by credit card so you have chargeback rights.

What to Do: Avoiding Home Improvement Frauds

Consumer loans for home improvement account for $120 billion annually and continue to be a leading source of consumer fraud. A common scenario for home improvement fraud is someone cold-calling you or ringing your doorbell, claiming they can give you a good price because they have just finished a job down the street and have materials left over.

New Mexico's attorney general, for example, received scores of complaints from consumers complaining of the repaving of their driveway or roof repairs. The attorney general found that the consumers were told that they could receive a greatly reduced price because there was material left over from another job in the neighborhood. State attorneys general around the country have received complaints of another fraud in which the contractor makes a cold call or contract informing you that your house has structural damage, roof damage, or other problems that need prompt remedial action. Do not contract with a contractor who has out-of-state license plates and unmarked trucks unless you have done your due diligence in checking references. Do not contract with any home improvement contractor without vetting his license and references and checking with prior customers.

Do not rely upon the bare assertion that a contractor has been recommended by someone you know. The greater the pressure on price or time, the more on guard you should be. Do comparison shopping by getting different prices and estimates on major home improvement projects. Check out the home contractor with the Better Business Bureau or your state's attorney general's office. Pay for any work with a check or credit card, not cash.

Example: Fast-Track That Wasn't. In a 2005 Ohio case, homeowners sued a contractor for failing to perform certain renovations on the plaintiffs' house. In that case, the contractor told the homeowners that work would be completed within eight to ten weeks of groundbreaking. More than a year later, the work was still not completed. The plaintiffs received a $50,000 settlement to recoup costs as well as what they paid another contractor to complete the work (*Dubusker v. the Dar-Tel Company, Inc., Fast-Trac Services, LLC.* No. 40300 [Ct. of Common Pleas, Cuyohaga Cty., Ohio, June 7, 2005]).

Home Improvement Contractor Rules

Many states have statutes protecting homeowners or tenants contracting for improvement services. Massachusetts, for example, requires contractors to provide consumers with a written agreement, including the description of the work and cost, where the price is greater than $1,000 (M.G.L.A. ch. 142A, §2). The Massachusetts statute also requires contractors to give consumers a work and payment schedule and a right to cancel the contract within three days (M.G.L.A. ch. 142A). Massachusetts's legislature also set up a Residential Contractor's Guaranty Fund that gives prevailing homeowners or tenants the right to recover up to $10,000 from the special fund if they are unable to collect from the contractor. The state will also frequently include a requirement that many home improvement plans require building permits or special licenses.

If a contractor violates home improvement regulations, he will also be liable under UDTPA because such a violation is likely be classified as an unfair or deceptive trade practice. In Massachusetts, a violation of the Home Improvement Contractors Rule is also considered a violation of Chapter 93A, which is Massachusetts's Little FTC Act. Check your state attorney general's office for similar protection against unfair or deceptive home contracting practices. Even if your state does not have a specific home contracting statute, the contractor or subcontractor will be in violation of an unfair or deceptive trade practices act for abandoning or failing to perform projects or disregarding plans or specifications in material respects. If your state has a specific statute prohibiting material misrepresentations, violations of building codes, or failing to pay for materials or services as a contractor, you can file a claim using the specific statute as well as the Little FTC Act. If your home contracting project involves only a few thousand dollars in financial loss or damages, you can file in small claims court. Otherwise, you will file claims in civil courts of general jurisdiction.

Manufactured Homes

Manufactured homes are defined as factory-built, as opposed to built on the home lot. HUD Home Construction and Safety Standards, also known as the HUD Code, regulate the homes' design and construction, strength and durability, transportability, fire resistance, and energy efficiency. HUD sets quality standards for heating, air conditioning, plumbing, thermal, and electrical systems and requires all manufactured homes to come with a written warranty covering (1) structural workmanship; (2) factory-installed plumbing, heating, and electrical systems; and (3) factory-installed appliances, which also may be covered by separate appliance manufacturer warranties.

These warranties do not typically cover the costs of setup and transportation of your manufactured home. You must get this insurance coverage through the retailer and installation contractor. Ask about warranties before you purchase a module or manufactured home.[14]

To prevail in a lawsuit against the manufacturer or seller of a mobile home, you must prove (1) the mobile home had substandard materials or workmanship at the time of the sale; (2) the defects in materials or workmanship were the cause of the damages; (3) the mobile home was unmerchantable (not fit for its ordinary purpose) at the time of the sale; and (4) damages. In a mobile home case, you can also cover the reasonable rental value of the use of substitute housing of the same class as the mobile home. In addition, you must prove that you notified the mobile home seller within a reasonable time after discovering the problems. In addition to a claim of merchantability, you may have an action for product liability, but you must show that the manufacturer was negligent in the design, construct, or installation of the mobile home.

Retail installment contracts are frequently involved in defective mobile home cases. A consumer may, for example, find that the lender/seller also violated the TILA or state law by not disclosing rate adjustments or other costs of credit. In many breach of warranty mobile home cases, the defects are so significant that the consumer may also claim treble damages and attorney's fees under her state's UDTPA (see Chapter 3).

Example: Manufactured Homes. Riley Homes, an Illinois manufacturer of prefabricated homes, was charged with violating the advertising provisions of TILA because it failed to disclose the finance charge and failed to state the rate as an annual percentage rate (APR), as required by TILA and its implementing Regulation Z. The settlement prohibited the company from violating any provisions of the TILA in the future. FTC advertising rules were also violated because the ads for Riley homes failed to state the APR. The company was also charged with placing ads stating "triggering" terms (the amount or percentage of any down payment, the number of payments, or the period of repayment; the amount of any payment; or the amount of any finance charge) but failing to disclose the information required by Regulation Z (the amount or percentage of the down payment, the terms of repayment, and the APR).

Example: Rescission of Manufactured Home. Consumers will frequently seek rescission of the contract as well as attorneys' fees and costs in these cases. In a recent Ohio case, the consumer received rescission of contract plus $91,100 for the cost of rescission (the $62,300 contract price and $28,800 representing monies spent attempting to correct problems with the residence), $10,000 for inconvenience and ancillary expenses, $55,568 in attorney fees, and $1,575 expert witness fees, for a total of $158,243. Although this amount was subject to setoff for a prior settlement with the manufacturer, the plaintiff was also awarded $36,986 in prejudgment interest (*Drenning v. Blue Ribbon Homes, Inc.*, No. 04-CV-000003 [Fulton County (Ohio) Ct. of Common Pleas, Jan. 6, 2006]).

Mobile Homes

The consumer laws governing the owning and renting of mobile homes are different from those governing other homes. This section explains your rights if you own or rent a mobile home. California's state Department of Housing and Community Development (HCD) licenses dealers, licenses and inspects mobile home parks, inspects manufactured home installations, issues certificates of occupancy, and processes and issues registration and titles for mobile and manufactured homes. You may address complaints to California's mobile home Ombudsman, P.O. Box 31, Sacramento, CA 95812-0031, telephone: 1-800-952-5275.

Illinois's Mobile Home and Landlord and Tenant Rights Act regulates the leasing of mobile homes or lots in mobile home parks. The state law defines a "mobile home" to cover any "structure designed for permanent habitation and so constructed as to permit its transport on wheels, temporarily or permanently attached to its frame, from the place of its construction to the location or subsequent locations at which it is intended to be a permanent habitation." Many other jurisdictions have similar definitions. Most jurisdictions no longer consider a structure a mobile home if placed on a permanent structure. If you remove the wheels, tongue, and hitch from your mobile home, it is no longer classifiable as a "mobile home." The mobile home statute was enacted because of a long history of abuses in the sale, lease, or rental of mobile homes (765 ILCS 745/1).

Example: Breach of Warranty Damages for Defective Mobile Home. In a Texas case, a family purchased a $29,500 doublewide mobile home from Liberty, manufactured by Melody, for their primary residence. The seller was unable to complete installation satisfactorily and has never joined the two halves. The plaintiffs filed suit against the seller and manufacturer, alleging defective installation and defective manufacturing because the two halves did not match on their mobile home. The plaintiffs' causes of action were the Manufactured Housing Standards Act, Texas Deceptive Trade Practices Act (DTPA), the Consumer Credit Code, the federal and state truth in lending acts, UCC Article 2 breach of warranty, common law negligence, and revocation of acceptance under UCC §2-608. The jury ruled for the plaintiffs, and with multiple damages under the DTPA and attorneys' fees, the plaintiff's verdict was substantial. The parties settled all claims for a confidential amount (*Guerra v. Liberty Manufactured Housing Inc.*, No. 83-CI-19, 072 [Texas 88th Dist. Ct. 1985]).

Consumer Rights in the Event of Foreclosure

Foreclosure of your home is one of those consumer problems for which you need legal counsel. If you are a low-income consumer, contact the LSC-affiliated organization in your area. Chapter 4 gives you guidance on how to get free legal services with LSC organizations or law school clinics. A homeowner may use contract or equitable defenses to defend against foreclosures. In a Texas case, the homeowner was not current in his account, but the jury found that the lender waived the late payment of installments by accepting multiple payments. In that case, a Texas jury awarded the tenant the reasonable market value, including improvements.

Notes

1. Federal Trade Commission, "Home Equity Loans: Buyer Beware," available at http://www.ftc.gov/bcp/conline/pubs/homes/eqscams.htm (accessed June 17, 2007).

2. Christopher W. Backley, et al., "License to Deal: Regulation in the Mortgage Broker Industry," Federal Reserve Bank of Minneapolis, Issue 3 (2006), available at http://www.minneapolisfed.org/pubs/cd/06-3/mortgage.cfm (accessed June 18, 2007).

3. Jonathan Saltzman and Marita Sacchetti, "Mortgage Brokers Shut Down by State: Deceptive Loan Practices Banned," *Boston Globe*, September 9, 2006, 1.

4. Federal Trade Commission, "Reverse Mortgages: Get the Facts before Cashing In on Your Home's Equity," available at http://www.ftc.gov/bcp/conline/pubs/homes/rms.htm (accessed June 17, 2007).

5. Housing and Urban Development, "Subprime Lending," available at http://www.hud.gov/offices/fheo/lending/subprime.cfm (accessed June 18, 2007).

6. HUD and U.S. Treasury, "Joint Report on Predatory Lending," available at http://www.hud.gov/offices/hsg/sfh/pred/predlnd1.cfm (accessed June 17, 2007).

7. Nuestra, Communidad Development Corporation, "Mortgage Terminology," available at http://www.nuestracdc.org/mortgage%20terminology.html (accessed June 17, 2007).

8. Alvin Harrell and Kurt Eggert, "Consumer Law Symposium on Responsibility and Reform," *Consumer Fin. L. Q.* 58 (2004): 214, 217.

9. Housing and Urban Development, "Do Not Be a Victim of Loan Fraud," available at http://www.hud.gov/offices/hsg/sfh/buying/loanfraud.cfm (accessed June 18, 2007).

10. Federal Deposit Insurance Corporation, "Examples of Predatory Lending," available at http://www.fdic.gov/consumers/consumer/news/cnsum02/examples .html (accessed June 18, 2007).

11. Housing and Urban Development, HUD-Treasury Task Force on Predatory Lending, "Curbing Predatory Home Mortgage Lending" (2000), available at http:// www.huduser.org/publications/hsgfin/curbing.html (accessed June 18, 2007).

12. Federal Trade Commission, "Loan Flipping," available at http://www.ftc .gov/bcp/conline/pubs/homes/eqscams.shtm (last visited June 18, 2007).

13. Charles Rabin, "Scam Puts Home Repairs in Limbo," *Miami Herald,* August 18, 2006, 1.

14. Federal Trade Commission, "Choosing a Home," available at http://www .ftc.gov/bcp/conline/pubs/homes/manufact/choosing.htm (accessed June 18, 2007).

14

Consumer Protection in Cyberspace and Identity Theft

Recently I received an email informing me that I was the winner of a multimillion-dollar Australian lottery. I must have been incredibly lucky because it is not every day that you can win a lottery that you do not enter. The email stated that I could receive my winnings if I would only send my account number so the funds could be transferred. As the old adage warns, "If it looks too good to be true, it probably is!" In addition, it was. This Internet solicitation was part of a fraudulent scheme that is also hatched by regular mail and by telephone. The Internet, however, can affect hundreds more individuals than mail and telephone schemes in the same instance. The Internet reaches millions, and even sites that seem "safe" have a high potential for fraud. For example, legitimate online auctions have millions of members but are known to have a high fraud rate.

Do Not Give Up Your Personally Identifiable Information

Never release personal information such as your credit card number, Social Security number, or bank account number over the Internet, especially if you receive an unsolicited email requesting this information. Even if the email indicates it is from a known company, there is a high chance this email was not sent from that company. Legitimate companies do not initiate requests with personally identifiable information. The rule never to release personal information over the Internet will prevent much consumer fraud. Never send money or give personal account numbers unless you can verify the recipient.

Example: Nigerian Email Solicitations. In 2005, more than 500 American consumers filed complaints with the FTC's Consumer Sentinel after being cheated by fraudulent foreign money offers. I received an email from a solicitor in England instructing me to provide my account information so he could wire me money from a Nigerian government official. The cybercriminal's letter stated:

> Dear Friend,
> My name is Chief Joseph Ankar, a 54-year-old politician in the Federal Republic of Nigeria. I am presently the party's National Treasurer, Board of Trustee for the ruling People's Democratic Party (PDP) of Nigeria. My party (the PDP), the biggest party in Africa is the ruling party in Nigeria having produced the President and an overwhelming majority in the National Assembly in the elections of 1999 till date. Another general election is coming up in February 2007 and I want to run for the senate in the coming election so as to be the senate President, as the slot has been allocated to my constituency. As you may know, electioneering cost lot money and I have been mandated to raise a specified sum of money for the party so as to have my ambition fulfilled.
> So far, with the assistance of my loyal aids [sic], I have been able to set aside the sum of US$9M (Nine Million United States Dollars) in an escrow account. This money was meant to be payment for some contractors that supplied vehicles and other materials to the party, and this is where you come in.
> This money would be transferred to you for payment for goods and services. The "DEAL" is that you will receive this money in your account, take 30 percent (US$2.7M) as your commission and send back to the party's account the remaining US$6.3M as endorsement for the party. Apart from your initial and immediate commission, you will be listed in the party's manifesto as co-supporter and you will be given a top priority in allocation of contracts once we win the election in 2007.
> I sincerely want you to take your time to read and digest this message for a proper understanding and I will avail you of further information and details once I hear from you.
>
> Sincerely,
> Chief Joseph Ankar

Countless consumers have received similar emails from Chief Ankar and his organized Nigerian crime ring. If it is too good to be true, it is a swindle. My sister received the following email solicitation, which is an example of a similar fraud:

> From: "norawilliams" <norawilliams@terra.com.mx>
> To: undisclosed-recipients:
> Subject: Re: I Need Your Urgent Reply (From Mrs. Nora Williams).
> Date: Sat, 7 Oct 2006 11:07:36 +0000
>
> Dear Sir,
> I got your address via the Internet. I have a proposal for you, this however is not mandatory nor will I in any manner compel you to honor it against your will.

I will start by introducing myself to you, my name is Nora Williams, a 43 years old woman, and I am a banker by profession and had worked with a bank as an Auditor in one of the leading banks West African Coast. Here in this bank existed a dormant account for the past 8 years which belong to a Syrian national who is now late, When we discovered that there had been no deposits nor withdrawals from this particular account for this long period, I and my two other colleagues decided to carry out a system investigation and discovered that non of the family member nor relations of the late Syrian man is aware of this account, This is the story in a nutshell.

Now we want to lift this funds out of the shores of this bank/country via diplomatic channel and as such, we need a reliable person whom we can build trust in to receive this fund on our behalf because considering our position here, it is will not be possible to transfer the fund from our bank. Be rest assured that the entire deal will be executed under legitimate arrangement and it is 100 percent risk free.

Thereafter, we had planned to destroy all related documents for this account, It is a careful network and for the past eleven months now, we have worked out everything to ensure a hitch-free operation, The amount is not so much, including all the accumulated interest the balance in this account stands at US$11.2million [*sic*] U.S. dollars.

Now our questions are:

1. Can you handle this project?
2. Can we give you this trust?
3. What will be your commission?

Consider this and get back to us as soon as possible. Finally, it is our humble prayer that the information as contained herein be accorded the necessary attention, urgency as well as the secrecy it deserves. We expect your urgent response if you can handle this project.

Respectfully yours,
Mrs. Nora A. Williams

When millions of Nigerian offers are made, it only takes a few thousand responses to result in fabulous transfers of wealth.

Another variation on the Nigerian letter from royalty is the letter asking for your help in transmitting wealth arising out of an estate of a wealthy Nigerian. The letter writer offers fabulous wealth to the recipient if they will help them deposit the funds in a U.S. bank account: yours. After you agree to help, the "official" will give you a princely sum if you will send him transfer or other fees. Cybercriminals typically offer to send a cashier's check (a fake one, that is) if you will return some of the money to them.

Meg Whitman, eBay's chief executive officer, states that the online auction site has more than 135 million subscribers. She placed this number in perspective by noting that if eBay were a nation-state, it would be among the top ten countries in population. An FTC report on consumer fraud concluded that Internet auctions topped the list of consumer complaints in 2005 (12 percent), followed by foreign money offers (8 percent). The FTC gives the following preventive consumer tips to protect against e-fraud:

- Be skeptical of unsolicited email offering credit reports. Keep an eye out for email from an atypical address, like XYZ123@website.net, or an email address ending in a top-level domain other than .com, like .ru or .de.
- Never open an email attachment unless it is from someone you know. It could contain a virus that can damage your computer and also spread to the computers of people in your address book.
- Check whether the company has a working telephone number and legitimate address. You can check addresses at websites like www .switchboard.com, and phone numbers through reverse lookup search engines like www.anywho.com.
- Check for misspellings and grammatical errors. Silly mistakes and sloppy copy—for example, an area code that does not match an address—often are giveaways that the site is a fraud. Look at the company's web address: Is it a real company's address, or it is a misspelled version of a legitimate company's web address?
- Check to see whether the email address matches the website address. That is, when you enter the company's web address into the browser, does it go to the sender's site or redirect you to a different web address? If it redirects you, that is a red flag that you should cease the transaction.
- Find out who owns the website by using a "Whose" search, such as the search at www.networksolutions.com.
- Exit from any website that asks for unnecessary personal information, like a personal identification number (PIN) for your bank account, the three-digit code on the back of your credit card, or your passport number and issuing country. Legitimate sites do not ask for this information.
- All legitimate sites will want to verify who you are and will respond to an electronic request for a credit report by asking you for an additional piece of information. If a site does not ask a follow-up question, the site is almost certainly a fake.
- Never respond to emails asking for personal or financial information, even though they appear to be coming from legitimate sources.
- Use only secure websites. A secure website features a "lock" icon on the browser's status bar, and the phrase "https" in the URL, to keep your information secure during transmission. In 2007, every legitimate website was a secure website.
- Watch your mailbox and credit card statements: If you have responded to a bogus site, you may never receive the credit report they offered for free. If you paid one of these sites for a credit report, your

credit card may never be charged. If you find that you have unauthorized charges, contact your financial institutions and credit card issuers immediately.

- Report suspicious activity to the FTC and the U.S. Secret Service. Send the actual spam to the Los Angeles Electronic Crimes Task Force at LA.ECTF.reports@usss.dhs.gov and to the FTC at spam@uce.gov. If you believe you have been scammed, file your complaint at www.ftc.gov and then visit the FTC's identity theft website (www.consumer.gov/idtheft) to learn how to minimize your risk of damage from any online fraudulent schemes.

The FTC as the Constable of Cyberspace

The FTC has been the most effective Internet police force, judging by its 2006 annual report. It is also one of the leaders against fraudulent and deceptive sales pitches on the Internet. The FTC has used various regulations to continue to police the Internet. The Controlling the Assault of Non-Solicited Pornography and Marketing Act of 2003 (CAN-SPAM Act) is a regulation that has not proved as effective as state laws in combating unwanted email solicitation. In 2006, the FTC filed numerous lawsuits to enforce the federal CAN-SPAM Act, but there have been only a handful of prosecutions. The FTC has also cracked down on online pornographers with a sweep against abuses of the FTC's Adult Labeling Act.

Recently, the FTC has expanded enforcement against "spyware," which is adware that automatically is downloaded on a consumer's computer without her knowledge or consent, by filing complaints against companies that use deceptive means to get consumers to download the spyware. It filed a complaint against Internet Media that tricked consumers into downloading exploitive software code masquerading as free software. Mail and fraud statutes also serve as a ground for enforcement against computer fraud crimes.

Not only does the FTC act as the Internet police, it also reports on the incident of fraud on the Internet. The FTC's 2006 Annual Report on Consumer Fraud and Identity Theft Complaint Data found that 60 percent of fraud complaints arose out of an initial Internet solicitation (45 percent from email and 15 percent from website solicitations).[1]

The Internet is a petri dish for fraudulent schemes and deceptive actions. In 2006 alone there were 45,587 consumer complaints about fraud arising out of Internet services and another 32,832 complaints about Internet auctions.[2]

This chapter analyzes the issues behind Internet fraud and offers practical advice to avoid being victimized in cyberspace. Internet fraud poses difficult issues for consumer protection because the fraudulent schemes are perpetrated beyond the reach of the law. There are many reasons that a cybercriminal cannot be prosecuted: an inability to identify the criminal, jurisdictional issues, or protection for Internet service providers (ISPs) who refuse to identify individuals due to First Amendment rights that may arise to protect that individual's identity. Not only can the schemes themselves be beyond the reach of the law, but the numbers of complaints are exceedingly high, resulting in millions of dollars of losses. Complaints filed with the FBI's Internet Crime Complaint Center (IC3) doubled from 2003 to 2004.

Why Cyberfraud Is Difficult to Prosecute

A cybercriminal may disappear at the click of the mouse into the recesses of cyberspace in an offshore-protected haven beyond the reach of legal process. Cyberspace poses greater consumer protection problems because businesses may have no physical location, no personal interaction, no customer service representation, and no "bricks-and-mortar" building where you can even send a complaint. The vast majority of consumers defrauded in cyberspace will never recover a single dollar in damages. With cyberspace fraud, a fence at the top of the cliff is worth much more than the ambulance in the valley below. Consumer complaints will seldom result in remedies that make the defrauded person whole. In fact, the best results offer only partial restitution to those defrauded on the Internet.

The direct victim of an Internet scheme may file a complaint, or a third party representing the complainant may file a complaint with the IC3, which processed more than 228,400 Internet-related consumer complaints nationwide in 2005.[3] Online auction fraud, nondelivery of merchandise, and credit/debit card fraud topped the list, along with cybercrimes such as computer intrusions, spam/unsolicited email, and child pornography. The FBI estimated the total dollar loss from all referred cases of Internet fraud was $183 million. The median amount lost by American consumers nationwide was $424.[4]

The FTC's Enforcement of Cyberspace

The Children's Online Privacy Protection Rule

The FTC regulates unfair or deceptive acts or practices in connection with the collection, use, or disclosure of personal information harvested from children at websites. Commercial websites will need to comply with the FTC's Children's Online Privacy Protection Rule, which implements the Children's Online Privacy Protection Act (COPPA) (Children's Online Privacy Protection Rule, 16 C.F.R. §312). Websites must comply with COPPA's regulations if they market games and other promotions to children under the age of thirteen. COPPA applies to any site that (1) requests that children submit personal information online; (2) enables children to make personal information publicly available through a chat room, message board, or other means; or (3) uses cookies or other identifying codes in tracking children's activity over the Internet (16 C.F.R. §312.2[a] [b] [c]).

The website operator must make a threshold determination of whether the website or online service is directed to children under thirteen. The FTC considers a number of factors in determining whether a given website targets children.

The most important factors include the subject matter (visual or audio content), the age of models on the site, the age of the actual or intended audience, and whether the site uses animated characters. The FTC considers an entity an "operator" depending on who owns, controls, and pays for the collection of information. COPPA applies to "individually identifiable information about a child that is collected online, such as full name, home address, email address, telephone number," or other means of identifying or contacting a child. If COPPA applies, the operator must "link to a notice of its information practices on the home page of the website or online service and at each area where it collects personal information from children."

Personal information is defined to include (1) an individual's first and last name, (2) a home or other physical address, (3) an email address or other online contact information, (4) a telephone number, (5) a Social Security number, (6) a persistent identifier such as a code, and (7) any other information concerning the child or the parents of that child that the operator collects online from the child. Personal information may be collected directly from a child or passively through devices such as cookies.

The FTC requires the site to obtain parental consent and give conspicuous notice of its information practices. A site must obtain verifiable parental consent *before* collecting a child's personal data. Parents have a right to review personal information provided by a child and delete the information or have it deleted. A website may not condition a child's participation in the website on the collection of personal information. A child's parents must be given the opportunity to restrain further use or collection of information.

A website must have reasonable security to protect the confidentiality, security, and integrity of personal information collected from children. The FTC's COPPA Rule gives websites a safe harbor so long as they comply with approved, industry-created guidelines.

The FTC's Mail Order Rule

The FTC's Trade Regulation Rule Concerning the Sale of Mail or Telephone Order Merchandise protects you when you order goods or services by telephone, by facsimile transmissions, or on the Internet. The FTC claims jurisdiction any time a business engages in the mail order sale and telephone order sale of merchandise in commerce, as "commerce" is defined in Section 4 of the FTC Act (15 U.S.C. §44). The FTC's Mail Order Rule, for example, has special rules when shipment is delayed (16 C.F.R. §435.1[a] [1]).

The Mail Order Rule requires sellers to offer the buyer, clearly and conspicuously and without prior demand, in a timely fashion, an option either to consent to a delay in shipping or to cancel the order and receive a prompt refund (16 C.F.R. §435.1[b] [2]). If your order is delayed, a refund must be offered. It is a violation of the Mail Order Rule if the firm issues company credit toward future purchases instead of making a refund (16 C.F.R. §435.2[e]).

Spyware

The FTC has filed a number of enforcement actions against spyware companies that install software on a consumer's computer, altering their browsers, home page, or search capabilities without the user's consent or even knowledge. The FTC contends that the use of spyware constitutes an unfair and deceptive trade practice under Section 5(a) of the FTC Act. The spyware company Opt in Trade was enjoined from installing software that changed the user's operating system without consent. The FTC entered into a settlement agreement that prohibits the company and its officers from exploiting security vulnerabilities of any computer operating systems. Opt in Trade is also prohibited from redirecting computers to different websites or web pages without the user's consent or authorization. Finally, the company agreed not to modify search engines or other application searches without the user's consent (*FTC v. Seismic Entertainment Production, Inc.*, No. 04-377-D [D.N.H., March 22, 2006]).

Spyware is widely used in unfair and deceptive trade practices. The Washington State attorney general filed a claim against Movieland.com for its abusive use of pop-up ads. The company used pop-up ads in the following manner. The consumer is given a trial period of the service and then is bombarded with pop-ups that appear at least hourly and subject the consumer to a 40-second payment demand that cannot be closed. These annoying messages are generated by software installed on their computers that cannot be easily removed. The movie ad barrage does not stop until the consumer pays $19.95 to $100.00. That is an example of an unfair and deceptive method of generating online revenue. Washington is one of the few states to have an anti-spyware amendment to its computer crime statute. Washington imposes fines of up to $2 million for deceptive practices such as planting software that appears when a consumer launches an Internet browser.

This anti-spyware statute also makes it unlawful to use deceptive means to harvest personally identifiable information or to record keystrokes made by a consumer and transfer that information to a business. It is illegal to plant software that extracts information from the owner or operator's hard drive. The anti-spyware statute prohibits deceptive means that prevent consumers from blocking the installation of or disabling pop-ups or other malware software. The Washington anti-spyware statute sanctions the deceptive removal or disabling of security, anti-spyware, or antivirus computer software installed on a computer. Relatively few states have the same statutory protections against spyware.

Identity Theft

If someone uses your name or personal information to seek money, credit, loans, goods, or services without your permission, you are a victim of identity theft.[5] In a single year, data theft placed the personal information of more than 55 million consumers at risk.[6] The methods for committing identity theft are diverse and continue to evolve. Dishonest employees may, for example, swipe your card for an actual purchase, and then surreptitiously attach a device that captures your financial information when you use an ATM or use your credit card. Identity theft may occur when a wrongdoer steals your wallet or purse. A thief may complete a change of address form to divert your mail to the criminal's location. Burglars may use information they find in your home to commit identity theft. Identity thefts are often a self-inflicted wound when criminals masquerading as legitimate businesses trick consumers into transmitting confidential information through email or phone. Consumer data may be hijacked when criminals use trickery to obtain telephone records, utility records, banking records, and other information directly from junior company service representatives.

New dangers of identity theft stem from outsourcing data to back processing outsourcing (BPOs) operations located in countries such as India, China, and the Philippines. In 2005, a British journalist publicized the potential for data theft at Indian offshore call centers by reportedly purchasing the personally identifiable information of hundreds of UK-based banking customers.[7] In the wake of this exposé, members of Britain's Parliament called for a halt to sending consumer data to India because of concerns over inadequate security.[8] Data entrusters such as financial institutions transmitting data to BPOs are in the best position to avoid offshore data heists, not consumers.

The United States, too, is suffering a rash of data insecurity incidents. In December 2006, the U.S. mega-retailer TJX discovered a data heist of colossal dimensions.[9] ChoicePoint, another large American corporation, recently compromised consumer data by selling personal information to cybercriminals masquerading as legitimate companies. Cybercriminals used a computer virus to gain illegal access to CardSystems Solution's computer system in order to steal 40 million credit card users' personal data. Citigroup Bank and Financial Services lost computer tapes containing the personal data of 3.9 million customers. MCI was victimized by the theft of records of 16,500 current and former employees when an employee's laptop computer was stolen from his automobile.[10]

Identity theft is enabled by careless disposal of bank and credit card information, but it may occur despite your best efforts. A dishonest employee, for example, may be bribed to transfer data to the wrongdoer. A more common form of data theft occurs through a process known as "social engineering," in which the criminal uses lies to persuade data handlers to release data to them. Consumers are also the direct victims of social engineering when they are telephoned or receive an email from a criminal posing as a bank, business, credit card company, charity, or other legitimate entity. The most common swindle is theft by pretext, accomplished when the criminal asks the consumer to verify their account number, credit card information, Social Security information, or other information. Most identity fraud occurs through these elaborate pretext schemes, as opposed to data lost through hackers stealing personal information.

Data heists may also occur when wrongdoers steal your mail, which includes your bank and credit card statements, credit card offers, new checks, or tax information. Personally identifiable data is obtained by going through company dumpsters, a practice called "dumpster diving." It is also common for thieves to masquerade as a landlord, employer, or other person in order to access your credit report.

Phishing

Identity theft on the Internet is generally accomplished through a process known as "phishing." Phishers send emails supposedly from legitimate companies that direct consumers to fake websites where they are asked to turn over confidential credit card account information, Social Security numbers, or other confidential information.

Once you know a few key items to look for in an email message, you can avoid most phishers and determine whether it is a legitimate email. If the email has a sense of urgency to it, then there is a high likelihood it is a false email.[11] Fake links, generic greetings, and poor grammar can also key a person into whether it is a spoof.[12]

Consumer Fraud and PayPal

PayPal is an Internet-based alternative payment system owned by eBay through which members can transfer money to other people or businesses for online auctions or purchases. Consumers should be aware of emails asking the recipient to help them process an eBay auction payment through the consumer's own PayPal account. The email promises to give the consumer a cut of 15 percent or more of all money transferred via a PayPal account. If the consumer agrees to the scheme, it is possible that they will not only lose their own money but also be subject to prosecution for the crime of money laundering. Unsolicited emails about your PayPal account are likely to be cybercriminals masquerading as PayPal employees.

PayPal indicates on its web page what to look for when receiving an email. Beware of any unsolicited emails that request any of the following information. Legitimate businesses will not request any of the following:

- Credit and debit card numbers
- Bank account information

- Driver's license numbers
- Passwords

Here is an example of a legitimate email from PayPal, as well as a likely "phishing" email message, both said to be sent from PayPal customer service. Both the emails indicate to the recipient that there was a change in security question answers to that person's PayPal account. However, there are some obvious differences. This is an example of an email sent to a PayPal member when that member updated her account information:

To: Jane Doe
From: service@paypal.com
Subject: PayPal Security Question and Answer Change

Dear Jane Doe,
    The security questions and answers for John Doe's PayPal account were changed on Oct. 12, 2006.
    If you did not authorize this change, please contact us immediately using the phone number found on the following page: https://www.paypal.com/us/contact-phone.
    Security Advisory: When you log in to your PayPal account, be sure to open a new web browser (e.g., Internet Explorer or Netscape) and type in the PayPal URL to make sure you are on the real PayPal website. For more information on protecting yourself from fraud, please review the Security Tips in our Security Center.
    Please do not reply to this email. This mailbox is not monitored and you will not receive a response. For assistance, log in to your PayPal account and click the Help link located in the top right corner of any PayPal page.

Thank you for using PayPal!
The PayPal Team
PayPal Email ID PP232

That same PayPal member, however, received another email from PayPal prior to changing her account information:

To: Jane Doe
From: "PayPal" service@paypal.com
Subject: PayPal Notification: Possible Account Theft

Dear Valued PayPal member,
    The security questions and answers for your PayPal account were changed. If you did not authorize this change, please contact us immediately using this link: https://www.paypal.com/srt1/s-default.
    However, you will need to update some of your records in our Resolution center. If not will result account suspension. Please update your records by October 14.

For more information on how to prevent fraud, please review the Security Tips in our Security Center.

Please do not reply to this email. This mailbox is not monitored and you will not receive a response. For assistance, log in to your PayPal account and click the Help link located in the top right corner of any PayPal page.

Thank you for using PayPal!
The PayPal Team
PayPal Email ID PP226

Aside from the misspellings and poor grammar in the spoof email, there are other differences that can alert you to email fraud. Both the emails are in response to security questions being changed in the person's account. However, the first email gives the customer a phone number to use to call if that person has any questions. It alerts the account member that the security questions were changed, but does not contain a sense of urgency or indicate that there is possible theft resulting from this change. The second email, however, creates a sense of urgency. The subject reads, "Possible Account Theft." This email also instructs the account member to update her accounts by October 14; failure to do so will result in suspension of her account. If you receive an email from PayPal that you believe to be a spoof email, forward the email to spoof@paypal.com, and PayPal will investigate the email.[13]

In September 2006, twenty-eight state attorneys general settled with California-based PayPal in a complaint about inadequate disclosures given customers about their service. Their complaint centered on PayPal's disclosures for the funding source for each purchase. PayPal was charged with withdrawing money from a consumer's bank account, even if users submitted their credit card information when signing up. The consumers registered complaints with their state attorney general after they learned that money had been withdrawn from their bank accounts only when they received their monthly bank statements. This financial transaction conflicted with their intention to use a credit card, as opposed to withdrawing money from their bank account. Other consumers complained that PayPal placed a hold on funds held in the user's PayPal account. Still others were confused about how to use PayPal's in-house dispute resolution programs and chargeback features. The settlement with the states requires PayPal to provider clear and conspicuous disclosures about the important terms and conditions before a consumer becomes a PayPal member. PayPal must make these disclosures at the time members initiate transactions. PayPal is also required to reorganize the format of its website and make changes to its use of hyperlinks and multipage documents. In the future, PayPal must provide its members with a clear choice of what method of payment they wish to use, whether credit card, debit card, or electronic funds transfers. Customers using PayPal should compare their informal resolution system with the favorable chargeback rights customers have under the federal Electronic Funds Transfers Act.

Preventing Identity Theft

Safeguarding Your Social Security Number

Your employer and financial institutions will need your Social Security number for wage and tax reporting purposes. Other businesses may ask you for your Social Security number to do a credit check if you are applying for a loan, renting an apartment, or signing up for utilities. Sometimes, however, they simply want your Social Security number for general record keeping. If someone asks for your Social Security number, ask:

> Why do you need my Social Security number?
> How will my Social Security number be used?
> How do you protect my Social Security number from being stolen?
> What will happen if I don't give you my Social Security number?

If you don't provide your Social Security number, some businesses may not provide you with the service or benefit you want. Getting satisfactory answers to these questions will help you decide whether you want to share your Social Security number with the business. The decision to share is yours.[14]

Safeguard Your Trash as Well as Mail

The FTC recommends that you take proactive steps against dumpster divers and identity thieves who may go through your trash or recycling bins to secure your private information. Purchase a shredder or tear all charge receipts, copies of credit applications, insurance forms, physician statements, checks and bank statements, expired charge cards that you're discarding, and credit offers you get in the mail.

Opt Out of Prescreened Credit Offers

Prescreened credit offers pose a risk of identity theft. The FTC suggests that you minimize risk by opting out of prescreened offers of credit in the mail. To do so, call 1-888-5-OPTOUT (1-888-567-8688). You can use the same toll-free number to opt out of all credit offers. You will be asked to provide your Social Security number, which consumer reporting companies need to match you with your file. The FTC recommends the following proactive steps in protecting your personal information:

1. Keep your personal information in a secure place at home, especially if you have roommates, employ outside help, or are having work done in your house. Keep your purse or wallet in a safe place at work; do the same with copies of administrative forms that have your sensitive personal information.
2. Ask about information security procedures in your workplace or at businesses, doctor's offices, or other institutions that collect your personally identifying information. Find out who has access to your personal information

and verify that it is handled securely. Ask about the disposal procedures for those records as well. Find out if your information will be shared with anyone else. If so, ask how your information can be kept confidential.[15]

If you are a victim of identity theft, you will suffer emotional and financial losses. However, if you take prompt remedial steps, you can mitigate your damages. The FTC recommends that you take the following prompt remedial steps:

1. Call and speak with someone in the security or fraud department of each company. Follow up in writing, and include copies (*not* originals) of supporting documents. It's important to notify credit card companies and banks in writing. Send your letters by certified mail, return receipt requested, so you can document what the company received and when. Keep a file of your correspondence and enclosures.
2. When you open new accounts, use new personal identification numbers (PINs) and passwords. Avoid using easily available information like your mother's maiden name, your birth date, the last four digits of your Social Security number or your phone number, or a series of consecutive numbers.
3. If the identity thief has made charges to or debits from your accounts or has fraudulently opened accounts, ask the company for the forms to dispute those transactions:

    For charges and debits on existing accounts, ask the representative to send you the company's fraud dispute forms. If the company doesn't have special forms, use the sample letter to dispute the fraudulent charges or debits. In either case, write to the company at the address given for "billing inquiries," *not* the address for sending your payments.

    For new, unauthorized accounts, ask if the company accepts the ID Theft Affidavit. . . . If not, ask the representative to send you the company's fraud dispute forms. If the company already has reported these accounts or debts on your credit report, dispute this fraudulent information. See Correcting Fraudulent Information in Credit Reports to learn how.
4. Once you have resolved your identity theft dispute with the company, ask for a letter stating that the company has closed the disputed accounts and has discharged the fraudulent debts. This letter is your best proof if errors relating to this account reappear on your credit report or you are contacted again about the fraudulent debt.[16]

Next, you need to take steps to contact all government agencies that issued you identification forms such as driver's licenses, passports, or Social Security numbers. For driver's licenses and other government-issued identification, contact the agency that issued the license or other identification document. Follow its procedures to cancel the document and to get a replacement. Ask the agency to flag your file so that no one else can get a license or any other identification document from them in your name.[17]

Next, contact each nationwide reporting company to place a *fraud alert* on your credit report. The FTC describes the initial and extended fraud alerts and what functions each perform:

An initial alert stays on your credit report for at least ninety days. You may ask that an initial fraud alert be placed on your credit report if you suspect you have been, or are about to be, a victim of identity theft. An initial alert is appropriate if your wallet has been stolen or if you've been taken in by a "phishing" scam. When you place an initial fraud alert on your credit report, you're entitled to order one free credit report from each of the three nationwide consumer reporting companies, and, if you ask, they will display only the last four digits of your Social Security number.

An extended alert stays on your credit report for seven years. You can have an extended alert placed on your credit report if you've been a victim of identity theft and you provide the consumer reporting company with an "Identity Theft Report," or ID Theft Affidavit. When you place an extended alert on your credit report, you're entitled to two free credit reports within twelve months from each of the three nationwide consumer reporting companies. In addition, the consumer reporting companies will remove your name from marketing lists for prescreened credit offers for five years unless you ask them to put your name back on the list before then.

To place either of these alerts on your credit report, or to have them removed, you will be required to provide appropriate proof of your identity: that may include your Social Security number, name, address and other personal information requested by the consumer reporting company.

When a business sees the alert on your credit report, they must verify your identity before issuing you credit. As part of this verification process, the business may try to contact you directly. That may cause some delays if you're trying to obtain credit. To compensate for possible delays, you may wish to include a cell phone number where you can be reached easily in your alert. Remember to keep all contact information in your alert current.[18]

The fraud alert prevents the phisher or other identity thief from opening up new accounts in your name. You should contact (1) Equifax (1-800-525-6285, www.equifax.com); (2) Experian (1-888-EXPERIAN, or 1-888-397-3742, www.experian.com); and (3) TransUnion (1-800-680-7289, www.transunion.com). FTC regulations give you the right to order one free credit report from each of the three reporting companies after you file the fraud alert. You also have the right to require the companies to display only the last four digits of your Social Security number, which reduces your probability of being victimized by future identity theft crimes. Next, file a complaint with your police department. The police report is an important piece of documentation in freezing collection efforts and proving your claim of identity theft. The FTC gives the following guidance:

> Then, get a copy of the police report or at the very least, the number of the report. It can help you deal with creditors who need proof of the crime. If the police are reluctant to take your report, ask to file a "Miscellaneous Incidents" report, or try another jurisdiction, like your state police. You also can check with your state Attorney General's office to find out if state law requires the

police to take reports for identity theft. Check the Blue Pages of your telephone directory for the phone number or check www.naag.org for a list of state Attorneys General.

What to Do: Filing a Complaint about Identity Fraud

The FTC is the chief constable of cyberspace and the best place to file an identity theft complaint. The commission's staff has developed a straightforward complaint form easily accessible online. The FTC enters Internet, telemarketing, identity theft, and other fraud-related complaints into Consumer Sentinel, the agency's secure, online database available to hundreds of civil and criminal law enforcement agencies worldwide. The website address for filing a general consumer complaint is https://rn.ftc.gov/pls/dod/wsolcq$.startup?Z_ORG_CODE=PU01. The FTC's website for filing online complaints about identity theft is https://rn.ftc.gov/pls/dod/widtpubl$.startup?Z_ORG_CODE=PU03.

When you go to your local police department to file a complaint, bring a printed copy of your ID theft affidavit form and your supporting documentation. Ask the officer to attach or incorporate the affidavit into their police report. Also ask the officer to sign the "Law Enforcement Report" section of your complaint form. If the officer wants more information about the ID theft affidavit, you can tell them it is available on the FTC website's section for law enforcement at the link for "Identity Theft Report." Ask the officer to give you a copy of the official police report with your ID theft affidavit attached or incorporated. (In some jurisdictions the officer will not be able to give you a copy of the official police report, but should be able to sign your affidavit and write the police report number in the "Law Enforcement Report" section.)

The ID theft affidavit can be used to supplement an automated police report. If you can file online an automated report, complete the "Automated Report Information" block of the ID theft affidavit. Attach a copy of any confirmation received from the police to your ID theft affidavit.[19]

Finally, monitor your credit reports and take other precautions to mitigate losses. A number of states give you the right to freeze your credit report in the wake of identity theft. In addition, consumers should file a report with the FTC, which has an online complaint form at www.consumer.gov/idtheft. You can file a complaint with the FTC using the online complaint form or call the FTC's Identity Theft Hotline, toll-free: 1-877-ID-THEFT (438-4338); TTY: 1-866-653-4261; or write Identity Theft Clearinghouse, Federal Trade Commission, 600 Pennsylvania Avenue, N.W., Washington, D.C. 20580.

Using the FTC's ID Theft Affidavit

You should complete an ID theft affidavit, which was developed by the FTC to make reporting identity theft easier. Once you close your accounts, you will have difficulty establishing new accounts opened in your name. A number of banks, financial institutions, and other companies accept the ID theft affidavit when you open a new account in your name after an identity crime. The ID theft affidavit has two parts. Part I of the affidavit asks you to provide information about yourself (name, Social Security number, driver's license, residence, telephone number, and the nature of the ID theft). You will be asked to attest whether you received the goods, money, services, or other benefits that were allegedly gained by the identity thief. You are subject to criminal prosecution if you make false claims of identity theft when you actually received what you ordered. You must also represent that you do not know who misused your information or identification documents. You will be asked to describe any information you have on the description of the fraud and how the identity thief gained access to your personal information. Part II describes the fraudulent accounts opened in your name.

You can download the ID theft affidavit at the FTC website.[20] The FTC recommends sending a separate ID theft affidavit along with supporting documents (driver's license, Social Security number, police report, etc.) to companies where accounts were opened in your name. Before you send an ID theft affidavit, be sure that you review disputed amounts with family members or friends who have may have had access to your account. The FTC recommends that the affidavits be sent as soon as possible—no later than two weeks after you discover the identity theft. Sleeping on your rights may result in your loss of rights to be reimbursed for disputed charges.

You should be as truthful and accurate as possible when completing the affidavit because a false affidavit can be used to prosecute you. Send the completed affidavit, along with appropriate documentation, to each creditor, bank, or company that allowed unauthorized purchases or where the identity thief sought unauthorized credit. The FTC recommends that you send the affidavit (along with documents) by certified mail with return receipt requested. That additional preventive measure prevents your creditors from claiming that they had no notice about accounts opened by thieves.

An identity theft report blocks fraudulent information from reappearing on your credit report. Once an ID theft report is made, companies cannot continue hounding you about collecting debt you do not owe. An ID theft report can be used to permanently block fraudulent information from appearing on your credit report. It's also needed to place an extended fraud alert on your credit report.

An ID theft report will generally have two parts:

1. Step one is a copy of a report filed with a local, state, or federal law enforcement agency, such as your local police department, your state attorney general, the FBI, the U.S. Secret Service, the FTC, and the U.S. Postal Inspection Service. There is no federal law requiring a federal agency to take a report about identity theft, but some state laws require local police departments to take reports. The law requires the report to

provide as much information as you can about the crime, including anything you know about the dates of the identity theft, the fraudulent accounts opened and the alleged identity thief. If you do not provide detailed information, it may be impossible for consumer reporting companies and creditors to comply with your requests.

2. Step two of an identity theft report depends on the policies of the consumer reporting company and the information provider (the business that sends information to the consumer reporting company). That is, they may ask you to provide information or documentation in addition to that included in the law enforcement report and that is reasonably intended to verify your identity theft. They must make their request within fifteen days of receiving your law enforcement report, or, if you already obtained an extended fraud alert on your credit report, the date you submit your request to the credit reporting company for information blocking. The consumer reporting company and information provider then have fifteen more days to work with you to make sure your identity theft report contains everything they need. They are entitled to take five days to review any information you give them. For example, if you give them information eleven days after they request it, they do not have to make a final decision until sixteen days after they asked you for that information. If you give them any information after the fifteen-day deadline, they can reject your identity theft report as incomplete, and you will have to resubmit your identity theft report with the correct information.

You may find that most federal and state agencies, and some local police departments, offer only "automated" reports, which do not require a face-to-face meeting with a law enforcement officer. Automated reports may be submitted online or by telephone or mail. If you have a choice, do not use an automated report. The reason? It's more difficult for the consumer reporting company or information provider to verify the information. Unless you are asking a consumer reporting company to place an extended fraud alert on your credit report, you probably will have to provide additional information or documentation when you use an automated report.[21]

Resolving identity theft is a time-consuming, costly, and frustrating process. The victims of identity theft will only rarely be compensated for their losses, which makes it even more important to construct a fence at the top of the hill versus cleaning up your credit report in the wake of a data heist.

Auction and Retail Schemes Online

A consumer-to-consumer (C2C) model facilitates both transactions between consumers who might otherwise face high transaction costs in finding buyers or sellers and transactions in goods not commonly available through retailers.

Online auctions such as eBay are popular C2C models, linking up consumer sellers with consumer buyers interested in auction jewelry, pens, collectibles, electronic equipment, artwork, books, and hundreds of thousands of other consumer goods.

Auctions may take the form of a traditional auction in which purchasers bid against each other, or a reverse auction in which purchasers name their price. A growing number of websites, such as Priceline.com, use "reverse auctions." A reverse auction permits a consumer to place a bid for a flight to Copenhagen, for example, at a price no greater than $500 one way. The reverse bidder specifies departure and return dates, departure and arrival airports, flight times, number of tickets, passenger names, maximum number of connections, airlines, price on offer, and the manner of delivery. If the airline accepts the offer price, the purchase is automatically charged to the visitor's credit card. The user must have typed their initials in an icon box to indicate that they have reviewed the terms and agree to abide by Priceline.com's terms and conditions.

Online auctions allow potential consumers to search the database for any items they would be interested in purchasing. Online auctions evolved four decades after the rules for sale by auction were drafted in Article 2 of the Uniform Commercial Code. UCC Article 2 rules for auctions were drafted to apply to human auctioneers selling goods in lots. The auctioneer's "falling of the hammer" constituted acceptance of the bidder's offer. A "live" auction has no close parallel in Internet auctions, though judges may extend UCC Article 2 rules to the online auction house.

Under the UCC rules, a court will look to the "usage of trade" to clarify the contracting parties' intent in light of established practices in the industry. The usage of trade for auctions generally takes the form of an auction "with reserve" or "without reserve." The traditional auction is "with reserve," meaning that the auctioneer has the discretion to reject the highest bid if it is too low; as a general rule, a sale is with reserve unless the goods are explicitly sold "without reserve."

In an online auction, there is no fall of the hammer signifying acceptance, but the operators of virtual or online auctions are developing their own industry practices for listing goods, documenting bid histories, communicating bidding guidelines, and dealing with liability. Online auction sellers frequently set minimum prices and sell their goods with reserve or without reserve. As in a "live" auction, a virtual auction "with reserve" permits the seller to withdraw the goods at any time. Unlike a live auction, however, there is no auctioneer to announce the completion of the sale. An auction without reserve means that the auctioneer cannot withdraw the goods unless no bid is made within a reasonable time. In either case, a bidder may retract his bid until the auctioneer announces the end of the bidding period. The existing rules for virtual auctions must be accommodated to the evolving online auction practices.

Online auctions are different from live auctions in various ways. In a live auction, there is less concern with the seller's reputation since the item is physically available for a potential buyer to inspect. However, a seller's reputation is of the utmost importance for an online auction. Online auctions use measures of a seller's reputation to build trust in C2C transactions. Consumers give online ratings of their satisfaction with their course of dealing with a given vendor. In a live auction, the buyer can inspect the lots of goods being auctioned. For obvious reasons, that cannot occur during an online auction. Other means to identify the items are used, such as digital photographs of objects being sold and descriptions of the item, but a photo of an item for sale is hardly the same thing as a hands-on inspection. As a result, there is a high potential for fraud during an online auction. State and federal regulators are increasingly scrutinizing online fraud on Internet auction sites.

The FTC's Consumer Sentinel uncovered that online auction sites and retail schemes are a leading source of Internet fraud. Few Americans can resist a bargain for luxury goods such as Coach purses, Mont Blanc pens, or Gucci jewelry. The most typical fraud is for the seller to secure payment and then deliver knockoffs or obvious fakes. The FTC's analysis of Consumer Sentinel data concludes that the most common online auction complaint is that the consumer either did not receive the item paid for or that the merchandise sent was worth far less than represented. Online auction houses disclaim responsibility for fraudulent sales transactions.

Not receiving the item paid for or receiving an item of lesser value is only one of the many types of fraud that can occur on an online auction site. Sellers can also be defrauded out of thousands of dollars. One typical scheme occurs when a buyer purchases a high-priced item and sends the seller a check for thousands more than the amount of the item sold.[22] The buyer will then ask the seller to refund the extra amount.[23] Later, it is discovered that the check from the buyer was counterfeit.[24] Another type of fraud that can occur, called "shilling," is when a seller bids on his own item to increase the price of that item.[25] Another variation of the online auction involves customers banding together in a group to increase their purchasing power. The greater the number of interested buyers seeking a particular item, the lower the price per purchaser.

When using online services, a buyer should be aware of how to safeguard himself or herself against fraud. EBay and other auction websites disclaim any responsibility for fraudulent sales. However, these services do provide some safeguards against fraud occurring on their websites. If you purchase goods through PayPal, a service owned by eBay, you are insured after the first $25 up to a maximum of $1,000. Auction houses use "private policing" to banish fraudulent sellers from cyberspace. EBay also uses informal social sanctions to patrol the marketplace. EBay's system of reputational ratings for sellers relies heavily on informal feedback in which dissatisfied buyers warn others through postings. Under the section "Reviews and Guides," located on the eBay website, a potential buyer can find posts of bad sales practices of sellers. For example, if you search for the term *fake*, you will find more than 1,200 messages telling you how to avoid fakes and warning you about dishonest sellers. In general, expensive consumer goods being sold at a low price tend to be knockoffs or fakes. If you conduct a website search using the word *Chinese*, most messages are warnings since such a high percentage of bad deals come from China. Frequently the Chinese item sells for a very small amount of money, but postage is in the double digits. If you are dissatisfied, you have to ship the item back to China and you receive the purchase price, not the shipping costs, which makes it a useless remedy when the seller states that you may return the item.

EBay has also used third-party verification services to vouch for certain sellers to guard against fraudulent auctions. These verification services, however, may not always be effective against preventing fraud. For example, the third-party verification service used by eBay, SquareTrade, "vouched" for the company Liquidation Universe, which was later accused of victimizing nearly 1,000 people in 2003.[26]

Often eBay con artists use "private" feedback, which stops victims from warning each other, so it is important for consumers to perform a wide variety of searches on a seller before buying high-priced items. Many victims, once they are aware that they have been deceived, will band together and form websites or various mailing list sites to get the message out to other potential buyers. A consumer victimized by a Tech-Surplus scam created the website www.techsurplusvictim.com to warn other buyers of the danger. The online warning states: "We're interested in stopping this type of behavior as quickly as possible, recovering our money and informing others of the issues surrounding these transactions."[27] I cannot stress enough that it is important to perform research on a seller before making a large purchase. You must obtain information about the seller before the auction ends, since the seller can change his ID after the auction closes.[28]

One of the shortcomings of eBay's informal warning system is that consumers may be reluctant to post negative evaluations because of the fear that sellers will retaliate with even worse feedback about them. Once a buyer posts a negative review, the seller may not accept a return or may retaliate in other ways, such as sending virus-laden messages, threats, or harassment. The danger of blowback may deter some consumers from posting negative reviews. The feedback system also may contain favorable reviews that are not true reviews but postings by a fraudulent seller.

EBay's Immunity from Liability

The eBay User Agreement requires its users to "read, agree with and accept all of the terms and conditions contained in this User Agreement and the Privacy Policy, which include those terms and conditions expressly set out below and those incorporated by reference," before they can access the eBay system. One of the terms of service for eBay is the absolute prohibition on seeking punitive damages under any doctrinal theory. EBay asserts that it has no liability for acts of third parties. EBay will likely assert immunity from any claim under Section 230 of the Communications Decency Act (CDA) of 1996. The most significant reason why there are so few consumers using the remedy of punitive damages in cyberspace is the blanket immunity granted ISPs by Congress.

One of the unintended consequences of the CDA is that it gives websites such as eBay the equivalent of an absolute immunity for a third party's unfair, deceptive, and predatory practices in cyberspace. Congress enacted Section 230 to protect the "infant industry" of online service providers, such as America Online, CompuServe, and Prodigy, from tort liability arising out of postings by customers. Section 230 of the CDA immunizes ISPs from torts committed by subscribers and third parties.

The courts have stretched ISP immunity to nearly every conceivable information-related tort, including invasion of privacy and negligence. The result has been that ISPs have prevailed in nearly every tort-related case since the mid-1990s. This broad immunity will likely protect eBay or any other website from liability for failing to detect or control third-party wrongdoing on their systems. If you use eBay, you do so at your own risk. In the vast majority of eBay fraud cases, the third-party wrongdoer or cybercriminal simply disappears in cyberspace with your money or merchandise. You may want to insure your transactions or pay by credit card so that you will have chargeback rights.

EBay's Fraud Protection Program

EBay devotes significant resources to its private policing of transactions, even though it has no real tort liability. EBay's interest is to ferret out cybercriminals to protect its service. In addition, eBay has developed a fraud protection insurance program. EBay does not permit you to receive fraud protection coverage unless you fulfill each of the following criteria:

- You are a winning bidder or fixed-price buyer of an item listed on the eBay site.
- Both you and the seller were members in good standing (feedback rating of zero or above) at the close of the listing.
- You are a member in good standing at the time you file a claim.
- Your item is legal and in accordance with eBay's listing policies and User Agreement.
- The final winning bid price of the item is over $25. Multiple listings cannot be combined into one claim to become eligible, even if purchased from the same seller. Items purchased through Multiple Item Auctions (Dutch Auctions) are eligible provided the combined value of all items purchased through a single listing is over $25.
- Payment was sent to the seller in good faith and proof of payment can be documented.

- You filed a Fraud Alert prior to seeking reimbursement through a Protection Claim.
- You have not exceeded the three claims per six months limit.
- If you paid with a credit card (either directly to the seller or through an online payment service), you must have already contacted your credit card issuer and sought reimbursement from the issuer prior to filing a claim.[29]

The eBay fraud protection coverage *does not apply* to the following:

- Any transaction that is paid for using cash or any other form of payment that cannot be documented;
- Any transaction that is paid for using money transfer services such as Western Union or Moneygram;
- Merchandise that has been altered, repaired, discarded or resold;
- Items damaged or lost in shipping;
- Items that are picked up or delivered in person;
- Items that are not sold via eBay, including purchases in which you are not identified as the winning bidder or fixed price buyer and reserve price listings where the reserve price was not met;
- Double or overpayment;
- Items significantly different from the listing;
- Intangible items (for example, online game items); and
- Any item where a claim has already been paid (partially or in full) through Paypal Buyer Protection.[30]

Complaints Filed with Law Enforcement Officials
In particularly egregious cases you should contact local, state, or federal law enforcement and file complaints. You should contact both your local and state police departments as well as the law enforcement officials in the perpetrator's town and state.

Filing a Complaint with the Shipper
If your item was shipped by the USPS, you may file a complaint at http://www.usps.com/websites/depart/inspect.

You may also file a consumer complaint with the Internet Crime Complaint Center at www.ic3.gov. Be prepared to explain why you were defrauded or victimized and what damages you suffered. Government complaints are unlikely to result in a restitution remedy, but the evidence of a government action may be useful in your private civil action.

Other Complaint Mechanisms
NFIC for Online Complaints. Consider filing a complaint with the National Fraud Information Center (NFIC). You can call the NFIC toll-free at

1-800-876-7060. The NFIC complaint can also be completed online at http://www.fraud.org/info/contactnfic.htm. The NFIC accepts complaints whenever there is an attempt to defraud consumers, either by telephone or by the Internet.

Traditional Businesses. If you have a standard bricks-and-mortar-type complaint with problems such as home improvement, auto sales, or other transactions that usually take place at consumers' homes or retail stores, file with your state attorney general's office or other agency. You might also consider filing a complaint with the Better Business Bureau at http://www.bbb.org.[31]

What to Do: Telemarketing Abuses

The FTC's Telemarketing Sales Rule prohibits "deceptive telemarketing acts or practices" (Telemarketing Sales Rule, 16 C.F.R. §310.3). The FTC Rule requires telemarketers to make material disclosures *prior* to a customer's payment for goods or services. The creditor must disclose the total costs to purchase, receive, or use any goods or services. Further, telemarketers must make specific disclosures about any material limitations or a condition to purchase goods or services. A telemarketer must also disclose its policy for "refunds, cancellations, exchanges or repurchases."

In any prize promotion, the telemarketer must give the odds of winning a prize and the factors used in calculating the odds, as well as costs or conditions to receive or redeem a prize. A telemarketer is liable for deceptive telemarketing acts, including the misrepresentation of information on costs and on limitations or conditions to purchase or use goods or services.

Place your telephone number on the FTC's Do Not Call Registry by calling 1-888-382-1222 or registering it online at www.donotcall.com. The National Do Not Call Registry gives you the right to opt out of receiving annoying telemarketing calls at home. Once you register, you should be able to screen out most calls if your name has been on the registry for thirty-one days. Sixty days after registering, companies from whom you have not purchased anything in the past eighteen months can be fined $500 the first time they call you and $1,000 for each additional call. You can also register your cell phone, and registration is effective for a five-year period.

To register your numbers, visit http://www.donotcall.gov/register/Reg.aspx. You can also file a complaint against fraudulent telemarketers by visiting https://www.donotcall.gov/Complain/ComplainCheck.aspx. The FTC offers the following guideposts for filing a Do Not Call complaint. You may not file a complaint against a telemarketer unless you have been listed on the FTC's Do Not Call Registry for a minimum of thirty-one days. Assuming you have met this requirement, your complaint must give the time and date of the call and the telephone number and/or name of the company that called you.

Consumers may also call the registry's toll-free number at (1-888-382-1222) to file a complaint (for TTY, call 1-866-290-4236). The FTC does not have jurisdiction to resolve individual consumer problems, but complaints can lead to civil penalties or law enforcement. Another option is for you to mail a complaint to the FTC's Do Not Call Registry's mailing address: National Do Not Call Registry, Attn: DNC Program Manager, Federal Trade Commission, 600 Pennsylvania Avenue, N.W., Washington, D.C. 20580. The FTC manages the Do Not Call Registry and has posted helpful guidance at http://www.ftc.gov/bcp/conline/pubs/alerts/dncalrt.htm. The FTC warns consumers not to contract with private companies that charge fees for registering them with the Do Not Call Registry, as they are likely to be frauds. However, the FTC does note that not all nuisance calls are within the jurisdiction of the registry.

Consumer law's remarkable quality of continually adapting old causes of action to new threats and dangers makes it an important institution of social control. Consumer law needs to be strengthened, not diminished, if it is to control abuses made possible by the Internet and other emergent social problems of the new century. Consumer law plays a key role in holding wrongdoers responsible for their misdeeds. A strong consumer law regime ensures that not even multibillion dollar corporations operate beyond the reach of the law. Consumer law is, as it always has been in the past few decades, forward-looking, with the ability to adapt to new social problems and conditions. Progressive consumer law brings common sense to the common law.

Notes

1. Federal Trade Commission, "Consumer Fraud and Identity Theft Complaint Data, January-December 2006," available at www.consumer.gov/sentinel/pubs/Top10Fraud2006.pdf (last visited June 17, 2007).

2. Ibid., 5.

3. The Internet Crime Complaint Center, "2005 Internet Report," available at http://www.ic3.gov/media/annualreport/2005_IC3Report.pdf (last visited June 17, 2007).

4. Federal Bureau of Investigation and National White Collar Crime Center, Internet Crime Complaint Center, 2005 Internet Crime Survey (visited August 10, 2006), http://www.ic3.gov/.

5. The information in this section draws in part from the superb FTC Guide, *Take Charge: Fighting Back against Identity Theft* (2007), available at http://www.ftc.gov/bcp/edu/pubs/consumer/idtheft/idt04.htm (accessed March 21, 2007).

6. Robert Paul Norman, "Using E-Commerce Insurance to Minimize Liability," *Internet Law and Practice* (November 2006): 1.

7. Andy Mukherjee, "Globalizing Law and Order," *International Herald Tribune*, January 11, 2007, available at http://www.iht.com/articles/2007/01/11/bloomberg/sxmuk.php (accessed February 7, 2007).

8. "British MPs React to Outsourcing Security Breach," *Outsourcing Times*, June 24, 2005, available at http://www.blogsource.org/2005/06/british_mps_rea.html (accessed February 1, 2007).

9. Paul F. Roberts, "Retailer TJX Reports Massive Data Breach: Credit, Debit Data Stolen, Extent of Breach Unknown," *Infoworld*, January 7, 2007, 1.

10. Ibid.

11. See https://www.paypal.com/cgi-bin/webscr?cmd=_vdc-security-spoof-outside.

12. Ibid.

13. Ibid.

14. FTC, *Take Charge.*

15. Federal Trade Commission, "Your National Resources about ID Theft," www.consumer.gov/idtheft/con_minimize.htm (last visited June 17, 2007).

16. Federal Trade Commission, "ID Theft: What It's All About," http://www.ftc.gov/bcp/edu/microsites/idtheft/consumers/defend.html (last visited June 17, 2007).

17. Federal Trade Commission (FTC), "Take Charge: Fighting Back Against Identity Theft," http://www.ftc.gov/bcp/edu/pubs/consumer/idtheft/idt04.shtm (last visited June 17, 2007).

18. Ibid.

19. Ibid.

20. See http://www.ftc.gov/bcp/conline/pubs/credit/affidavit.pdf.

21. Ibid.

22. P. S. McLean et al., "Phishing and Pharming and Trojans—Oh My!" *Utah B.J.,* April 19, 2006, 28, 29.

23. Ibid.

24. Ibid.

25. F. Manjoo, "EBay Fraud Law: Any Takers?" available at www.wired.com/news/business/0,1367,44831,00.html (accessed October 7, 2006).

26. B. Sullivan, "Man Arrested in Huge eBay Fraud," MSNBC.com, available at www.msnbc.msn.com/id/3078461/print/1/displaymode/1098 (accessed October 7, 2006).

27. I. Steiner, "eBay Auction Fraud Spawns Vigilantism Trend," available at http://www.auctionbytes.com/cab/abn/y02/m10/il2/s01.

28. See http://www.manleylabs.com/containerpages/16x2FRAUD.html.

29. EBay, "Online Fraud Reporting Form," available at http://cgi1.ebay.com/aw-cgi/eBayISAPI.dll (accessed August 10, 2006).

30. Ibid.

31. These tips for coping with online fraud are given by the Internet Crime Complaint Center, available at http://www.ic3.gov/preventiontips.aspx (accessed August 10, 2006).

Appendix A:
State General Consumer
Protection Statutes

Alabama: Consumer Fraud Act, Ala. Code §§8-19-1 *et seq.*
Alaska: Consumer Protection Act, Alaska Stat. §§45.50.471 *et seq.*
Arizona: Consumer Fraud Act, Ariz. Rev. Stat. §§44-1521 *et seq.*
Arkansas: Deceptive Trade Practices Act, Ark. Code §§4-88-101 *et seq.*
California: Consumer Legal Remedies Act, Cal. Civ. Code, §§1750 *et seq.*
Colorado: Consumer Protection Act, Colo. Rev. Stat. §§6-1-101 *et seq.*
Connecticut: Unfair Trade Practices Act, Conn. Gen. Stat. §§42-110(a) *et seq.*
Delaware: Uniform Trade Practices Act, Del. Code tit. 6, §§2531 *et seq.*
District of Columbia: Consumer Protection Procedures Act, D.C. Code Ann.
    §§28-3901 *et seq.*
Florida: Deceptive and Unfair Trade Practices Act, Fla. Stat. ch. 501.201 *et seq.*
Georgia: Fair Business Practices Act, O.C.G.A. §§10-1-390 *et seq.*
Hawaii: Uniform Deceptive Trade Practices Act, Haw. Rev. Stat. 481A-1 *et. seq.*
Idaho: Idaho Consumer Protection Act, Idaho Stat. §48-601
Illinois: Consumer Fraud and Deceptive Business Practices Act, Ill. Comp. Stat.
    Ann. §§505/1 *et seq.*
Indiana: Deceptive Consumer Sales Act, Ind. Code Ann. §§24-5-0.5-1 *et seq.*
Iowa: Consumer Fraud Act, Iowa Code Ann. §§714.16 *et seq.*
Kansas: Consumer Protection Act, Kan. Stat. Ann. §§50-623 *et seq.*
Kentucky: Consumer Protection Act, Ky. Rev. Stat. §§367.110 *et seq.*
Louisiana: Unfair Trade Practices and Consumer Protection Law, La. Rev. Stat. Ann.
    §§51:1401 *et seq.*
Maine: Uniform Deceptive Trade Practices Act, Me. Rev. Stat. Ann. tit. 10, §§ 213 *et
    seq.*
Maryland: Maryland Consumer Protection Act, Md. Com. Law Code Ann.
    §§13-101 *et seq.*
Massachusetts: Regulation of Business Practices for Consumer Protection,
    M.G.L.A., ch. 93A.

Michigan: Consumer Protection Act, Mich. Comp. Laws Ann. §§445.901 *et seq.*
Minnesota: Deceptive Trade Practices Act, Minn. Stat. §§325D.44 *et seq.*
Mississippi: Consumer Protection Act, Miss. Code Ann. §§74-24-1 *et seq.*
Missouri: Merchandising Practices, Mo. Rev. Stat. §§407.010 *et seq.*
Montana: Unfair Trade Practices and Consumer Protection, Mont. Code, §§30-14-101 *et seq.*
Nebraska: Consumer Protection Act, Neb. Rev. Stat. §§59-1601 *et seq.*
Nevada: Deceptive Trade Practices Act, Nev. Rev. Stat. §§87-302 *et seq.*
New Hampshire: Regulation of Business Practices for Consumer Protection, N.H. Rev. Stat. §§358-A, *et seq.*
New Jersey: Consumer Fraud Act, N.J. Stat. Ann. §§57-12-1 *et seq.*
New Mexico: Unfair Practices Act, N.M. Stat. Ann. §§57-12-1 *et seq.*
New York: New York's Executive Law, N.Y. Exec. §§349 *et seq.*
North Carolina: Unfair and Deceptive Trade Practices Act, N.C. Gen. Stat. §75-1.1 *et seq.*
North Dakota: Consumer Fraud Act, Consumer Fraud and Unlawful Credit Practices, N.D. Cent. Code §51-15-01 *et seq.*
Ohio: Deceptive Trade Practices Act, Ohio Rev. Code §4165 *et seq.*
Oklahoma: Deceptive Trade Practices Act, Okla. Stat. tit. 22, §1080 *et seq.*
Oregon: Unlawful Trade Practices Act, Ore. Rev. Stat. §646.605 *et seq.*
Pennsylvania: Unfair Trade Practices and Consumer Protection Law, Pa. tit. 73 §201 *et seq.*
Rhode Island: Unfair Trade Practice and Consumer Protection Act, R.I. Gen. Laws 6-13.1-1 *et seq.*
South Carolina: Unfair Trade Practices Act, 39-5-10 *et seq.*
South Dakota: Deceptive Trade Practices and Consumer Protection Law, S.D. Codified Laws §§37-24-35 *et seq.*
Tennessee: Consumer Protection Act, Tenn. Code Ann. 47-18-101 *et seq.*
Texas: Deceptive Trade Practices and Consumer Protection Act, Tex. Bus. and Com. Code §§17.41 *et seq.*
Utah: Unfair Practices Act, Utah Code §§13-5 *et seq.*
Vermont: Consumer Fraud Act, Vt. Stat. Ann. Tit. 9, §§2451 *et seq.*
Virginia: Consumer Protection Act of 1977, Va. Code §§59-1-196 *et seq.*
Washington: Unfair Business Practices—Consumer Protection, Wash. Rev. Code §19.86 *et seq.*
West Virginia: Consumer Credit and Protection Act, W. Va. Code §46A-6-101 *et seq.*
Wisconsin: Deceptive Trade Practices and Consumer Protection Act, Wis. Stat. §100.20 (2003).
Wyoming: Consumer Protection Act, Wyo. Stat. §§40-12-101 *et seq.*

Appendix B:
Locating Legal Advice and
Low-Income Legal Services

The source for most of this information is the Federal Citizen Information Center (FCIC) administered by the General Services Administration. You can easily update this information by searching online using terms such as, by way of example: "Alabama, Office of the Attorney General." You can also find updated information at the FCIC website: http://consumeraction.gov/caw_problems_legal.shtml. If you need an attorney to advise or represent you, ask friends and family for recommendations. You can also contact the lawyer referral service of your state, county, or city bar association, listed in your local phone directory or online.

Websites such as www.abalawinfo.org (American Bar Association), www.uslaw .com, www.thelaw.com, www.freeadvice.com, and www.nolo.com may help you with answers to general legal questions. A peerless source of information on consumer law rights and remedies is www.consumer.gov. ATLA.org is a good source of information for any tort-related causes of action you might have. Information on consumer product recalls can be found at the Consumer Protection Safety Commission: http://www.cpsc.gov. An omnibus collection of links offering a gateway to consumer protection law is found at Consumer World: http://www.consumerworld.org/ pages/agencies.htm. The FTC makes available user-friendly summaries of the most important federal statutes at http://www.ftc.gov. The Federal Reserve website provides the best available information on commercial paper, negotiable instruments, and check collection: http://www.federalreserve.gov/consumers.htm. For information on state-specific legal questions, try the website of the National Association of Consumer Agency Administrators (www.nacaa.net).

If you cannot afford a lawyer, you may qualify for free legal help from a Legal Aid or Legal Services Corporation office. These offices generally offer legal assistance about such things as landlord-tenant relations, credit, utilities, family matters (e.g., divorce and adoption), foreclosure, home equity fraud, Social Security, welfare, unemployment, and workers' compensation. If the Legal Aid office in your area does not handle your type of case, it may refer you to other local, state, or national organizations that can provide help.

To find the Legal Aid office nearest to you, check a local telephone directory or contact:

National Legal Aid and Defender Association
1625 K Street, N.W., 8th Floor
Washington, DC 20006
Telephone: 202-452-0620
Fax: 202-872-1031
Website: www.nlada.org

To find the LSC office nearest you, check a local telephone directory or contact:

LSC Public Affairs
3333 K St., N.W., 3rd Floor
Washington, DC 20007
Telephone: 202-295-1500
Fax: 202-337-6797
Website: www.lsc.gov

Appendix C:
State Consumer
Protection Agencies

The addresses, phone numbers, and email addresses for state attorneys general and each state's chief consumer protection agency are reprinted below. You may also obtain county and local agency contact information at the Federal Citizen Information Center (FCIC) administered by the General Services Administration. You can easily update this information by searching online, using terms such as, by way of example: "Alabama, Office of the Attorney General." You can also find updated information at the FCIC website: http://consumeraction.gov/caw_state_resources.shtml. You can find the contact information for United States Attorneys at the United States Department of Justice Website at http://www.usdoj.gov/usao/offices/index.html.

The contact information listed in this appendix is updated as of June 2007.

Alabama
Office of the Attorney General
11 South Union St.
Montgomery, AL 36130
Telephone: 334-242-7335
Toll-free: 1-800-392-5658
Website: www.ago.state.al.us

Alaska
Consumer Protection Unit
Office of the Attorney General
1031 West 4th Ave., Suite 200
Anchorage, AK 99501-5903
Telephone: 907-269-5100
Toll-free: 1-888-576-2529
Fax: 907-276-8554
Website: www.law.state.ak.us

Arizona
Office of the Attorney General
1275 West Washington St.
Phoenix, AZ 85007
Telephone: 602-542-5025
Telephone: 602-542-5763 (Consumer Information and Complaints)
Toll-free: 1-800-352-8431
Fax: 602-542-4085
Website: www.azag.gov

Consumer Protection
Office of the Attorney General
400 West Congress South Bldg., Suite 315
Tucson, AZ 85701
Telephone: 520-628-6504
Toll-free: 1-800-352-8431
Fax: 520-628-6530
Website: www.azag.gov

Arkansas
Office of the Attorney General
323 Center St., Suite 200
Little Rock, AR 72201
Telephone: 501-682-2007 (General)
Telephone: 501-682-2341 (Consumer Hotline)
Toll-free: 1-800-482-8982 (Do Not Call Program)
Toll-free: 1-800-448-3014 (Crime Victims Hotline)
Toll-free: 1-877-866-8225 (In-State Do Not Call Program)
TTY: 501-682-6073
Fax: 501-682-8118
Website: www.ag.state.ar.us

California
California Department of Consumer Affairs
1625 North Market Blvd.
Sacramento, CA 95834
Telephone: 916-445-1254; 916-445-4465
Telephone: 916-445-2643 (Correspondence and Complaint Review Unit)
Toll-free: 1-800-952-5210
TTY: 916-322-1700 or Toll-free: 1-800-326-2297
Website: www.dca.ca.gov

California Department of Consumer Affairs
10240 Systems Pkwy.
Sacramento, CA 95827
Telephone: 916-255-4300
Toll-free: 1-800-952-5210
TTY: 916-322-1700

Fax: 916-255-1369
Website: www.autorepair.ca.gov

Office of the Attorney General
Public Inquiry Unit
P.O. Box 944255
Sacramento, CA 94244-2550
Telephone: 916-322-3360
Toll-free: 1-800-952-5225
TTY: 916-324-5564
Fax: 916-323-5341
Website: www.caag.state.ca.us

Colorado
Consumer Protection Division
Office of the Attorney General
1525 Sherman St., 5th Floor
Denver, CO 80203-1760
Telephone: 303-866-5079
Toll-free: 1-800-222-4444
Fax: 303-866-5443
Website: http://www.ago.state.co.us/index.cfm

Connecticut
Department of Consumer Protection
165 Capitol Ave.
Hartford, CT 06106
Telephone: 860-713-6050
Fax: 860-713-7243
Website: http://www.ct.gov.

Delaware
Fraud and Consumer Protection Division
Office of the Attorney General
Carvel State Office Building
820 North French St.
Wilmington, DE 19801
Telephone: 302-577-8600
Toll-free: 1-800-220-5424
TTY: 302-577-6499
Fax: 302-577-2496
Website: www.state.de.us/attgen/

District of Columbia
Office of Consumer Protection
Department of Consumer and Regulatory Affairs
941 N. Capitol Street, NE
Washington, DC 20002

Telephone: 202-442-4400
Fax: 202-442-8390
Website: www.dcra.dc.gov

Office of the Attorney General for the District of Columbia
441 4th St., NW, Suite 450 N
Washington, DC 20001
Telephone: 202-442-9828
Fax: 202-727-6546
Website: http://occ.dc.gov/

Department of Consumer and Regulatory Affairs
Government of the District of Columbia
941 North Capitol St., NE
Washington, DC 20002
Telephone: 202-442-4400
Citywide Call Center: 202-727-1000
Fax: 202-442-9445
Website: dcra.dc.gov

Florida
Office of the Attorney General
PL-01 The Capitol
Tallahassee, FL 32399-1050
Telephone: 850-414-3600
Toll-free: 1-866-966-7226
TTY: 1-800-955-8771
Fax: 850-488-4483
Website: myfloridalegal.com

Multi-State Litigation and Intergovernmental Affairs
Office of the Attorney General
PL-01 The Capitol
Tallahassee, FL 32399-1050
Telephone: 850-414-3300
Toll-free: 1-866-966-7226
TTY: 1-800-955-8771
Fax: 850-410-1630
Website: myfloridalegal.com

Division of Consumer Services
2005 Apalachee Parkway
Tallahassee, FL 32301
Telephone: 850-488-2221
Toll-free: 1-800-435-7352
Fax: 850-410-3839
Website: www.800helpfla.com

Georgia
Governor's Office of Consumer Affairs
2 Martin Luther King, Jr., Dr., Suite 356
Atlanta, GA 30334
Telephone: 404-656-3790
Toll-free: 1-800-869-1123
Fax: 404-651-9018
Website: www2.state.ga.us/gaoca

Hawaii
State Offices
Department of Commerce and Consumer Affairs
345 Kekuanaoa St., Room 12
Hilo, HI 96720
Telephone: 808-933-0910
Fax: 808-933-8845
Website: http://www.hawaii.gov/dcca

Office of Consumer Protection
Department of Commerce and Consumer Affairs
235 South Beretania St., Room 801
Honolulu, HI 96813-2419
Telephone: 808-586-2636
Fax: 808-586-2640
Website: http://www.hawaii.gov/dcca/areas/ocp/

Idaho
Consumer Protection Unit
Office of the Attorney General
650 West State St.
Boise, ID 83720-0010
Telephone: 208-334-2424
Toll-free: 1-800-432-3545
Fax: 208-334-2830
Website: www.state.id.us/ag

Illinois
1001 East Main St.
Carbondale, IL 62901
Telephone: 618-529-6400
Toll-free: 1-800-243-0607
TTY: 618-529-0607 or Toll-free: 1-877-675-9339
Fax: 618-529-6416
Website: www.illinoisattorneygeneral.gov

Consumer Fraud Bureau
100 West Randolph, 12th Floor
Chicago, IL 60601

Telephone: 312-814-3000
Toll-free: 1-800-386-5438
TTY: 312-814-3374
Fax: 312-814-2593
Website: www.illinoisattorneygeneral.gov

Indiana
Consumer Protection Division
Office of the Attorney General
Indiana Government Center South
302 West Washington St.
Indianapolis, IN 46204
Telephone: 317-232-6201
Toll-free: 1-800-382-5516 (Consumer Hotline)
Fax: 317-232-7979
Website: www.in.gov/attorneygeneral

Iowa
Consumer Protection Division
Office of the Iowa Attorney General
1305 East Walnut St., 2nd Floor
Hoover Building
Des Moines, IA 50319
Telephone: 515-281-5926
Toll-free: 1-888-777-4590
Fax: 515-281-6771
Website: www.IowaAttorneyGeneral.org

Kansas
Consumer Protection and Antitrust Division
Office of the Attorney General
120 S.W. 10th, 2nd Floor
Topeka, KS 66612-1597
Telephone: 785-296-3751
Toll-free: 1-800-432-2310
TTY: 785-291-3767
Fax: 785-291-3699
Website: www.ksag.org

Kentucky
1024 Capital Center Dr., Suite 200
Frankfort, KY 40601
Telephone: 502-696-5389
Toll-free: 1-888-432-9257
Fax: 502-573-8317
Website: ag.ky.gov

Office of the Attorney General
Consumer Protection Division

8911 Shelbyville Rd.
Louisville, KY 40222
Telephone: 502-429-7134
Fax: 502-429-7129
Website: http://ag.ky.gov/consumer/

Louisiana
Office of the Attorney General
P.O. Box 94005
Baton Rouge, LA 70804-9005
Telephone: 225-342-7013
Toll-free: 1-800-351-4889
Fax: 225-326-6499
Website: www.ag.state.la.us

Maine
Office of Consumer Credit Regulation
35 State House Station
Augusta, ME 04333-0035
Telephone: 207-624-8527
Toll-free: 1-800-332-8529
TTY: 1-888-577-6690
Fax: 207-582-7699
Website: www.mainecreditreg.org

Office of the Attorney General
6 State House Station
Augusta, ME 04333
Telephone: 207-626-8800
Fax: 207-626-8812
Website: www.maine.gov

Maryland
Consumer Protection Division
Office of the Attorney General
200 Saint Paul Place, 16th Floor
Baltimore, MD 21202-2021
Telephone: 410-528-8662 (Consumer Complaints)
Telephone: 410-576-6550 (Consumer Information)
Telephone: 410-528-1840 (Health Advocacy unit)
Toll-free: 1-888-743-0023
TTY: 410-576-6372
Fax: 410-576-7040
Website: www.oag.state.md.us/consumer

Massachusetts
10 Park Plaza, Suite 5170
Boston, MA 02116
Telephone: 617-973-8700 (General Information)

Telephone: 617-973-8787 (Consumer Hotline)
Toll-free: 1-888-283-3757
TTY: 617-973-8790
Fax: 617-973-8798
Website: www.mass.gov/Consumer

Consumer Protection and Antitrust Division
Office of the Attorney General
One Ashburton Place
Boston, MA 02108
Telephone: 617-727-8400 (Consumer Hotline)
TTY: 617-727-4765
Fax: 617-727-3265
Website: www.mass.gov/ago

Michigan
Consumer Protection Division
Office of Attorney General
P.O. Box 30213
Lansing, MI 48909
Telephone: 517-373-1140
Toll-free: 1-877-765-8388
Fax: 517-241-3771/373-3042
Website: www.michigan.gov/ag

Minnesota
Consumer Services Division
Office of the Attorney General
1400 Bremer Tower
445 Minnesota St.
St. Paul, MN 55101
Telephone: 651-296-3353
Toll-free: 1-800-657-3787
TTY: 651-297-7206 or Toll-free: 1-800-366-4812
Fax: 651-282-2155
Website: www.ag.state.mn.us/consumer

Mississippi
Consumer Protection Division
Office of the Attorney General
P.O. Box 22947
Jackson, MS 39225-2947
Telephone: 601-359-4230
Toll-free: 1-800-281-4418
Fax: 601-359-4231
Website: www.ago.state.ms.us

Department of Agriculture and Commerce
121 North Jefferson St.

P.O. Box 1609
Jackson, MS 39201
Telephone: 601-359-1111
Fax: 601-359-1175
Website: www.mdac.state.ms.us

Missouri
Consumer Protection and Trade Offense Division
P.O. Box 899
1530 Rax Court
Jefferson City, MO 65102
Telephone: 573-751-6887
Telephone: 573-751-3321
Toll-free: 1-800-392-8222
TTY: 1-800-729-8668
Fax: 573-751-7948
Website: www.ago.state.mo.us

Montana
Department of Justice
1219 8th Ave.
P.O. Box 200151
Helena, MT 59620-0151
Telephone: 406-444-4500
Toll-free: 1-800-481-6896
Fax: 406-444-9680
Website: doj.mt.gov/consumer

Nebraska
Office of the Attorney General
Department of Justice
2115 State Capitol
P.O. Box 98920
Lincoln, NE 68509
Telephone: 402-471-2682
Telephone: 402-471-3891 (Spanish)
Toll-free: 1-800-727-6432
Toll-free: 1-888-850-7555 (Spanish)
Fax: 402-471-0006
Website: www.ago.state.ne.us

Nevada
Consumer Affairs Division
1850 East Sahara Ave., Suite 101
Las Vegas, NV 89104
Telephone: 702-486-7355
Toll-free: 1-800-326-5202
TTY: 702-486-7901

Fax: 702-486-7371
Website: www.fyiconsumer.org

555 E. Washington Ave., Suite 3900
Las Vegas, NV 89101
Telephone: 702-486-3420
Fax: 702-486-3768
Website: ag.state.nv.us

New Hampshire
Consumer Protection and Antitrust Bureau
Office of the Attorney General
33 Capitol St.
Concord, NH 03301
Telephone: 603-271-3641
Toll-free: 1-888-468-4454
TTY: 1-800-735-2964 (New Hampshire Only)
Fax: 603-223-6202
Website: www.doj.nh.gov/consumer/index.html

New Jersey
Division of Consumer Affairs
Department of Law and Public Safety
P.O. Box 45027
Newark, NJ 07101
Telephone: 973-504-6200
Toll-free: 1-800-242-5846
TTY: 973-504-6588
Fax: 973-648-3538
Website: www.state.nj.us/lps/ca/home.htm

New Mexico
P.O. Drawer 1508
407 Galisteo
Santa Fe, NM 87504-1508
Telephone: 505-827-6060
Toll-free: 1-800-678-1508
Fax: 505-827-6685
Website: www.ago.state.nm.us

New York
Bureau of Consumer Fraud and Protection
Office of the Attorney General
State Capitol
Albany, NY 12224
Telephone: 518-474-5481
Toll-free: 1-800-771-7755
TTY: 1-800-788-9898

Fax: 518-474-3618
Website: www.oag.state.ny.us

5 Empire State Plaza, Suite 2101
Albany, NY 12223-1556
Telephone: 518-474-8583 (Capitol Region)
Toll-free: 1-800-697-1220
Fax: 518-474-2474
Website: www.nysconsumer.gov

Consumer Frauds and Protection Bureau
Office of the Attorney General
120 Broadway, 3rd Fl.
New York, NY 10271
Telephone: 212-416-8300
TTY: 1-800-788-9898 or 212-416-8893
Fax: 212-416-6003
Website: my.boatus.com/consumer/dept.asp?ID=169

North Carolina
Consumer Protection Division
Office of the Attorney General
9001 Mail Service Center
Raleigh, NC 27699-9001
Telephone: 919-716-6000
Toll-free: 1-877-566-7226
Fax: 919-716-6050
Website: www.ncdoj.com

North Dakota
Office of the Attorney General
600 E. Boulevard Ave., Dept. 125
Bismarck, ND 58505
Telephone: 701-328-3404
Toll-free: 1-800-472-2600
TTY: 1-800-366-6888
Website: www.ag.state.nd.us

Ohio
Consumer Protection Section
Office of the Attorney General
30 East Broad St., 17th Floor
Columbus, OH 43215-3428
Telephone: 614-466-4320
Toll-free: 1-800-282-0515
TTY: 614-466-1393
Fax: 614-728-7583
Website: www.ag.state.oh.us

Office of the Ohio Consumers' Counsel
10 W. Broad St. 18th Floor Suite 1800
Columbus, OH 43215
Telephone: 614-466-8574 (outside OH)
Toll-free: 1-877-PICK-OCC (1-877-742-5622)
Website: www.pickocc.org

Oklahoma
Office of the Attorney General
313 N.E. 21st Street
Oklahoma City, OK 73105
Telephone: 405-521-3921
Fax: 405-521-6246
Website: http://www.oag.state.ok.us/

Oregon
Department of Justice
1162 Court Street, NE
Salem, OR 97301-4096
Telephone: 503-378-4400
TTY: 503-378-5938
Website: http://www.doj.state.or.us/

Pennsylvania
Office of Attorney General
16th Floor, Strawberry Square
Harrisburg, PA 17120
Telephone: 717-787-3391
Toll-free: 1-800-441-2555
Toll-free: 1-877-888-4877 (Health Care Section)
Fax: 717-787-8242
Website: www.attorneygeneral.gov

Office of the Consumer Advocate
555 Walnut Street
5th Floor, Forum Place
Harrisburg, PA 17101-1923
Telephone: 717-783-5048 (Utilities only)
Toll-free: 1-800-684-6560
Fax: 717-783-7152
Website: www.oca.state.pa.us

Puerto Rico
Centro Gubernamental Roberto Sanchez Vilella
Edificio Norte
Apartado 41059, Estacion Minillas
San Juan, PR 00940-1059
Telephone: 787-722-7555

Fax: 787-726-0077
Website: www.daco.gobierno.pr

Rhode Island
Consumer Protection Unit
Department of the Attorney General
150 South Main St.
Providence, RI 02903
Telephone: 401-274-4400
TTY: 401-453-0410
Fax: 401-222-5110
Website: www.riag.state.ri.gov

South Carolina
P.O. Box 11549
Columbia, SC 29211
Telephone: 803-734-3970
TTY: 803-734-4877
Fax: 803-734-4323
Website: www.scattorneygeneral.org

Department of Consumer Affairs
3600 Forest Drive, Suite 300
P.O. Box 5757
Columbia, SC 29250-5757
Telephone: 803-734-4200
Toll-free: 1-800-922-1594
TTY: 1-800-735-2905
Fax: 803-734-4286
Website: www.scconsumer.gov

Ombudsman
Office of Executive Policy and Program
1301 Gervais St., Suite 710
Columbia, SC 29201
Telephone: 803-340-7105
Toll-free: 1-866-340-7105
Fax: 803-734-0799
Website: www.myscgov.com

South Dakota
Office of the Attorney General
1302 E. Hwy. 14, Suite 3
Pierre, SD 57501-8503
Telephone: 605-773-4400
Toll-free: 1-800-300-1986
TTY: 605-773-6585

Fax: 605-773-7163
Website: www.state.sd.us/atg

Tennessee
Division of Consumer Affairs
500 James Robertson Pkwy., 5th Floor
Nashville, TN 37243-0600
Telephone: 615-741-4737
Toll-free: 1-800-342-8385
Fax: 615-532-4994
Website: www.state.tn.us/consumer

Office of the Attorney General
P.O. Box 20207
Nashville, TN 37202-02071
Telephone: 615-741-1671
Fax: 615-532-2910
Website: attorneygeneral.state.tn.us/cpro/cpro

Texas
Austin Regional Office
P.O. Box 12548
Austin, TX 78711-2548
Telephone: 512-463-2100
Toll-free: 1-800-621-0508
Fax: 512-473-8301
Website: www.oag.state.tx.us

Dallas Regional Office
Office of the Attorney General
1412 Main Street, Suite 810
Dallas, TX 75202
Telephone: 214-969-5310
Fax: 214-969-7615
Website: www.oag.state.tx.us

El Paso Regional Office
Office of the Attorney General
401 East Franklin Ave., Suite 530
El Paso, TX 79901
Telephone: 915-834-5800
Fax: 915-542-1546
Website: www.oag.state.tx.us

Houston Regional Office
Office of the Attorney General
808 Travis, Suite 300
Houston, TX 77002-1702

Telephone: 713-223-5886
Toll-free: 1-800-252-8011
Fax: 713-223-5821
Website: www.oag.state.tx.us

Lubbock Regional Office
Office of the Attorney General
4630 50th Street, Suite 500
Lubbock, TX 79414-3520
Telephone: 806-747-5238
Fax: 806-747-6307
Website: www.oag.state.tx.us

McAllen Regional Office
Office of the Attorney General
3201 North McColl Road, Suite B
McAllen, TX 78501-1685
Telephone: 956-682-4547
Toll-free: 1-800-252-8011
Fax: 956-682-1957
Website: www.oag.state.tx.us

San Antonio Regional Office
Office of the Attorney General
115 East Travis St., Suite 925
San Antonio, TX 78205-1605
Telephone: 210-224-1007
Toll-free: 1-800-252-8011
Fax: 210-225-1075
Website: www.oag.state.tx.us

Utah
Division of Consumer Protection
Department of Commerce
160 East 300 South
Box 146704
Salt Lake City, UT 84114-6704
Telephone: 801-530-6601
Fax: 801-530-6001
Website: www.consumerprotection.utah.gov

Vermont
Office of the Attorney General
104 Morrill Hall
University of Vermont
Burlington, VT 05405
Telephone: 802-656-3183
Toll-free: 1-800-649-2424

Fax: 802-656-1423
Website: www.atg.state.vt.us

Food Safety and Consumer Protection
Vermont Agency of Agriculture, Food, and Market
116 State St., Drawer 20
Montpelier, VT 05620-2901
Telephone: 802-828-2436
Fax: 802-828-5983
Website: www.vermontagriculture.com

Virgin Islands
Golden Rock Shopping Center
Christiansted
St. Croix, VI 00820
Telephone: 340-773-2226
Fax: 340-778-8250
Website: www.dlca.gov.vi

Department of Licensing and Consumer Affairs
Property and Procurement Bldg.
No. 1 Sub Base, Room 205
St. Thomas, VI 00802
Telephone: 340-774-3130
Fax: 340-776-0675
Website: www.dlca.gov.vi

Virginia
Antitrust and Consumer Litigation Section
Office of the Attorney General
900 East Main St.
Richmond, VA 23219
Telephone: 804-786-2116
Toll-free: 1-800-451-1525
Fax: 804-786-0122
Website: www.oag.state.va.us

Washington
1125 Washington St., SE
Olympia, WA 98504-0100
Toll-free: 1-800-551-4636
Website: www.atg.wa.gov/

Bellingham Consumer Resource Center
(Island, San Juan, Skagit, and Whatcom Counties)
Office of the Attorney General
103 East Holly St., Suite 308
Bellingham, WA 98225-4728

Telephone: 360-738-6185
Toll-free: 1-800-551-4636
Fax: 360-738-6190
Website: www.atg.wa.gov

Kennewick Consumer Resource Center (Southeast Washington)
Office of the Attorney General
500 N. Morain St., Suite 1250
Kennewick, WA 99336-2607
Telephone: 509-734-7140
Toll-free: 1-800-551-4636
Fax: 509-734-7475
Website: www.atg.wa.gov

Seattle Consumer Resource Center
(King, Snohomish, Clallam and Jefferson Counties)
Office of the Attorney General
900 Fourth Ave., Suite 2000
Seattle, WA 98164-1012
Telephone: 206-464-6684
Toll-free: 1-800-551-4636
Fax: 206-464-6451
Website: www.atg.wa.gov

Office of the Attorney General
1116 West Riverside
Spokane, WA 99201-1194
Telephone: 509-456-3123
Toll-free: 1-800-551-4636
Fax: 509-458-3548
Website: www.atg.wa.gov

West Virginia
Consumer Protection Division
Office of the Attorney General
812 Quarrier St., 6th Floor
P.O. Box 1789
Charleston, WV 25326-1789
Telephone: 304-558-8986
Toll-free: 1-800-368-8808
Fax: 304-558-0184
Website: www.wvago.us

Wisconsin
2811 Agriculture Dr.
P.O. Box 8911
Madison, WI 53708-8911
Telephone: 608-224-4949

Toll-free: 1-800-422-7128 (WI)
TTY: 608-224-5058
Fax: 608-224-4939
Website: www.datcp.state.wi.us

Wyoming
Consumer Protection Unit
Office of the Attorney General
123 Capitol, 200 W. 24th Street
Cheyenne, WY 82002
Telephone: 307-777-7841
Toll-free: 1-800-438-5799
Fax: 307-777-6869
Website: attorneygeneral.state.wy.us

Appendix D: Filing a Consumer Complaint with a Federal Agency

If you have a complaint about a problem with a product, service, or company, you can file a complaint with the relevant federal agency online. Federal agencies that oversee the industries listed below use your feedback to prompt product recalls, launch investigations, and develop new regulations. Agencies accept complaints via email, postal mail, or directly through their websites. Consumer.gov has online forms addressing each of these common consumer problems within the sphere of application of federal (and often state) consumer law.

Airline Accessibility or Discrimination
Airline Baggage and Service
Airline Overbooking
Airline Ticket Prices
Airline—Other Issues and General Complaints
Alcohol, Tobacco, and Firearms
Animal Feeds and Products (Veterinary)
Auctions
Auctions—International
Auto Dealers
Automobile—Vehicles and Equipment
Banks—Federal Savings and Loans/Savings
Banks—With National or "N.A." in the Name
Banks—Internet Banking
Banks—State-Chartered Banks
Banks—Others in the Federal Reserve System
Buying from Foreign Companies
Cell Phones, Pagers, Wireless
Charities
Child Car Seats
Companies—General Consumer Complaints

Consumer Products—Except Automobiles, Food, Drugs, Cosmetics, and Medicine
Cosmetics
Credit Unions
Disabilities—Architectural Barriers Act Access Violations. For other ADA issues, visit the ADA home page at http://www.ada.gov/
Employment
Environmental Violators
Financial Aid for Students
Food—Except Meat and Poultry
Health Clubs and Exercise Equipment
Home Improvement
Housing Discrimination
Internet Fraud—FBI
Internet Fraud—FTC
Meat and Poultry
Medical Drugs and Products Sold Online
Medicine, Drugs, Medical Devices
Occupational Safety and Health Administration
Online Services, Websites, E-Commerce
Online Services, Websites, E-Commerce—International
Retail Stores
Securities
Spam, or Junk E-Mail
Telephone Service and Telemarketers
Trade Barriers
Vaccines

Multipurpose Complaint Form: Federal Trade Commission

Use the Multipurpose Complaint Form to submit a complaint to the FTC Bureau of Consumer Protection about a particular company or organization. This form may also be used to submit a complaint to the FTC concerning media violence. The information you provide is up to you, but keep in mind that the more information you provide, the more likely it is that the agency will refer, respond to, or investigate your complaint or request. Federal agencies cannot obtain an individual remedy, but there have been a number of cases in which the FTC has obtained a settlement on behalf of a class of consumers resulting in restitution. You can find updated information on how to file a FTC complaint at https://rn.ftc.gov/pls/dod/wsolcq$.startup.

Example: Consumer Complaint about Discrimination. If you suffered discrimination on the basis of your race, sex, age, or gender while flying, you can file a complaint with the U.S. Department of Transportation (USDOT). You can fill out the USDOT form and send it via email, or you may print out a disability/accessibility complaint form from http://airconsumer.ost.dot.gov/forms/382form.pdf or a discrimination complaint form from http://airconsumer.ost.dot.gov/forms/disform.pdf and mail in.

Describe the incident, including where it occurred. If your complaint has to do with your disability, include the names of those involved or of any witnesses. Describe the nature of the disability and any accommodations that were required. In the case of airline flights, provide details (including dates) of any contacts prior to the flight date on which assistance was requested. State when the passenger checked in for the flight(s). If your complaint has to do with discrimination, describe the incident, including where it occurred. If possible, include the names of those involved or of any witnesses. Describe any efforts to resolve the complaint through the airline's complaint resolution official or other airline staff.

Appendix E:
Federal Agencies with a
Mission to Protect Consumers

This list includes only those agencies with a significant consumer law role and has been adapted for this topic. For the most current addresses, consult http://www .consumeraction.gov/selected.shtml. Many of these agencies will have procedures for investigating consumer complaints.

Consumer Product Safety Commission (CPSC)
4330 East West Highway
Bethesda, MD 20814
Toll-free: 1-800-638-CPSC (2772) (CPSC Hotline)
TTY: 1-800-638-8270
Fax: 301-504-0051
Email: info@cpsc.gov
Website: www.cpsc.gov
Website: www.recalls.gov (Information on all government conducted recalls)

To get information on product recalls or report a dangerous product or product-related injury, call CPSC's Hotline (Spanish-speaking staff available), visit its website, or send an email. Visit www.recalls.gov for information about all recalls conducted by the federal government. To order free publications, visit CPSC's website or write to the address above, Attention: Publications Request.

Federal Aviation Administration
AIR Consumer Protection Division (Airline service complaints)
C-75, Room 4107
Washington, DC 20590
Telephone: 202-366-2220
TTY: 202-366-0511
Email: airconsumer@dot.gov
Website: www.airconsumer.ost.dot.gov

Federal Communications Commission (FCC)
Consumer and Governmental Affairs Bureau (CGB)
445 12th St., SW
Washington, DC 20554
Toll-free: 1-888-CALL-FCC (1-888-225-5322)
TTY: 1-888-TELL-FCC (1-888-835-5322)
Fax: 1-866-418-0232
Email: fccinfo@fcc.gov
Website: www.fcc.gov

FCC accepts public inquiries; informal complaints; and questions regarding cable, radio, satellite, telephone, television, and wireless services. Mobile phone carriers, for example, are urging the Federal Communications Commission to preempt state regulations of early termination fees, which is an important consumer issue.

Federal Deposit Insurance Corporation (FDIC)
Division of Supervision and Consumer Protection
Consumer Response Center
2345 Grand Boulevard, Suite 100
Kansas City, MO 64108
Telephone: 703-562-2222 (Virginia Residents)
Toll-free: 1-877-ASK-FDIC (1-877-275-3342)
TTY: 1-800-925-4618
Fax: 816-234-9060
Website: www.fdic.gov

FDIC handles questions about federal deposit insurance coverage and complaints about FDIC-insured state banks that are not members of the Federal Reserve System.

Federal Motor Carrier Safety Administration
400 7th St., SE
Washington, DC 20590
Telephone: 202-366-2519
Toll-free: 1-800-832-5660
TTY: 1-800-877-8339
Website: www.fmcsa.dot.gov
Website: www.fmcsa.dot.gov/factsfigs/moving.htm (Information about your
   rights when moving)

Consumers may and are encouraged to submit household goods commercial complaints to the Federal Motor Carrier Safety Administration by calling toll-free, 1-888-DOT-SAFE (368-7238). This same toll-free number may be used to report dangerous safety violations involving a commercial truck or bus.

Federal Reserve System
Division of Consumer and Community Affairs
Board of Governors of the Federal Reserve System
20th and C Sts., NW
Washington, DC 20551

Telephone: 202-452-3693 (Complaints Only)
Telephone: 202-452-3204 (Public Affairs)
TTY: 202-452-3544
Website: www.federalreserve.gov

The Board of Governors handles consumer complaints about state-chartered banks and trust companies that are members of the Federal Reserve System.

Federal Trade Commission (FTC)
Bureau of Consumer Protection
Division of Consumer and Business Education
600 Pennsylvania Ave., N.W.
NJ-2267
Washington, DC 20580
Toll-free: 1-877-FTC-HELP (1-877-382-4357)
TTY: 1-866-653-4261
Website: www.ftc.gov

The FTC works for the consumer to prevent fraudulent, deceptive, and unfair business practices in the marketplace and to provide information to help consumers spot, stop, and avoid them. To file a complaint or to get free information on consumer issues, visit the website or call the toll-free numbers above. The FTC enters Internet, telemarketing, identity theft, and other fraud-related complaints into Consumer Sentinel, a secure online database available to hundreds of civil and criminal law enforcement agencies in the United States and abroad.

Food and Drug Administration
5600 Fishers Lane
Rockville, MD 20857-0001
Toll-free: 1-888-INFO-FDA (463-6332)
Toll-free: 1-888-723-3366
Website: www.fda.gov

Housing and Urban Development
Home Mortgage Insurance Division
451 7th St., SW, Room 9266
Washington, DC 20410
Telephone: 202-708-2121
Fax: 202-708-4308
Website: www.hud.gov

Housing and Urban Development
Office of Affordable Housing Programs
451 7th St., SW, Room 7164
Washington, DC 20410
Telephone: 202-708-2685
Toll-free: 1-800-998-9999 (Community Connections)
Fax: 202-708-1744
Website: www.hud.gov

Housing and Urban Development
Office of Fair Housing and Equal Opportunity
451 7th St., SW, Room 5204
Washington, DC 20410-2000
Telephone: 202-708-4252
Toll-free: 1-800-669-9777 (Complaints Hotline)
TTY: 1-800-927-9275
Fax: 202-708-4483
Website: www.hud.gov/complaints/housediscrim.cfm

Housing and Urban Development
Office of Manufactured Housing Program
Office of Deputy Assistant Secretary for Regulatory Affairs and
    Manufactured Housing
451 7th St., SW, Room 9164
Washington, DC 20410-8000
Telephone: 202-708-6423
Toll-free: 1-800-927-2891
Fax: 202-708-4213
Email: mhs@hud.gov
Website: www.hud.gov/offices/hsg/sfh/mhs/mhshome.cfm
    (Manufactured Housing)
Website: www.hud.gov/offices/hsg/sfh/mps/mpshome.cfm
    (Minimum Property Standards)

The Manufactured Housing Program is a consumer protection program that regulates the construction of certain factory-built housing units called "manufactured homes," formerly known as "mobile homes." HUD works with thirty-seven states to respond to consumer complaints. The Minimum Property Standards establish certain minimum standards for buildings constructed under HUD housing programs, including new single-family homes, multifamily housing, and health care–type facilities. HUD standards are relevant in breach of warranty lawsuits arising out of defective mobile homes. If a mobile home violates a minimum statutory standard, that evidence will also be relevant to a claim of negligent design or strict product liability.

Housing and Urban Development
Office of RESPA and Interstate Land Sales
Office of the Deputy Assistant Secretary for Regulatory Affairs and
    Manufactured Housing
451 7th St., SW, Room 9158
Washington, DC 20410
Telephone: 202-708-0502
Toll-free: 1-800-217-6970 (Home Buyer Assistance)
Fax: 202-708-4559
Email: hsg-respa@hud.gov
Website: www.hud.gov/offices/hsg/sfh/res/respa_hm.cfm (RESPA)
Website: www.hud.gov/offices/hsg/sfh/ils/ilshome.cfm
    (Interstate Land Sales)

The Office of RESPA and Interstate Land Sales handles complaints and provides information regarding real estate loan transactions and borrower rights under the Real Estate Settlement Procedures Act (RESPA). The Interstate Land Sales program protects consumers from fraud and abuse in the sale or lease of land. The Interstate Land Sales Full Disclosure Act requires land developers to register subdivisions of 100 or more nonexempt lots with HUD and to provide each purchaser with a disclosure document called a Property Report. The Property Report contains relevant information about the subdivision and must be delivered to each purchaser before the signing of the contract or agreement.

U.S. Postal Inspection Service
Criminal Investigations Service Center
ATTN: Mail Fraud
222 S. Riverside Plaza, Suite 1250
Chicago, IL 60606-6100
Website: www.usps.gov/postalinspectors

If you believe you have been the victim of a crime involving the U.S. mail or need assistance with postal-related problems of a law enforcement nature, you should contact your nearest Postal Inspection Service office. Addresses and telephone numbers can be found in the government pages of your telephone book or by visiting the Postal Inspection Service website.

Index